D1621364

47,50

Developmental Toxicology

Developmental Toxicology

Edited by Keith Snell

PRAEGER

Published in 1982 by Praeger Publishers
CBS Educational and Professional Publishing
A Division of CBS, Inc.
521 Fifth Avenue, New York, NewYork 10175 U.S.A.

Library of Congress Catalog Number: 81-15370
ISBN: 0-03-060408-7

0123456789 056 987654321

Printed in Great Britain

Contents

Preface

Since the 1930s and the work of Hale and Warkany on birth defects produced by variations in dietary vitamin A, it has been recognised that the developing fetus is particularly vulnerable to adverse influences in the environment. Studies of malformations at birth remained largely in the hands of paediatricians who, for instance, quickly established the connection between rubella infection in early pregnancy and the birth of severely affected infants. However, it was through the tragic events of 1962, when dramatic increases in the incidence of phocomelia in newborn infants in Germany, the United Kingdom, Japan, and other countries were traced to the use of the apparently non-toxic sedative thalidomide by pregnant women, that toxicologists were brought face to face with the devastating possibility of chemically-induced developmental abnormalities.

It had been shown earlier that chemotherapeutic agents could cause damage to the developing organism, but the absence of any known examples of drug-induced birth defects had produced an air of complacency which was reinforced by the lack of any specific regulatory requirements for safety evaluation in this area. The magnitude of the thalidomide tragedy, affecting some 10 000 malformed children, was sufficient to cause an immediate, and some would say hasty, reaction by government drug regulatory agencies throughout the world to construct a test protocol which would detect potential teratogenic substances that might give rise to anatomical malformations. Such empirically based protocols paid scant attention to the spectrum of possible developmental abnormalities that may befall the developing organism and more recent revised regulatory guidelines require investigations that include reproduction studies, teratology studies and postnatal studies.

The latter category is noteworthy in that it raises two fundamental issues in developmental toxicology. One is the recognition that development, and the susceptibility of the developing organism, is not confined to the prenatal phase of life but continues during postnatal life. This is a particularly significant concept for toxicology in the light of the known transmission of therapeutic agents and environmental pollutants to the suckling infant in the breast milk of the nursing mother, the so-called translactational route of exposure (cf. transplacental exposure). The other is the question of the latency of developmental toxic responses which may only become overtly manifest as maturation proceeds. Thus, although the critical toxic event itself may have occurred during gestation, the defect or disturbance may be functional rather than structural and may not be revealed until these functions and other associated processes are brought into action at a later maturational stage, often in the postnatal period. Moreover, for toxic interactions which are initiated postnatally, the eventual derangement may not occur until much later in life. In these cases, where cause and effect are temporally separated, it is difficult to explore the mechanisms just by examining the end-results. It is equally difficult to devise testing procedures which would be able to detect the full range of possible developmental toxic phenomena.

The aim of this book is to provide a forum for a discussion of the inter-actions between toxic agents and developmental processes. It is not a recipe book for test procedures for detecting teratogenicity or develop-mental toxicity. Rather it seeks to show the current status of various aspects of research in developmental toxicology which should comprise the background knowledge required to approach the problem of the detection of such hazards in a rational fashion governed by scientific rather than empirical considerations. It is axiomatic in toxicology, and developmental toxicology is no exception, that the discipline as a whole is made up of many varied specialist areas of expertise. It is important for the scientific advancement of the subject that these individual specialisms should be intelligible to each other so that their contributions can be properly evaluated. In this spirit the various contributors to the book have been charged with the task of presenting a review of their specialist area which should not only describe the current research efforts in that area and the concepts which are emerging, but also place these in perspective and discuss them in a way which will allow them to be appreciated by the non-specialist in that area.

The book, then, is aimed at a broad readership which will include practising toxicologists, especially those concerned with evaluating develop-mental hazards whether their role is in the laboratory or in the legislative departments of government and industry. It will also include those research scientists who are interested in the effect of toxic agents on the processes of mammalian development and the mechanisms of such interactions. Hopefully, this book will also be read by those members of the medical profession, particularly paediatricians, who are faced with the consequences of the untoward effects of therapeutic and environmental agents on the developing human organism. Finally, it is intended that the book should prove useful to those students in universities and young scientists in industrial training who are embarking on a career in toxicology and who would benefit from an overview of the current preoccupations of developmental toxicology.

The book begins with a consideration of various aspects of teratology, particularly the use of model systems using techniques *in vitro*. These are proving useful in dissecting the mechanistic events of teratogenesis free from the secondary events which can lead to ambiguity with studies *in vivo* (Beck). The applications of some of these *in vitro* systems for use in testing chemicals for teratogenic potential are described by Brown and Fabro. The use of *in vitro* cell culture systems for exploring the nature and timing of teratogenic susceptibility is illustrated with reference to examples of known teratogens by Clayton and Zehir. Williams discusses the biological and biochemical bases for teratogenic actions. One of the factors determining the susceptibility of the developing organism to developmental toxicity in general is the manner and extent to which chemical substances are distributed (Ullberg *et al.*) or undergo bioactivation or detoxification (Pelkonen; Juchau) in the materno-placental-fetal unit. Bioactivation is a key factor in determining the carcinogenicity of many agents and Kleihues discusses the effect of carcinogens on the developing organism, with particular emphasis on tumours of the nervous system and the mechanisms which determine carcinogenic susceptibility. Functional developmental aberrations which only become manifest at later periods after the original toxic insult are illustrated by examples of behavioural teratogenicity (Vorhees and Butcher) and of biochemical or metabolic teratogenesis and developmental toxicity (Snell). This final chapter also describes the possible use of developmental biochemical parameters (particularly enzymes) in the early detection of developmental aberrations induced by developmental toxicants and carcinogens (Snell).

As editor of the book I am indebted to my colleagues and co-authors for the enthusiastic and diligent manner in which they approached their various contributions. Even if, in certain cases, the gestation period proved somewhat longer than expected, the finished articles more than justified their conception. I am grateful to Tim Hardwick of Croom Helm for prompting the initial implantation and for guiding the whole conceptus on its journey into life. I should also like to acknowledge with thanks the ministering efforts and secretarial co-operation of Prue Levers and Janet Cole in assisting with the delivery. In the end of course, as with any newly created being, this book must justify its existence on its own merits. It is my hope that they approach closely the original aspirations.

Keith Snell
Toxicology Division,
Biochemistry Department,
University of Surrey,
Guildford

CHAPTER ONE

MODEL SYSTEMS IN TERATOLOGY RESEARCH
Felix Beck

CONTENTS

I. Introduction

Broadly speaking, teratology research falls into two main categories. The first is essentially concerned with identifying extrinsic and intrinsic factors responsible for embryopathies. In pursuing such objectives account is taken not only of the biological effects of potentially embryotoxic agents in isolation but also of the so-called *dramatype* of the experimental animal used (i.e. the combination of the maternal phenotype with the multiple environmental factors which play upon it) as well as a consideration of the embryonic genotype and its contribution in facilitating or hindering the action of agents which tend to disturb development. Clearly the widest application of this type of work is in the testing of drugs and other consumer products for possible embryopathic effects. A quartet of effects are relevant in this context; namely, fetal death (with consequent resorption or abortion), fetal malformation (true teratologies in the morphological sense) abnormalities of function (perhaps associated with faulty histogenesis) and intra-uterine growth retardation.

The second principal aim of teratology research is the precise elucidation of the natural history of a congenital disorder. Here Wilson's (1977) subdivision of the process into an initial mechanism (such as a gene mutation) which leads to a pathogenic event (for example impeded morphogenetic movement) with a subsequent final defect being produced by a restricted number of common pathways (such as too few cells to effect localised morphogenesis) is a useful concept, though it is probably incomplete and oversimplified.

Teratology research, therefore, is a wide field with an important unifying inference – namely its value as an applied discipline in the study of embryopathy relevant to man and economically important domestic animals. Teratology experiments are usually not performed on farm animals or man and for this reason particular attention must be paid to the relevance of the experimental model used. This chapter will be devoted to a critical analysis of many of the experimental plans available to us. Particular attention will be paid to an analysis of the questions which any particular model is capable of answering as well as to its advantages and limitations.

II. *In Vivo* Systems

A. *Screening for Potentially Embryopathic Agents*

The rat is the species most often used for routine studies. In most drug screening protocols, *in vivo* data obtained from this animal makes up an important part of submissions to government agencies with respect to teratogenic potential. Such studies usually take the form of a three-phase reproduction study such as that described by Schardein (1976). In phase one males are treated for 60 days and females for 14 days before mating. Pregnant females are then treated throughout gestation; half are killed at mid-pregnancy and their embryos examined while the other half go to term and suckle their offspring. Weanlings are killed and post mortems are performed. Phase 1 is therefore designed to study gonadal effects, effects on the ovarian cycle, mating, conception rates, late gestation, parturition and lactation as well as providing an overall crude screen for teratogenicity. Phase two is specifically designed to test teratogenic potential, the drug being administered at various doses between 6 and 15 days of gestation – i.e. during the major organogenetic period in the rat. Dams are killed near term and their fetuses are examined grossly as well as for visceral and skeletal malformations. A note is made of resorption sites. In phase 3 treatment is during the final third of pregnancy and through to weaning, thereby focusing attention on late fetal maturation and growth, parturition and lactation.

   Though reproduction and teratology studies performed over a wide dose range (usually at least three dose levels) in rats provide the basis of most investigations into the embryopathic potential of environmental factors, experience (most notably with thalidomide) has shown that such studies can often prove inadequate because the rat does not react in the same way as man. In other words, the model is inadequate. There are many possible reasons for this. The pharmacodynamics of an agent, its maternal metabolism, fetal metabolism and the embryonic capacity for recovery from the effects may differ greatly between species and even more fundamentally between mammalian families and orders.

A factor which is often neglected is the unique method of placentation in the *Rodentia* which *of itself* is likely to introduce complications when a teratogenic agent acts upon the physiological peculiarities of the inverted yolk sac placental system characteristic of this order (see Beck and Lloyd, 1977). An important factor to bear in mind when thinking about placentation in the context of teratology is the switchover point from histiotrophic nutrition to haemotrophic nutrition. By this I mean the changeover from the time when the early embryo is dependent upon the intracellular breakdown of a pabulum of maternal cells and secretions to sustain itself to the point when it has developed a circulation of its own and is therefore able to transfer solutes across a 'placental membrane' from the maternal to the fetal circulation. Haemotrophic embryonic nutrition to a greater or lesser extent replaces histiotrophic nutrition but it does so at different points during gestation and embryonic development in various species (Beck 1976a, 1980).

Therefore, if a potential teratogen acts principally (say) upon the 'placental membrane' it will constitute a danger to man where haemotrophic nutrition is developed precociously, while an agent acting upon special aspects of intracellular degradation of endocytosed histiotroph may give a 'false-positive' result in rats — where the 'inverted yolk sac' is responsible for histiotrophic nutrition via liquid pinocytosis until at least the 20-25 somite stage or in the ferret where bulk endocytosis (phagocytosis and pinocytosis) sustains the embryo probably until at least the 35 somite stage. A fuller account of the factors are given by Beck and Lloyd (1977).

Clearly, therefore, the demonstration of embryopathic effects (or their lack) cannot be indiscriminately extrapolated between species. This should not be construed as implying that *in vivo* screening is without value in reproductive toxicology. It merely implies that a model becomes effective only if some assessment of possible methods and sites of action of an agent under investigation are established. The appropriate species may then be selected and any unexpected findings in other species can be properly evaluated in terms of their potential applicability to man. UK guidelines require testing on two species, one of which is other than a rodent. This is a sensible arrangement, its only weakness being that the

15

rabbit (a closely related order with many metabolic and placental characteristics similar to the rat) tends to be used as a second species rather than (say) a carnivore such as the ferret or an ungulate such as the pig. Clearly, simian primate models are ideal but economic and biological reasons make these animals unavailable except in special circumstances, usually when a specific and important drug requires thorough evaluation after equivocal results obtained from other species. Wilson (1973) gives some 'sample protocols' for use with dogs, pigs and monkeys and these are of value when considering the use of a 'second species'.

The reader is referred to Palmer (1978) and Wilson (1978a) for a detailed analysis of the various factors to be taken into account in designing subprimate drug-screening protocols.

B. *The Study of Teratogenic Mechanisms*

Adinolfi *et al.* (1976) and Seller *et al.* (1979) have made excellent use of a mouse mutant known as 'curly tail' (Grüneberg, 1954) as a model for the pathogenesis of spina bifida and anencephaly in man. The similarity between the neural tube defects seen in 'curly tail' and those occurring in man is close (Embury *et al.*, 1979). Lesions predominate at either end of the central nervous system so that both exencephaly and spina bifida are found. As in the human, an excess of female fetuses is affected. Polyhydramnios and raised amniotic alpha-fetoprotein concentrations are concomitant findings. The precise degree of similarity in the pathogenesis of the neural-tube defect is, of course, impossible to determine. Grüneberg (1954) suggested that the condition in the curly tail mouse resulted from the effects of a recessive gene (ct) with modifiers and the suggestion that in the human, polygenic inheritence influenced by numerous unidentified environmental factors causes the congenital defect (Carter, 1969) is an attractive one. For this reason the model is an intriguing one for testing various extraneous factors on the expression of the genotype – see, for example, the effect of Vitamin A (Seller *et al.*, 1979). Furthermore, a thorough examination of the earliest morphological and biochemical abnormalities manifest by these animals (grossly affected or otherwise) might well shed light upon the human conditions. Here, then, is a prime example of a simple *in vivo* model which, if intelligently applied, can give meaningful results of potential clinical value.

In vivo systems in small polycoitus animals can be used to study the complex relationship between fetal death and fetal malformation which is

16

often observed in nature. An example is provided by the different biological effects observed after subcutaneous administration of two isomeric acid *bis*azo dyes Trypan blue and Niagara blue 4B. Their formulae are given below (Fig. 1.1); both are taken up by the mammalian reticulo-endothelial system and possibly exert their embryopathic effects in inhibiting nutritionally important endocytosis of macromolecules by extraembryonic membranes (the visceral layer of the yolk sac in the case of rats) (Williams *et al.*, 1976). The serum levels after a single injection of each drug are different and this difference in pharmacokinetics is probably connected with the difference in their action. Thus a sustained plasma level of about 200mg/100ml is probably necessary to achieve the prolonged deprivation of nutrients required to produce a teratogenic effect. This is achieved by a single subcutaneous injection of 50mg/kg body weight Trypan blue but requires 200mg/kg body weight Niagara blue 4B. The latter dose results in an immediate rise in serum levels to 50mg/100ml (Fig. 1.2), which appears to cause rapid embryonic death – possibly by alteration of the osmotic relationships in the immediate vicinity of the embryo. Thus, although both compounds probably cause an inhibition of histiotrophic nutrition, one is predominantly embryolethal and the other predominantly teratogenic when administered at the 'optimum teratogenic dose' (Beck and Lloyd, 1964). This is illustrated in Figure 1.3, which shows the results of an experiment in which one series of rats was injected with Trypan blue and another with Niagara blue 4B at 8.5 days' gestation (the time of maximal susceptibility). Groups of animals were then killed at 11.5, 14.5 and 20.5 days' gestation. Clearly, the immediate embryolethal effect was relatively minor for Trypan blue while for Niagara blue 4B the high serum levels immediately killed most affected fetuses (a higher dose would have killed them all). Trypan blue did, however, sufficiently interfere with embryonic nutrition for a large number of embryos to develop abnormally and these were clearly recognisable at 11.5 days of gestation. By 14.5 days many of the malformed embryos had died by a process of intrauterine natural selection and this was further accentuated at 20.5 days.

Thus the pharmacokinetics of two closely related dyes resulted in different embryotoxic effects. The same principles would presumably hold good for other related agents and the model is therefore of value beyond that of an investigation concerned with the teratogenic effects of acid *bis*azo dyes. Clearly, before the system was capable of wide extrapolation basic similarities of metabolism, pharmacokinetics and mode of action of the agent between rats and man would have to be presumed but many of these parameters are capable of easy verification.

17

Figure 1.1: The Structural Formula of Trypan Blue and Niagara Blue 4B.

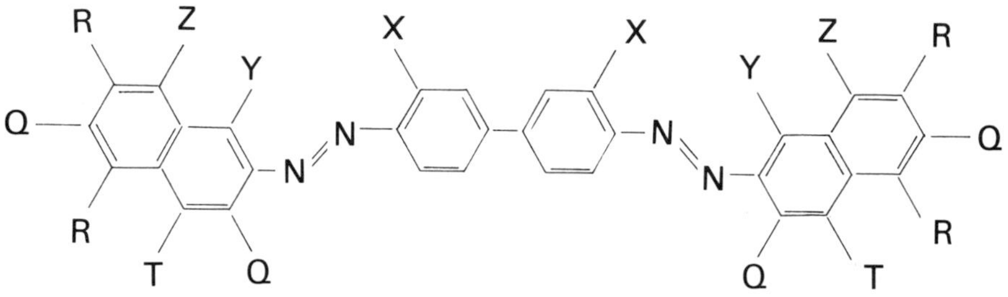

Name	No.	Substituents					
		X	Z	Q	R	Y	T
Trypan blue	23,850	CH_3	NH_2	SO_3Na	H	OH	H
Niagara blue 4B	24,400	OCH_3	NH_2	SO_3Na	H	OH	H

Source: *Colour Index* (2nd ed.), Society of Dyers and Colourists, Bradford.

Berry and Germain (1975) have drawn attention to the advantages of using polygenically determined anomalies in animals as models for simulating teratogenic mechanisms in man. Carter (1965), Edwards (1969) and Fraser (1977a) have pointed out that most human malformations occur as a result of an interaction of (possibly multiple) environmental factors combining with a polygenically determined predisposition which together push a developing organism beyond a 'teratogenic threshold' (Fig. 1.4) Leck *et al.* (1968) have indicated that this concept implies that given a normal distribution of the tendency to produce a defect and a well-defined 'threshold' the mean predisposition need only be slightly altered (possibly by a change in only a single variable) for a resulting dramatic change in the incidence of the malformation in the population to occur. This was very clearly demonstrated by Fraser (1977b) who shows what at first sight may appear to be apparent synergism between two teratogens which are merely acting additively (Fig. 1.5).

It is clearly useful to have a model in which subthreshold incipient 'teratogenic' effects may be measured. Such a system exists in the sensitivity exhibited in the size of the third molar tooth in the mouse to subthreshold effects of the rodent teratogen aspirin. The tooth size can

Figure 1.2: Maternal Serum levels of Trypan Blue and Niagara Blue 4B after Subcutaneous Injection.

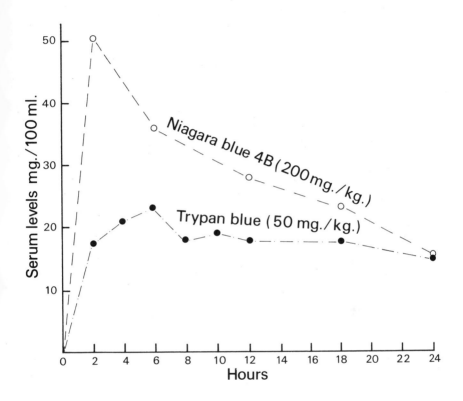

readily be measured (Berry and Germain, 1972) and if during development the anlage falls below a certain threshold level it will fail to develop altogether. There exists here, then, a potential model system for screening 'weak' teratogens *at sub-teratogenic concentrations.* The system is described by Berry and Nickols (1979) and may form a useful model for situations including a variety of 'weak teratogens'.

Figure 1.3: Effect of Two Azo Dyes on Pregnancy in the Rat after Injection at 8.5 Days. The rats were examined at 11.5, 14.5 and 20.5 days and the number of malformed and resorbed fetuses noted. A decrease in abnormalities can be observed with a corresponding increase in resorptions. N, normal embryos; A, abnormal embryos; R, resorptions.

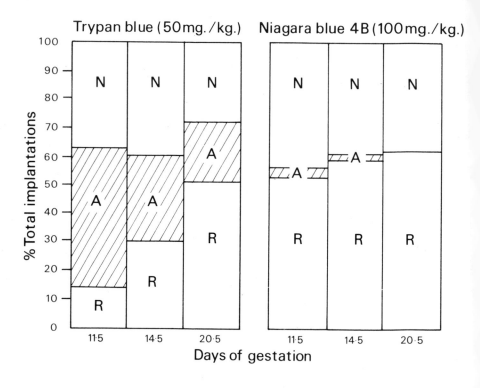

III. Some Model Systems to Study Teratogenic Mechanisms Using Surgical Techniques

Three approaches will serve to illustrate the part that surgical techniques play in teratological research.

Egg transfer techniques are a powerful tool for evaluating the genetic background relevant to the effects of an embryopathic agent. Most malformations are the result of polyfactorial systems composed of multiple

Figure 1.4: The Multifactorial/Threshold Model for Cleft Palate

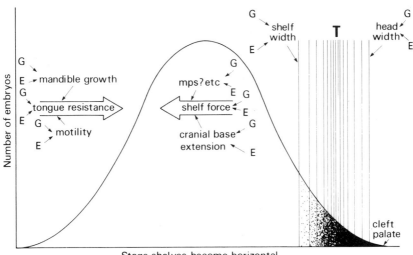

Key: G = genetic factors; E = environmental factors
Source: Wilson (1977, 83), with permission.

environmental factors interacting with a polygenetic predisposition to the congenital malformation in question. The situation is often a discontinuous one that either a gross malformation exists, or it does not. This is well illustrated by Fraser's (1977a) studies on the multifactorial/threshold model for cleft palate (Fig. 1.4). It may be contrasted with the malformation which represents the extreme form of a continuous physical variation (e.g. in spina bifida, where some symptomless forms of incipient spina bifida occulta represents no more than hypoplastic conditions of certain vertebrae). Even here, however the situation is not so clear as it may first appear (*viz*; bifid uvula probably represents a minor form of palatal cleft).

The genetic components in such situations may reside in the ovum, either in its genome and/or in its cytoplasm (which of course is of maternal origin); alternatively, it may be a uterine (such as position, parity, blood supply, etc.) or other purely maternal somatic factor. Egg transfer experiments between susceptible and resistant strains to certain malformations combined with administration of the appropriate environmental teratogen often help to clarify such situations. A purely paternal genetic factor may

Figure 1.5: Hypothetical Diagram Illustrating Apparent Synergism between Two Teratogens that Interact Additively

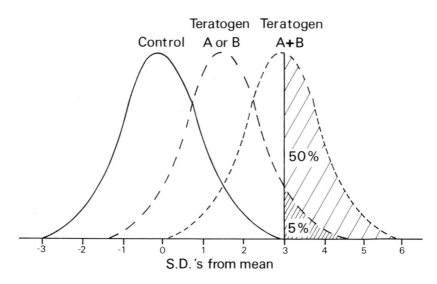

Source: Wilson (1977, 452), with permission.

first be eliminated at the F_1 stage by appropriate crossing experiments; very few such situations are found to exist and one is usually faced with having to decide the relative influence attributable to control of the maternal somatic phenotype by her genotype (McLaren and Michie, 1958) or alternatively to possible extranuclear factors transmitted through the egg cytoplasm (Verrusio *et al.*, 1968). A relevant example is quoted by Beck (1976a). Marsk *et al.*, (1971) transferred A/Jax mouse ova to CBA foster mothers and later treated these with cortisone. There was a 100% occurrence of cleft palate but preliminary data when CBA eggs were transferred to A/Jax mothers gave only 20% palatal clefts after the same treatment — results which are similar to A/Jax and CBA developing in the uterus of their natural mothers. Since reciprocal cross-breeding experiments showed a maternal influence on the incidence of cortisone-induced palatal cleft, cytoplasmic factors may in this case contribute to the effect of cortisone treatment. Few unequivocal cases of cytoplasmic inheritance of teratogen susceptibility have as yet been established; most maternal factors seem to be connected with the maternal soma. Nevertheless, it is clear that egg transfer techniques and complementary analyses using

22

back-crossing techniques (Verrusio *et al.*, 1968; Bornstein *et al.*, 1970) could be used to analyse maternal factors by essentially complementary methods.

Surgical techniques directly applied to the late embryo or fetus, especially in small animals, are not much used in teratology though one wonders what may be achieved using marsupials as test species. Some germinal experiments, not primarily teratological in nature, have been carried out by Maizell and Isaaca (1970), but in general the methods have been little exploited. In primitive marsupial forms (e.g., the South American opossum *Didelphis albiventris*) the young are born as little more than late somite embryos which become attached to the teat where they are easily accessible to surgical intervention. The pouch young – for example – still function on mesonephric kidneys, there are no islets of Langerhans in the pancreas, the hind limb is an early limb bud at birth and in general most organs are in a primitive state of histogenesis. It can only be a matter of time before such species assume their proper role in teratological research concerned with teratogenic mechanisms, particularly at the later (histogenetic) stages of development.

Other surgical techniques, however, have been successfully used in eutherian mammals. Intrauterine embryopathy, especially growth retardation, may well be the result of fetal malnutrition due to maternal vascular deficiency. This can be easily investigated in the rat, where the uterus is supplied by only two vessels (the ovarian and uterine artery). Brent and Franklin (1960) first took advantage of this by acute vascular clamping of the uterine vessels for varying periods of time. They produced a 16.7% congenital malformation rate at 9 days' gestation when clamping exceeded 90 minutes but no effects after only 30 minutes. Cooling the uterus to 4°C (George *et al.*, 1967) allows the clamping procedure to be increased to 2.5 hours without appreciable fetal mortality or malformation. Cooling need only affect the uterus and the mother may be at a normal temperature. This is therefore a most useful technique for studying short-term maternal treatment with a teratogen while effectively isolating the conceptus. In many cases results relevant to the site of action of the agent may be obtained as well as other useful information, including pharmacokinetics, secondary teratogenic effects, the relevance of intermediate metabolites, etc. The method has been extensively applied in experiments to determine the effects of maternal radiation while shielding the post-implantation embryo (Brent and McLaughlin, 1960). The results indicate that irradiation teratogenesis almost certainly results from a direct effect on the embryo (no effect was observed when embryos were shielded and the

23

mother irradiated except at radiations > 400r). Uterine vascular clamping for 45 minutes on day 9 (a subteratogenic stimulus) protects against teratogenic doses of radiation – probably by causing hypoxia. The technique and its applications is well reviewed by Barr and Brent (1978).

Wigglesworth (1964) permanently interrupted flow along the uterine artery late in gestation in the rat. This experimental procedure is designed to study the effects of chronic ischaemia on development. The effect is principally on fetal weight? it is greatest when performed late in gestation, and the results resemble human 'small for dates' babies in that (for example) lung maturity reflects gestational age rather than body weight (Wigglesworth, 1964; Blanc, 1967). The interpretation of results is not easy; the effect depends partly upon uterine position and partly upon the fact that the uterine artery is not an end artery so that the circulation improves with time as collaterals develop from the ovarian pole.

IV. Some Model Systems Using *In Vitro* Techniques

In vitro systems are essentially too simple in biological terms to provide a complete model for a teratological event. Their value lies in isolating and investigating the constituent elements of a teratological situation. Three examples out of many possible ones (Wilson, 1978b) will be discussed here in some detail.

A. *Embryo Culture*

Culture systems for whole rat embryos have been developed by New (for reviews see Brown and Fabro, Chapter 2; New, 1978) which are undoubtedly the most effective methods presently available. In special cases modifications of New's basic techniques have been used (Chatot *et al.*, 1980) and some other species have been successfully cultured (Clarkson *et al.*, 1969). Further significant advances will probably be made in this field and improvements are continually being reported. Basically, the embryo is cultured inside its own intact extraembryonic membranes and it is found that at certain stages (e.g. between 9.5 and 11.5 days in the rat) growth *in vivo* and *in vitro* is identical in quality and quantity.

We therefore have an excellent system for separating the mother and the fetoplacental unit in a teratogenic system. Furthermore, it is possible to demonstrate whether an agent which is teratogenic if given to the mother directly affects the embryo or whether it does so in part or completely through one of its metabolites or due to maternal bioactivation. Thus Fantel *et al.* (1979) found that 10-day embryos *in vitro* were unaffected by cyclophosphamide concentrations as high as $250\mu g/ml$ in the culture serum. However, $6.25\mu g/ml$ of the drug produced abnormal embryos if a hepatic microsomal fraction and co-factors for a mono-oxygenase system were also added to the serum. Clearly, cyclophosphamide is not active unless maternal activation first takes place.

It would seem that there is also considerable potential here for the elements of an *in vitro* drug screening system, although I have already indicated that *in vivo* tests will always continue to provide the necessary basic information. Conceivably, however, batches of chemicals or materials containing potent contaminants might be tested in this way.

The teratogenic potential of various human sera might conceivably be assessed by this means and in this respect it is interesting that by using this method we have shown that both sodium salicylate (McGarrity *et al.*, 1981) and trypan blue (Moore and Gulamhusein, 1981) are teratogenic when added to the culture medium at the level at which they are 'naturally' teratogenic in rat serum *in vivo*.

B. *Organ Culture*

Embryonic organs may be maintained for protracted periods of time, usually greatly in excess of the restricted duration for which whole embryo cultures can be maintained. During this period they can often be made to undergo considerable differentiation and such systems may be used to investigate the primary mode of action of teratogens (Aydelotte and Kochhar, 1972). The mouse limb-bud is perhaps the most widely used model in this type of work but some aspects of palatogenesis (Pourtois, 1966) and tooth culture (Thesleff, 1977) have also been used. Kochhar (1975) has reviewed the fate of mouse limb explants exposed to a series of teratogenic agents. The materials he used produced reasonably specific effects on limb-bud development which in many cases roughly mimicked their *in vivo* effect. This gives one hope that such an approach may sometimes be of value not only in identifying the primary site of action of a drug, but also form a starting point for an investigation of the mode of action of a teratogen at the molecular level. Mouse limb-buds grow well for about 6 days and more recently we (Gulamhusein *et al.*, 1980) have succeeded in obtaining equally comprehensive morphological development in ferret limb-buds cultured for 18 days. This makes it possible to devise experiments in which organ rudiments are exposed to teratogenic agents for quite protracted periods.

Organ culture systems are in general much more sensitive than other *in vitro* systems. They also serve to accentuate a limited number of the polyfactorial forces which combine to make a perfectly formed organ *in vivo*. These characteristics act both to the advantage of the system but also constitute a weakness. Thus it is difficult to conceive of a comprehensive organ culture screening system for drugs. At the same time, however, this avenue of approach may well set the pace for numerous investigations into the precise mode of action of a teratogen — be it direct or indirect, mediated by a metabolite or directly due to a drug, specific in its action or the result of relatively non-specific growth retardation, etc.

The placenta is a difficult organ to culture for protracted periods of time; nevertheless short-term maintenance systems have been developed which allow the measurement of various biochemical systems and their disruption by potential teratogens. Thus Beck and Lloyd (1966) suggested that trypan blue was teratogenic in rats by virtue of its action on the visceral yolk sac placental system. The dye is concentrated in the visceral yolk sac epithelium and inhibits several lysosomal enzymes (Beck *et al.*, 1967). At first the mode of action was thought to lie in the deprivation of the embryo of vital nutrients because of the inability of the yolk sac to catabolise endocytosed biopolymers. More recent studies of the effect of trypan blue on 17.5 day rat yolk sac in short-term culture show that while trypan blue does indeed act as an intralysosomal inhibitor (Davies *et al.*, 1969) it exerts an even more profound effect on the process of endocytosis itself (Williams, Chapter 4). Since yolk sac morphology is virtually unchanged electron microscopically throughout gestation one is perhaps justified in extrapolating the results obtained from 17.5 day yolk sacs to the state of affairs present at 8.5 days' gestation. When this is done it seems more likely that the dye interferes with embryonic nutrition by inhibiting the pinocytic uptake of macromolecules (Williams *et al.*, 1976). Whichever turns out to be the main cause of inhibition of embryonic nutrition at the susceptible period (8.5 days) the point at which teratogenic effects may be mediated by a disturbance of placental function and at which these effects may be investigated biochemically *in vitro* is important in a model system for the investigation of teratogenic mechanisms.

C. *Cell Culture*

Cell cultures in certain circumstances can provide an index of toxicity of agents introduced into the culture system and may therefore be used as a sort of 'eukaryotic Ames test'. Clayton (Chapter 3) has developed such systems to a considerable degree and is now engaged in the task of relating *in vitro* with *in vivo* effects. Again, there seems to be little chance of developing a comprehensive screening test for teratogens by these means but undoubtedly there is great potential for the investigation of the mechanisms of toxicity of external agents on embryonic cells and perhaps in establishing the fundamental mode of action of certain teratogenic agents. Fetal liver organ culture systems have been developed by Nau and Liddiard (1978). They allow for monitoring of the development of detoxifying systems and are thus of clear relevance to teratogenesis. This is part of a larger field which is discussed in Chapters 6 and 7 and previously in a volume entitled 'Role of Pharmacokinetics in Prenatal and Perinatal Toxicology' (Neubert *et al.*, 1978).

V. Conclusion

The title of this contribution embraces the whole subject of teratology apart from epidemiological and clinical studies. It has therefore been possible to indicate only some of the major growing points in teratological research. What emerges is that we have progressed considerably from the relatively crude *in vivo* experiments of the 1950s and 1960s even though no viable alternative for *in vivo* drug screening seems feasible at this time. I have not attempted to deal with the emerging subject of behavioural teratology. The status of presently performed tests in this field require very careful evaluation before meaningful extrapolation to human brain function can be accepted (see Vorhees and Butcher, Chapter 9). Furthermore, the field of postnatal development has not been considered; there seems little doubt that prenatal influences can adversely affect the considerable degree of postnatal growth and morphogenesis which occurs (see Chapters 9 and 10). This subject also undoubtedly requires extensive investigation in the near future.

Model Systems in Teratology Research

Acknowledgement

The author is indebted to the Medical Research Council for a grant in aid of research.

References

Adinolfi, M., Beck, S., Embury, S., Polani, P.E. and Seller, M.J. (1976) *J. Med. Genet.*, *13*, 511-13
Aydelotte, M.B. and Kochhar, D. (1972) *Develop. Biol.*, *28*, 191-201
Barr, M. and Brent, R.L. (1978) in *Handbook of Teratology* (Wilson J.G. and Fraser, F.C., eds.), Vol. 4, pp. 275-304, Plenum Press, New York
Beck, F. (1976a) *Br. Med. Bull.*, *32*, 53-8
—— (1976b) *Env. Health Persp.*, *18*, 5-12
Beck, F. (1980) in *Developmental Toxicity* (Kimmel, C.A. and Buelke-Sam, J., eds.), Raven Press, New York, (in press)
Beck, F. and Lloyd, J.B. (1964) *Nature (London)*, *201*, 1136-7
Beck, F. and Lloyd, J.B. (1966) *Advan. Teratol. 11*, 131-93
Beck, F. and Lloyd, J.B. (1977) in *Handbook of Teratology* (Wilson, J.G. and Fraser, F.C., eds.), Vol. 3, pp. 155-86, Plenum Press, New York and London
Beck, F., Lloyd, J.B. and Griffiths, A. (1967) *Science*, *157*, 1180-2
Berry, C.L. and Germain, J. (1972) *J. Path.*, *108*, 35-45
Berry, C.L. and Germain, J. (1975) in *Teratology – Trends and Applications* (Berry, C.L. and Poswillo, D., eds.), pp. 83-102, Springer, Berlin
Berry, C.L. and Nickols, C.D. (1979) *Arch. Toxicol.*, *42*, 185-90
Blanc, W.A. (1967) *Pediatr. Res.*, *1*, 218
Bornstein, S., Trasler, D.G. and Fraser, F.C. (1970) *Teratology*, *3*, 295-8
Brent, R.L. and Franklin, J.B. (1960) *Science*, *132*, 89-91
Brent, R.L. and McLaughlin, M.M. (1960) *Am. J. Dis. Child.*, *100*, 94-102
Carter, C.O. (1965) *Progr. Med. Genet.*, *4*, 59-84
—— (1969) *Br. Med. Bull.*, *25*, 52-7
Chatot, C.L., Klein, N.W., Piatek, J. and Pierro, L.J. (1980) *Science*, *207*, 1471-3
Clarkson, S.G., Doering, J.V. and Runner, N.M. (1969) *Teratology*, *2*, 181-6
Davies, M., Lloyd, J.B. and Beck, F. (1969) *Science*, *163*, 1454-6
Edwards, J.H. (1969) *Br. Med. Bull.*, *25*, 58-64
Embury, S., Seller, M.J., Adinolfi, M. and Polani, P.E. (1979) *Proc. Roy. Soc. Lond. B.*, *206*, 85-94
Fantel, A.G., Greenaway, J.C., Juchau, M.R. and Shepard, T.H. (1979) *Life Sci.*, *25*, 67-72
Fraser, F.C. (1977a) in *Handbook of Teratology* (Wilson, J.G. and Fraser, F.C., eds.), Vol. 1, pp. 75-96, Plenum Press, New York
—— (1977b) in *Handbook of Teratology* (Wilson, J.G. and Fraser, F.C., eds.), Vol. 1, pp. 445-63, Plenum Press, New York
George, E.F., Franklin, J.B. and Brent, R.L. (1967) *Proc. Soc. Exp. Biol. Med.*, *124*, 257-60
Grüneberg, H. (1954) *J. Genet.*, *52*, 52-67
Gulamhusein, A.P., Beck, F. and Zimmerman, B. (1980) *J. Anat.*, *131*, 347-54
Kochhar, D.M. (1975) *Teratology*, *11*, 273-88
Leck, I., Record, R.G., McKeown, T. and Edwards, J.H. (1968) *Teratology*, *1*, 263-80
Maizell, M. and Isaaca, J.J. (1970) *Am. Zool.*, *10*, 141-55
Marsk, L., Theorell, M. and Larsson, K.S. (1971) *Teratology*, *4*, 494 (Abstract)
Moore, W. and Gulamhusein, A.P. (1981) *J. Anat.* (in press)
McGarrity, C., Samani, N., Beck, F. and Gulamhusein, A.P. (1981) *J. Anat.* (in press)
McLaren, A. and Michie, D. (1958) *J. Embryol. Exp. Morphol.*, *6*, 645-59
New, D.A.T. (1978) *Biol. Rev.*, *53*, 81-122
Nau, H. and Liddiard, C. (1978) in *Role of Pharmacokinetics in Prenatal and Perinatal Toxicology* (Neubert, D., Merker, H.J., Nau, H. and Langman, J., eds.), pp. 76-90, Georg Thieme, Stuttgart

Neubert, D., Merker, H.-J., Nau, H. and Longman, J. (1978) *Role of Pharmacokinetics in Prenatal and Perinatal Toxicology*, Georg Thieme, Stuttgart

Palmer, A.K. (1978) in *Handbook of Teratology* (Wilson, J.G. and Fraser, F.C., eds.), Vol. 4, pp. 215-53, Plenum Press, New York

Pourtois, M. (1966) *J. Embryol. Exp. Morphol., 16*, 171-82

Schardein, J.L. (1976) *Drugs as Teratogens*, pp. 9-33, CRC Press, Cleveland, Ohio

Seller, M.J., Embury, S., Polani, P.E. and Adinolfi, M. (1979) *Proc. Roy. Soc. Lond. B., 206*, 95-107

Thesleff, I. (1977) in *Methods in Prenatal Toxicology* (Neubert, D., Merker, H.-J. and Kwasigroch, T.E., eds.), pp. 252-62, Georg Thieme, Stuttgart

Verrusio, A.C., Pollard, D.R. and Fraser, F.C. (1968) *Science, 160*, 206-7

Wigglesworth, J.S. (1964) *J. Path. Bact., 88*, 1-13

Williams, K.E., Roberts, G., Kidston, M.E., Beck, F. and Lloyd, J.B. (1976) *Teratology, 14*, 343-54

Wilson, J.G. (1973) *Environment and Birth Defects*, pp. 195-205, Academic Press, New York and London

—— (1977) in *Handbook of Teratology* (Wilson, J.G. and Fraser, F.C., eds.), Vol. 1, pp. 47-74, Plenum Press, New York and London

—— (1978a) in *Handbook of Teratology* (Wilson, J.G. and Fraser, F.C., eds.), Vol. 4, pp. 255-73, Plenum Press, New York and London

—— (1978b) in *Handbook of Teratology* (Wilson, J.G. and Fraser, F.C., eds.), Vol. 4, pp. 135-53, Plenum Press, New York

CHAPTER TWO

THE *IN VITRO* APPROACH TO TERATOGENICITY TESTING
Nigel A. Brown and Sergio E. Fabro

CONTENTS

Contents

I. Introduction

A. *Definition of the Approach*

Investigations in toxicology may be divided into those in which the primary aim is to identify hazardous substances (e.g. toxicity testing) and those where the mechanism of toxicity is the object of study. There is, of course, much overlap between the two approaches and they are mutually inter-dependent, but the distinction is useful to define the scope of this chapter. The goal of toxicity testing is to identify hazardous agents, to define the conditions (dose, time, route of exposure, susceptible species, etc.) under which they will exert their toxicity and to estimate the potential effects on human health. This chapter will review those *in vitro* systems which have potential application as tests for the identification of teratogenic substances. That is not to suggest that studies of the mechanisms of teratogenicity are not of paramount importance. Knowledge of toxic mechanisms may allow the prediction of toxicity, based upon chemical structure or reactivity, and may also permit preventive, ameliorative or curative measures to be devised. As will be discussed, suitable *in vitro* test systems cannot be defined without considering the mechanism of toxicity.

Numerous *in vitro* techniques have been utilised in investigations of particular processes or pathways of the teratogenic response. Many cell culture techniques and cell-free biochemical systems fall into this category and since these are covered elsewhere in this volume (Chapters 1, 3 and 4), they will not be considered here.

The In Vitro Approach to Teratogenicity Testing

B. *Rationale for* In Vitro *Tests for Teratogenicity*

The currently accepted tests for teratogenicity comprise the administration of the test agent to pregnant rodents or lagomorphs with examination of the progeny near term. These whole-animal *in vivo* tests have developed to a relatively standardised form and are utilised world-wide. They suffer, however, from two serious problems: they are expensive and time con-suming to perform, and the extrapolation of the results to the human population is confounded by the well-known species variation in terato-genic response (Wilson, 1977). The number of compounds which must be tested for teratogenicity has increased dramatically with the continuous development of therapeutic, cosmetic and food-additive chemicals. In addition, there are increasing governmental regulations in many countries which require more rigorous toxicity testing of those industrial and commercial agents to which the human population could conceivably be exposed. It is clearly unrealistic to attempt to perform complete *in vivo* teratogenicity tests on each and every one of these chemicals. Thus, cheaper, quicker, more efficient, but nevertheless reliable tests must be developed. These tests may sometimes function only as a pre-screen for the detection of compounds which may require further, more exhaustive, testing. In other cases, a risk-benefit decision may be made based upon the result of *in vitro* testing. If an *in vitro* test can be established which satisfies these requirements and also aids the extrapolation of test data to the human population, a significant advance in toxicology will have been achieved.

C. *Selection of Suitable Test Systems*

In addition to the practical features required of an *in vitro* system (low cost, ease of performance, etc.), any prospective test for teratogenicity must meet certain scientific criteria. An understanding of the mechanism of production of a toxic lesion is a prerequisite for the formulation of a suitable *in vitro* test system. For example, the short-term 'Ames' test for carcinogens (Ames *et al.*, 1975) measures mutation frequency as an indi-cator of carcinogenicity. This is thought to be an appropriate test since, for many agents, somatic mutation is considered to be the common initial insult leading to neoplasia. Significant problems exist in defining a suitable test for teratogenicity since relatively little is known of the initial insults which lead to abnormal development. Indeed, it has been suggested that faced with the vast array of congenital syndromes, disorders, defects and variations, the search for unifying mechanisms in teratogenicity is likely to be disappointing (Wilson, 1977). Nevertheless, the known primary sites of teratogenic action and their potential pathogenic consequences can be listed (Fig. 2.1).

Figure 2.1: Potential Sites of Teratogenic Insult

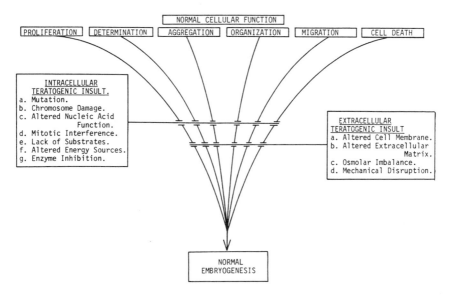

A teratogenic agent may act at one or more initial sites (only some of which are shown). The initial insult may result in a change in one or more of the normal cellular functions, e.g. reduced proliferation, inhibited cell migration. This, in turn, may lead to abnormal embryogenesis. Data from Saxén (1976) and Wilson (1977).

Given the fact that the initial action of an uncharacterised agent could be exerted at any one of these multiple sites, two approaches may be taken in devising a generally applicable test system. On the one hand, a battery of tests could be assembled, each of which would evaluate one of the potential sites of teratogenic insult. Some interesting possibilities for individual tests have been described. For example, a cell-adhesion assay has recently been proposed for evaluation of cell-surface function and has been shown to detect a variety of teratogenic substances (Braun *et al.,* 1979). However, the overall 'battery' approach is unlikely to be feasible, since a large number of individual tests would have to be carried out, contradicting the 'low cost' and 'ease of performance' requirements for a suitable system. In the alternative approach, a test system would incorporate all of the processes of growth and differentiation, so that any teratogenic agent would produce a response, regardless of its mechanism of action (i.e., there would be few false-negatives). Thus, single systems must be identified which include the processes of cell multiplication, determination/induction, aggregation, morphogenetic movement, cell death, etc. Currently, only two types of systems satisfy these criteria; those using developing embryos (or portions of embryos) and those utilising regenerating tissue. These potential *in vitro* tests for teratogenicity are summarised in Table 2.1 and are discussed in turn in the following sections.

Table 2.1: *In Vitro* **Systems with Potential Application as Tests of Teratogenicity**

Sub-Mammalian Systems	
Invertebrate Embryos	— Nematoda (e.g. *Caenorhabditis elegans*) Cnidaria (e.g. hydra) Echinodermata (e.g. sea urchin, sand dollar) Insecta (e.g. drosophila)
Vertebrate Embryos	— Pisces (e.g. medaka, zebra fish) Amphibia (e.g. frog, salamander) Aves (e.g. chick, quail)
Mammalian Systems	
Isolated Whole Embryos	— Pre-implantation Post-implantation
Isolated Embryonic Organs	— Limb-buds Palate

II. Potential *In Vitro* Tests for Teratogenicity

A. *Sub-Mammalian Systems*

(i) Invertebrates. Adult and embryonic stages of several invertebrate species can be maintained in the laboratory in large numbers and provide

model systems in many areas of biological research. For several years, the nematode *Caenorhabditis elegans* has been a model organism in studies of the control of embryonic development. The cell lineages of both embryonic (Deppe *et al.*, 1978) and post-embryonic (Sulston and Horvitz, 1977) development have been elucidated, giving a precise map of differentiation from the fertilised egg to the 900 cell adult. This model has been widely used in studies of genetic control in development and a comprehensive map of its genome is available (see Moerman and Baillie, 1979; Hodgkin *et al.*, 1979). While the extensive background information suggests that this organism may be useful in studies of abnormal development, it has yet to be evaluated as a potential test for teratogenicity.

An interesting system has recently been described which uses regeneration of a cnidarian organism as a test for teratogenic potential (Johnson, 1980). The adult hydra *Attenuata* can be disrupted into individual cells and centrifuged to form a pellet which will ultimately reform into a complete organism. The system has been used in an investigation of the relative toxicities of known teratogens to the adult organism and the regenerating 'synthetic embryo' with good, albeit preliminary, correlation with mammalian data (Johnson, 1980).

The embryology and development of certain echinoderms, particularly the sand dollar and sea urchin (Gross *et al.*, 1972) are well characterised, and these species may be easily cultured in large numbers (Hinegardner, 1969). Although they have not been systematically examined as potential screening systems, these organisms have been used in experimental embryology, particularly in studies of antimetabolite effects on embryogenesis (Karnofsky and Basch, 1960; Lallier, 1965).

Within the class Insecta, the drosophila (fruit fly) is familiar to all students of biology (Demerec, 1950) and its embryonic development has been well described (Bodenstein, 1950; Poulson, 1950). The use of this species in genetic studies is well known and, recently, short-term tests for mutagenicity have been developed using this system (Würgler *et al.*, 1977). Again, the extensive genetic and developmental background data suggest that this may be a suitable organism for teratogenicity studies but it has not been comprehensively evaluated.

(ii) Vertebrates − Pisces and Amphibia. A major portion of the discipline of aquatic toxicology concerns the assessment of toxicity to fish and amphibians (see, for example, Marking and Kimerle, 1979; Vernberg *et al.*, 1977). An integral part of these studies is the evaluation of the effects of chemicals on the development of eggs, embryos and larvae (e.g. Birge *et al.*,

The In Vitro Approach to Teratogenicity Testing

1979; Leung and Bulkley, 1979). Thus, much information is available on the toxicity of xenobiotics to aquatic organisms and the methodology is available for embryotoxicity testing in these lower vertebrates (Birge and Black, 1977). In addition, the normal development of fish, newts, salamanders and frogs has been the subject of classic embryological studies and detailed treatises can be found in many standard texts. Recently, there has been much interest in xenobiotic disposition and metabolism in fish (e.g. Melancon *et al.*, 1977; Statham *et al.*, 1978) and even in the possible elimination of contaminants in eggs during spawning (Guiney *et al.*, 1980). All of these data suggest that lower vertebrates, particularly those varieties of fish which can be easily maintained in the laboratory, such as zebra fish, medaka or minnows, may be suitable test systems in teratology. Indeed, early experimental teratology studies often used fish as models (see Wilson, 1978). More recently, the teratogenic effects of drugs such as tolbutamide (Smithberg, 1962) and environmental pollutants such as 2,4,5-T (2,4,5-trichlorophenoxyacetic acid) (Schreiweis and Murray, 1976) have been studied in aquatic species. However, as with the invertebrate models, there has been no systematic study of the possible use of lower vertebrates as test systems in teratogenicity.

(iii) Vertebrates − Aves. Avian embryos, particularly the chick embryo, have contributed enormously to experimental embryology and there is a vast amount of literature describing their development and their use as model systems (e.g. Patten, 1951; Hamburger and Hamilton, 1951; Freeman and Vince, 1974). Much has been said of the possible use of the chick embryo as a test for teratogenicity but the predictive value of the chick model has repeatedly been doubted (Karnofsky, 1965; Koll, 1966). The recommendations of the WHO (1967) are perhaps most widely quoted:

Mice, rats and rabbits are the test animals most frequently used. They have been selected primarily on the basis of prior experience with teratogenic agents and of the availability of these animals in most laboratories. Otherwise, the choice is arbitrary in the absence of any indication, as yet, of a species with a susceptibility close to that of man.

The chick embryo contributes greatly to basic embryological knowledge. However, for the screening of drugs for teratogenicity, its use is not recommended. It is too sensitive to a wide range of agents and affords no parallel with the anatomical and physiological relationship existing between a pregnant mammal and her conceptus.

38

However, as the list of chemicals which must be tested has grown to an intolerable burden, the chick embryo has received more favourable review (Gebhardt, 1972; Jelinek, 1977; Wilson, 1978).

Several authors have described protocols in which the chick is utilised in a predictive test for teratogenicity. Those of Karnofsky (1955), McLaughlin *et al.* (1963), Gebhardt (1972) and Wilson (1978) are essentially similar. White Leghorn eggs incubated in commercial apparatus at 30°C are usually used. To administer the test agent, a hole is bored in the egg, which may be subsequently resealed with wax or Parafilm. The test agent may be administered to the yolk sac, subgerminal cavity, allantois, amnion or air chamber depending upon the physicochemical properties of the compound and the individual preference of the investigator (Gebhardt, 1972; Wilson, 1978). Opinions on the most appropriate treatment time vary from 0 hours of incubation (McLaughlin *et al.*, 1963) to 30 hours (Wilson, 1978), 48 hours (Kaplan and Grabowski, 1967), or 96 hours (Karnofsky, 1955; Gebhardt, 1972). The chick may be examined for abnormalities at any time during incubation, at hatching, or may be allowed to mature to evaluate functional normality. Wilson (1978) has provided a detailed summary of appropriate dose schedules and sacrifice times.

Recently, a more rapid chick embryotoxicity screening test has been proposed (Jelinek, 1977) based upon the caudal morphogenetic system. In this technique, agents are administered directly below the caudal region of the embryo, which is at Hamburger-Hamilton stage 10 or 11. After a 24-hour incubation, the length of the caudal trunk is measured and used as a quantitative estimate of embryotoxicity. In a preliminary test of the system, 17 drugs were screened and reasonable correspondence with whole-mammal data was reported (Jelinek, 1977).

It is not appropriate to attempt to summarize the vast literature which exists describing the adverse effects of chemicals on the chick embryo. Suffice it to say that probably more compounds have been evaluated in this system that in all the other *in vitro* systems combined. Gebhardt (1972) has summarised much of the chick information, particularly in those cases in which comparisons with mammalian embryotoxic effects were possible.

B. *Mammalian Systems*

(i) Whole-Embryo Culture: Pre-Implantation. Mammalian conceptuses can be maintained in culture for limited periods of time and with variable

degrees of success, starting at any stage of gestation from fertilised zygote to mature fetus. Culture techniques for the early mammalian conceptus, from the one cell to blastocyst stages, are well established (Daniel, 1971). Indeed, the mammalian conceptus at this stage can be removed from the dam, maintained *in vitro* for several days and re-implanted into a pseudo-pregnant surrogate dam with complete development to term (e.g. Staples, 1971). While these techniques are elegant and most successful, they have proved to be of limited value to the teratologist, in contrast to their extensive use in developmental biology (Daniel, 1971). Several authors have reported that embryos at the early pre-implantation stages are largely refractory to treatment with teratogenic agents (Staples, 1975). High doses may result in death of the embryo, but there have been few instances of congenital malformations as a result of insult to the blastocyst (Wilson, 1978).

The culture of mammalian conceptuses over the implantation period has generally proved to be difficult (McLaren and Hensleigh, 1975). In a series of elegant studies, Hsu (see Hsu, 1973, 1979, 1980) has perfected techniques which allow mouse blastocysts to be grown *in vitro* to the early somite stage. While this is a powerful tool for developmental studies, the technique is too complex for routine use and the low percentage survival rate (approximately 50%) would prove to be a large problem in an *in vitro* test. The remainder of this section will deal exclusively with the culture of post-implantation mammalian embryos.

(ii) Whole-Embryo Culture: Post-Implantation. Most studies used the rat embryo and the embryonic ages used in this section refer to the rat. Reference will be made to other species where appropriate. (Embryonic ages are calculated assuming that zero age was the midpoint of the mating period. When duration of pregnancy is referred to, day 1 is the day on which a positive vaginal smear or copulatory plug was detected.) The rat conceptus completes implantation at 7.5-8 days of age, when the embryo is at the egg cylinder stage. Subsequent development proceeds through the following stages: age 8.5 days, primitive streak; 9 days, pre-somite neurula; 9.5 days, first somites, brain folds (Figs. 2A, 3A); 10.5 days, 10-14 somites, yolk-sac circulation (Figs. 2B, 3B); 11.5 days, tail-bud embryo, 26-30 somites, forelimb bud (Figs. 2C, 3C); 12.5 days, complete embryo, 40-42 somites (Figs. 2D, 3D); 13.5 days, early fetus, 48-50 somites. Techniques are available which will support embryonic growth for periods from 24 hours to 4 days over any portion of this post-implantation embryonic phase. All these methods have similar protocols: the dam is sacrificed, the whole

Figure 2.2: Rat Conceptuses Prepared for Whole-embryo Culture. In each case, Reichert's membrane has been removed leaving the yolk sac, containing the amnion and embryo, and the ectoplacental cone. A: 9.5 days, complete conceptus (right) and embryo and allantois (left); B: 10.5 days; C: 11.5 days; D: 12.5 days.

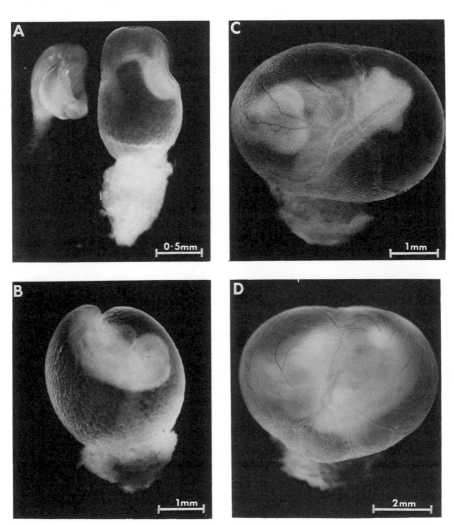

Figure 2.3: Rat Embryos, Showing the Development Obtained During Whole-embryo Culture. A: Embryo as explanted at 9.5 days; B: Embryo, as explanted at 10.5 days; C: 11.5 day embryo (equivalent to 48 hours of culture from 9.5 day stage); D: 12.5 day embryo (equivalent to 48 hours of culture from 10.5 day stage).

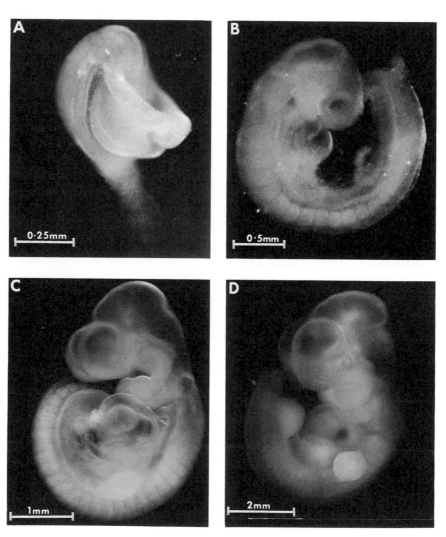

uterus is removed and implantation sites are dissected from the uterine wall. With the aid of a dissecting microscope and micro-forceps, the maternal decidual tissue is torn away, leaving the whole conceptus enclosed within the trophoblastic Reichert's membrane. This membrane is then torn open or removed entirely and the conceptus (as shown in Figure 2) is transferred to the culture medium. Techniques differ with respect to the apparatus which contains the medium, the medium itself and the gas phase of the system.

(a) *Static Methods.* In these systems, the conceptus is placed in the nutrient medium on a watch-glass which is contained in a petri dish. The dish is normally lined with a wet, absorbent material to provide a humidified atmosphere and the whole system is housed within a gas-tight chamber filled with the appropriate gas mixture. New and Stein (1964) originally described a supportive clot of fowl plasma and embryo extract with a nutrient medium of dilute embryo extract. However, homologous serum seems to be the most successful medium (New, 1966), as is the case in most embryo culture techniques. When homologous serum is used, immediate centrifugation (Steele, 1972) and heat inactivation (Steele and New, 1974) prevent the formation of double hearts in early embryos (7.5 and 8.5 days). Serum has been diluted with Waymouth's medium (Clarkson et al., 1969), dialysed and then supplemented with glucose (Gunberg, 1976).

Static culture techniques are most successful with early (7.5-9.5 day) rat embryos but, at best, survival of embryos for more than 24 hours is poor and growth does not approximate that *in vivo*. Survival of early somite embryos, as determined by heart beat and yolk sac circulation, is about 60% at 24 hours and less for longer culture periods (New and Stein, 1964; Berry, 1971; Morriss and Steele, 1977). Growth of 5 somite embryos, measured by protein content, is significantly retarded compared with that obtained *in vivo* (Berry, 1968). When compared with other techniques, these static methods have serious limitations for use in teratological investigations, because of the high rate of embryonic death and the less than optimal growth rates. Nevertheless, useful information has been generated using these procedures.

Deuchar has provided a detailed description of axial rotation in rat embryos and of the reconstruction ability of axial tissue (Deuchar, 1971, 1975). The direct embryotoxicity of trypan blue (Turbow, 1966), 6-aminonicotinamide (Turbow and Chamberline, 1968), vitamin E (Steele et al., 1974), the anaesthetic Avertin (Kaufman and Steele, 1976), retinol and retinoic acid (Morriss and Steele, 1974, 1977) have all been demonstrated in static-medium experiments. In addition, antibodies to the contractile proteins of rat heart have been shown to be lethal to embryos in culture (Berry, 1971).

(b) *Circulating Methods.* In attempts to improve the development of embryos over that obtained in static cultures, several techniques have been described which enable medium to be circulated around an immobilised conceptus (New, 1967; Robkin *et al.*, 1972; Tamarin and Jones, 1968; Givelber and DiPaolo, 1968). In principle, all the techniques are similar and follow a concept introduced by Nicholas (1938). The conceptus is explanted, as described previously, attached by Reichert's membrane to gauze or wire mesh and installed in a chamber through which oxygenated culture medium is circulated. Various media have been used including homologous sera (New, 1967; Givelber and DiPaolo, 1968), human serum (Robkin and Shepard, 1972) and serum diluted with Eagle's medium (Tamarin and Jones, 1968) or Tyrode's solution (Cockroft, 1973). Generally, greater dilution of serum is tolerated in circulating systems than in either static or rotating methods (Cockroft, 1973).

Because of the complexity of the apparatus and the limited number of embryos which can be handled, circulating systems are not ideal for use in teratogenicity testing. However, they do offer two distinct advantages. Firstly, embryos can be monitored continuously, which permits cinematography of development (see New, 1978a) or measurement of embryonic heart rate (Robkin and Shepard, 1972). Secondly, circulation systems support the growth of late organogenesis embryos (13.5 or 14.5 days), especially if the yolk sac is cut and the embryo is exposed directly to the medium (Cockroft, 1973, 1976).

Shepard and his colleagues have made extensive use of circulating systems in studying the effects of autonomic drugs on the embryonic heart (Robkin *et al.*, 1974; Robkin *et al.*, 1976b), the effect of hypoxia and carbon monoxide (Shepard *et al.*, 1969; Robkin *et al.*, 1976a) and glucose utilisation in aerobic and anaerobic metabolism (Robkin and Shepard, 1972; Robkin *et al.*, 1972; Tanimura and Shepard, 1970). The direct embryotoxicity of vitamin A has been examined using a circulator system (Morriss and Steele, 1974), although this method was not observed to be superior to either watch-glass or roller-bottle methods (Morriss and Steele, 1974, 1977).

(c) *Roller-Bottle Methods.* Roller-bottles or rotating bottles seem to offer the greatest possibility for the use of whole mammalian conceptuses in an *in vitro* test for teratogenicity. In these systems, the conceptus is explanted, Reichert's membrane is removed and the conceptus is submerged in culture medium which is contained in a suitable bottle. The gas phase of the bottle is equilibrated with a mixture of oxygen, carbon dioxide and nitrogen and the bottle is installed within a roller apparatus or a rotating disk. The technique was introduced by New and his colleagues (New *et al.*, 1973) and the rotating modification was described by Kochhar (1975). Since its introduction, this system has been used extensively by several groups of investigators (see New, 1978a, b; Kochhar, 1980, for reviews).

Homologous rat serum which has been prepared after immediate centrifugation and which is heat-inactivated (New *et al.*, 1976a) provides optimal growth of rat embryos. Human serum (Fantel *et al.*, 1979) or human serum supplemented with glucose has been used (Chatot *et al.*, 1980) but growth is less than that obtained with rat serum. Several different gassing procedures have been used and there is general agreement that early embryos (less than 10 days) require low (about 5%) oxygen concentrations (New *et al.*, 1976a), which must be steadily increased as the embryo matures to a maximum of 95% O_2 at and above ages of 12.5 days (Cockroft, 1977). Gases can either be changed periodically (Brown *et al.*, 1979) or continuously varied using a suitable flow apparatus (New and Cockroft, 1978). Recently, the first steps have been taken in the production of a defined medium for the whole rat-conceptus roller system by the supplementation of extensively dialysed serum with various nutrients (Cockroft, 1979).

The growth of embryos explanted at 9.5 days (Fig. 2.3A) and cultured for 48 hours is indistinguishable from that *in utero* (11.5 days – Fig. 2.3C) over the equivalent period (New *et al.*, 1976b) and almost all cultured embryos survive the culture process. Growth of older embryos is retarded, presumably due to the lack of chorio-allantoic placental flow of nutrients. The yolk sac placentation appears to be sufficient to maintain earlier embryos. Younger embryos (7.5 days or 8.5 days) can be grown with some success, for periods up to 5 days (Buckley *et al.*, 1978). However, survival of these embryos is much reduced (about 50%), compared with those explanted at 9.5 days.

Studies of the effects of the following agents on embryonic development have used the roller-bottle technique, and most have used one or two day cultures to the 11.5 day stage:

Copper (Webb and Coppola, 1976); 5-bromodeoxyuridine (Agnish and

Kochhar, 1976); glucose (Cockroft and Coppola, 1977); retinol and retinoic acid (Morriss and Steele, 1977); carbon monoxide (Robkin and Cockroft, 1978); hyperthermia (Cockroft and New, 1978); ethanol (Brown *et al.*, 1979); oxygen (Morriss and New, 1979); cyclophosphamide (Fantel *et al.*, 1979); cytosine arabinoside and ribavirin (Kochhar, 1980); cadmium and cyclophosphamide (Klein *et al.*, 1980); cancer chemotherapeutic agents and anticonvulsants (Chatot *et al.*, 1980). Finally, recent studies of the embryotoxicity of diabetic serum and hyperglycemia have utilised mouse embryos in rotator culture (Sadler, 1979, 1980a, b).

(d) *Mode of Treatment.* In using the isolated embryo as an *in vitro* test for teratogenicity, a major drawback is that the maternal xenobiotic metabolising systems are removed. Thus, the profound influence that biotransformation may have on teratogenic potential is obscured. This may not be a problem if the aim of the study is to establish the direct embryotoxicity of a drug or agent (e.g., Brown *et al.*, 1979) or to complement known *in vivo* data (e.g., Morriss and Steele, 1977). However, for predictive testing of compounds of unknown potential, metabolic transformation must be taken into consideration. Three different approaches have been proposed: (1) testing of the parent compound and known metabolites; (2) addition of a metabolising system to the culture system; (3) culturing in serum from animals treated with the agent.

In circumstances where the metabolism of a compound is documented, particularly if its transformation in man is established, the first approach may be the most profitable. An example of this is the study of the anticonvulsant trimethadione, a known human teratogen, which is extensively *N*-demethylated in man. In testing the parent compound and the metabolite dimethadione in a rat-embryo culture system, it was shown that the metabolite exerts greater embryotoxicity than does the parent compound (Brown and Fabro, 1979). This approach is *not* appropriate if a reactive intermediate is suspected as the ultimate teratogen. Addition of hepatic homogenate or post-mitochondrial supernatant (S9) fraction is a standard approach in mutagenicity tests where metabolic activation is required. The same approach has been taken in the embryo culture system and it has been shown that cyclophosphamide exerts embryotoxic effects only in the presence of the S9 fraction (Fantel *et al.*, 1979). As in other tests which utilise this approach, it must always be remembered that metabolic profiles may be different in *in vitro* and *in vivo* systems, and the profiles may vary significantly with enzyme preparations from different species. It should, however, be possible to include a metabolising system from human tissues into these systems.

A third approach is to culture embryos in serum prepared from animals pre-treated with the agent under testing. Recent studies of cadmium and cyclophosphamide embryotoxicity have demonstrated that this is a workable approach and have shown that a compound may exert differing effects when administered in this way, compared with direct addition to untreated serum (Klein *et al.,* 1980). A drawback of this approach is that the treated serum may vary from control serum, in addition to the presence of the agent and its metabolites. Serum changes may be produced by a toxic effect of the agent upon the treated animals. Care should be taken to exclude this possibility before attributing a toxic effect to the direct action of the agent. Nevertheless, the technique is an attractive one, since it allows the use of serum from human subjects treated with drugs or other toxicants. It was recently shown that the serum of patients undergoing therapy with cancer chemotherapeutic agents or anticonvulsants exerted significant embryotoxic effects on cultured rat conceptuses (Chatot *et al.,* 1980), although the chemical nature of the embryotoxic agent was not investigated.

(e) *Evaluation of Results.* An obvious prerequisite of any test is that it should have suitable end-points to define whether the answer is positive or negative and, perhaps, to quantify the magnitude of the effect. Satisfactory criteria for the development of embryos have been difficult to define (New, 1978a). Evaluation of whether an embryo has 'survived' the culture can be made from the presence of a normal heartbeat and active yolk-sac blood circulation, but this is hardly enough. Embryonic growth is relatively easy to measure and several parameters are suitable, including: crown-rump length, head length and embryonic protein or DNA content (New, 1978a; Brown *et al.,* 1979). Gross structural defects are also easily observed, but more subtle developmental abnormalities may not be. Recently, a system was proposed which is specifically designed to evaluate the differentiation and morphogenesis of cultured embryos (Brown *et al.,* 1980a; Brown and Fabro, 1980). A morphological score is calculated for a conceptus from the defined stages of development of a series of specific embryonic features. The score gives a numerical value for development and will indicate any developmental retardation, since in normal embryos the score correlates closely with embryonic age. By careful reference to the normal stages of development for each organ primordium, subtle dysmorphogenesis can also be detected.

A major problem in whole-conceptus culture is the viability of the yolk sac and its circulation. In our laboratories, virtually all embryotoxic agents are also observed to be toxic to the yolk sac, at equal or even lower doses. Since an embryo which develops for any length of time within an abnormal yolk sac does not develop normally, any yolk-sac effects must be taken into account. Thus, data may be presented only on those conceptuses which have a functional yolk-sac circulation at the end of the culture period (e.g. Fantel *et al.,* 1979). Alternatively, when presenting incidences of malformation, some indication should be given of what proportion were from abnormal yolk sacs. The relationships of yolk-sac damage *in vitro* to the actions of the agent *in vivo* are not yet established.

C. *Organ Culture*

(i) Embryonic and Fetal Organs. A wide range of embryonic organs can be explanted and grown in culture. Table 2.2 lists those organs which have been successfully maintained *in vitro*, with appropriate sample references. The vast majority of these systems would not, however, be appropriate as testing techniques. This is primarily because of the limited development which is achieved *in vitro* since organs are explanted at an advanced stage of differentiation. Many of these organ systems do play an important role in the study of biochemical and histological development, but this is beyond the scope of this article. In the specific investigation for oro-facial anomalies, organ culture has proven particularly useful both in the study of palate fusion (Lahti *et al.,* 1972; Saxén and Saxén, 1975) and palate rotation (Wee *et al.,* 1976; Zimmerman, 1976). Of all the embryonic organs, limb-buds have proven most amenable to *in vitro* culture and would seem to present the best possibility of a workable test system.

(ii) Limb-buds. The techniques for the embryonic organs, including limb-buds, have been developed from the classic methods devised by Trowell (1954, 1959, 1961). The initial report of limb-bud culture was made by Kochhar (Aydelotte and Kochhar, 1972) and the technique has been utilised extensively by his group (see Kochhar, 1975, 1976; Kochhar *et al.,* 1980) and by the group headed by Neubert (see Neubert and Barrach, 1977b, for review). In these studies, the mouse has been the main source of material but rat and rabbit limb-buds can also be cultured (Lessmöllmann *et al.,* 1976).

The development of limb-buds *in vitro* is critically dependent upon the embryonic stage at which the culture is initiated. The most complete

Table 2.2: Mammalian Embryonic or Fetal Organs which may be Maintained *In Vitro*

Organ (species)	Reference
Limb-bud (mouse, rat, rabbit)	See text
Palatal shelves (mouse)	Saxén and Saxén (1975) Fairbanks and Kollar (1974) Lahti *et al.* (1972)
Palate (whole-embryo, mouse)	Wee *et al.* (1976)
Bone (mouse) (rat)	Fell and Weiss (1965) Biggers *et al.* (1961)
Kidney (mouse)	Crocker and Vernier (1970)
Lens (human)	Karkinen-Jääskeläinen *et al.* (1975)
Liver (human)	Räihä and Schwartz (1973)
Lung (rat)	Funkhouser *et al.* (1976)
Müllerian duct (rat)	Josso (1971)
Testes, ovaries (rabbit, rat)	Holyoke and Beber (1958)
Teeth (mice)	Koch (1974) Koller (1976)

Modified from Neubert and Barrach, 1977a.

development is achieved with forelimb-buds explanted from embryos at the 40-43 somite stage (cf. Fig. 2.3D; Neubert and Barrach, 1977b). Limb-buds are dissected from explanted embryos and placed on membrane filters which are supported by metal grids. The grids are placed in petri dishes and sufficient culture medium is added to wet only the underside of the filter. Culture is performed in a humidified 5% CO_2-air atmosphere at 37°C. The original medium was a mixture of 75% Bigger's medium with 25% fetal calf serum (Aydelotte and Kochhar, 1972); however, a chemically defined medium has now been described (Lessmöllman *et al.*, 1976). Maximum growth of limb-buds is obtained by the sixth day of culture when cartilagenous rudiments of scapula, humerus, radius, ulna and phalanges have been formed (Kochhar and Aydelotte, 1974; Neubert *et al.*, 1974a).

Recently, a second technique for limb-bud culture has been described (Neubert and Barrach, 1977b). In this method, limb-bud explantation and the culture medium are as described above but the organs are maintained in a roller-bottle system similar to that described for whole-embryo culture. The development of the paw anlagen appears to be slightly better in this system, compared with the Trowell technique (Neubert and Barrach, 1977b).

Most investigations which have used limb-bud culture have focused upon characterisation of the system or upon biochemical studies of teratogenic mechanisms and it is not appropriate to summarise this data here. Reference may be made to reviews by Kochhar (1975, 1976) and Neubert (Neubert *et al.,* 1976; Merker, 1975). Several authors have suggested that limb-bud culture may be an appropriate test for terato-genicity, but there have been no systematic investigations of its potential. However, the problem of the lack of xenobiotic metabolism in the system has been addressed and several techniques have been proposed to over-come this difficulty. Treatment may be made *in utero* followed by sacrifice of the dam, explantation of embryos and culture of limb-buds. This approach was used in a study of 5-bromodeoxyuridine teratogenicity, but the survival of limb-buds was poor, perhaps because of an impaired ability to attach to the filter membrane (Neubert *et al.,* 1974b). Utilising a similar protocol, exposure to retinoic acid *in utero* led to abnormal development of limb-buds in culture (Kochhar and Aydelotte, 1974). An alternative approach is to add serum prepared from treated animals to the culture medium, as has been described for whole-embryo culture. It has been suggested that the agent under study can be pre-incubated with a liver microsomal preparation and the necessary co-factors and that a suitably filtered sample may then be added to the culture medium. Limb-bud toxicity due to activated cyclophosphamide has been described following this procedure (Neubert and Barrach, 1977b). As was discussed for the whole-embryo culture system, a drug metabolising fraction may be added directly to the culture medium. It has been shown that microsomes or post-mitochondrial supernatant are both capable of activating cyclo-phosphamide to aklylating metabolites in a limb-bud system but both preparations were found to be toxic themselves (Manson and Simons, 1979). In contrast, co-cultured hamster embryo cells were non-toxic and continued to metabolise cyclophosphamide to toxic products for a period of three days (Manson and Simons, 1979).

The suitability of limb-bud culture as a test of teratogenicity has been doubted (Wilson, 1978) since the development of the organ does not closely parallel development *in vivo*. Growth is considerably retarded *in vitro*, the morphological stage attained in 6 days of culture is equivalent to approximately 3 days *in utero* (Neubert *et al.,* 1974a). While all the cartilagenous rudiments of the forelimb do develop during culture, they are distorted compared with the normal organ *in vivo* (Aydelotte and Kochhar, 1972). Significant biochemical and histological differences between limb-buds *in vitro* and *in vivo* have also been described (Merker, 1975; Neubert *et al.*, 1974a, 1976). Nevertheless, differentiation *in vitro* is consistent and reproducible and deviations due to treatment can be clearly detected. A scoring system has been devised to quantitate the differentiation of limb-buds *in vitro*. Each bone rudiment and each digit is assigned a score (maximum 30) based upon its development, with a total limb score of 300 being ideal (Neubert *et al.*, 1977). This system permits statistical analysis of treatment effects as well as facilitating the detection of abnormalities.

III. Advantages and Disadvantages of the *In Vitro* Approach

In the study of mechanisms of teratogenicity, *in vitro* techniques have clear practical and theoretical advantages over whole-animal studies. Some of these advantages are listed in Table 2.3 and particular mention should be made of the radioisotopic and other biochemical studies which are facilitated by using *in vitro* techniques. The potential advantages of the *in vitro* approach in teratogenicity testing are more difficult to evaluate. Most of the tests described in this chapter offer the advantages of speed and ease of operation and are relatively inexpensive to perform. However, whether they offer a predictive advantage over standard testing *in vivo* is uncertain. One of the major differences between these *in vitro* test systems and either the whole-animal or the human situation is the absence of the complex maternal-fetal-placental relationships. Herein lies a paradoxical dichotomy of advantages and disadvantages. On the one hand, much of the species differences, and indeed individual differences, in teratogenic response are thought to be due to disparate xenobiotic distribution, pharmacokinetics and biotransformation. In general, *in vitro* tests permit the exact regulation of level and time of exposure and the precise nature of the agent is known since little or no metabolism takes place. Metabolites can be individually tested or a bioactivation system may be added if it is appropriate. The confounding maternal factors of nutritional and hormonal balance are excluded, as is the placental 'barrier'. Litter differences in the developmental stage of *in vivo* test embryos may also contribute to variability in whole animal tests and this factor can be well controlled in tests *in vitro*. All of these comments suggest that an *in vitro* test may be

51

Table 2.3: **Advantages and Disadvantages of** *In Vitro* **Techniques in Teratology**

Advantages	Disadvantages
Confounding factors excluded — maternal, nutritional, hormonal.	Complex *in vivo* interactions are ignored.
Direct embryotoxicity may be studied	Whole-animal pharmacokinetics are ignored.
Exact concentrations can be defined	Maternal xenobiotic metabolism is absent.
Exact time of exposure can be defined.	
Biochemical and radioisotopic studies are facilitated.	Development *in vitro* may be 'abnormal'.
Exact developmental stage can be defined	Only limited periods of mammalian embryogenesis may be studied.
Placental 'barrier' is eliminated	
Microsurgical manipulation is facilitated.	
Continuous observation of embryos is possible.	
Human tissues may be used.	
Embryonic/fetal metabolism can be studied.	

Modified from Saxén and Saxén (1975); Neubert and Barrach (1977a).

capable of a reasonable prediction of human health hazard if there is some knowledge of the dose, time and nature of human conceptus exposure. At least, a well-controlled *in vitro* test can give a precise estimate of teratogenic potential under defined and precisely known conditions.

However, an adverse human embryonic reaction is ultimately the product of the complex maternal-conceptus-placental interactions, direct embryotoxicity, or both. Thus the absence of these interactions may reduce the predictive capacity of *in vitro* tests and the described advantages are transformed into disadvantages. The ultimate resolution of this paradox will be possible only when sufficient data are available to allow scientific comparisons of the effects of a series of agents for which there are human, whole animal and *in vitro* data. We are far from that point.

IV. Summary and Conclusions

The evaluation of health hazards from toxicity testing relies upon the degree to which the test system reflects the response of the human organism. Suitable tests can be designed when the underlying processes which result in toxicity are understood and can be incorporated into the test system. For teratogenic response, these processes are not known and therefore the only criterion for selecting a test is that its biological properties approximate the human situation as closely as possible. Since routine use of primates is clearly impractical, rodents and lagomorphs are the standard test systems for teratogenicity and they are, indeed, the only tests used in regulatory decision-making around the world. However, the need to develop alternative systems is clear. In summarising the potential tests an attempt has been made to cover all workable possibilities but with a bias toward mammalian systems (as argued above).

Each of the potential tests has its own attributes and limitations. From the practical perspective, invertebrate, lower vertebrate and avian test systems offer the opportunity to use large numbers of animals with technical ease and low cost. The mammalian systems of whole-embryo culture and organ culture are certainly more complex, more time-consuming and more expensive but are nevertheless superior in these areas to the standard procedures *in vivo*. These practical considerations should not cloud the scientific evaluation of the appropriateness of testing techniques. Specific problems are attached to each of the systems; e.g., the protective layers of fish and amphibian eggs may impair delivery of the test agent. Similarly, the administration of highly lipophilic agents to aquatic species is often difficult. The normality of development *in vitro* is an important factor for explanted mammalian tissue. Whole conceptus development can closely approximate growth *in utero* but explanted organ differentiation (e.g. limb buds) is less similar to 'natural' development. A limitation of the whole-embryo system is that only restricted periods of growth can be maintained, largely because of the lack of placental function. The periods which are satisfactorily supported (early organogenesis) are often the most sensitive to environmental insult, but the manifestations of toxicity may not appear until later in gestation or, alternatively, repair of damage may occur.

The relationship between adult and embryonic toxicities must be considered when using any of these *in vitro* tests. The question should not be 'Is this agent embryotoxic?' since the answer will be 'Yes!' for all compounds, provided the dose can be made appropriately large. The question which requires answering is 'Can this agent exert embryotoxic effects at doses which are not toxic or lethal to the maternal/adult organism?' Thus a comparison between adult toxicity and embryotoxicity must be made. This factor is often ignored, even in whole animal tests, but recent suggestions have been made to use a quantitative embryonic/adult comparison in risk assessment (Brown *et al.*, 1980b; Johnson, 1980; Fabro *et al.*, 1981).

Clearly, there are few *a priori* scientific reasons to favour the use of any one of these *in vitro* systems. The establishment of a suitable system must rest on pragmatic validation with a range of well characterised compounds. This pre-requisite is largely satisfied for the chick system and yet opinions vary widely on the suitability of the chick as a test system. Some of the controversy may exist because proper consideration has not been given to the importance of xenobiotic metabolism, route of administration and adult/embryo toxicities, as has been discussed in this chapter. Even with a great deal of new data, these systems will probably never replace the pregnant mammal as the primary system for teratogenicity testing and, indeed, this should not be their purpose. However, some of the techniques do offer the promise of suitability as rapid pre-screening procedures and they should be actively evaluated.

References

Agnish, N.D. and Kochhar, D.M. (1976) *J. Embryol. Exp. Morphol.*, *36*, 623-38

Ames, B.N., McCann, J. and Yamasaki, E. (1975) *Mutat. Res.*, *31*, 347-64

Aydelotte, M.B. and Kochhar, D.M. (1972) *Develop. Biol.*, *28*, 191-201

Berry, C.L. (1968) *Nature (London)*, *219*, 92-3

Berry, C.L. (1971) *J. Embryol. Exp. Morphol.*, *25*, 203-12

Biggers, J.D., Gawtkin, R.B.L. and Heyner, S. (1961) *Exp. Cell Res.*, *25*, 41-53

Birge, W.J. and Black, J.A. (1977) *EPA Report EPA-560/5-77-002*, US Environmental Protection Agency, Washington, DC

Birge, W.J., Black, J.A., Hudson, J.E. and Bruser, D.M. (1979) in *Aquatic Toxicology, ASTM STP 667* (Marking, L.L. and Kimerle, R.A., eds.), pp. 131-47, American Society for Testing and Materials

Bodenstein, D. (1950) in *Biology of Drosophila* (Demerec, M., ed.), pp. 275-367, John Wiley, New York

Braun, A.G., Emerson, D.J. and Nichinson, B.B. (1979) *Nature (London)*, *282*, 507-9

Brown, N.A. and Fabro, S. (1979) *Proc. Ann. Meeting Soc. Gynecol. Invest.*, *26*, 132

Brown, N.A. and Fabro, S. (1981) *Teratology* (in press)

Brown, N.A., Goulding, E.H. and Fabro, S. (1979) *Science*, *206*, 573-5

Brown, N.A., Goulding, E.H. and Fabro, S. (1980a) *Teratology*, *21*, 30A

Brown, N.A., Kao, J. and Fabro, S. (1980b) *Lancet*, *1*, 660-1

Buckley, S.K.L., Steele, C.E. and New, D.A.T. (1978) *Develop. Biol.*, *65*, 396-403

Chatot, D.L., Klein, N.W., Piatek, J. and Pierro, L.J. (1980) *Science*, *207*, 1471-3

Clarkson, S.G., Doering, J.V. and Runner, M.N. (1969) *Teratology*, *2*, 181-6

Cockroft, D.L. (1973) *J. Embryol. Exp. Morphol.*, *29*, 473-83

—— (1976) *Develop. Biol.*, *48*, 163-72

Cockroft, D.L. (1977) in *Methods in Prenatal Toxicology* (Neubert, D., Merker, H.-J. and Kwasigroch, T.E., eds.), pp. 231-405, Georg Thieme, Stuttgart
—— (1979) *Reprod. Fertil., 57*, 505-10
Cockroft, D.L. and Coppola, P.T. (1977) *Teratology, 16,* 141-6
Cockroft, D.L. and New, D.A.T. (1978) *Teratology, 17,* 277-84
Crocker, J.F.S. and Vernier, R.L. (1970) *Science, 169,* 485-6
Daniel, J.C. (1971) *Methods in Mammalian Embryology.* Freeman and Company, San Francisco
Demerec, M. (1950) *Biology of Drosophila.* John Wiley, New York
Deppe, U., Schierenberg, E., Cole, T., Krieg, C., Schmitt, D., Yoder, B. and von Ehrenstein, G. (1978) *Proc. Natl. Acad. Sci. U.S.A. 75,* 376-80
Deuchar, E.M. (1971) *J. Embryol. Exp. Morphol., 25,* 189-201
Deuchar, E.M. (1975) *J. Embryol. Exp. Morphol., 33,* 217-26
Fabro, S., Haseman, J. and Brown, N.A. (1981) *Teratogen. Mutagen. Carcinogen.* (in press)
Fairbanks, M.D. and Koller, E.J. (1974) *Teratology, 9,* 169-78
Fantel, A.G., Greenaway, J.C., Juchau, M.R. and Shepard, T.H. (1979) *Life Sci., 25,* 67-73
Fell, H.B. and Weiss, L. (1965) *J. Exp. Med., 121,* 551-60
Freeman, B.M. and Vince, M.A. (1974) *Development of the Avian Embryo.* Chapman and Hall, London
Funkhouser, J.D., Hughes, E.R. and Peterson, R.D.A. (1976) *Biochem. Biophys. Res. Comm., 70,* 630-6
Gebhardt, D.O.E. (1972) *Advan. Teratol., 5,* 97-111
Givelber, H.M., DiPaolo, J.A. (1968) *Nature (London), 220,* 1131-2
Gross, P., Humphreys, T. and Anderson, E. (1972) *The Sea Urchin: Developmental Urchin,* MSS Information Corporation, New York
Guiney, P.D., Lech, J.J. and Peterson, R.E. (1980) *Toxicol. Appl. Pharmacol., 53,* 521-9
Gunberg, D.L. (1976) *Teratology, 14,* 65-70
Hamburger, V. and Hamilton, H.L. (1951) *J. Morphol., 88,* 49-82
Hinegardner, R.T. (1969) *Biol. Bull., 137,* 465-75
Holyoke, E.A. and Beber, B.A. (1958) *Science, 128,* 1082
Hodgkin, J., Horvitz, H.R. and Brenner, S. (1979) *Genetics, 91,* 67-91
Hsu, Y.-C. (1973) *Develop. Biol., 33,* 403-11
—— (1979) *Develop. Biol., 68,* 453-61
—— (1980) *Develop. Biol., 76,* 465-74
Jelinek, R. (1977) in *Methods in Prenatal Toxicology* (Neubert, D., Merker, H.-J. and Kwasigroch, T.E., eds.), pp. 381-6, Georg Thieme, Stuttgart
Johnson, E.H. (1980) *Teratology, 21,* 47A
Josso, N. (1971) *J. Clin, Endocrinol. Metab., 32,* 404-9
Kaplan, S. and Grabowski, C.T. (1967) *J. Exp. Zool., 165,* 325-36
Karkinen-Jääskeläinen, M., Saxén, L., Vaheri, A. and Leinikki, P. (1975) *J. Exp. Med., 141,* 1238-44
Karnofsky, D.A. (1955) *Stanford Med. Bull., 13,* 247-59
Karnofsky, D.A. (1965) in *Teratology Principles and Techniques* (Wilson, J.G. and Warkany, J., eds.), pp. 194-213, University of Chicago Press, Chicago
Karnofsky, D.A. and Basch, R.S. (1960) *J. Biophys. Biochem. Cytol., 7,* 61-71
Kaufman, M.H. and Steele, C.E. (1976) *Nature (London), 260,* 782-4
Klein, N.W., Vogler, M.A., Chatot, C.L. and Pierro, L.J. (1980) *Teratology, 21,* 199-208
Koch, W. (1974) *Anat. Rec., 178,* 393-4
Kochhar, D.M. (1975) *Teratology, 11,* 273-88
Kochhar, D.M. (1976) in *Tests of Teratogenicity In Vitro* (Ebert, J.D. and Marois, M., eds.), pp. 485-94, North-Holland, Amsterdam
—— (1980) *Teratogen. Mutagen. Carcinogen., 1,* 63-74
Kochhar, D.M. and Aydelotte, M.B. (1974) *J. Embryol. Exp. Morphol., 31,* 721-34
Kochhar, D.M., Penner, J.D. and Knudsen, T.B. (1980) *Toxicol. Appl. Pharmacol., 52,* 99-112
Koll, W. (1966) *Arzneimittel Forsch., 16,* 1251-63
Koller, E.J. (1976) The use of organ cultures of embryonic tooth germs for teratological studies. in *Tests of Teratogenicity In Vitro* (Ebert, J.D. and Marois, M., eds.), pp. 303-34, North-Holland, Amsterdam
Lahti, A., Antila, E. and Saxén, L. (1972) *Teratology, 6,* 37-42
Lallier, R. (1965) *J. Embryol. Exp. Morphol., 14,* 181-9

The In Vitro Approach to Teratogenicity Testing

Lessmöllmann, U., Hinz, H. and Neubert, D. (1976) *Arch. Toxicol., 36,* 169-76
Leung, T.S. and Bulkley, R.V. (1979) *Bull. Environm. Contam. Toxicol., 23,* 236-43
Manson, J.M. and Simons, R. (1979) *Teratology, 19,* 149-58
Marking, L.L. and Kimerle, R.A. (1979) *Aquatic Toxicology.* American Society for Testing and Materials, Philadelphia
Melancon, M.R., Jr., Saybolt, J. and Lech, J.J. (1977) *Xenobiotica, 7,* 633-40
Merker, H.-J. (1975) in *New Approaches to the Evaluation of Abnormal Embryonic Development* (Neubert, D. and Merker, H.-J., eds.), pp. 161-99, Thieme-Edition Publishing Sciences Group, Inc., Berlin
Moerman, D.G. and Baillie, D.P. (1979) *Genetics, 91,* 95-103
Morriss, G.M. and New, D.A.T. (1979) *J. Embryol. Exp. Morphol., 54,* 17-35
Morriss, G.M. and Steele, C.E. (1974) *J. Embryol. Exp. Morphol., 32,* 505-14
—— and —— (1977) *Teratology, 15,* 109-20
McLaren, A. and Hensleigh, H.C. (1975) in *The Early Development of Mammals* (Balls, M. and Wild, A.E., eds.), pp. 45-60, Cambridge University Press, Cambridge
McLaughlin, J., Jr., Marliac, J., Verret, M.J., Mutchler, M.K. and Fitzhugh, O.G. (1963) *Toxicol. Appl. Pharmacol., 5,* 760-71
New, D.A.T. (1966) *J. Reprod. Fertil., 12,* 509-24
—— (1967) *J. Embryol. Exp. Morphol., 17,* 513-25
—— (1978a) *Biol. Rev., 53,* 81-122
—— (1978b) in *Handbook of Teratology* (Wilson, J.G. and Fraser, F.C., eds.), pp. 95-133, Plenum Press, New York
New, D.A.T. and Cockroft, D.L. (1978) *Experentia, 35,* 138-40
New, D.A.T. and Stein, K.F. (1964) *J. Embryol. Exp. Morphol., 12,* 101-11
New, D.A.T., Coppola, P.T. and Cockroft, D.L. (1976a) *J. Reprod. Fertil., 48,* 219-22
New, D.A.T., Coppola, P.T. and Cockroft, D.L. (1976b) *J. Embryol. Exp. Morphol., 36,* 133-44
New, D.A.T., Coppola, P.T. and Terry, S. (1973) *J. Reprod. Fertil., 35,* 135-8
Neubert, D. and Barrach, H.-J. (1977a) in *Methods in Prenatal Toxicology* (Neubert, D., Merker, H.-J. and Kwasigroch, T.E., eds.), pp. 202-9, Georg Thieme Publishers, Stuttgart
Neubert, D. and Barrach, H.-J. (1977b) in *Methods in Prenatal Toxicology* (Neubert, D., Merker, H.-J. and Kwasigroch, T.E., eds.), pp. 241-51, Georg Thieme Publishers, Stuttgart
Neubert, D., Merker, H.-J. and Tapken, S. (1974a) *Naunyn-Schmiedeberg's Arch. Pharmacol., 286,* 251-70
Neubert, D., Tapken, S. and Merker, H.-J. (1974b) *Naunyn-Schmiedeberg's Arch. Pharmacol., 286,* 271-82
Neubert, D., Merker, H.-J., Barrach, H.-J. and Lessmöllmann, U. (1976) in *Tests of Teratogenicity In Vitro* (Ebert, J.D. and Marois, M., eds.), pp. 335-48, North-Holland, Amsterdam
Neubert, D., Lessmöllman, U., Hinz, N., Dillmann, I. and Fuch, G. (1977) *Naunyn-Schmiedeberg's Arch. Pharmacol., 298,* 93-105
Nicholas, J.S. (1938) *Anat. Rec., 70,* 199-210
Patten, B.M. (1951) *Early Embryology of the Chick* (4th ed.), The Blakiston Company, New York
Poulson, D.F. (1950) in *Biology of Drosophila* (Demerec, M., ed.), pp. 168-274, John Wiley, New York
Räihä, N.C.R. and Schwartz, A.L. (1973) *Enzyme, 15,* 330-9
Robkin, M.A., Beachler, D.W. and Shepard, T.H. (1976a) *Environ. Res., 12,* 32-7
Robkin, M.A. and Shepard, T.H. (1972) *In Vitro, 8,* 151-60
Robkin, M.A. and Cockroft, D.L. (1978) *Teratology, 18,* 337-42
Robkin, M., Shepard, T.H. and Baum, D. (1974) *Teratology, 9,* 35-44
Robkin, M.A., Shepard, T.H. and Dyer, D.C. (1976b) *Proc. Soc. Exp. Biol. Med., 151,* 799-803
Robkin, M.A., Shepard, T.H. and Tanimura, T. (1972) *Teratology, 5,* 367-76
Sadler, T.W. (1979) *J. Embryol. Exp. Morphol., 49,* 17-25
—— (1980a) *Teratology, 21,* 339-47
—— (1980b) *Teratology, 21,* 349-56
Saxén, L. (1976) *J. Embryol. Exp. Morphol., 36,* 1-12
Saxén, I. and Saxén, L. (1975) in *New Approaches to the Evaluation of Abnormal Embryonic Development* (Neubert, D. and Merker, H.J., eds.), pp. 84-98, Thieme-Edition Publishing Sciences Group, Berlin

The In Vitro Approach to Teratogenicity Testing

Schreiweis, D.O. and Murray, G.J. (1976) *Teratology, 14,* 287-90

Shepard, T.H., Tanimura, T. and Robkin, M. (1969) *Teratology, 2,* 107-10

Smithberg, M. (1962) *Am. J. Anat., 111,* 205-13

Staples, R.E. (1971) in *Methods in Mammalian Embryology* (Daniel, J.C., ed.), pp. 190-204, Freeman and Company, San Francisco

Staples, R.E. (1975) in *New Approaches to the Evaluation of Abnormal Embryonic Development* (Neubert, D. and Merker, H.-J., eds.), pp. 71-81, Thieme-Edition Publishing Sciences Group, Berlin

Statham, C.N., Elcombe, C.R., Szyjka, S.P. and Lech, J.J. (1978) *Xenobiotica, 8,* 65-71

Steele, C.E. (1972) *Nature New Biol., 237,* 150-1

Steele, C.E. and New, D.A.T. (1974) *J. Embryol. Exp. Morphol., 31,* 707-19

Steele, C.E., Jeffery, E.H. and Diplock, A.T. (1974) *J. Reprod. Fertil., 38,* 115-23

Sulston, J.E. and Horvitz, H.R. (1977) *Develop. Biol., 56,* 110-56

Tamarin, A. and Jones, K.W. (1968) *Acta Embryol. Morphol. Exp., 10,* 288-301

Tanimura, T. and Shepard, T.H. (1970) *Proc. Soc. Exp. Biol. Med., 135,* 51-4

Trowell, O.A. (1954) *Exp. Cell Res., 6,* 246-8

—— (1959) *Exp. Cell Res., 16,* 118-47

—— (1961) in *La Culture Organotypique,* pp. 237-49, Edition de Centre National de la Recherche Scientifique, Paris

Turbow, M.M. (1966) *J. Embryol. Exp. Morphol., 15,* 387-95

Turbow, M.M. and Chamberlain, J.G. (1968) *Teratology, 1,* 103-8

Vernberg, F.J., Calabrese, A., Thurber, F.P. and Vernberg, W.B. (1977) *Physiological Responses of Marine Biota to Pollutants,* Academic Press, New York

Wee, E.L., Wolfson, L.G. and Zimmerman, E.F. (1976) *Develop. Biol., 48,* 91-103

Webb, F.T.G. and Coppola, P.T. (1976) in *Recent Developments in Contraceptive Technology* (Laumas, K.R., ed.), pp. 35-42, Ankur Publishing House, New Delhi

Wilson, J.G. (1977) in *Handbook of Teratology* (Wilson, J.G. and Fraser, F.C., eds.), Vol. 1, pp. 47-74, Plenum Press, New York

—— (1978) in *Handbook of Teratology* (Wilson, J.G. and Fraser, F.C., eds.), pp. 135-54, Plenum Press, New York

World Health Organization *Technical Report Ser.* 167, No. 364

Würgler, F.E., Sobels, F.H. and Vogel, E. (1977) in *Handbook of Mutagenicity Test Procedures* (Kilbey, B. *et al.,* eds.), pp. 335-73, Elsevier/North Holland Biomedical Press, Amsterdam

Zimmerman, E.F. (1976) in *Tests of Teratogenicity In Vitro* (Ebert, J.D. and Marois, M. eds.), pp. 449-61, North Holland, Amsterdam

CHAPTER THREE

THE USE OF CELL CULTURE METHODS FOR EXPLORING TERATOGENIC SUSCEPTIBILITY

Ruth M. Clayton and Ahmet Zehir

CONTENTS

Contents

I. Introduction

According to data summarised by Hemminki *et al.*, in 1979, there were then some 63 000 chemicals in common use, and around 1 000 (or 2 000 according to Shepard, 1979), new compounds are marketed each year. About 7 000 had been tested for carcinogenicity when they wrote, and Maugh (1978) estimated the rate of such necessary tests at around 500 a year. The only source of direct information on the teratogenic effects of various substances on humans is epidemiological, so that it rests on an accumulation of family tragedies (Taussig, 1962; Saxén and Rapola, 1969; Weatherall and Haskey, 1976).

Although both micro-organisms and eukaryote cells are now used in tests of mutagenicity or carcinogenicity (McCann *et al.*, 1975; Purchase *et al.*, 1976), such systems have not been considered suitable for teratogenicity testing. Mutagens and carcinogens may have properties which also make them potential teratogens (Harbison, 1978; Brusick, 1978), but many teratogens are not carcinogens or mutagens (Miller, 1977; Brusick, 1978; Shepard, 1979). This is to be expected: the production of a teratogenic effect is the result of the exposure of a pregnant female to an agency which may damage any part of the interacting and changing systems of the embryo or fetus. A temporary, perhaps even a minor, interference with a crucial embryonic process such as inductive contacts or the migration and sorting of cells may have consequences which may lead to multiple effects, and to gross changes in the morphology and function of various structures and organs, which have been affected during the course of their development. The response to teratogenic agencies is characterised by

61

different periods of fetal sensitivity, physiological variables affected by the routes, times and duration of drug administration, and the range of exposure levels. Tests for teratogenicity therefore pose special problems. The currently approved tests of new drugs and other agencies for possible teratogenic effects on the human fetus generally include the examination for morphopathology and for histopathology of very large numbers of rodent fetuses of various ages, obtained from pregnant females injected or fed with suspected teratogenic substances, at different stages of pregnancy and at different dose levels. There are, however, different levels of susceptibility between species, and indeed some agencies do not affect all species. For this reason, some investigations now use more than one rodent species, and occasionally a small number of some non-rodent, such as the rabbit or the dog. Large numbers of animals must be exposed to obtain a statistically significant result.

Apart from their slowness and expense, experimental assays on intact animals lead to a number of quite serious problems. Some variability in results springs directly from the processes of embryonic development, but other problems are the product of evolutionary divergence between species. These have been discussed in detail elsewhere (Clayton, 1980), but some of the problems are outlined here.

This article does not attempt to be a complete review. Some major problems in testing for embryotoxicity, and problems in *in vitro* testing will be outlined, and a few examples given of results obtainable from cell-based assays, both from the literature and our own experiments.

II. Genetic Variables

Species differences include such features as placental structure as well as pharmacogenetic characteristics. Such differences may not affect the response to some drugs, but may be of major importance for others. (A well-known example of species difference in response is that of thalidomide; Schumacher *et al.,* 1968; Scott *et al.,* 1977).

There are also numerous reports of strain differences in susceptibility to particular teratogens occuring within a species. Examples include responses to galactoflavin (Kalter and Warkany, 1959), to 6-aminonicotinamide (Goldstein *et al.,* 1963), and to corticosteroids (Kalter, 1965; Biddle and Fraser, 1977, 1979), to diphenylhydantoin (Gibson and Becker, 1968), to alcohol (Randall and Taylor, 1979; Chernoff, 1980), and to insulin (Cole and Trasler, 1980).

The possibility that the genotype of an animal may confer either relative unresponsiveness or especial hazard with respect to a particular teratogen has implications both for the necessary conduct of tests and for problems confronting the human population. Genetic variants in man which predispose to adverse effects of drugs (which are acceptable to the population at large) are found in increasing numbers (see for example, Vesell, 1976; Propping, 1978). Such genetic variation is known for several substances which are known teratogens, such as alcohol, phenothiazines, anticonvulsants, anti-malarials, halothane, barbiturates, dicoumarol, etc. In principle (Clayton, 1980) one would anticipate that a fetus homozygous for a susceptible function in a physiologically normal heterozygous mother may be at risk from an agent pharmacologically acceptable to the mother. In addition, the genotype of the mother may affect the circulating levels of a given drug and the duration of exposure of the fetus. Rapid metabolisers will presumably expose their fetus, of whatever genotype, to less hazard than slow metabolisers of a potentially hazardous substance. Several lines of evidence point to this as a real possibility, and a few examples may be outlined.

Phenytoin (diphenylhydantoin) causes a dose-dependent incidence of cleft palate in mice (Elshove, 1969), and can lead to a cluster of defects in man, which include mental defect, cleft lip, cleft palate, dysmorphic facies, congenital heart defects and other changes (Shapiro *et al.*, 1976; Hanson, *et al.*, 1976). Hanson *et al.* (1976) found an incidence of severe effects in 11% and less severe effects in 33%, including impaired intellectual performance. (Discussion of the teratogenicity of phenytoin and other anticonvulsants can be found in Ajodhia and Hope, 1973; and Smith, 1977.) Agencies increasing the rate of metabolism of phenytoin decrease its teratogenicity in mice, those that decrease the rate of metabolism increase teratogenicity (Harbison and Becker, 1970). Strain differences in susceptibility have also been observed in mice (Gibson and Becker, 1968; Johnston *et al.*, 1979), and genetic variants for the rate of metabolism of phenytoin in man are known (reviewed by Propping, 1978). The drug accumulates in genetically slow metabolisers, increasing the risk of toxic side effects. Since maternal plasma phenytoin is rapidly equilibrated with the fetal plasma (Mirkin, 1971), it is likely that the hazard to the fetus will be increased in slow metabolisers.

Alcohol teratogenesis is dose-dependent in the mouse (Randall and Taylor, 1979), and Chernoff (1980) found that the risk of alcohol teratogenesis differed between inbred strains of mice exposed to the same dose. This risk was related to the maternal alcohol concentration, which is regulated by genetically different levels of activity of alcohol dehydrogenase. Thus fetal damage is greatest in the offspring of low metabolisers. Alcohol causes direct damage to the rodent fetus (Brown *et al.*, 1979), but other mechanisms are also possible (Chernoff, 1980), one via a possible change in cellular NAD/NADH ratios after induction of alcohol dehydrogenase, another via the formation of acetaldehyde which is teratogenic to mice (O'Shea and Kaufman, 1979).

Alcohol is teratogenic in man (Jones *et al.*, 1973; Mulvihill and Yeager, 1976; Ouellette *et al.*, 1977), and genetic variants in the efficiency of alcohol metabolism are also known (reviewed by Vesell, 1976; Propping, 1978). The relative importance of maternal genotype and of the level of alcohol intake probably depend on the values of both these variables in any individual case.

A condition in which the relative contributions to fetal hazard of maternal and fetal genotypes depend, in any pregnancy, on their respective genotypes, was investigated in the mouse by Shum *et al.* (1979). In the mouse there is a locus (Ah) which controls the inducibility of arylhydrocarbon hydroxylase and cytochrome P450. This locus affects the response to polycylic aromatic hydrocarbons (see Nebert and Felton, 1976), and it has also been shown to be correlated with teratogenesis by this class of compounds (Lambert and Nebert, 1977). The alleles Ah^d and Ah^b are distinguished by the inducibility of this enzyme and the several enzymes associated with cytochrome P450. This regulates the production of carcinogenic intermediates from polycyclic hydrocarbon compounds. Mice homozygous for Ah^b (responders) produce toxic metabolites, and Shum *et al.* (1979) showed that a mother of this genotype exposes her fetuses, whether heterozygotes or homozygous responders, to equal risk. However, in a homozygous Ah^d (non-responding) mother, the heterozygous (Ah^d/Ah^b) fetus is more affected than the homozygous Ah^d fetus.

This enzyme system is found in a wide variety of fetal tissues although it is highest in the liver (see Shum *et al.*, 1979, for further references), and sensitive and resistant genotypes may be assayed in cultures of such cell types as express this enzyme (Nebert, 1973). A similar locus exists in man (Atlas *et al.*, 1976; Kellerman *et al.*, 1975; Nebert and Felton, 1976). Shum *et al.* (1979) also discuss the possibility that the inducibility of P450 may be included in the metabolic pathways of a wide range of substances and may be significant in determining the teratogenic potential of such teratogens as anticonvulsants, anticoagulants, oral contraceptives, etc. Genetic variants for the metabolism of these substances are already known, and if this view is substantiated it would point to a complex regulation of risk for any teratogen, governed by maternal dose and maternal genotype, both for the immediately relevant locus but also for other loci (such as Ah) and fetal genotype.

Other single-gene differences which affect teratogenic risk include muscular dystrophy, in the chick, which is associated with a genetic defect in acetylcholinesterase which renders the embryo more sensitive than normal to the teratogenic effect of cholinomimetic drugs (Landauer *et al.*, 1976), and the production of exencephaly among the range of responses to a teratogenic dose of insulin in mice. The frequency of this condition, affected by two different genes (Cd and Rf), are both recognised by skeletal effects (Cole and Trasler, 1980). Genetic differences in response to insulin have also been reported by Smithberg and Runner (1963), and we have found striking differences in response to insulin of cells of different genotypes in cell culture conditions (Clayton *et al.*, 1976; Clayton *et al.*, 1980; and see Section VIII C.).

Other examples may be expected to come to light in the future, and one might speculate as to the possible risk to individuals with such genetic idiosyncracies as are exemplified by some variants of the X-linked locus for glucose 6-phosphate dehydrogenase (G6PD) in man, which confer sensitivity of affected males to sulphonamides, analgesics, antimalarials and certain other drugs, many of which are teratogenic to animals and some of which are teratogenic to man. A male fetus may be at some risk if the physiologically normal heterozygous mother ingests any of these substances at a period critical for the fetus.

III. Developmental Variables

It has been amply demonstrated that the incidence and nature of teratogenic defects depend on the stage of development of the fetus at the time of insult. The earliest effects will include failures of implantation or early fetal loss which will be recorded as reduced fecundity or reduced litter size. Eye and brain defects will occur earlier than forelimb defects and these, in turn, will occur earlier than hind-limb defects (Kochhar, 1973; Nelson, 1960; Nowack, 1965; Russel, 1950; Wilson *et al.*, 1953; Palmer, 1974; Saxén and Rapola, 1969; Wilson, 1973; Shepard, 1979; Goldman, 1979). The sequence of processes required for the determination, morphogenesis and differentiation of any structure is normally spread out over a period of embryonic life, so that an overlapping series of curves may be drawn, each representing a relatively protracted period of susceptibility for an embryonic structure, with a peak period of maximum sensitivity, when the teratogenic dose required to produce a given defect is lowest (for examples, see Chapters 1 and 4).

IV. The Cell as Target

A teratogenic substance must exert its immediate effect on the cells of the embryo or fetus by affecting cellular properties, unless the effects are wholly secondary to a change in maternal physiology or placental function, or to an extrinsic change in fetal physiology. Modifications of cell division leading to changes in relative growth rate, or cell orientation or adhesion, could affect necessary inductive contacts, or lead to disproportionate growth. An increase or decrease in the rate of cell death will have morphological consequences: either by a loss or diminution in cell number which cannot be regulated, or by a failure to eliminate cells which are 'programmed' to die in specific regions as part of a morphogenetic process. Changes in properties of the cell surface or of extracellular components will affect cell contact, cell recognition, adhesiveness or cell movement. A teratogen may act by blocking a receptor site, or affecting the synthesis of extracellular matrix, or the integrity of a component of the cytoarchitecture. Modified cell-surface properties have been shown to exist in several mutants with severe developmental defects (see Bennett, 1975; Clayton, 1980). Finally, a teratogen may affect cell inducibility or interfere with cell metabolism, (for example as an enzyme poison, inhibitor, or as a metabolic analogue) or affect the synthesis of nucleic acids or proteins.

The developmental anomalies after any of these types of change may include both direct and indirect consequences. Cellular sensitivity to the action of a teratogen, and the possible developmental consequences, may vary according to the time of insult and the developmental processes affected. This subject is discussed by Saxén (1976a, b), Moscona (1976), and Clayton, (1980).

Restricted periods of sensitivity for a particular defect imply either that a specific vulnerable process is occuring temporally or that a biochemical characteristic does not appear before a certain stage of differentiation.

In whole-animal tests, each potential teratogen must be assayed over a wide range of doses and the tests must span the whole period of fetal development. Culture-based assays, on the other hand, can assess the effect of a substance on differentiation in a relatively short time, and sample representative tissues; for example, a pre-cartilage rudiment can stand in for all differentiating pre-cartilage rudiments over the whole embryonic period.

An example would be the effect of vitamin A on cells in the early stage of chondrogenesis (Lewis *et al.*, 1978). Since the initiation of chondrogenesis in the limb follows an orderly sequence along a proximodistal gradient it is not surprising that the precise effect on the limb depends on the period of drug administration. All the evidence from cell culture studies points to an important regulatory effect of vitamin A on the differentiating chondrocyte cell surface, probably by regulating the synthesis of specific glycoproteins. (Vitamin A is discussed further in Section VIII A.) The proposition that the action of a substance on the cell surface is one of the possible mechanisms of teratogenesis may be illustrated by a few brief examples.

At 5 days of incubation, the chick embryo retina is a simple neuro-epithelium. If it is explanted into culture it develops normal histiotypic organisation and cell differentiation; furthermore, dissociated cells, if permitted to reassemble, show histiotypic reassembly and cell differentiation. In both cases, glutamine synthetase is inducible by hydrocortisone. (Monroy and Moscona, 1980, review the considerable body of experimental work on this system.) 5-Bromodeoxyuridine(BUdR) is teratogenic, producing a range of defects according to the time of administration: the CNS is particularly vulnerable (Chaube and Murphy, 1968; Ruffolo and Ferm, 1965). Brief exposure of 5-day embryo retina to BUdR in culture leads to very disorganised histogenesis, indicating a failure of cell recognition and assembly. The cells adhere, but do so non-selectively, and glutamine synthetase induction is impaired or prevented (Mayerson and Moscona, 1979; Moscona and Moscona, 1979).

Cleft palate has been obtained in mice after high doses of diazepam (Valium) (Miller and Becker, 1975), but rats were not affected (Beall, 1972). There is some evidence that an increased incidence of cleft palate may occur in children exposed to diazepam during the first trimester (Saxén and Saxén, 1975; Aarskog, 1975). Clark and Ryan (1980) tested a number of benzodiazepines on a line of Friend cells in culture and found diazepam one of the two most active in affecting induction. They consider that this effect is mediated via changes in the cell surface, in which the lipophilic benzodiazepines are soluble, and suggest that the teratogenic effects of tranquillisers in large doses may be related to this effect.

The possibility that many teratogens may act by affecting cell-surface properties is also supported by the inhibition by teratogens of the attachment of tumour cells to lectin-coated surfaces (Braun *et al.*, 1979), and by the teratogenic effect of concanavalin A (Con A) on the rabbit fetus (De Sesso *et al.*, 1977). The range of morphological defects are presumably related to the known quantitative differences in the distribution of Con A or other lectin-type binding in different tissues (Robertson *et al.*, 1975), to the changes in such distribution during differentiation (Kleinshuster and Moscona, 1972), and to the effect of blocking these sites on such cellular activities as cell migration (Moran, 1974).

V. *In Vitro* Assays

A cell-based assay would require that there be a necessary relationship between fetal morphology, cell function, cell interactions and detectable aspects of cell biochemistry. Evidence which indicates that this is the case has been reviewed and discussed by Clayton (1980). Cell tests are possible in principle because different types of embryonic or fetal cells grown in appropriate conditions may continue to demonstrate specific characteristics, including the capacity for reassembly of histiotypic organisation, inducibility, and differentiation as judged by the development of characteristic ultrastructure and cell products (for reviews see Kaighn, 1976; Morris, 1976; Clayton, 1980). Several investigators have tested *in vitro* assay systems (see Nebert, 1973; Rajan, 1974; Kochhar, 1975; Beck, 1976; Clayton, 1976, 1980; Kaighn, 1976; Karkinnen-Jääskeläinen and Saxén, 1976; Morris, 1976; Saxén, 1976a, b; Shepard and Pious, 1978; Wilk *et al.*, 1980).

The major advantage of *in vitro* assays for teratogens are their greater rapidity than whole-animal tests. They could also be applied to scarce primate material. Organ cultures require growth measurements and histological investigation. Cell cultures, being more homogeneous (and being also exposed to the possible teratogenic agent more homogeneously) are more suited to biochemical assay, but cell behaviour, cell-cell recognition properties, histiotypic assembly and cell replication can also be measured accurately. However, the drug must be applied to the cells in the correct biochemical form and at concentrations equivalent to those experienced by fetal cells *in vivo*. A concentration in the culture dish derived directly from the dose per body weight of the mother does not allow for the effects of maternal-fetal partition, or of rapid elimination by the mother, which would rapidly reduce the fetal dose. The *in vivo* doses of several drugs producing limb teratology in the mouse, calculated as mg/g body weight, appear to bear no relationship to the dose in μg/ml found to produce definite effects in limb organ culture systems (Kochhar, 1975). For example the required *in vitro* concentration of 6-aminonicotinamide was 100μg/ml and the hydroxyurea 10μg/ml, but the *in vivo* concentrations were 25μg/g and 3mg/g respectively.

A serious problem for organ and cell culture systems (see Clayton, 1976, 1980) is the form in which the substance should be presented, since some substances administered to the mother *in vivo* do not exert their teratogenic effects directly on the fetus, but through a toxic or persistent metabolite, while other substances which are toxic *in vitro* may be metabolised to a harmless agent *in vivo*. This problem of administration of drugs in the correct form to cultured cells has been approached in two ways: by using the amniotic fluid of drug-injected mothers as culture medium, which allows for metabolism and partitioning (Clayton, 1980), or by adding the drug together with a maternal liver postmitochondrial fraction and a NADPH-generating system in a dialysis sac and suspending this in the culture medium which permits metabolism to occur (Wilk *et al.*, 1980). Cell behaviour was recorded in both sets of experiments; the differentiation of neural crest cells into pigment cells or neurones and the amount of stainable matrix synthesised by chondrocytes was used as a further index by Wilk *et al.* (1980) and the effect on the profiles of accumulated protein and of protein synthesis by Clayton (1976, 1980). In both sets of experiments a correlation was found between the teratogenicity of a compound and its effect in cell culture.

VI. Substances with Little or No Effect

A. *Chlordiazepoxide*

At sufficiently high doses almost any normally innocuous substance would be expected to affect cultured embryonic cells. The necessity for caution in setting up cell-based assay systems may be illustrated by the effect of a minor tranquilliser, the benzodiazepine chlordiazepoxide HCl (Librium), which was not found to be a teratogen in one study (Hartz *et al.*, 1975) and only slightly teratogenic in another (Milkovich and van den Berg, 1974).

We have not observed any morphological effects in chick embryos injected at 4 days' incubation with 0.5mg or 1.25mg per egg. Calculating the relative dose on the basis of the average weights of a human adult and a chick egg is most unsatisfactory, since the 4-day embryo is only a fraction

Figure 3.1: The Effect of Chlordiazepoxide (Librium) on Embryos and Cultured Cells. A: 17-day chick embryos, cleared skeletons. Left, untreated; right, injected with 2mg Librium per egg at 8 days' incubation. No effects were observed at doses from 0.5mg to 1mg per egg. At 1.5mg per egg a very slight reduction in size was found in some embryos. 2.5mg/egg was embryo-lethal. B: Limb fibroblasts from 8-day embryos, transferred to medium containing Librium on day 4, with medium changes every 2-3 days, and harvested on day 12. Accumulated proteins were separated by SDS poly-acrylamide gel electrophoresis (as in Laemmli, 1970). (a) 25μg/ml Librium; (b) 50μg/ml Librium; (c) control. Two proteins are affected, actin and another protein as yet not unambiguously identified. C: Kidney fibroblasts from 8-day chick embryos, transferred to medium containing Librium on day 4, with medium changes every 2-3 days, and harvested on day 12. (a) 25μg/ml Librium; (b) 50μg/ml Librium; (c) control. Actin is affected. D: 16-day lens epithelium cultures from 1-day-old chicks. Transferred to medium containing Librium on day 6, with medium changes every 2-3 days and harvested on day 16. (a) Control; (b) 25μg/ml Librium; (c) 50μg/ml Librium; (d) 75μg/ml Librium. At the highest dose the lower molecular weight δ-actin and some β-crystallins are diminished. Close inspection shows components affected.

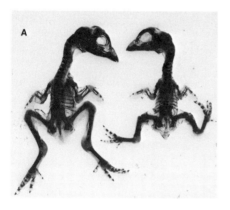

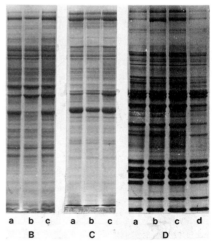

a b c   a b c   a b c d
B   C   D

of the weight of the egg, and no allowance is made in either case for drug distribution in the various compartments of man or egg, nor of turnover. In the absence of pharmacokinetic data on Librium in the egg, it may still be noted that on this per weight basis these doses are 10 and 20 times higher than a particularly high daily intake of 60mg for an adult (15 and 30mg daily is a more likely dose). The true excess is probably considerably greater. However, at 2mg and 2.5mg per egg an overall reduction in embryonic body size was obtained (Fig. 3.1), and there was 70% lethality at 2.5mg/egg. In cell culture, a range of unphysiological high-dose concentrations were tested, but effects on the cells were not seen below $50\mu g/ml$ for limb fibroblasts and $75\mu g/ml$ for lens epithelium. At these values, which are not less than 40 and 60 times a high human dose, an apparently specific effect was observed: a marked diminution of actin in limb and kidney fibroblasts and in lens epithelium (Fig. 3.1). Additional changes in lens epithelium were also observed. The available translatable actin-mRNA was found to be diminished by exposure of limb fibroblasts to very high concentrations of Librium (Fig. 3.2).

An effect on postnatal learning ability has been reported for anti-convulsants and tranquillisers (see Voorhees and Butcher, Chapter 9). Hartz *et al.* (1975) found no evidence for a diminution of IQ levels in children after Librium treatment of their mothers. Although we have not yet assessed the effect of Librium on brain cultures, we observed an effect, at $50\mu g/ml$, on 10-day cultures of 8-day chick embryo neural retina, when there are abundant neurones with axonal connections (Fig. 3.3A). However, no effect was observed on such cultures at a later stage of growth, when the neuronal cells are no longer present and the culture comprises only neuroepithelial cells (Okada, 1976; Clayton *et al.*, 1977).

B. *Meprobamate*

Meprobamate, a substituted propanediol, may only rarely have teratogenic effects, but the evidence is not unambiguous (Milkovich and van den Berg, 1974). We have not found it to produce morphological effects on chick embryos *in ovo*, but 0.8mg/egg was embryotoxic to 30% of 4.5-day embryos and 10% of 8-day embryos. At 20 or $40\mu g/ml$ no effects were observed in cell culture, and at $60\mu g/ml$ it was cytotoxic. At $50\mu g/ml$ it did not affect the protein profiles of the cells tested, with the exception of a slight effect on one component only (of molecular weight between 23 and 30K daltons) in limb fibroblasts.

71

Figure 3.2: Fluorograph of Translation Products of mRNA from 12-Day Cultures of Limb Fibroblasts. Culture medium contained 50μg/ml Librium, as in Fig. 3.1. Procedures as in Thomson *et al.* (1979). Arrows indicate proteins affected in Librium treated cultures (B) compared with control cultures (A).

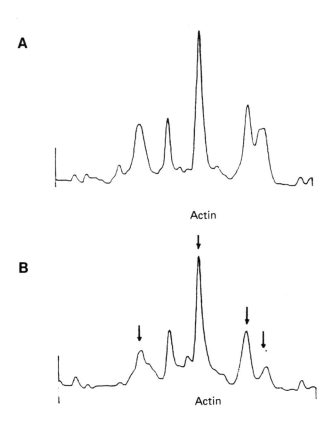

Figure 3.3: A. The Effect of Several Substances on 10-Day Cultures of Neural Retina Established from 8-Day Chick Embryos. Both neuroepithelium and neurones are normally present in 8-day embryo neural retina cultures at this stage. (a) Control; (b) phenytoin (Epanutin), 50μg/ml; (c) chloroquine sulphate (Nivaquine), 4μg/ml; (d) chlordiazepoxide HC1 (Librium), 50μg/ml. Close inspection reveals the components affected. Actin is severely affected by Nivaquine.
B. The Effect of Several Substances on 16-Day Cultures of Lens Epithelium from 1-Day-Old Chicks. (a) Control; (b) phenytoin (Epanutin), 50μg/ml; (c) meprobamate (Equanil), 50μg/ml. Actin is diminished, and the higher molecular weight δ-crystallin is depressed by Epanutin. Meprobamate does not affect the protein profile. Close inspection reveals the components affected.

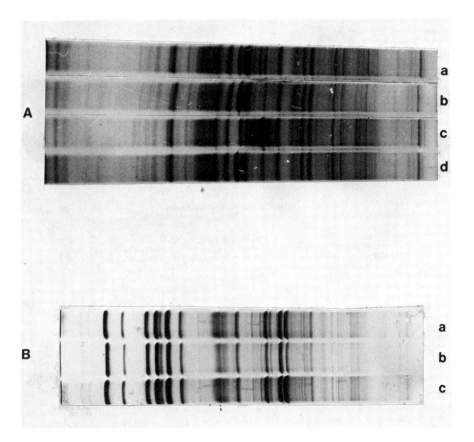

VII. Toxic Effects

A. *Diphenylhydantoin*

Diphenylhydantoin or phenytoin (Epanutin) is an anticonvulsant which prevents both cardiac arhythmia and epileptic discharges. It acts by stabilising cell membranes, thus affecting Na^+/K^+ flux (Kizer *et al.*, 1970). Anticonvulsants are teratogenic (Lefebvre *et al.*, 1972; Ajodhia and Hope, 1973), and this has been suggested to be due to folic acid antagonism (Netzloff *et al.*, 1979).

We did not observe gross abnormalities in 17-day chick embryos *in ovo* injected at 4 days' incubation with 0.25mg per egg, when 5% lethality was obtained, but some embryotoxicity appeared at 0.5mg/egg, with a 41% incidence of death. This dose was 100% embryotoxic at 2 days' incubation and 30% at 8 days' incubation. No effects were discernible in cultured cells at concentrations of 20 or $40\mu g/ml$, but $60\mu g/ml$ was cytotoxic. At $50\mu g/ml$, effects were observed on cultured cells. Again, actin was affected in all cells, but other effects were found in lens epithelium and neural retina. In lens epithelium the ratio of the 50K dalton and 45K dalton δ-crystallin polypeptides is strongly affected by the drug (Fig. 3.3B). This ratio is known to be modified by changing the Na^+/K^+ balance (Piatigorsky, 1980), so that this effect would seem to be reasonably related to the action of phenytoin.

We have observed a diminution in axon formation and outgrowth in cell cultures of 8-day chick embryo brain and neural retina (A. Zehir and R.M. Clayton, unpublished work). Brain-cell proteins are still to be tested, but (as with high levels of Librium) we observed that 10-day cultures of neural retina, containing both neuroepithelium and neurones with axonal connections are affected (Fig. 3.3A) but later cultures, when all neurones have been lost, are not affected.

B. *Daunomycin*

Daunomycin has been used as an antibiotic and in cancer chemotherapy; it is teratogenic in the rabbit and rat (Thompson *et al.*, 1978). We found that at sub-cytotoxic concentrations it produced distortions of the profile of protein synthesis in cultured cells, of each of three different genotypes, but the patterns of response were quantitatively different for each genotype (Clayton *et al.*, 1976).

C. *6-Aminonicotinamide*

Nicotinamide analogues are teratogenic, causing a variety of defects in mice and chicks, including cleft palate and skeletal defects. Genetic differences in sensitivity to 6-aminonicotinamide have been found (Goldstein *et al.*, 1963; Biddle and Fraser, 1979). Caplan (1970, 1972) was able to relate the effects observed on chick development *in ovo* to those obtained on limb cells in culture conditions, and showed that the differentiation of mesoderm into muscle and chondrogenic cells is inhibited. Seegmiller *et al.* (1980) have shown that cartilage epiphyses *in vitro* in medium supplemented with 6-aminonicotinamide synthesise chondrotin sulphate with a reduced molecular weight and the sulphate moeity in an abnormal position. Similar changes were found in myogenic cultures (Caplan, 1972a). 6-Aminonicotinamide was also found to affect the protein profile of lens cells in culture (Clayton, 1976, 1980) and to affect the protein profiles of neural retina, limb and kidney fibroblasts in culture (C. Smart and R.M. Clayton, unpublished work).

D. *Chloroquine*

Chloroquine sulphate (Nivaquine) is used as an antimalarial drug and also for rheumatoid arthritis, when the daily dose may be from 200 to 400mg. Retinopathy is among the more common toxic side effects in adults, and the teratogenic effects reported include damage to the 8th nerve and cochlea, mental retardation, neonatal convulsions and posterior column defects (Maltz and Naunton, 1968). At 200-300ng per egg, we observed no effects in the 4.5- and 8-day embryo, but 400ng/egg was embryotoxic to 100%, 67% and 28% of 2-, 4.5- and 8-day embryos, respectively. In cell culture, we found that $2\mu g/ml$ was without discernible effect, and above $4\mu g/ml$ Nivaquine was cytotoxic. At $4\mu g/ml$, cultures survived if exposed only once; cells survived and a number of specific effects were observed, the same protein being affected in lens epithelium, (Fig. 3.4E), neural retina (Fig. 3.4C), and brain cultures (Fig. 3.4D). Several components are affected in neural retina (Fig. 3.4C). In early cultures a new pair of bands normally appears in SDS gels (molecular weights 50-55K daltons); these are abolished by Nivaquine. In later cultures, two components of about 40K daltons appear, which are lost on Nivaquine treatment (Fig. 3.4C-E). Cell morphology is also affected (Fig. 3.4A and B).

Figure 3.4: The Effect of Chloroquine Sulphate (Nivaquine) on Cultured Embryonic Cells. The effects of Nivaquine on 16-day neural retina cell cultures, established from 8-day chick embryos. A. Control culture: neuronal cells have disappeared, as is normal at this stage, leaving neuro-epithelium. B. Treated once with Nivaquine at $4\mu g/ml$ on day 14, cells are abnormal and nuclei swollen. C. 30-day cultures set up as above, harvested and analysed as described in Fig. 3.1. (a) Controls; (b) treated once with Nivaquine as in B above, on day 29; (c) treated once with Nivaquine as in B above, on day 15. D. 30-day cultures set up from 8-day chick embryo brain, harvested and analysed as above. (a) Controls: neuronal cells survive for about 15 days, but at this stage the cultures are largely neuro-epithelium; (b) treated with Nivaquine as above on day 29; (c) treated with Nivaquine as above on day 15. E. 16-day lens epithelial culture set up from 1-day-old chick lens (as in Eguchi *et al.,* 1975), harvested on day 15 and analysed as above. (a) Controls; (b) treated with Nivaquine as above on day 15.

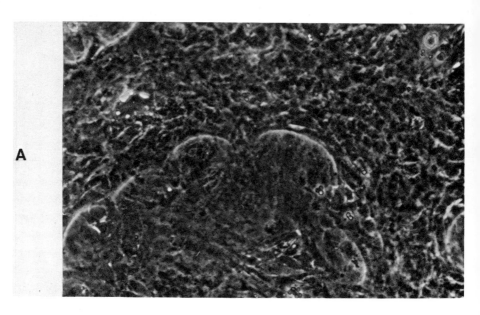

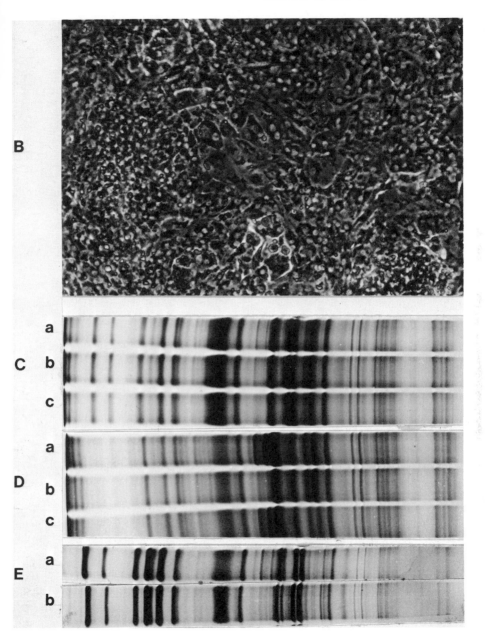

E. *Cobalt*

Cobaltous chloride caused 'brain softening' and defective eye development including anophthalamia and microphthalamia, and anaemia (Ridgway and Karnofsky, 1952; Kury and Crosby, 1968). It reduces concentrations of haem and cytochrome P450 in intact rats (Guzelian and Bissell, 1976), and in monolayer primary cultures of rat hepatocytes (Guzelian and Bissell, 1976).

We observed dose- and stage-dependent lethality to cobaltous chloride: mortality in the 2-day chick embryo rose from 32% at 0.05mg/egg to 75% at 0.1mg/egg and 100% at 0.3mg/egg. However the 4.5-day embryo was more resistant, the lethality being 47% at 0.1mg/egg and 51% at 0.3mg/egg. Furthermore, the 8-day embryo was not killed by 0.1mg/egg: lethality at 0.3mg/egg was 34% and at 0.5mg/egg 44%. Although no red cell counts were made, the very marked pallor of these embryos would be compatible with the previously reported anaemia.

At 0.3mg/egg, chick embryos injected at 4.5 days developed lens opacities by 7-8 days; those injected on the eighth day developed lens opacities by 9-10 days (Fig. 3.5A). The survivors also had thin limbs.

In cell culture it is cytotoxic above $4\mu g/ml$, but limb and kidney fibroblasts are more affected than neural retina or lens cells. Actin is affected in kidney cells and one band is absent in polyacrylamide gel analyses of treated lens cells (A. Zehir and R.M. Clayton, unpublished work; Fig. 3.5B).

F. *Lead*

Lead salts are teratogenic in chicks, hamsters, rats and mice (Ridgway and Karnofsky, 1952; Butt *et al.,* 1952; Ferm and Carpenter, 1967; Murakami *et al.,* 1954; McClain and Becker, 1975). Reduction of body size, brain damage, and posterior axial defects including the urorectocaudal syndrome have all been reported. In man there is some evidence of an increase in fetal deaths (Angle and McIntyre, 1964), and of lead-associated mental retardation (Moore *et al.,* 1977).

We observed stage- and dose-related embryotoxicity for chick embryos injected with lead nitrate. Embryos injected at 2 days' incubation developed spinal and caudal defects, those injected at 4 or 8 days developed brain defects including hydrocephaly and exencephaly. At 2 days' incubation, 0.025mg/egg produced 10% lethality, rising to 24% at 0.05mg/egg, and 50% at 0.1mg/egg. Older embryos were less susceptible; 4.5-day embryos

Figure 3.5: The Effect of Cobaltous Chloride. A. 8-day embryo lenses, seen from the anterior face (phase contrast x 200) and focused below the epithelium. (a) Control lens; (b) lens from embryo treated with cobaltous chloride at 0.3mg/egg at 4.5 days. B. 12-day cultures of lens epithelium set up from 1-day-old chicks. Harvested and analysed as in Fig. 3.1. (a) Control cultures; (b) treated with 2μg/ml cobaltous chloride at 11 days; (c) treated with 4μg/ml cobaltous chloride at 11 days.

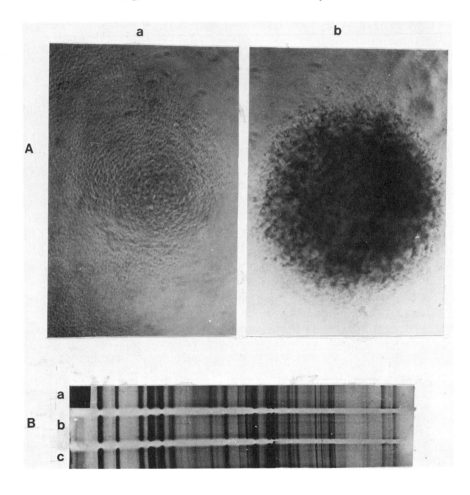

were not killed at 0.05mg/egg, but 18% lethality was obtained at 0.1mg/egg and 24% at 0.2mg/egg. By 8 days of incubation, 0.1mg/egg led to 2% lethality, and 0.2mg/egg to only 7.5%. In cell culture, levels of $6\mu g/ml$ were cytotoxic to all tissues, at $5\mu g/ml$ brain and neural retina cells were affected. The effects seen on polyacrylamide gel electrophoresis were similar to those observed with chloroquine sulphate for these two tissues.

VIII. Effects Including Changes in Differentiation

A. *Vitamin A*

The importance of vitamin A and related substances in regulating developmental processes is evident from the teratogenic effects obtained in animals both by deprivation and by excess. The commonest effects of hypovitaminosis A in the rat include ocular and urinogenital defects, but cardiac and other anomalies are also common (Wilson *et al.*, 1953; Kalter, 1968). Hypervitaminosis A and retinoic acid produce a wide range of effects depending on the state of development of the fetus (Cohlan, 1954; Wilson *et al.*, 1953; Kalter, 1968; Shenefelt, 1972; Geelen, 1979). The effects include skeletal anomalies, cleft palate, eye defects and neural-tube defects. In the early embryo there is interference with closure of the neural tube (Giroud and Martinet, 1956), but later treatment affects learning and motor ability (see Vorhees and Butcher, Chapter 9).

Sporn *et al.* (1976) review the evidence that retinoids including vitamin A regulate the normal differentiation of many epithelial cells. The effect on epithelial growth, differentiation and metaplasia has been studied in organ culture for several systems besides the chondrogenic cells already mentioned, for example prostate (Lasnitzki, 1962), epidermis (Sporn *et al.*, 1975), somite, notochordal cells, and mesoderm in general (Marin-Padilla and Ferm, 1965; Marin-Padilla, 1966).

Teratogenic effects include limb defects, and vitamin A can be shown to interfere with chondrogenesis *in vivo* (Dingle *et al.*, 1966; Kochhar, 1973). Limb rudiments cultured in vitamin A excess develop abnormally (Nakamura, 1977; Rajan, 1974) and cartilage matrix is lost (Fell and Dingle, 1963; Kochhar and Aydelotte, 1974). The effects of vitamin A on limb differentiation is produced only during the period of early chondrogenesis; direct effects on chondrocytes in cell culture have been shown with matrix synthesis being inhibited (Shapiro and Poon, 1976; Vasan and

Lash, 1975). Lewis *et al.* (1978), using organ culture, found that growth in the presence of vitamin A preserves the type of cell-cell contacts, and the presence of a glycoprotein characteristic of prechondrocyte mesenchyme. The appearance of a high molecular weight glycoprotein and changes in cell-to-cell contacts and in the intercellular matrix characterising chondrocyte differentiation were prevented.

B. *N-Methyl-N-nitro-N-nitrosoguanidine*

N-Methyl-N-nitro-N-nitrosoguanidine (MNNG), an alkylating agent, is both mutagenic and carcinogenic. It has been shown to have teratogenic effects in mice (Inouye and Murakami, 1978), with multiple defects of brain, skeleton and palate. It has been shown to cause transdifferentiation in the amphibian eye (Eguchi and Watanabe, 1973), and we have found that it disturbs the pattern of protein synthesis in both lens and neural retina cells in culture. The quantitative changes in protein profiles differed for the two genotypes tested. Exposure to $7\mu g/ml$ MNNG for 1 hour also produces distortions in the pathway of differentiation and transdifferentiation of these cells in culture (Clayton *et al.*, 1980). 8-day chick embryo neural retina in cell culture can give rise to neuronal cells, pigment cells or lens under appropriate culture conditions (Eguchi, 1976; Okada, 1976; Clayton, 1978). We have found that the effect of exposure to a subcytotoxic dose of MNNG depends on the state of differentiation that the cells have acquired during their period of cell culture. Early exposure (at 9 and 11 days after plating) totally prevents the differentiation of pigment cells which normally appear from about day 30 onwards, delays the appearance of lens cell differentiation by 7-10 days, and also leads to a late reappearance of neuronal cells, which are not normally seen after about 16-18 days in normal culture conditions. Exposure to MNNG at a later stage (19 and 21 days) leads to a delay of 10 days or more in pigment-cell appearance, which are abnormal and die after a few days. The appearance of lens cells is only slightly delayed, and again neurone-like cells reappear at a late stage. Thus the effect of MNNG is to affect the future pathways of differentiation of embryonic cells (determination) (Clayton *et al.*, 1980; C. Patek and R.M. Clayton unpublished work).

C. *Insulin*

Insulin has not been found to be teratogenic in rats, but defects of brain, skeleton or both are produced in rabbits, mice and chicks (reviewed by Kalter, 1968; Landauer, 1972). Genetic differences in responses of mice to insulin have been described above (Section II). We have confirmed all the teratogenic effects for the chick *in ovo* reported by Landauer (1972). At 2 days' incubation 37% and 57% of embryos were killed by doses of one and two IU of insulin, respectively. The lower dose was not lethal to 4.5- and 8-day embryos, but lethality of the higher dose remained the same.

In addition to the age- and dose-dependent lethality and the skeletal and other effects, we also observed that insulin *in ovo* causes cataract, (Fig. 3.6). We have explored the reasons for this effect by examining the response of lens epithelium to insulin *in vitro*.

Insulin stimulates mitosis in a wide range of tissues such as liver, (Gerschenson *et al.*, 1972), chondrocytes, (Hajek and Solursh, 1974), fibroblasts, (Paul and Pearson, 1960), myoblasts (Kumegawa *et al.*, 1980) and lens epithelium (Reddan *et al.*, 1972), although in lens cell sheets from the early embryo it promotes cell elongation: a process which characterises lens fibre cell differentiation (Piatigorsky *et al.*, 1973). We find that the genotype of the cell may affect the growth rate response to insulin (Fig. 3.7a and b). Insulin affects the survival of neurones in culture (reviewed by Waymouth, 1977). It also affects microtubule assembly (Soifer *et al.*, 1971; Piatigorsky, *et al.*, 1973) and nucleic acid and protein metabolism (Hickey and Klein, 1970). Insulin binds to membranes, including the plasmalemma and Golgi membranes (Carpenter *et al.*, 1979), nuclear membranes and both rough and smooth endoplasmic reticulum (Goldfine *et al.*, 1978).

In the lens cell, the effect of insulin is to change the relative balance of crystallins synthesised, and in lens epithelium from embryos and 1-day-old chicks the proportion of δ-crystallin is increased (Milstone and Piatigorsky, 1977; de Pomerai and Clayton, 1978; de Pomerai *et al.*, 1978). This effect is also obtained in lens cells transdifferentiating from neural retina cells in culture (de Pomerai and Clayton, 1980). However, many other crystallins are also affected by insulin treatment (Clayton *et al.*, 1976, 1980; and Fig. 3.8). This response is modified by the genotype of the cell (Clayton *et al.*, 1976, 1980). These changes are effected by changes in the available mRNA population, for example the amount of δ-crystallin-mRNA increases preferentially in the 6-day-old embryo lens (Milstone *et al.*, 1976). We find that other crystallin-mRNAs are also affected in 1-day old lens non-coordinately, and this effect is also modulated by the genotype (Clayton *et al.,* 1980; and Figs. 3.9, and 3.10).

Figure 3.6: The Effect of Insulin on the Chick Lens *In Vivo.* The centre area of whole lenses of 17-day chick embryos are seen from the anterior surface, with focus just below the anterior epithelium (phase contrast x 200). A. Control: the types of the fibre cells are seen in orderly array. B. Lens from embryo injected at 4.5 days' incubation with 2 IU of insulin. Swollen, disorganised cells are seen in the centre of the lens, replacing the fibres.

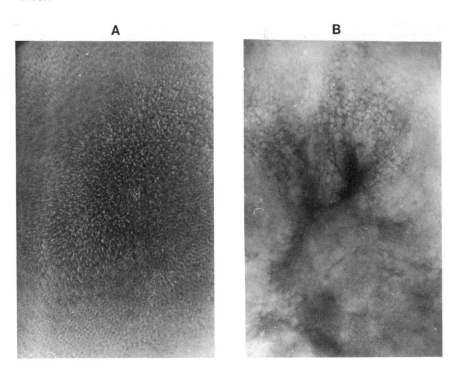

Figure 3.7: The Effect of Insulin on Cell Growth *In Vitro*. Growth curves of 1-day-old chick lens epithelium cells in culture, conditions as in Eguchi *et al.* (1975). Dotted lines, control cultures; solid lines, grown in medium containing insulin.

Cells were transferred to medium containing 10μg/ml insulin, which was replaced every 3 days. Insulin stimulates growth but the Hy-2 genotype response is slight, that of Db more marked.

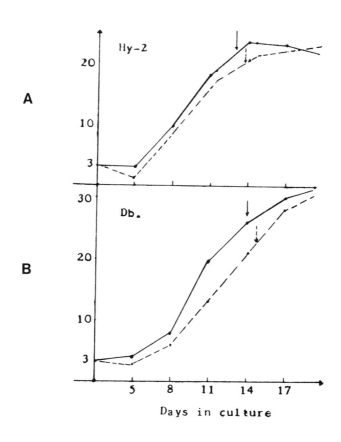

Figure 3.8: The Effect of Insulin on Protein Synthesis in Cell Culture. Traces obtained by integrating densitometer from fluorographs of SDS polyacrylamide gel electrophoretic separation of proteins from cultured lens cells from 1-day-old chick Db genotype cells, grown as in Fig. 3.7, labelled for 3 hours with ^{3}H-amino acid mixture and harvested on day 13, as described in Thomson *et al.* (1979). A. Control. B. Cells transferred to medium containing $10\mu g/ml$ insulin and transferred every 3 days as for Fig. 3.7. Arrows indicate proteins most affected.

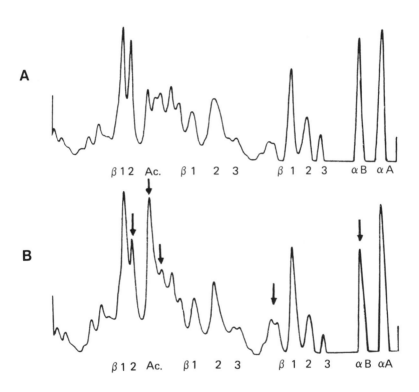

Figure 3.9: Fluorographic Analysis of the Effect of Insulin on mRNA Translation in Cell Culture. Fluorographs of SDS polyacrylamide gel electrophoresis of products translated in a cell-free system from mRNA obtained from cultures of 1-day-old lens epithelium, grown and analysed as described for Figs. 3.7 and 3.8. (a) Control cells; (b) insulin-treated cells. A. Db genotype. B. Hy-2 genotype.

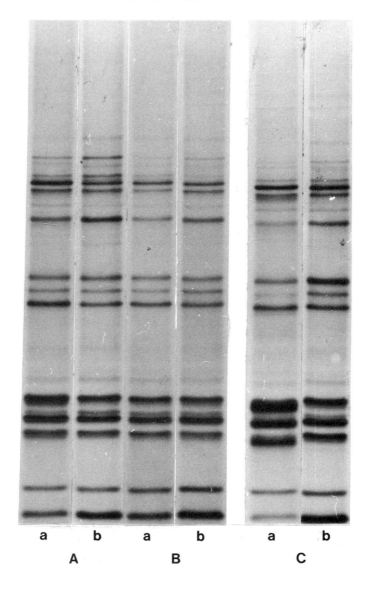

Figure 3.10: Densitometric Analysis of the Effect of Insulin on mRNA Translation in Cell Culture. Showing the reduced effect of insulin treatment on more differentiated cultures. Db lens epithelial cells from 1-day-old chick embryos, harvested on 15 days when mature lentoids are developed in the cultures. All procedures as in Thomson *et al.* (1979). A. Translation products of mRNA from control cells. B. Translation products of mRNA from insulin-treated cells. Arrows indicate proteins most affected.

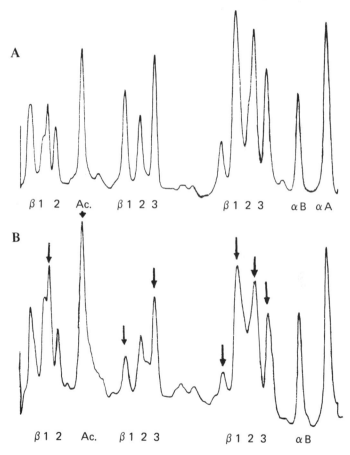

The Use of Cell Culture Methods

IX. Conclusions

There seems to be reason to be optimistic regarding the possibility both of using *in vitro* assays as preliminary tests of compounds (and probably to apply these to human material), and of using such methods to elucidate some of the primary actions of a teratogen. However, both problems require that the question of the form of the drug and the relevant dose be investigated fully, for the reasons given above (Section V). It is very likely that teratogens which exert their effect indirectly, for example by affecting maternal physiology, may not be testable by *in vitro* methods. On the other hand, some problems not considered suitable for *in vitro* investigation may nevertheless be accessible. One such problem may be that of low-level neurotoxic effects.

Gross disturbances in neuroanatomy, intelligence or neurological function do not cause difficulties in assessment, but assessment of lesser changes in postnatal behaviour or in learning capacity, which could be expected as part of the spectrum of impairment, may lead to difficulties or conflicting reports, (see Vorhees and Butcher, Chapter 9, for discussion). Learning or behavioural deficits have been reported in rats after halothane administration in the second trimester (Smith *et al.*, 1978), subjecting the pregnant female to continued stress which would be expected to affect maternal endocrinology (Barlow *et al.*, 1979), and after exposure to alcohol (Bond and Digusto, 1976), or to some psychotropic drugs (see Buelke-Sam and Kimmel, 1979; Mello, 1975; Kolata, 1978; and Vorhees and Butcher, Chapter 9, for discussions). Buelke-Sam and Kimmel discuss the problems of different systems of measurement of performance. A different approach might be to assess the effect of a suspected substance on neuronal outgrowth, and synaptic connections, in cell or tissue culture systems. This possibility is suggested by the effect of some teratogens on fetal brain cells in mice (Manning *et al.*, 1971; Langman and Cordell, 1977). Barbiturates are teratogenic in animals (McColl *et al.*, 1963) and may lead to a dose-related diminution in learning capacity (Martin and Mackler, quoted in Smith, 1977), and a reduction in embryo brain-cell number (Manning *et al.*, 1971). We have made preliminary observations of the effects of barbiturates on protein synthesis in neural retina (Clayton, 1980), and of phenytoin, chloroquine and lead on brain and neural retina, (Figs. 3.3 and 3.4; and A. Zehir and R.M. Clayton, unpublished work), and changes in growth, differentiation in culture and protein profiles of neuronal cells may be of relevance in this context.

The development of cellular techniques for assessment of teratogens

88

may prove to be relevant not only to fundamental problems of development and cell biology, but also to help in providing a rapid assessment of hazards with a sociobiological effect which produce both physical and intellectual handicap in the human population.

Acknowledgements

We are indebted to J. Sinclair for generously undertaking some evaluations of dose-dependent effects of teratogens in cell culture; to J. Jack for technical assistance, and we are especially indebted to M. Alexander, D. Brown and L. Dobbie for their indispensible and generous help with the preparation of this manuscript.

We are grateful to Stirling Poultry Products, the Poultry Research Centre, and D.B. Marshall for a supply of fertile eggs of various strains.

Our work has been supported by the M.R.C. and the Humane Research Trust. A. Zehir is supported by a postgraduate scholarship from the Turkish Government.

References

Aarskog, D. (1975) *Lancet, 2,* 921
Ajodhia, J.M. and Hope, G.M. (1973) *Pharmaceutical J., 1,* 566-8
Angle, C.R. and McIntyre, M.S. (1964) *Am. J. Dis. Child., 108,* 436-9
Atlas, S.A., Vesell, G.S. and Nebert, D.W. (1976) *Cancer Res., 36,* 4619-30
Barlow, S.M. Knight, A.F. and Sullivan, F.M. (1979) *Teratology, 19,* 105-10
Beall, J.R. (1972) *Canad. Med. Assoc. J., 106,* 1061
Beck, F. (1976) *Br. Med. Bull., 32,* 53-8
Bennet, D. (1975) *Cell, 6,* 441-54
Biddle, F.G. and Fraser, F.C. (1977) *Genetics, 85,* 289-302
Biddle, F.G. and Fraser, F.C. (1979) *Teratology, 19,* 207-12
Bond, N.W. and Diguisto, E.L. (1976) *Psychopharmacologia (Berlin), 46,* 163-5
Braun, A.G., Emerson, D.J. and Nichinson, B.B. (1979) *Nature (London), 282,* 507-9
Brown, N.A., Goulding, E.H. and Fabro, S. (1979) *Science, 206,* 573-5
Brusick, D.J. (1978) *Environ. Health Persp., 24,* 105-12
Buelke-Sam, J. and Kimmel, C.A. (1979) *Teratology, 20,* 17-29
Butt, E.M., Pearson, H.E. and Simonsen, D.G. (1952) *Proc. Soc. Exp. Biol. Med., 79,* 247-9
Caplan, A.I. (1970) *Exp. Cell Res., 63,* 341-52
—— (1972) *Develop. Biol., 28,* 71-83
—— (1972a) *Exp. Cell Res., 70,* 185-95
Carpenter, J.L., Gordon, P., Barrazone, P., Freychet, P., Le Cam, A. and Orci, L. (1979) *Proc. Nat. Acad. Sci. U.S.A., 76,* 2803-7
Chaube, S. and Murphy, M.L. (1968) *Advan. Teratol., 3,* 181-237
Chernoff, G.F. (1980) *Teratology, 22,* 71-5
Clark, G.D. and Ryan, P.J. (1980) in *Tissue Culture in Medical Research* (Richards, U.J. and Rajan, K.T., eds.), pp. 79-86, Pergamon Press, Oxford
Clayton, R.M. (1976) in *Tests of Teratogenicity In Vitro* (Ebert, J.D. and Marois, M., eds.), pp.

The Use of Cell Culture Methods

473-83, Elsevier, Amsterdam

—— (1978) in *Stem Cells and Tissue Homeostasis* (Lord, B.I., Potter, C.S. and Cole, R.J., eds.), pp. 115-38, Cambridge University Press, Cambridge

—— (1980) in *Alternatives in Drug Research* (Rowan, A. and Stratman, C., eds.), pp. 153-73, Macmillan, London

Clayton, R.M., Bower, D.J., Clayton, P.R., Patek, C.E., Randall, F.E., Sime, C., Wainwright, N.R. and Zehir, A. (1980) in *Tissue Culture in Medical Research* (Richards, R.J. and Rajan, K.T., eds.), Vol. II, pp. 185-94, Pergamon Press, Oxford and New York

Clayton, R.M., Odeigah, P.G., De Pomerai, D.I., Pritchard, D.J., Thomson, I. and Truman, D.E.S. (1976) in *Biology of the Epithelial Lens Cells in Relations to Development, Ageing and Cataract* (Courtois, Y. and Regnault, F., eds.), pp. 123-36, Les Colloques de L'I.N.S.E.R.M., Paris

Clayton, R.M., De Pomerai, D.I. and Pritchard, D.J. (1977) *Develop. Growth Differ., 19,* 319-27

Cohlan, S.Q. (1954) *Pediatrics, 13,* 556-69

Cole, W.A. and Trasler, D.G. (1980) *Teratology, 22,* 125-39

Desesso, J.M. and Jordan, R.L. (1977) *Teratology, 15,* 199-212

Dingle, J.L., Fell, H.B. and Lucy, J.A. (1966) *Biochem. J., 98,* 173-81

Eguchi, G. (1976) *CIBA Found. Symp., 40,* 241-58

Eguchi, G. and Watanabe, K. (1973) *J. Embryol. Exp. Morphol., 30,* 63-71

Eguchi, G., Clayton, R.M. and Perry, M.M. (1975) *Develop. Growth Differ., 17,* 395-413

Elshove, J. (1969) *Lancet, 2,* 1074

Fell, H.B. and Dingle, J.T. (1963) *Biochem. J., 87,* 403-8

Ferm, V.H. and Carpenter, S.J. (1967) *Exp. Mol. Pathol., 7,* 208-13

Geelen, J.A.G. (1979) *Crit. Rev. Toxicol., 6,* 351-75

Gerschenson, L.E., Okigaki, T., Andersson, M., Molson, J. and Davidson, M.B. (1972) *Exp. Cell Res., 71,* 49-58

Gibson, J.E. and Becker, B.A. (1968) *Cancer Res., 28,* 475-80

Giroud, A. and Martinet, M. (1956) *Arch. Anat. Micr. Morph. Exp., 45,* 77-98

Goldfine, I.D., Jones, A.L., Hradek, G.T., Wong, K.Y. and Mooney, J.S. (1978) *Science, 202,* 760-3

Goldman, A.S. (1979) *Clin. Perinatol., 6,* 203-18

Goldstein, M., Pinsky, M.F. and Fraser, F.C. (1963) *Genet. Res., 4,* 258-65

Guzelian, P.S. and Bissell, D.M. (1976) *J. Biol. Chem., 251,* 4421-7

Hajek, A.S. and Solursh, M. (1974) *Gen. Comp. Endoc., 25,* 432-46

Hanson, J.W., Myrianthopoulos, N.C., Harvey, M.A.S. and Smith, D.W. (1976) *J. Pediatr., 89,* 662-8

Harbison, R.D. (1978) *Environ. Health Persp., 24,* 87-100

Harbison, R.D. and Becker, B.A. (1970) *J. Pharm. Exp. Ther., 175,* 283-8

Hartz, S.C., Heinonen, O.P., Shapiro, S., Siskind, V. and Slone, D. (1975) *N. Engl. J. Med., 292,* 726-8

Hemminki, K., Sorsa, M. and Vainio, H. (1979) *Scand. J. Work. Environ. Health, 5,* 307-27

Hickey, E.D. and Klein, N.W. (1971) *Teratology, 4,* 453-60

Inouye, M. and Murakami, U. (1978) *Teratology, 18,* 263-8

Johnston, M.C., Sulik, K.K. and Dudley, K.H. (1979) *Teratology, 19,* 33A

Jones, K.L., Smith, D.W., Ulleland, C.N. and Streissguth, A.P. (1973) *Lancet, 1,* 1267-71

Kaighn, M.E. (1976) in *Tests of Teratogenicity In Vitro* (Ebert, J.D. and Marois, M., eds.), pp. 73-90, Elsevier, Amsterdam

Kalter, H. (1965) in *Teratology: Principles and Techniques* (Wilson, J.G. and Warkany, J., eds.), pp. 57-80, University of Chicago Press, Chicago

Kalter, H. (1968) *Teratology of the Central Nervous System*, pp. 35-40, University of Chicago Press, Chicago

Kalter, H. and Warkany, J. (1959) *Physiol. Rev., 39,* 60-115

Kameyama, Y. (1964) *Ann. Rep. Res. Inst. Environ. Med. Nagoya Univ., 13,* 49

Karkinnen-Jääskeläinen, M. and Saxén, L. (1976) in *Tests of Teratogenicity In Vitro* (Ebert, J.D. and Marois, M. eds.), pp. 275-84, Elsevier, Amsterdam

Kellerman, G., Luyten-Kellerman, M. and Shaw, C.R. (1975) *Am. J. Hum. Genet., 25,* 327-31

Kizer, S.J., Cordon, V.M., Brendel, K. and Bresler, R. (1970) *J. Clin. Invest., 49,* 1942-8

Kleinshuster, S.J. and Moscona, A.A. (1972) *Exp. Cell Res., 70,* 397-410

Kochhar, D.M. (1973) *Teratology, 7,* 289-98

—— (1975) *Teratology, 11,* 273-88

90

Kochhar, D.M. and Aydelotte, M.B. (1974) *J. Embryol. Exp. Morphol., 31,* 721-34
Kolata, O.B. (1978) *Science, 202,* 732-4
Kumegawa, M., Ikeda, E., Hosoda, S. and Takuma, T. (1980) *Develop. Biol., 79,* 493-9
Kury, G. and Crosby, R.J. (1968) *Toxicol. Appl. Pharmacol., 13,* 199-206
Laemmli, U.K. (1970) *Nature, 227,* 680-5
Lambert, G.H. and Nebert, D.W. (1977) *Teratology, 16,* 147-54
Landauer, W. (1972) *Teratology, 5,* 129-36
Landauer, W., Clark, E.M. and Larner, M.M. (1976) *Teratology, 14,* 281-6
Langman, J. and Cardell, E.L. (1977) *Teratology, 17,* 15-30
Lasnitzki, I. (1962) *Exp. Cell. Res., 28,* 40-51
Lefebvre, E.B., Haining, M.D. and Labbe, R.F. (1972) *N. Engl. J. Med., 286,* 1301-2
Lewis, C.A., Pratt, R.M., Pennypacker, J.P. and Hassell, J.R. (1978) *Develop. Biol., 64,* 31-47
McCann, J., Choi, E., Yamasaki, E. and Ames, B.W. (1975) *Proc. Natl. Acad. Sci. USA, 72,* 5135-9
McColl, J.D., Globus, M. and Robinson, S. (1963) *Experientia, 19,* 183-4
McLain, R.M. and Becker, B.A. (1975) *Toxicol. Appl. Pharmacol., 31,* 72-82
Manning, D.E., Stout, A.G. and Zemp, J.W. (1971) *Fed. Proc. Fed. Am. Soc. Exp. Biol., 30,* 495, Abstract
Marin-Padilla, M. (1966) *J. Embryol. Exp. Morphol., 15,* 261-9
Marin-Padilla, M. and Ferm, V.H. (1965) *J. Embryol. Exp. Morphol., 13,* 1-8
Matz, G.J. and Naunton, R.F. (1968) *J. Am. Med. Assoc., 206,* 910
Maugh, T.H. (1978) *Science, 201,* 1200-5
Mayerson, P. and Moscona, A.A. (1979) *Differentiation, 13,* 173-84
Mello, N.K. (1975) *Fed. Proc. Fed. Am. Soc. Exp. Biol., 34,* 1832-4
Milkovitch, L. and van den Berg, B.J. (1974) *N. Engl. J. Med., 291,* 1268-71
Miller, R.W. (1977) *J. Natl. Cancer Inst., 58,* 471-4
Miller, R.P. and Becker, B.A. (1975) *Toxicol. Appl. Pharmacol., 32,* 53-61
Milstone, L.M. and Piatigorsky, J. (1977) *Exp. Cell. Res., 105,* 9-14
Milstone, L.M., Zelenka, P. and Piatigorsky, J. (1976) *Develop. Biol., 48,* 197-204
Mirkin, B.L. (1971) *J. Pediatr., 78,* 329-38
Monroy, A. and Moscona, A.A. (1980) *Introductory Concepts in Developmental Biology,* pp. 128-206, University of Chicago Press, Chicago
Moore, M.R., Meredith, P.A. and Goldberg, A. (1977) *Lancet, 1,* 717-19
Moran, D. (1974) *Exp. Cell. Res., 86,* 365-73
Morris, J.E. (1976) in *Tests of Teratogenicity In Vitro* (Ebert, J.D. and Marois, M., eds.), pp. 107-48, Elsevier, Amsterdam
Moscona, A.A. (1976) in *Tests of Teratogenicity In Vitro* (Ebert, J.D. and Marois, M., eds.), pp. 67-72, Elsevier, Amsterdam
Moscona, M. and Moscona, A.A. (1979) *Differentiation, 13,* 165-72
Mulvihill, J.J. and Yeager, A.M. (1976) *Teratology, 13,* 345-8
Murakami, U., Kameyama, Y. and Kato, T. (1954) *Nagoya J. Med. Sci., 17,* 74-88
Nakamura, H. (1977) *Teratology, 16,* 195-202
Nebert, D.W. (1973) *Clin. Pharmacol. Ther., 14,* 693-9
Nebert, D.W. and Felton, J.S. (1976) *Fed. Proc. Fed. Am. Soc. Exp. Biol., 35,* 1133-41
Nelson, M.M. (1960) in *Congenital Malformations* (Wolstenholme, G.E.W. and O'Connor, C.M., eds.), pp. 134-51, J. and A. Churchill, London
Netzloff, M.L., Streiff, R.R., Frias, J.L. and Rennert, O.M. (1979) *Teratology, 19,* 45-9
Nowack, E. (1965) *Humangenetik, 1,* 516-36
Okada, T.S. (1976) in *Tests of Teratogenicity In Vitro* (Ebert, J.D. and Marois, M., eds.), pp. 91-105, Elsevier, Amsterdam
O'Shea, K.S. and Kaufman, M.H. (1979) *J. Anat., 128,* 65-76
Ouellette, E.M., Rosett, H.L., Rosman, N.P. and Weiner, L. (1977) *N. Engl. J. Med., 10,* 528-30
Palmer, M.A.K. (1974) in *Experimental Embryology and Teratology* (Woollam, D.H.M. and Morriss, G.M., eds.), pp. 16-33, Elek Science, London
Paul, J. and Pearson, E.S. (1960) *J. Endocrinol., 21,* 287-94
Piatigorsky, J., Rothschilds, S.S. and Wollberg, M. (1973) *Proc. Natl. Acad. Sci. USA, 70,* 1195-8
Piatigorsky, J. (1980) in *Curr. Top. Eye Res., 3,* 1-39
De Pomerai, D.I. and Clayton, R.M. (1978) *J. Embryol. Exp. Morphol., 47,* 179-93
De Pomerai, D.I. and Clayton, R.M. (1980) *Develop. Growth Differ., 22,* 49-66

The Use of Cell Culture Methods

De Pomerai, D.I., Pritchard, D.J. and Clayton, R.M. (1977) *Develop. Biol., 60,* 416-27
Propping, P. (1978) *Rev. Physiol. Biochem. Pharmacol., 83,* 123-73
Purchase, I.F.H., Longstaff, E., Ashby, J., Styles, J.A., Anderson, D., Lefevre, P.A. and Westwood, F.R. (1976) *Nature (London), 264,* 624-7
Rajan, K.T. (1974) *Experimental Embryology and Teratology* (Woollam, D.H.M. and Morriss, G.M., eds.), pp. 65-89, Elek Science, London
Randall, C.L. and Taylor, W.J. (1979) *Teratology, 19,* 305-11
Reddan, J.R., Harding, C.V., Rothstein, H., Crotty, M.W., Lee, P. and Freeman, N. (1972) *Ophthal. Res., 3,* 65-82
Ridgway, L.P. and Karnofsky, D.A. (1952) *Annls. N.Y. Acad. Sci., 55,* 203-15
Robertson, M., Neri, A. and Oppenheimer, S. (1975) *Science, 189,* 639-40
Ruffolo, P.R. and Ferm, V.H. (1965) *Lab. Invest., 14,* 1547-53
Russell, L.B. (1950) *J. Exp. Zool., 114,* 545-602
Saxén, I. and Saxén, L. (1975) *Lancet, 2,* 498
Saxén, L. (1976a) in *Tests of Teratogenicity In Vitro* (Ebert, J.D. and Marois, M., eds.), pp. 262-84, Elsevier, Amsterdam
—— (1976b) *J. Embryol. Exp. Morphol., 36,* 1-12
Saxén, L. and Rapola, J. (1969) *Congenital Defects,* Holt, Rinehart and Winston, New York
Schumacher, H.D.A., Blake, J.M.G. and Gillette, J.R. (1968) *J. Pharmacol. Exp. Ther., 160,* 189-200
Scott, W.J., Fradkin, R. and Wilson, J.G. (1977) *Teratology, 16,* 333-6
Seegmiller, R.E., Horwitz, A.L. and Dorfman, A. (1980) *J. Embryol. Exp. Morphol., 59,* 207-16
Shapiro, S., Hartz, S.C., Siskind, V., Mitchell, A.A., Slone, D., Rosenberg, L., Monson, R.R. and Heinonen, O.P. (1976) *Lancet, 1,* 272-5
Shapiro, S.S. and Poon, J.P. (1976) *Arch. Biochem. Biophys., 174,* 74-81
Shenefelt, R.E. (1972) *Teratology, 5,* 103-8
Shepard, T.H. (1979) *Curr. Prob. Pediatr., 10,* 5-42
Shepard, T.H. and Pious, D. (1978) in *Handbook of Teratology* (Wilson, J.G. and Fraser, F.C., eds.), Vol. 4, pp. 71-93, Plenum Press, New York
Shum, S., Jensen, N.M. and Nebert, D.W. (1979) *Teratology, 20,* 365-78
Smith, D.W. (1977) *Am. J. Dis. Child., 131,* 1337-9
Smith, R.F., Bowman, R.E. and Katz, J. (1978) *Anaesthesiology, 41,* 319-23
Smithberg, M. and Runner, M. (1963) *Am. J. Anat., 113,* 479-89
Soifer, D., Braun, T. and Hechter, O. (1971) *Science, 172,* 269-71
Sporn, M.B., Clamon, G.H., Dunlop, N.M., Newton, D.L., Smith, J.M. and Saffiotti, U. (1975) *Nature (London), 253,* 47-50
Sporn, M.B., Dunlop, N.M., Newton, D.L. and Smith, J.M. (1976) *Fed. Proc. Fed. Am. Soc. Exp. Biol., 35,* 1332-8
Taussig, H.B. (1962) *J. Am. Med. Assoc., 180,* 1106-14
Thompson, D.J., Molello, J.A., Strebing, R.J. and Dyke, I.L. (1978) *Teratology, 17,* 151-8
Thomson, I., De Pomerai, D.I., Jackson, J.F. and Clayton, R.M. (1979) *Exp. Cell Res., 122,* 73-81
Vasan, N. and Lash, J.W. (1975) *Calc. Tiss. Res., 19,* 99-107
Vesell, E.S. (1976) in *Psychotherapeutic Drugs* (Usden, E. and Forrest, I.S., eds.), pp. 169-73, M. Dekker, New York and Basel
Waymouth, C. (1977) in *Cell, Tissue and Organ Cultures in Neurobiology* (Federoff, S. and Hertz, L., eds.), pp. 631-43, Academic Press, New York
Weatherall, J.A.C. and Haskey, J.C. (1976) *Br. Med. Bull., 32,* 39-44
Wilk, A.L., Greenberg, J.H., Horigan, E.A., Pratt, R.M. and Martin, G.R. (1980) *In Vitro, 16,* 269-76
Wilson, J.G. (1973) *Environment and Birth Defects,* Academic Press, New York
Wilson, J.G., Roth, C.B. and Warkany, J. (1953) *Am. J. Anat., 92,* 189-217

CHAPTER FOUR

BIOCHEMICAL MECHANISMS OF TERATOGENESIS
Kenneth E. Williams

CONTENTS

I. Introduction

Before attempting to review our current very limited understanding of the biochemical basis of teratogenesis, it is probably wise to give some general impression of the place that biochemical studies occupy in the overall approach to the investigation of human birth defects. Considered out of such context, the unfortunate impression may be given that the biochemical approach is distinctly separate, superior or merely more fashionable than any other approach. An inevitable consequence of such artificial isolation would be to invite wasted effort through conducting biochemical experiments directed at answering physiologically irrelevant questions. However, properly integrated biochemical experiments can extend and challenge the findings from studies based on, say, morphological and ultrastructural techniques alone so that richer, more penetrating findings should accrue to those who tackle the problems in this field on an interdisciplinary basis (Bass *et al.*, 1970). Also, in a relatively young science like teratology where a large mass of experimental data has now been gathered, but where the theoretical basis of the subject still consists of little more than half a dozen 'rules of thumb' (Wilson, 1973), hypotheses couched in epidemiological, morphological, pharmacokinetic, biochemical or any other terms are desperately needed. Only by advancing fresh hypotheses and by testing them rigorously (so that most are discarded but a few develop) will the science avoid being suffocated by an ever-increasing mass of factual observations and meet some of its more pressing needs. Central amongst these needs is the requirement for some basis for rationalizing the observed very large interspecies variability in the teratogenic response of different mammals to a given teratogenic agent. This problem is exemplified by the failure of rodents and other non-primate species to respond to thalidomide in the same manner as both man and simian primates (Wilson, 1973; Schardein, 1976) although rodents are usually more responsive to teratogenic agents than are rhesus monkeys (Wilson, 1971). It is important to establish whether such variability can be explained in terms of differences in general physiology, reproductive physiology, pharmacokinetic factors or differences in placentation between the species, rather than simply to ascribe the variability to intrinsic differences in the sensitivity of the embryogenic processes of the different species to a given teratogenic insult (see Wilson *et al.,* 1975). Without a better understanding of this aspect of the subject, extrapolation from laboratory animals to man will remain hazardous and the screening of drugs for teratogenic potential will be in danger of degenerating into an expensive but meaningless ritual rooted in arbitrary legal requirements.

II. General Considerations in Formulating Teratogenic Mechanisms

Certain basic difficulties in the field of teratology have been responsible for the slow rate of progress in formulating mechanisms and continue to cause problems in both the design of experiments and in the interpretation of results from the literature.

When incriminating a particular agent in the causation of human congenital defects other causes must be eliminated with certainty. This basic requirement is often difficult to satisfy in practice. Thalidomide was an exceptional agent in that human exposure to it occurred in a precipitous manner and the amelia induced had a low 'spontaneous' incidence in human populations so that an upsurge in its incidence was rapidly detected (Lenz, 1965). Epidemiological studies have also been responsible for incriminating rubella and one or two other environmental agents like methyl mercury. However, from past experience it seems likely that, unless massive prospective studies are begun, the epidemiological approach will in future be capable of identifying only a few potent environmental teratogens released by some accident of the thalidomide type. It seems unlikely that epidemiological studies alone will ever be capable of identifying mildly teratogenic agents, ether natural or man-made, that are already widespread in the environment. This is because there is usually a greater overlap between genetically- and environmentally-induced defects than was found in the case of thalidomide, so that it is difficult to distinguish the additional effects of an environmental agent against a 'background noise' of similar effects of genetic origin.

A. *Genetic Considerations*

Epidemiological studies indicate that some 20% of human malformations have a known major genetic component (Wilson, 1973). Within this group are found some of the more severe malformations caused by chromosomal abnormalities; about two-thirds of these affect sex chromosomes, while the biggest contributor to the autosomal sub-group is the trisomy responsible for Down's syndrome (mongolism). Some mild malformations (e.g. an extra digit, deafness) that are compatible with an unimpaired reproductive capacity, show a simple Mendelian dominant pattern of inheritance. Similarly, many of the inborn errors of metabolism have been shown to exhibit a simple Mendelian recessive pattern of inheritance with full penetrance, but many of the common malformations (e.g. cleft palate, spina bifida and anencephaly), although known to run in families, have less straightforward patterns of inheritance so that alternative genetic models are compatible with the available data. Amongst the alternative models that have appeared to explain these malformations are polygenic and multifactorial models (Carter, 1969; Smith and Aase, 1970). In the latter it is proposed that an environmental agent acts in conjunction with genetic factors to cause the malformation (Carter, 1974). Human twin studies serve to indicate that many common malformations are not completely determined by genetic factors (Fig. 4.1). In fraternal twins the incidence of malformations is, as expected, no greater than in other sibs, but in the case of monozygotic twins the concordance is far less than the figure of 100% expected from an entirely genetically determined mechanism (Smith and Aase, 1970). It appears that in the case of one half of the monozygotic twins an environmental 'trigger' acted on one twin but not the other.

Animal studies serve to confirm, in a more rigorous experimental manner, the conclusion that there is a strong interaction between environmental agents and genotype. For example, administration of cortisone to a number of strains of mice during pregnancy (keeping both the dose and the day of gestation constant) leads to a very different response to the drug in the different strains (Table 4.1). At one extreme CBA mice show only 12% malformations whereas, at the other, strain A animals show a 100% incidence at the same dose (Kalter, 1965). Such findings indicate

Figure 4.1: Concordance of Common Malformations in Twins. Monozygotic (hatched) and Dizygotic (stippled).

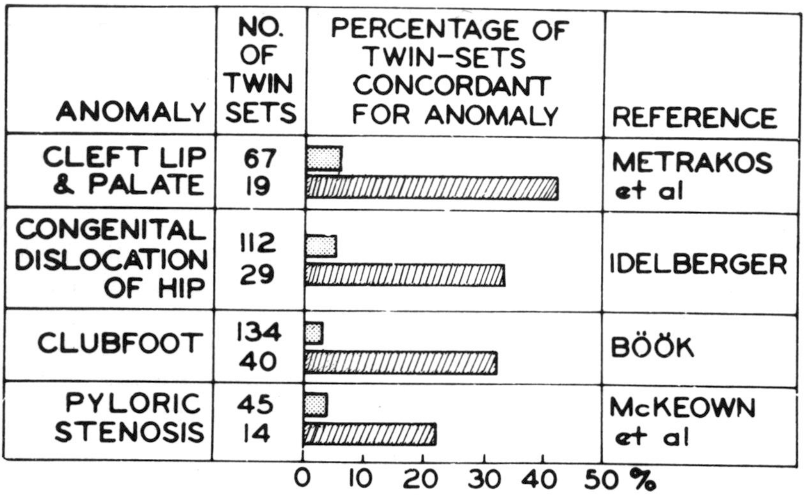

ANOMALY	NO. OF TWIN SETS	PERCENTAGE OF TWIN–SETS CONCORDANT FOR ANOMALY	REFERENCE
CLEFT LIP & PALATE	67 / 19		METRAKOS et al
CONGENITAL DISLOCATION OF HIP	112 / 29		IDELBERGER
CLUBFOOT	134 / 40		BÖÖK
PYLORIC STENOSIS	45 / 14		McKEOWN et al

0   10   20   30   40   50 %

Source: Smith and Aase (1970), with permission.

Table 4.1: Incidence of Cortisone-induced Cleft Palate in Different Strains of Inbred Mice

Strain	Percent
CBA	12
C57BL	19
C3H	68
DBA	92
A	100

From H. Kalter, in *Teratology. Principles and Techniques*. (J.G. Wilson and J. Warkany, eds.), University of Chicago Press, Chicago 1965.

that interactions between the given environmental agent and the particular mammalian genotype are important. It is thus against a complex background of genetic effects that any effects from environmental teratogenic agents must be considered.

B. *Developmental Considerations*

A second, highly complex set of factors, that permeates the whole subject of teratology and which ultimately separates it from conventional pathology and toxicology arises from the rapidly changing nature of the target tissue(s) during gestation. Whereas pathological changes in adult animals are likely to arise from the breakdown of homeostatic mechanisms, the complex, sequential nature of the changes that occur in the mammalian embryo during the course of development and the highly dynamic nature of most structures lead to a much greater scope for the perturbation of events than exists in the relatively static end-products of development that are found in the adult (Saxén, 1976).

From animal studies, in which a constant dose of a given agent has been administered to a given species at different stages of gestation, two important concepts emerge that do not feature in the toxicology of the adult. First, the concept that there are periods of development when the embryo is either highly sensitive or relatively resistant to the induction of malformations by an established teratogenic agent so that at different times during gestation a given dose of the agent may either kill the embryo or leave it completely undamaged (Wilson, 1973). At other stages of development the same dose of agent may damage the embryo which, however, remains viable. In this case the embryo either fully repairs minor damage by compensatory growth (Snow and Tam, 1979) so as to develop normally, or it fails to effect a complete repair of more severe damage and continues to grow so that a structural defect is present at birth. (One consequence of this factor is that in mammals that produce many offspring from a single pregnancy, asynchronous development of litter mates will lead to their differential susceptibility after a single acute exposure of the mother to a teratogenic agent so that normal, malformed and dead fetuses can all be found in the same litter towards the end of gestation. Any genetic differences between litter mates will serve to exacerbate this effect.)

The second useful concept that emerges from such animal studies is that of a teratogenic range. When an agent is administered to the maternal animal in increasing amounts it first shows a 'no effect' range followed by

Figure 4.2: Effects of Increasing the Dosage of a Teratogenic Agent

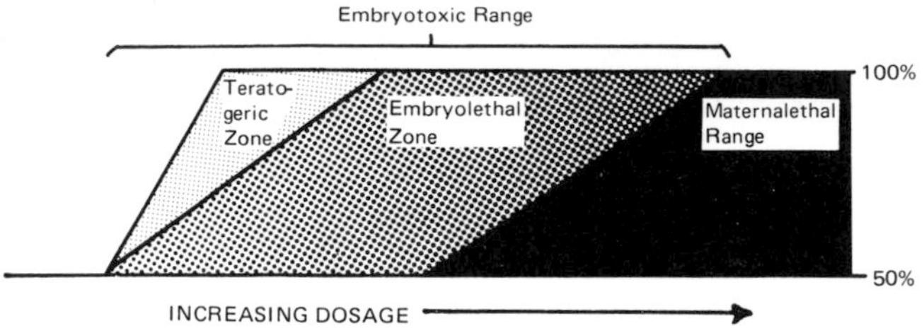

Source: Wilson (1973), with permission.

an embryotoxic range that overlaps with the teratogenic range (Fig. 4.2) (but cf. Chapter 9). As the dose is increased still further, an embryolethal range is passed through before maternal deaths are induced. In general it is observed that the embryo is more sensitive than the mother to the drug (Wilson, 1973) and that there may be quite a narrow dose range, somewhere between the embryonic 'no effect' level and the 100% embryolethal level, in which malformations can be induced.

C. Pharmacokinetic Considerations

If the relationship between the mother and the embryo is examined then the route to the fetus of an agent administered to the mother will be shown to be neither direct nor passive (Fig. 4.3). If the mother detoxifies or excretes an active agent extremely rapidly it may fail to do more than traverse the placenta in very small quantities for a short period of time; hydroxyurea is an example of such an agent, but interesting differences in serum half-lives between the rat and the rhesus monkey have been reported (Wilson *et al.*, 1975). If the drug is not rapidly excreted by the mother and the placenta is not resistant to permeation by the teratogenically active form of a particular drug then its concentration in the fetal tissues may approach that reached in the maternal blood-stream. However, the blood-brain barrier of the fetus may be less effective than in the adult (Mirkin, 1970) so that certain drugs may be much more potent to the fetus. Likewise, the embryo could concentrate the toxic metabolite and become very adversely affected while the mother experiences no ill effects.This could occur if the drug in the form administered to the mother is not teratogenic but persists in the maternal system and can penetrate the fetoplacental unit where it becomes metabolised to a teratogenic form

100

Figure 4.3: Relation of Maternal and Embryonic Circulatory Systems. The importance of the placenta in the exchange of metabolites and drugs between the embryo/fetus and the mother is emphasised. Placental permeability may change during gestation and hence be an important pharmacokinetic variable.

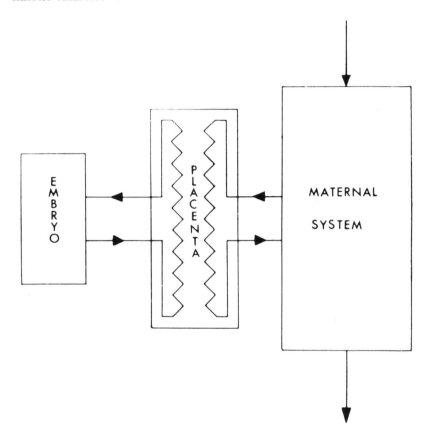

Source: Wilson *et al.* (1975); Dencker (1979), with permission.

that cannot readily be either detoxified by the embryo or passed back across the placenta into the maternal system. For further discussion of this point, see Chapter 5.

D. *Other Considerations*

Two or more agents at mild or non-teratogenic doses that have little or no effect when administered separately may undergo potentiative interactions when administered together to form a teratogenically effective combined agent. Animal studies have shown such potentiation to be more than just a theoretical possibility. For example, Wilson (1964) quotes a report that mice fasted for 24 hours on day 9 of pregnancy show a malformation rate unaltered from the 'spontaneous' rate of 1%, while those treated with cortisone on days 11-13 shown an incidence of 24%. On a simple additive basis, giving both treatments together would lead to an expected incidence of 25% malformations, whereas in practice simultaneous treatment leads to a 76% incidence (i.e. three times the simple additive effect). It has also been shown that a high incidence of malformations results on administering a mixture of actinomycin, 5-fluorouracil and cyclophosphamide at concentrations that, individually, are non-teratogenic (Wilson, 1964). These findings indicate that similar effects should be borne in mind when considering the human situation, where 4% of women have been reported as receiving ten or more medications during a single pregnancy (Mirkin, 1970) and many women are exposed to more than three drugs in the first trimester.

A further consideration is that during pregnancy there is usually a high natural wastage of 'spontaneous' congenital malformations (Table 4.2), so that the percentage of common structural malformations found at term is usually much lower than that found in 2-month-old human embryos (Nishimura *et al.*, 1968). Hence any agent that interferes with spontaneous

Table 4.2: Gross Malformations in Second-Month Embryos and Newborn Infants

Malformation	α − 2nd month (%)	β − Newborn (%)	α/β
Anencephaly	0.169	0.062	2.3
Spina bifida	0.172	0.019	9.1
Cyclopia	0.274	0.006	45.7
Cleft lip	1.471	0.178	8.3
Polydactyly	0.909	0.098	9.3

Source: Nishimura, H., Takano, K., Tanimura, T. and Yasuda, M. (1968) *Teratology,* *1,* 281

Figure 4.4: Possible Environmental (Non-Genetic) Ways of Inducing Abnormal Development

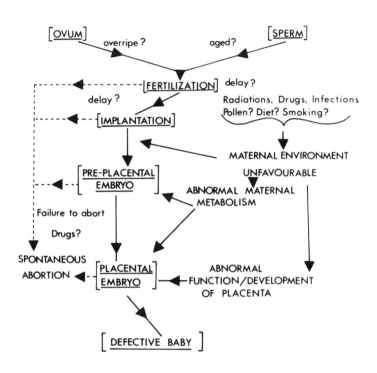

abortion can act to increase the incidence of malformations at term even if it is not directly responsible for the induction of the defect.

If the possible ways of inducing malformations in mammals are summarised (Fig. 4.4) then a complex network of possible sites of disturbance of developmental processes can be constructed. From the time of formation of the primordial ovum through to the end of pregnancy (or even beyond, if behavioural development is also considered) there are ways in which development can be influenced by environmental factors. If an infectious agent or drug renders the maternal environment unfavourable the agent may act either by being passed on directly to the implanted embryo, or some aspect of maternal metabolism may be disturbed by the agent so that a secondary metabolic imbalance affects the embryo. In the post-implantation embryo, the agent may act by perturbing some aspect of placental function rather than by acting directly on the mother or embryo. Changing dietary factors and pollen levels suggest ways in which reported weak seasonal variations (Elwood, 1975) in the incidence of certain malformations could arise. The paternal environment also appears to be important in the induction of defects since Hansmann *et al.* (1979) have shown that the offspring of mice in which the male alone was acutely exposed to fairly low doses of X-rays showed elevated levels of chromo-somal abnormalities in fetuses on day 9.5 of gestation. Thus occupational exposure to mutagenic or teratogenic agents may be of significance in men as well as in women.

E. *Identification of the Primary Teratogenic Event*

With the above factors in mind it is possible, in theory at least, to define the event(s) that we would like to identify when formulating biochemical mechanisms of teratogenesis. If our understanding of normal reproductive physiology was complete, then concentrations of hormones, metabolites, etc. could be compared between normal and abnormal development, permitting the identification of the primary abnormal physiological event (the primary insult) that leads to an *irreversible* sequence of abnormal morphological events. It is important to stress the irreversible nature because, if damage is reversible and heals, developmental events may be delayed but, on repair, they would proceed normally so that no defect would be detectable at birth (Snow and Tam, 1979). It is therefore desirable to try to identify the abnormal physiological event(s) responsible for a sequence of abnormal morphological events which, as development continues, cause the appearance of the characteristic features of a particu-lar syndrome that are apparent at or after birth. This theoretical objective is one at which we can aim when studying human malformations. Sur-prisingly, there is one group of abnormalities in which the primary physio-logical event can be defined quite precisely in biochemical terms. These are the inborn errors of metabolism that arise from either the absence of a particular enzyme or the production of a structurally altered, non-functional fôrm of the enzymic protein (Stanbury *et al.*, 1972). In such abnormalities it is still difficult to explain the secondary pathological and bizarre behavioural effects (Anderson *et al.*, 1977) associated with a number of these syndromes in terms of the known missing enzyme alone. This suggests that, with regard to overall action, secondary effects are as important as primary effects in determining the precise nature of the final pattern of damage.

III. The Mechanistic Approach to Teratology

The major known cause of human malformations is genetic transmission (Wilson, 1973), but this accounts for only some 20% of all recorded malformations. After the appearance of an index case, genetic counselling may help to reduce the risk of further similiar malformations within a given family, but little can be done in general terms to alter the genetic composition of human populations and thereby reduce the incidence of malformations that are entirely genetically determined. However, if amongst the largest group (65-75% of the total) currently with no known cause interactions of unrecognised environmental agents with susceptible genotypes are important, then these malformations would be entirely preventable if the environmental 'triggers' could be identified and eliminated. [Reports (see Morriss, 1980) that multivitamin supplements significantly reduced the incidence of neural-tube defects when given to pregnant women who had previously given birth to an infant with such a defect give some encouragement to those who are exploring this general approach.] Similarly, identification of an essential member of a multi-component agent, whose members interact potentiatively, would permit inactivation of the agent on eliminating just one component.

To identify such environmental agents, investigators have turned to animal models for indications; consequently, sizeable catalogues (Shepard, 1976; Kalter, 1968) have now been compiled that list agents known to be teratogenic in one or more species of mammal. Further additions to such catalogues are largely superfluous since it is now well established that exposure of the pregant mammal to a wide variety of drugs (Schardein, 1976) and other environmental influences, such as dietary deficiency, hypoxia and radiations (Morriss, 1979), can have adverse effects on development of the embryo. Moreover, the classical dose-response studies have brought as much confusion as enlightenment, through the strongly differing responses of different mammalian species to a given agent, so that extrapolation from animal studies to the human situation has remained an extremely imprecise exercise. Investigators have therefore been forced to look more closely at the mode of action of a given agent in a susceptible species and to establish the cellular and subcellular effects induced in the embryonic tissues during the critical stages of development and then to decide which effects are important in the pathogenesis of the defect. If equivalent effects are absent in the non-susceptible species, this implies that they are indeed important, although the question of the reason for the interspecies difference remains. (In the simplest case the difference could arise from maternal pharmacokinetic factors; in less obvious cases there may be subtle interspecies differences in embryogenic mechanisms.)

When potentially important morphological changes have been identified, the pharmacologist and biochemist can suggest possible ways in which such changes could have been induced at the molecular level. A knowledge of both the structure of the agent and its established effects in the adult organism serve as a starting point in such speculations. However, an agent may influence important embryonic events (e.g. cell migration or cell-cell interactions) by actions that would not be amongst those normally reported in even well-documented studies of the effects of the agent on adult tissues. Recently, Brown *et al.* (1979) have established a correlation between the ability of drugs (other than those known to inhibit macro-molecular synthesis) to act as teratogens and their ability to inhibit adhesion of mouse ovarian tumour cells to concanavalin A-coated plastic surfaces; although caution is needed in interpreting findings of this type (see next section for general comment), such experiments suggest new lines of inquiry that could be extended in more relevant test systems. If it is suggested that a particular agent is teratogenically active because of a specific property (e.g. it inhibits a particular enzyme or arrests mitosis) then, other things being equal, analogues of the agent showing different degrees of effectiveness in a suitable assay system would be expected to show corresponding ranking as teratogens. Also, blocking an essential pathway or a process at different points should have the same gross effects on developmental processes.

IV. Strategies in Investigating Mechanisms

As mentioned above, studies of the mode of action of teratogens in whole animals are complicated by the metabolic and pharmacokinetic factors associated with the maternal and placental systems. For example, differences in placentation may be responsible for some of the interspecies variability in teratogenic response (see Chapter 1 and Beck and Lloyd, 1977). Attempts have therefore been made to simplify the experimental systems to see whether, on elimination of the maternoplacental system, the embryonic tissues themselves show intrinsic differences in susceptibility to teratogens. Over the last decade certain groups, notably New and co-workers at Cambridge and groups in the Free University of Berlin, have been active in developing *in vitro* systems to isolate variables (New *et al.*, 1976; New, 1978; Bass *et al.*, 1970; Neubert and Merker, 1975; see Chapters 1 and 2). By the use of techniques of this type it is possible to take either an embryo, together with some of its placental membranes, or some part of the embryo itself (e.g. limb-buds, or palatal shelves) and culture these *in vitro* to produce nomal, progressive development. The advantages of such isolated embryo or embryonic tissue systems are: the developmental stage can be observed directly and related to any effects; the concentration of the drug in the medium remains constant (maternal metabolism and excretion having been eliminated); placental concentration gradients are abolished; and maternal or placental metabolite production is prevented. Moreover, it may be ethically acceptable to study organs from aborted human embryos in such systems (Rajan, 1974).

The disadvantages are that, on removal of an embryo from its placental membranes, it can only be cultured *in vitro* with a beating heart for about 3 or 4 days, so that only a limited period of development can be studied. Furthermore, on isolating an organ its blood supply is interrupted so that during subsequent culture *in vitro*, even under the most favourable conditions, the rate of development is usually greatly retarded relative to that *in vivo* (Merker in Neubert and Merker, 1975). Also, even with increased oxygen pressures, it may prove impossible to produce adequate oxygen tensions at the centre of tissues more than a few millimetres in thickness without reaching excessive oxygen tensions in the surface cells. In addition it has been shown that manipulation of the partial pressure of oxygen can itself induce abnormal development in cultured embryos (Morriss and New, 1979). Clearly, much careful empirical work is needed to establish those culture conditions that permit not only survival of the embryo but also allow normal development to continue *in vitro* for a useful period of time (New *et al.*, 1976; New, 1978). This approach also requires detailed morphological and ultrastructural assessment to be made to ensure that, in the absence of agents, the observed sequence of developmental changes closely parallels that which occurs *in vivo*. However, interesting results have recently been reported (Chatot *et al.*, 1980) showing that human serum from individuals undergoing treatment with a known or suspected teratogen induces more developmental defects in rat embryos cultured *in vitro* than does human serum from untreated individuals. Extension of such studies offers a possible means of identifying the drug metabolites responsible for teratogenic effects.

A danger inherent in the *in vitro* approach is that the findings from studies of isolated tissues or embryos may be totally irrelevant to the situation *in vivo* (Morriss, 1979), so that they only provide supporting evidence which must be viewed in a wider context. However, the study of limb-buds and palatal shelves in this manner is of obvious appeal in trying to define the mechanisms of action of drugs that show thalidomide-like effects or induce cleft palate. One important basic question that can be answered by the growth of isolated organs is whether, *in vitro*, such structures will develop normally in isolation without the influence of nervous signals or hormonal messages from elsewhere in the embryo. It is thus possible to examine, at a different level, certain questions to do with problems like normal fusion of the palate or failure of fusion which may result in the production of a central cleft.

From observations *in vivo* Walker and Fraser (1956) and Fraser (1957) proposed that differential growth rates may be an important factor in the production of palatal clefts (Fig. 4.5). Thus if the oral cavity starts to grow rapidly before the two palatal shelves have touched and fused and if the rate of growth of the oral cavity outstrips the rate of growth of the palatal shelves the latter can never meet and a cleft will remain. On culturing palatal shelves *in vitro* Saxén (1973) showed that shelves taken from a sensitive strain of mouse, strain A (one that gives a 100% incidence of a cleft palate *in vivo* on administering cortisone), the control shelves fuse well ahead of those treated with cortisone at a dose of 1mg/ml (Fig. 4.6). In contrast, if shelves from a resistant strain (CBA, that gives only 12% incidence of cleft palate when pregnant animals are treated with cortisone *in vivo*) are examined in equivalent experiments, cortisone treatment does not retard closure to anywhere near the same extent as in the sensitive strain (Fig. 4.7). Thus, in this example, the differential malformation rate in the two strains *in vivo* seems to be at least partly due to a genetically determined differential sensitivity of the embryonic target tissue to the effects of cortisone.

V. Examples of Biochemically Formulated Mechanisms

A. *Thalidomide (α-phthalimidoglutarimide)*

Because of the impact of this one hypnotic drug on the subject of teratology,

Figure 4.5: Schematic Illustration of the Movements and Fusion of the Palatal Shelves in the Mammalian Embryo. The palatal shelves, originally situated vertically on either side of the tongue (A), move to a horizontal position (B) and become fused in the midline (C).

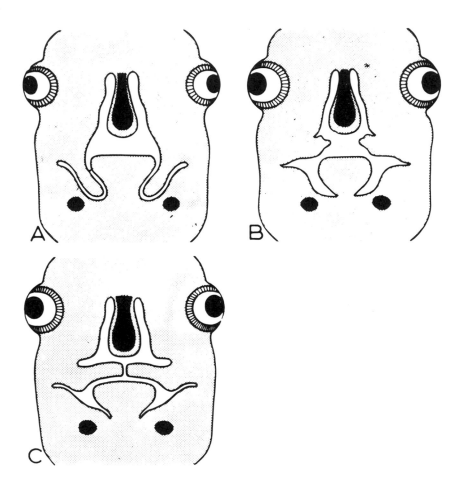

Source: Saxén and Rapola (1969), with permission.

Figure 4.6: The Effect of Cortisol (1.0μg/ml) on *In Vitro* Closure of the Palatal Shelves of 13-day-old Mouse Embryos of Strain A. Cumulative index: Fraction of closed palates observed at 6-hour intervals.

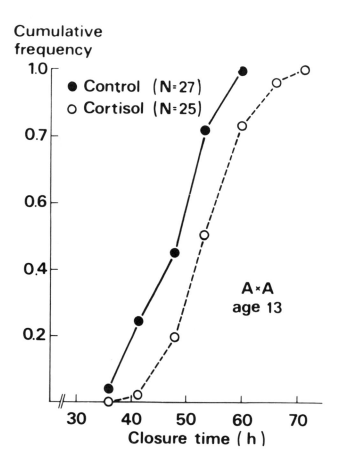

Source: Saxén (1973), with permission.

Figure 4.7: The Effect of Cortisol (1.0µg/ml) on *In Vitro* Closure of the Palatal Shelves of Mouse Embryos of Strain CBA. Embryos were used at the same developmental stage (13-) as 13-day-old strain A embryos (Figure 4.6).

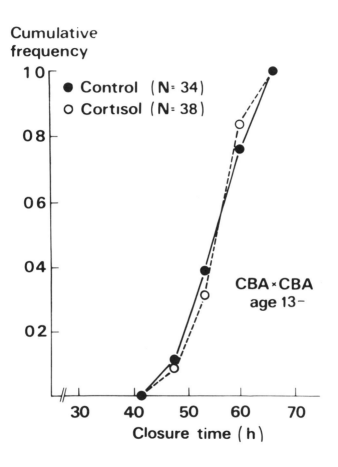

Source: Saxén (1973), with permission.

it would be expected that two decades later its mechanism of action would have been conclusively established. The close structural relation of thalidomide to glutamic acid led to the early suggestion that some of the 10 or more metabolites of the drug act as competitive antagonists of glutamic acid/glutamine; alternatively, it may act through antimitotic effects, which it shows against human leucocytes in culture (Woollam, 1965). At a more speculative level, Neubert (see Bass *et al.,* 1970) has suggested that thalidomide owes its species-specific effects to a feature of the general physiology of primates, namely their lack of L-gulonolactone oxidase activity, which determines their requirements for dietary ascorbate (Nishikimi and Udenfriend, 1977). This in turn leads both to the specific effects on the limbs and to the higher sensitivity of primates to the toxic effects of thalidomide, compared with other species, through protocollagen proline hydroxylase, an ascorbate-dependent enzyme which plays a key role in collagen formation, becoming the target for the drug. (As yet the evidence for this mechanism is not very substantial, but if valid it would be predicted that guinea-pigs and some bats would also be expected to be susceptible to the induction of amelia by thalidomide because of their known ascorbate dependence.) Schardein (1976) lists interference with folic acid metabolism, intercalation between base pairs of DNA and acylation of subcellular components as alternative modes of action advanced by other groups of investigators, so that there is little or no agreement on the molecular basis of the action of this compound.

However, McCredie (1976) has advanced a compelling set of arguments linking the limb-reduction deformities of the fetus and the peripheral sensory neuropathy in adults that are both induced by this drug, and suggests that thalidomide acts primarily on the neural crest within the embryo so that sensory nerve damage is the key effect and destroys the trophic function of the nerves so that limb deformities arise as secondary events. This elegantly presented hypothesis deserves testing rigorously at the molecular level using a highly susceptible primate as the experimental animal to establish whether mitotic arrest in the neural crest occurs or cell migration is prevented.

The ingestion of hypnotics/sedatives in early pregnancy is likely to continue, in particular up to the time that a woman is certain that she is pregnant. Thalidomide was effective in the interval 21-36 days after conception (Schardein, 1976), so any future sedatives or hypnotics that share the unwanted effects of thalidomide will pose a serious threat to at least this group of women even if their prescription to women known to be pregnant is banned.

B. *Agents that Interfere with Nucleic Acid Synthesis/Function*

The rapidly changing needs for gene products during embryogenesis have been demonstrated in a dramatic manner by Klose (see Neubert and Merker, 1975) who showed, by protein mapping studies, that in mouse embryos somewhere in the region of 356 soluble proteins can be isolated on day 9, whereas on day 14 at least 408 proteins are present. However, during this period 53 proteins (largely those of high molecular weight) disappear and 105 new proteins appear. In other words, many genes are being switched on and off over short intervals of time during periods of rapid differentiation and growth, so that agents that interfere even transiently with the production of new species of RNA, and so deprive the embryo of a specific gene product at some sensitive stage in organogenesis, could well act in the manner shown in Figure 4.8. If one specific example of such an agent, hydroxyurea — a compound that has been investigated extensively by Kochhar (see Neubert and Merker, 1975) — is considered then this compound is found to be a very potent, fast-acting teratogen that induces a very high incidence of limb defects as well as other severe malformations (e.g. cleft palate) when administered to mice on the appropriate days of gestation. It has been proposed that the mechanism of action of hydroxyurea is to interfere reversibly with the enzyme ribonucleotide reductase, the enzyme that converts ribose to deoxyribose during the formation of deoxyribonucleotides, so that there is a deficiency of deoxyribonucleoside triphosphates for incorporation into DNA (Fig. 4.9). Thus it is suggested that, through interfering with a critical enzyme, hydroxyurea disturbs nucleic acid synthesis and that this is its mechanism of action as a teratogen. However, other workers (e.g. Krowke and Bochert, 1975) have suggested that this agent inhibits nucleic acid synthesis in a less specific manner.

Saxén and Rapola (1969), Wilson (1973) and Schardein (1976) all give useful summaries of agents whose interference with nucleic acid synthesis and function renders them among the most potent teratogens on record. Analogues of nucleic acid bases (e.g. 5-bromouracil and 8-azoguanine), agents that prevent DNA-dependent RNA synthesis (e.g. actinomycin D) and agents that inhibit RNA translation (e.g. puromycin) have all been reported to be teratogenic, indicating that prevention of gene expression at any of a number of stages can lead to a similar end-result.

Figure 4.8: Sites of Action of Different Antagonists of Nucleic Acid Metabolism

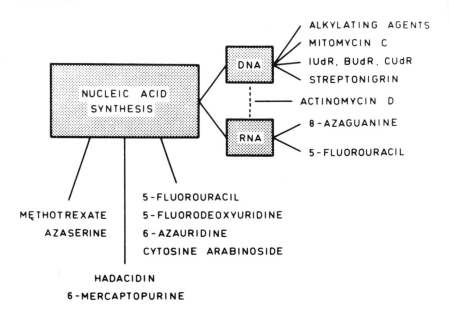

Source: Saxén and Rapola (1969), with permission.

C. *Antimetabolites*

The nicotinamide analogue, 6-aminonicotinamide, and the L-glutamine analogue, 6-diazo-5-oxo-L-norleucine, are examples of antimetabolites that have been investigated in detail and shown to be teratogenic in a number of mammalian species (Schardein, 1976); the latter compound is a particularly potent teratogen in the rat.

In the rat at least, 6-aminonicotinamide (6-AN) probably acts in part by interfering with the pentose-phosphate pathway, which has been demonstrated in the rat embryo during the active stages of organogenesis (Bass *et al.*, 1970). By following the fate of ^{14}C-labelled glucose in the 13-day rat embryo, Köhler and Brand (see Bass *et al.*, 1970) showed the oxidative route through the pentose-phosphate pathway to be marginally active (so that it is vulnerable to agents that decrease the flux through it), but that it is capable of forming amounts of ribose 5-phosphate adequate for the

Figure 4.9: Postulated Mode of Action of Hydroxyurea

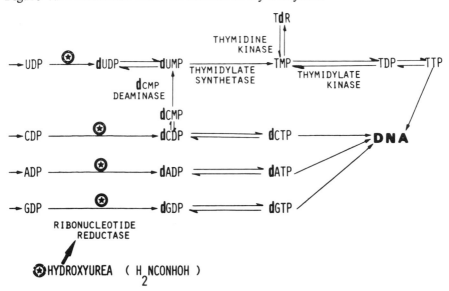

Source: Neubert and Merker (1975), with permission.

synthesis *de novo* of all the nucleotides required for incorporation into nucleic acids. In contrast, the amounts of NADPH (required for reductive cellular biosynthesis) formed by this route are probably inadequate for embryonic needs. Administration of 6-aminonicotamide leads to the build-up of one of the intermediates in the oxidative route through the pentose-phosphate pathway so that the net rate of nucleic acid synthesis is decreased, an action that is compatible with the severe growth retardation induced by this compound. In addition to the competitive blocking of 6-phospho-gluconate dehydrogenase, Merker (see Bass *et al.*, 1970) has shown this agent to produce rather bizarre effects in the nuclear region of cells from ectodermal tissue in the embryo. Large fluid-filled cavities appear around the nucleus so that it appears to float in a pool of liquid. Thus it is quite possible that nuclear activity in ectodermal tissue is generally disrupted. Such changes may reflect differences in metabolic activity in different germ layers of the embryo and in turn explain why this agent induces cleft palate as the major defect.

Ritter *et al.* (1975) examined the levels of ATP in embryos from rats treated with a teratogenic dose of 6-AN and in embryos from rats that were also give a protective dose of nicotinamide 1-4 hours after the teratogen. Up to 48 hours after such treatments unprotected embryos showed up to a 50% decrease in ATP concentrations relative to untreated embryos, whereas nicotinamide given 1 hour after the 6-AN prevented more than a 20% fall. Similarly, treatment of animals with 2,4-dinitrophenol (an agent known to interfere with ATP generation) produced up to a 20% fall in embryonic ATP concentrations, but induced no malformations. Such findings suggest that only when ATP values fall by about 20-50% from normal is there sufficient disruption of general cell function to induce permanent damage resulting in malformations.

Investigations of the effects of the L-glutamine analogue 6-diazo-5-oxo-L-norleucine (DON), indicate that it both inhibits a specific step in the synthesis of purines, required for DNA and RNA formation, and also blocks the utilisation of L-glutamine in transamidination reactions, so preventing the formation of hexosamines for incorporation into glycos-aminoglycans for glycoprotein synthesis. Studies with mouse limb-buds grown in culture (Aydelotte and Kochhar, 1975) indicate that the amount of damage induced by DON can be reduced by simultaneous exposure to L-glutamine. However, *in vivo* administration of L-glutamine (Greene and Kochhar, 1975) was not effective in preventing malformations in the manner that nicotinamide reduced the incidence of 6-AN induced malformations, so the action of DON as a teratogen may not be limited to blocking reactions involving L-glutamine.

D. *Agents that Interfere with Placental Function*

Whatever their precise mechanism of action, the above agents probably act by crossing the placenta and acting directly on embryonic tissues. This view is supported by the demonstration (Rowinski *et al.,* 1975) that mouse blastocysts incubated *in vitro*, in the presence of concentrations of inhibitors of RNA and protein synthesis sufficient to prevent the develop-ment of inner cell mass derivatives, were without effect on the development of the outer, primary trophoblast cells, so that the outer-cell layer remained intact but was penetrated by the agents. Such findings may also give the impression that cells of the placental tissues are unlikely candidates as targets for teratogens.

However, there are probably a number of teratogenic agents whose excessive size or charge prevents them from crossing the placental mem-branes and reaching embryonic tissues; they thus act indirectly on the embryo. For example, trypan blue, a large polar molecule that is unable to freely permeate cell membranes, gives a spectrum of severe structural malformations when administered to pregnant rodents. The compound has been investigated extensively by Beck, Lloyd and co-workers (see Chapter 1; Beck and Lloyd, 1966). It shows an optimum teratogenic dose of about 50mg/kg body weight in the rat and gives an increased resorption rate when the dose is further increased. A characteristic of this dye is that significant amounts of it do not reach or accumulate within the embryonic tissues, but large amounts of it concentrate in the visceral yolk sac of the egg cylinder. Moreover, it shows an unusually abrupt cut-off in its action which coincides with the time at which the chorio-allantoic placenta is established (Fig. 4.10). This led Beck and Lloyd to make their initial proposal relating to the mechanism of action of this compound as a teratogen, namely that it interferes with the nutrition of the embryo

Figure 4.10: Malformation Rate in Rat Fetuses when a Given Dose of Trypan Blue is Administered at Different Stages of Gestation

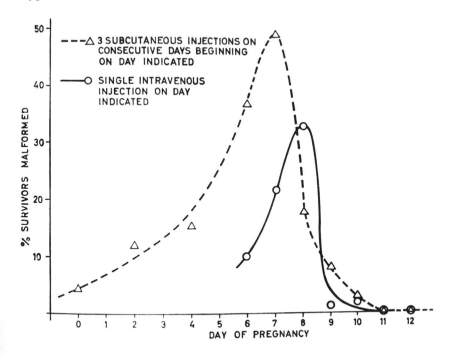

Source: Beck and Lloyd (1966), with permission.

(Beck *et al.*, 1967). Rodents are thought to obtain a substantial amount of the monomeric biochemical units, required by the embryo during growth and development, by degrading macromolecules of maternal origin within the lysosomal system of the visceral yolk sac, a process that has been termed 'embryotrophic nutrition'. Since trypan blue administered to pregnant rats accumulates extensively in the vacuolar system and was found *in vitro* to inhibit a number of lysosomal enzymes, the initial proposal for the mechanism of action of the dye as a teratogen was that it inhibited lysosomal enzymes *in vivo*, thereby reducing the flux of nutrients made available to the embryo by the process of embryotrophic nutrition (Beck *et al.*, 1967). This mechanism has much in common with the anti-metabolite- or enzyme inhibition-induced deficiencies in essential metabolites described in the previous section.

By culturing visceral yolk sacs removed from pregnant rats late in gestation it has been possible to explore this proposal further. Isolated yolk sacs incubated *in vitro* rapidly hydrolyse ^{125}I-labelled proteins are added to the culture medium so that the quantity of trichloroacetic acid-soluble (non-protein-precipitable) radioactivity in the medium rises rapidly. On further examination of the hydrolysis products by gel chromatography it was shown that the yolk sac has the ability to degrade proteins to the level of amino acids and release these back into the culture medium. When trypan blue was added to the medium at concentrations similar to those found in the maternal blood-stream *in vivo* after the administration of the optimum teratogenic dose of the dye (50mg/kg body weight), a sharp decrease in the rate of hydrolysis of the protein was observed. The inhibition of hydrolysis was dose dependent over the concentration range of dye found in the bloodstream after the administration of the optimum teratogenic dose. When the levels of radioactivity in the tissue were examined, the control tissue showed a steady-state level beyond the first hour of incubation, but when trypan blue was added to the medium a rapid depletion of the amount of non-hydrolysed protein within the tissue was observed (Williams *et al.*, 1976). This is entirely the opposite effect to that predicted if trypan blue acts as an intralysosomal inhibitor of protein hydrolysis, and suggests that in the *in vitro* system the dye does not act primarily on intralysosomal digestion but interferes with the ingestion of protein into the lysosomal system of the yolk sac. However, the net effect on the embryo is identical with that produced by an inhibition of lysosomal enzymes, namely that the embryo receives a reduced flux of essential metabolites in the period before the chorio-allantoic placenta has become functional and this transient deprivation of nutrients at a critical stage of development is the cause of the malformation. Thus the revised hypothesis merely shifts the site of the primary insult from the lysosomal system to the mechanism of pinocytic uptake of macromolecules.

The experimental findings supporting the modified hypothesis are also compatible with the permeation of the yolk sac by small metabolites being inhibited by the dye, but as yet there is no evidence to either support or refute this suggestion. However, Zawoiski (1975) has observed that the administration of L-glutamic acid to trypan blue-treated pregnant rats affords protection against the induction of exencephaly in the off-spring. Since the arguments in favour of the embryotrophic nutrition hypothesis are still not conclusive, other possible mechanisms of action of trypan blue deserve to be explored (Hamburgh *et al.*, 1975).

Trypan blue is probably not the only agent to act on the placental membranes. Because of their size, the various tissue antisera (including anti yolk-sac sera) that have been shown to be potent teratogens by Brent and co-workers (Brent *et al.*, 1971, 1975; Jensen *et al.*, 1975) are unlikely to reach embryonic tissues at the critical stages of development, and thus may well act by interfering with some aspect of yolk-sac function (New and Brent, 1972; Goetze *et al.*, 1975).

VI. Conclusions

The above mechanisms, set in the context of the general problem of human malformations, are intended to be representative of the stage the subject has reached rather than to be a comprehensive list of all biochemical mechanisms ever formulated. But, even from a cursory examination of a small number of examples, certain trends emerge. The tight schedule of events in mammalian development appears to leave the embryo susceptible to the induction of defects if a transient lack of metabolites is severe enough and persists for a sufficient interval. The choice of metabolite (e.g. ATP, purine, hexosamine or amino acid) does not appear to be as critical as the period in which it is in short supply. However, we are currently struggling to offer satisfactory explanations as to why different teratogenic agents, administered to a single species of inbred mammal at a given stage of gestation, elicit significantly different patterns of malform-ations. Likewise, as yet we have little true idea of the root causes of the marked interspecies differences in response to a given agent administered at equivalent stages of development (see e.g. Wilson *et al.*, 1975). Our methodology is becoming more sophisticated (Neubert *et al.*, 1977), but our working hypotheses must keep pace and become more comprehensive as the results of well-planned studies of embryogenic, pharmacokinetic and biochemical factors become available. Our success or failure in this challenging task will determine whether we will be able to devise valid tests, based on laboratory animals and their tissues, that will permit the positive identification and possible elimination of environmental agents that pose a threat to the unborn human infant.

Acknowledgements

The author wishes to thank those who have kindly permitted the quotation of figures and tables from their published work.

References

Anderson, L., Dancis, J., Alpert, M. and Herrmann, L. (1977) *Nature (London), 265,* 461-3
Aydelotte, M.B. and Kochhar, D.M. (1975) *Differentiation, 4,* 73-80
Bass, R., Beck, F., Merker, H.-J., Neubert, D. and Randhahn, B. (1970) *Metabolic Pathways in Mammalian Embryos during Organogenesis and its Modification by Drugs,* Freie Universitat, Berlin
Beck, F. and Lloyd, J.B. (1966) *Adv. Teratol., 1,* 131-93
Beck, F. and Lloyd, J.B. (1977) *Handbook in Teratology,* Vol. 3, *Comparative, Maternal and Epidemiological Aspects* (Wilson, J.G. and Fraser, F.C., eds.), pp. 155-86, Plenum Press, New York/London
Beck, F., Lloyd, J.B. and Griffiths, A. (1967) *Science, 157,* 1180-2
Böök, J.A. (1948) *Hereditas, 34,* 289-300
Braun, A.G., Emerson, D.J. and Nichinson, B.B. (1979) *Nature (London), 282,* 507-9
Brent, R.L., Johnson, A.J. and Jensen, M. (1971) *Teratol., 4,* 255-75
Brent, R.L., Jensen, M., Koszalka, T.R. and Leung, C.C.K. (1975) *Teratology, 11,* 14a
Carter, C.O. (1969) *Br. Med. Bull., 25,* 52-7
Carter, C.O. (1974) *Devel. Med. Child Neurol., 16,* Suppl. 32, 3-15
Chatot, C.L., Klein, N.W., Piatek, J. and Pierro, L.J. (1980) *Science, 207,* 1471-3
Dencker, L. (1979) in *Advances in The Study of Birth Defects,* Vol. 1, *Teratogenic Mechanisms* (Persaud, T.V.N., ed.), pp. 1-18, MTP Press, Lancaster
Elwood, J.M. (1975) *Br. J. Prev. Soc. Med., 29,* 22-6
Goetze, T., Franke, H., Oswald, B., Schlag, B. and Goetze, E. (1975) *Biol. Neonate, 27,* 221-31
Greene, R.M. and Kochhar, D.M. (1975) *J. Embryol. Exp. Morphol., 33,* 355-70
Hamburgh, M., Erlich, M., Nathanson, G. and Pesetsky, I. (1975) *J. Exp. Zool., 192,* 1-12
Hansmann, I., Zmarsly, R., Probeck, H.D., Schäfer, J. and Jenderny, J. (1979) *Nature (London), 280,* 228-9
Idelberger, K. (1951) *Die Erbpathologie der sogenannten angeborenen Huftverenkung,* Urban und Schwarzenburg, Munich
Jensen, M., Koszalka, T.R. and Brent, R.L. (1975) *Develop. Biol., 42,* 1-12
Kalter, H. (1965) in *Teratology, Principles and Techniques* (Wilson, J.G. and Warkany, J., eds.), pp. 57-80, University of Chicago Press, Chicago
—— (1968) *Teratology of the Central Nervous System,* University of Chicago Press, Chicago
Krowke, R. and Bochert, G. (1975) *Naunyn-Schmiedeberg's Arch. Pharmacol., 288,* 7-16
Lenz, W. (1965) in *Embryopathic Activity of Drugs* (Robson, J.M., Sullivan, F.M. and Smith, R.L.,

eds.), pp. 182-5, Churchill, London

McCredie, J. (1976) *Med. Hypoth., 2,* 63-9

McKeown, T., MacMahon, B. and Record, R.G. (1952) *Arch. Dis. Child., 27,* 386-90

Metrakos, J.D., Metrakos, K. and Baxter, H. (1958) *Plast. Reconstr. Surg., 22,* 109-22

Mirkin, B.L. (1970) *Postgrad. Med.,*(January), 91-6

Morriss, G.M. (1979) in *Maternal Effects in Development* (Newth, D.R. and Balls, M., eds.), pp. 351-73, Cambridge University Press

—— (1980) *Nature (London, 284,* 121-3

Morriss, G.M. and New, D.A.T. (1979) *J. Embryol. Exp. Morphol., 54,* 17-35

Neubert, D. and Merker, H.-J. (1975) *New Approaches to the Evaluation of Abnormal Embryonic Development,* Georg Thieme, Stuttgart

Neubert, D., Merker, H.-J. and Kwasigroch, T.E. (1977) *Methods in Prenatal Toxicology,* Georg Thieme, Stuttgart

New, D.A.T. (1978) *Biol. Revs., 53,* 81-122

New, D.A.T. and Brent, R.L. (1972) *J. Embryol. Exp. Morphol., 27,* 543-53

New, D.A.T., Coppola, P.T. and Cockroft, D.L. (1976) *J. Reprod. Fertil., 48,* 219-22

Nishikimi, M. and Udenfriend, S. (1977) *Trends Biochem. Sci., 2,* 111-13

Nishimura, H., Takano, K., Tanimura, T. and Yasuda, M. (1968) *Teratology, 1,* 281-90

Rajan, K.T. (1974) *Exp. Embryol. Teratol., 1,* 65-89

Ritter, E.J., Scott, W.J. and Wilson, J.G. (1975) *Teratol., 12,* 233-8

Rowinski, J., Solter, D. and Koprowski, H. (1975) *J. Exp. Zool., 192,* 133-42

Saxén, I. (1973) *Archs Oral Biol., 18,* 1469-79

Saxén, L. (1976) *J. Embryol. Exp. Morphol., 36,* 1-12

Saxén, L. and Rapola, J. (1969) *Congenital Defects,* Holt, Rinehart and Winston, New York

Schardein, J.L. (1976) *Drugs as Teratogens,* CRC Press, Florida

Shepard, T.H. (1976) *Catalog of Teratogenic Agents* (2nd edition), Johns Hopkins University Press, Baltimore and London

Smith, D.W. and Aase, J.M. (1970) *J. Pediatr., 76,* 653-9

Snow, M.H.L. and Tam, P.P.L. (1979) *Nature (London), 279,* 555-7

Stanbury, J.B., Wyngaarden, J.B. and Fredrickson, D.S. (eds.), (1972) *The Metabolic Basis of Inherited Disease,* 3rd edn., McGraw-Hill, New York

Walker, B.E. and Fraser, F.C. (1956) *J. Embryol. Exp. Morphol., 4,* 176-89

Walker, B.E. and Fraser, F.C. (1957) *J. Embryol. Exp. Morphol., 5,* 201-9

Williams, K.E., Roberts, G., Kidston, M.E., Beck, F. and Lloyd, J.B. (1976) *Teratology, 14,* 343-54

Wilson, J.G. (1964) *J. Pharmacol. Exp. Therapeut., 144,* 429-36

—— (1971) *Fed. Proc. Fed. Am. Soc. Exp. Biol. 30,* 104-9

—— (1973) *Environment and Birth Defects,* Academic Press, New York/London

Wilson, J.G., Scott, W.J., Ritter, E.J. and Frandkin, R. (1975) *Teratology, 11,* 169-78

Woollam, D.H.M. (1965) *Proc. Roy. Soc. Med., 58,* 497-571

Zawoiski, E.J. (1975) *Toxicol. Appl. Pharmacol., 31,* 191-200

121

CHAPTER FIVE

THE DISTRIBUTION OF DRUGS AND OTHER AGENTS IN THE FETUS
Sven Ullberg, Lennart Dencker and Bengt Danielsson

CONTENTS

Contents

I. Introduction

Most chemical agents pass from the mother to the fetus but to differing extents and at different rates. The majority of those which damage the fetus are likely to cause their adverse effect directly in the fetus – in the tissues which are affected. Evidence for this is that a number of substances accumulate selectively in the critical fetal tissues.

Some harmful agents, however, hardly reach the fetus at all but accumulate in the yolk sac and placenta (see Williams, Chapter 4). There is a strong indication that they exert their damage by interfering with fetal nutrition. The apparently active transport of some nutrients to the fetus seems to be a delicate mechanism which can be easily damaged by toxic agents. The distribution of various nutrients and the effect on this by harmful chemicals is therefore of major interest.

The normal development of a fetus may also be disturbed by a primary effect on the maternal organism, for instance by interference with progesterone or glucocorticoid production, or by changing the blood sugar concentration.

This review is based mainly on results obtained from distribution studies in experimental animals performed by the whole-body autoradiographic technique (Ullberg, 1954, 1977).

In such experiments a series of pregnant animals are usually injected with a single intravenous dose. The distribution pattern is recorded photographically in sections through whole removed fetuses or, more often, through the whole pregnant animal. The variation with time of the distribution pattern in the fetus or in the whole pregnant animal can thus be followed. The rapidity with which a substance is taken up by the fetus and leaves it is registered. The possible accumulation and retention in individual fetal organs can be observed.

Diffusion of soluble compounds is avoided and the technique is therefore accessible to investigations of such chemicals. With low-temperature autoradiography volatile substances can also be studied.

The observations made are generally qualitative but some investigations have been complemented by quantitative determinations.

If a substance is metabolised in the body the original compound and the labelled metabolites will be registered. The autoradiographic experiments may then be combined with a separation of the metabolities. In cases where drug metabolites are believed to be covalently bound to tissue components the unbound drug may be washed away by selected solvents and the residual radioactivity registered.

The most common experimental animal has been the mouse. However, cryomicrotomes are now available which allow the sectioning of animals as large as a pregnant monkey in the 5 kg range.

Most experiments have been performed when the animal is at a relatively late stage of gestation. The results from these studies apply more to fetal toxicity than to malformations. Recently, however, the distribution of many substances has also been studied during the organogenetic period (Dencker, 1976, 1979).

A few review articles have appeared dealing with the autoradiographic distribution of drugs during pregnancy. A short review was previously presented (Ullberg, 1973). Waddell and Marlowe (1976) published a comprehensive review of the complete literature in the field. A recent paper (Dencker, 1979) was specifically aimed at comparing early and late stages of gestation.

II. Selection and Transport of Nutrients

The transfer to the fetus of substances which through evolution have been accessible to the mammalian body seems to be regulated in a relatively rational way. Substances which play a physiological role are positively selected compared with non-physiological or harmful ones. Many substances which are essential for the developing fetus are apparently transported actively by carrier proteins and some are rather strongly accumulated in the fetus compared with the mother. The passage of most non-physiological natural environmental substances, on the other hand, is retarded so that they appear in the foetal organs in considerably lower concentrations than in the maternal tissues.

Substances which undergo favourable placental transfer include several vitamins, amino acids, monosaccharides, DNA precursors (nitrogenous bases, such as thymidine), and some microelements.

Of the halides, iodide is concentrated in the fetus while bromide is partially retarded. There are, on the other hand, many similarities between the distribution patterns of these two halides. Thus bromide like iodide, has a tendency to accumulate in the thyroid and the gastric mucosa both in the adult and the fetus. Fluoride is also retarded but its distribution differs due to its strong affinity to bone. In a similar way iron is favoured, while the chemically related ruthenium and cobalt are retarded. The essential metal zinc is accumulated in the fetus, while others which belong to the same group in the periodic table, cadmium and mercury (HG^{2+}), are almost totally prevented from reaching the fetus. Similar but less pronounced differences are found when sodium is compared with rubidium and caesium. There is also a discrimination of strontium and barium compared with calcium, although it is less efficient.

We may thus talk about the experienced placenta with respect to substances which have been present in the environment during the evolution of the species. For synthetic substances it is suspected that the frequency of mistakes is higher. The transport of essential nutrients seems to be carried out by specific mechanisms, which may include carrier proteins. Such mechanisms may be rather vulnerable.

The substance which has been found to accumulate most in the fetus, vitamin B_{12}, may serve as a sensitive indicator of placental function. Its placental transport is blocked by stereostructurally related agents (Flodh, 1968), and preliminary studies (B. Danielsson and L. Dencker, unpublished work) have shown that it can also be retarded by cadmium (which accumulates in the placenta but does not reach the fetus).

A. *Vitamins*

Drugs and other foreign substances are known to pass rather freely to the fetus if they are fat soluble. With vitamins, the opposite tendency seems to dominate. The fat-soluble vitamins A and E are rather slowly and sparsely transferred compared with such fat-soluble drugs as short-acting barbiturates. Some water-soluble vitamins, on the other hand, are accumulated in the fetus. Examples are B_{12} (Ullberg *et al.*, 1967), B_6 (B. Danielsson, unpublished work), B_1 (Hammarström *et al.*, 1966), and C (Hammarström, 1966). The vitamin which leads this group is B_{12}, which can be accumulated more than a hundredfold, if a low dose is given to the mother. The pattern of fetal accumulation of vitamin B_{12} is illustrated in Figure 5.1 and proceeds in two steps. First there is a very rapid accumulation in the placenta to reach a concentration several hundred times the average maternal concentration (Fig. 5.2). Then there is a lag phase which varies in length from fetus to fetus and which is followed by a rather slow but consistent further one-way transport to the fetus. The peak in the fetal concentration is reached after 4 days. After 4 hours, when the fetal concentration has just exceeded the maternal concentration, the level is very low in the maternal blood but high in the fetal blood. Vitamin B_{12} is chemically stable in the body, so that the radioactivity represents exclusively the intact substance. The vitamin which reaches the fetus is not rapidly accumulated in any fetal storage organ. The placental 'pump' is saturable and the transport is depressed by vitamin B_{12} analogues.

The fetal distribution pattern resembles the adult pattern, especially in late gestation. The highest concentration in both the maternal and fetal body is found in some endocrine organs. The accumulation of vitamin B_{12} can also be observed in early pregnancy, when the yolk sac seems to be responsible for the transfer. A tremendous accumulation of vitamin B_{12} in the yolk sac of the rat was observed by Padykula *et al.* (1966) and in the rabbit by Deren *et al.* (1966). In our autoradiograms, an accumulation of B_{12} is seen even in the ovarian follicle.

It thus seems as if there are receptors or carriers in suitable amounts distributed strategically in various sites with the purpose of supplying the egg-embryo-fetus with this essential vitamin. The carrier mechanism (including the intrinsic factor) which is needed for intestinal absorption of vitamin B_{12} is sometimes defective. In a similar way, fetal damage may be caused by a disturbed transport of vitamin B_{12} or some other essential nutrient to the fetus.

Ascorbic acid (vitamin C) accumulates both in the maternal and fetal brain, retina and adrenal. The concentration in these fetal tissues was higher than in the maternal, but the fetal distribution pattern was, as is often the case, simpler than the maternal since many sites of accumulation which are found in the adult organism are lacking in the fetus (Hammarström, 1966).

Vitamin A has attracted much interest in teratology since an excess or a deficit are both known to produce malformations. A metabolite of vitamin A, retinoic acid, is known to be a more potent teratogen than vitamin A

Figure 5.1: Vitamin B_{12} : This Sequence of Three Pictures Illustrates the Successive Accumulation of Vitamin B_{12} (Labelled with ^{58}Co) in Mouse Fetuses. Vitamin B_{12} is first rapidly accumulated in the placenta, which apparently has a very large receptor capacity for B_{12}. The further transfer to the fetus is slow. After 4 hours, when the fetal concentration has just exceeded that of the maternal, the concentration is low in the maternal blood but high in the fetal blood. The peak fetal concentration is not reached until after 4 days.

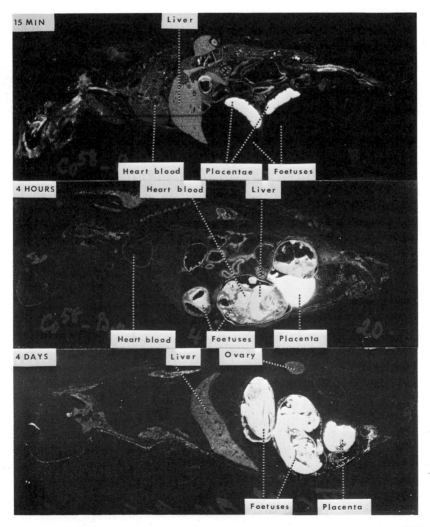

Figure 5.2: Vitamin B_{12} : Accumulation of Vitamin B_{12} in the Placenta and in the Fetus. Content of radioactive substance in the collected placentas, fetuses and remaining carcass as a percentage of the total retained dose 15 minutes to 24 hours after injection of $^{58}Co - B_{12}$ (Dose: 50ng).

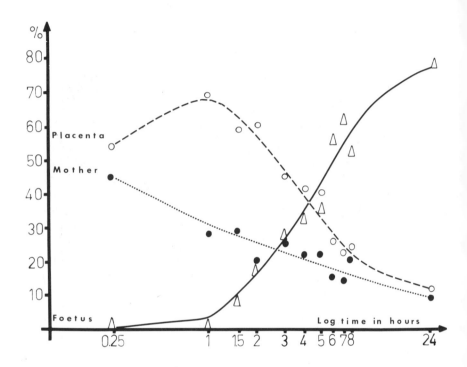

itself (Kochhar, 1967). However, retinoic acid can maintain embryogenesis in vitamin-A deficient rats during organ formation up to day 14 but not later (Howell *et al.,* 1964). In the early embryo (Dencker, 1979), vitamin A (retinol or retinyl acetate) reaches a high concentration in the neuro-epithelial tissues (parts of the brain, spinal chord and retina). The pattern of vitamin A shows many similarities with that of thymidine during early and mid-gestation. A localisation can thus be seen in the lungs and liver and in the heart and large vessels on day 13 in mice for both substances (Fig. 5.3). This may indicate a participation of vitamin A in cell proliferation during this period. Retinoic acid showed an even higher uptake in the neuroepithelium (Fig. 5.4) than vitamin A (retinyl acetate). This was

Figure 5.3: Vitamin A: Enlarged Autoradiogram of Mouse Uterus on Day 13 of Gestation, 4 Hours after Maternal Injection of 15-[^{14}C]-Retinyl Acetate. The pattern of uptake in the embryo is dominated by the spinal chord, developing retina, liver, lung-buds, heart and large vessels. This pattern corresponds to that of thymidine at the same stage of development.

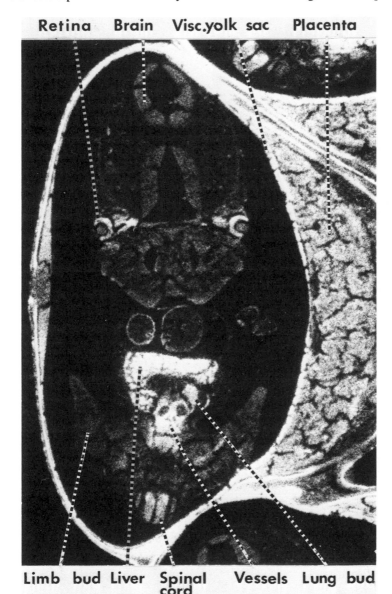

131

Figure 5.4: Retinoic acid: Part of a Mouse Uterus on Day 10 of Gestation, 4 Hours after the Injection to the Mother of 15-[^{14}C] -Retinoic Acid. As can be seen, there is a regional accumulation in the neuroepithelium in some parts of the embryonic neural tube, a consistent finding throughout organogenesis.

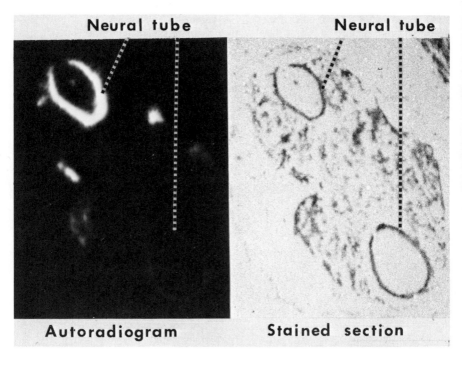

especially true for the outer brain layers, where growth is rapid during days 9-13. In contrast to vitamin A, it did not localise significantly in the lung and liver.

Both vitamin A and retinoic acid are known to participate in the synthesis of glycoproteins (DeLuca, 1977). Both an over- and under-production of glycoproteins may be hazardous for normal embryonic development.

The kinetics of vitamin A are known to be determined by carrier proteins. However, the carrier system has a limited capacity and if doses of vitamin A are given which exceed this capacity, excessive concentrations may reach the embryo due to its fat solubility (Vahlquist *et al.*, 1973; Takahashi *et al.*, 1977).

B. *Thymidine and Amino Acids*

Thymidine and a few amino acids have been studied at certain days throughout gestation (L. Dencker, unpublished work). The pattern varies considerably with gestational age due to the difference in rates of cell proliferation and growth of the embryonic-fetal structures. Results from such investigations may be used as a reference for other compounds. The application of fetotoxic substances may also selectively change the thymidine or amino acid incorporation patterns. Due to their growth, most fetal tissues show a higher uptake than the corresponding maternal tissues. Thymidine is also strongly accumulated in maternal tissues where rapid cell growth takes place: the bone marrow, lymphatic organs, gastrointestinal tract, gonads and hair follicles. In the fetus, these tissues accumulate thymidine less actively.

The different amino acids are to a certain extent individual, but in general they give similar patterns. In the adult, the exocrine pancreas dominates the picture as it is the most active protein synthesising organ in the body. Accumulation of amino acids in the fetal pancreas is not seen until late in pregnancy, but generally the fetus shows a higher uptake than the mother.

C. *Amino Acid Analogues*

The analogue parafluorophenylalanine (Garzo *et al.*, 1962) behaves like the related natural amino acid phenylalanine. It is transported similarly, being accumulated in the fetus and utilised for protein synthesis. The methionine analogue ethionine (Hansson and Garzo, 1961), behaves similarly kinetically, although it is to a large extent non-utilisable in protein synthesis. Most of the labelled ethionine was extractable from both the fetal and maternal portions of the whole-body sections. However, it was still accumulated rather strongly in the fetuses and after 4 hours the concentration in fetal tissues was significantly higher than in maternal tissues. Also, iodinated phenylalanines (mainly 4-iodophenylalanine) which seem not at all to be incorporated into proteins, nevertheless show some similarities in their kinetics to natural amino acids (Ullberg and Blomquist, 1968). Thus they are rather selectively taken up by the adult pancreas and also accumulate in the fetus. In the latter there is an especially strong accumulation in the lens of the eye. A similar accumulation, although weaker, is seen in the newborn but not in the adult, which indicates that it is age or growth related.

133

D. *Glucose*

Glucose rapidly crosses the placenta and 5-10 minutes after intravenous injection to the mother, the fetal concentration exceeds the maternal. In the adult, there is a rapid accumulation in the brain, which apparently is function related, because a similar accumulation is not seen in the fetal brain (S. Ullberg, unpublished work).

E. *Iron*

Iron shows a strong and rapid accumulation in the placenta and a relatively rapid further transport to the fetuses, although this proceeds more rapidly in some placentas than in others. In the mother, the highest accumulation of radioactive-iron is seen in the bone marrow, but in the early embryo the main site of accumulation is the visceral yolk sac and, in the late-term fetus, the liver. This probably reflects the changes with time in the localisation of haemoglobin synthesis. The fetal tissues show an over-all higher concentration than the maternal tissues (Ullberg *et al.*, 1961).

F. *Zinc*

The essential metal zinc has been shown to be required for normal fetal development, a deficiency resulting in severe malformations (Hurley and Swenerton, 1966). It is transferred rapidly to the fetus but is not significantly accumulated there. With varying gestational age, its distribution pattern changes very much like that of thymidine, which may be related to its participation in enzymes engaged in replication and cell growth (Dencker, 1976).

G. *Halide Ions*

Fluoride differs from the other halide ions by being rather selectively accumulated by the bone. The physiologically important iodide ion is the only halide ion which reaches a higher overall concentration in the fetus than in the dam (Fig. 5.5). It is also concentrated much more than bromide in the ovarian follicles and in the thyroid of both the mother and the late fetus. A similarity between iodide and bromide is the tendency of both

134

Figure 5.5: Iodine: Active Transport of Iodide (^{125} I) to Mouse Fetus. After one hour, fetus 1 but not fetus 2 has a higher concentration than the mother. Accumulation in fetus 1 is localised in the gastric mucosa.

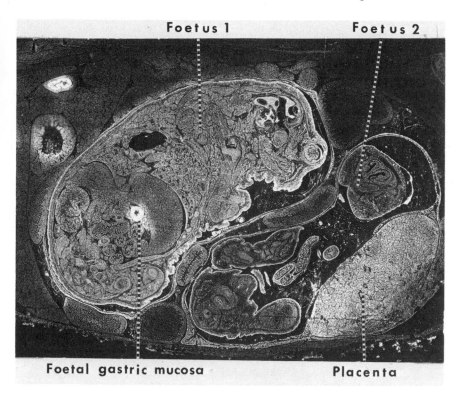

to be secreted in the maternal and fetal gastric juice and to a smaller extent also in the saliva (Ullberg *et al.*, 1964).

H. *Hormonal Substances*

Endogenous substances such as hormones are distributed very specifically in the mammalian body. A large number of hormones have been studied and only limited information can be presented here. Comprehensive studies have been made on the fate of some steroid hormone precursors (Appelgren, 1967). Both cholesterol and ^{14}C-pregnenolone accumulated very selectively in the maternal adrenal cortex and in the ovarian corpora lutea, but hardly entered the fetus.

The physiological oestrogen oestradiol (Ullberg and Bengtsson, 1963) and the synthetic hormone diethylstilboestrol (Bengtsson and Ullberg, 1963) are very similarly distributed in adult females. They are both accumulated in target organs such as the uterine wall and the vagina. However, oestradiol showed a marked fetal accumulation, while the placental passage of diethylstilboestrol was partially blocked.

[14]C-progesterone is found in the mouse fetus to accumulate rather distinctly in the adrenal cortex (Fig. 5.6), which may be related to the rapid metabolism of progesterone by the fetal adrenal. It seems to use progesterone as a precursor in the formation of adrenal cortical steroids. Also when given to previable male human fetuses of about 6 months age (Bengtsson *et al.*, 1964), a dominant localisation was found in the adrenal cortex. In addition, interesting localisations were found in the testes, the pituitary, parts of the brain, and (astonishingly enough) in the thyroid and thymus.

Figure 5.6: Progesterone: Autoradiogram of Human Male Fetus of about 6 Months of Age after Intramuscular Injection of 4-[14 C]-progesterone. Note the marked uptake by the adrenal cortex, where ^{14}C-progesterone is probably used in the production of cortical steroids.

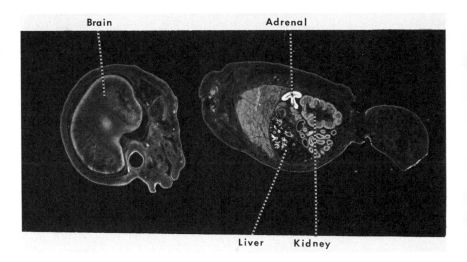

A synthetic compound with hormonal properties, a diphenylethene derivative (Hanngren *et al.*, 1965), was distributed very similarly to ^{14}C-pregnenolone. It localised extremely selectively in the ovarian corpora lutea where it was found to interfere with progesterone formation. The accumulation of this substance at sites of steroid hormone formation is probably due to an enzyme affinity. Appelgren (1969) found histochemically, using whole-body sections, that it blocked the $\triangle$-5-3-β-hydroxy-steroid dehydrogenase, which transforms pregnenolone into progesterone. The enzyme affinity is probably due to a sterostructural resemblance between the natural substrate for this enzyme, pregnenolone, and the diphenylethene drug. The enzyme activity was temporarily blocked as long as the binding lasted. The small amount which penetrated into the fetus localised mainly in the adrenal cortex.

Chlormadinone acetate (CAP = 6-chloro-6-dehydro-17-acetoxypro-gesterone) is a very potent oral gestagen and a constituent in some oral contraceptive agents. Appelgren (1972) found chlormadinone to concentrate in the maternal corpora lutea and in the adrenal cortex of both the mother and the fetus.

III. Foreign Substances

Most nutrients are transferred in a one-way direction to the fetus, many by an active transport mechanism, and are more or less permanently incorporated into the fetal tissues. Non-physiological drugs and most environmental pollutants, on the other hand, oscillate from the mother through the placenta to the fetus and then back again. When the pendulum has swung over to the fetus and the return stroke begins, the fetus should have the opportunity to pass the mother and achieve a higher concentration; but it seldom does. A few such cases are given as examples below.

High fat solubility and small molecular size generally seem to favour passage to the fetus. Highly ionized drugs such as quaternary bases pass very slowly to the fetus and are sometimes not found at a detectable concentration. Also, some toxic metals such as inorganic mercury (Hg^{2+}) (Berlin and Ullberg, 1963a) and cadmium (Berlin and Ullberg, 1963b) are largely prevented from reaching the fetal tissues. The distribution picture varies considerably from one substance to another. As a general rule, it may be said that the placenta is more discriminatory to foreign substances in early than in late gestation, at least in rodents (Dencker, 1976, 1979).

Thus, for salicylic acid there is a 50 per cent increase in the fetal concentration at day 18 compared with day 12, measured 4 hours after intravenous injection to the mother. This is probably a reflection of a continuous attenuation of the cellular layers of the placenta which divide the maternal and fetal circulations, and also factors like changes in the blood flow rate. For some other drugs, e.g. 2,4,5,-T (2,4,5-trichloro-phenoxyacetic acid) (Dencker, 1976), biphenyl (Brandt, 1977), and diethylstilboestrol (A. Lindgren and L. Dencker, unpublished work), there may be a 20- to 40-fold increase in the fetal concentration from day 12 to day 18. For diethylstilboestrol, this is partly due to the metabolism and subsequent conjugation in the fetus, which increases dramatically with age. This is clearly seen from the accumulation in the fetal liver and excretion to the fetal intestine in late gestation (McLachlan, 1977; A. Lindgren and L. Dencker, unpublished work). Also, biphenyl is probably increasingly metabolised, as non-volatile radioactivity accumulates in the fetal tissues late in gestation (Brandt, 1977). For these drugs, and especially for 2,4,5-T (which is not considered to be appreciably metabolised), additional explanations have to be found. It is obvious that the yolk-sac placenta, which is the only such structure developed before day 11-12 in rodents, will almost completely discriminate against drugs like 2,4,5-T, diethylstilboestrol and biphenyl but let drugs like salicylic acid pass. The chorio-allantoic placenta, which is successively developing from this time on, will considerably increase the net transfer of drugs hitherto discriminated against, while the onset of chorio-allantoic function will cause less increase in the concentration of drugs which pass earlier through the yolk-sac placenta.

A. *Barbiturates*

The short-acting barbiturates, being highly fat soluble, will immediately reach a high concentration in the adult brain and induce an anaesthetic effect. They can therefore be suspected of crossing the placenta rapidly and of reaching a high concentration in the fetal brain. However, this does not happen. The most plausible reason seems to be that during the time required for placental passage there is a redistribution in the maternal body with an increasing concentration in fat and other tissues. This causes a rapid decrease in the blood concentration and lowers the amount of drug available for transport to the fetus. The fetal brain, as opposed to the maternal brain, contains a low concentration initially which slowly increases. However, maternal concentrations are never reached, either in the whole fetal body or specifically in the fetal brain. The highest concentration in the fetus is seen in the liver (Schechter and Roth, 1967; Sarteschi *et al.*, 1973).

If we compare thiopental with the long-acting barbiturates such as phenobarbital (Waddell, 1971) or barbital (Lal *et al.*, 1964), we find that transfer to the fetus proceeds more slowly. The highest concentration is found in the liver and brain, followed by the adrenal cortex and myocardium. At term, an excretory pattern with accumulation in the fetal bile and intestinal lumen is apparent. Also in the case of long-acting barbiturates, the fetal brain concentrations do not reach maternal values. For ^{14}C-pentobarbital, however, Waddell (1972) has found a higher concentration in the fetus than in the mother after 3 hours. He ascribes this finding mainly to a very rapid elimination from the mother.

B. *Benzodiazepines*

The popular tranquillisers diazepam (Valium) and chlordiazeposide (Librium) have been investigated extensively (Sarteschi *et al.*, 1973; van der Kleijn, 1969; Idänpään-Heikkilä *et al.*, 1971). Their distribution patterns show similarities to those of the long-acting barbiturates. The peak in fetal concentration is reached rather late, generally after several hours. The fetal brain, liver and myocardium show the highest concentration. Later on a localisation in fetal fat dominates, together with an excretory pattern.

The distribution is qualitatively similar in all species studied, but some differences are found between the monkey and small rodents. There is a more pronounced uptake and a longer retention in the central nervous system of the monkey. Even after 24 hours, there is high activity in the brain of the monkey. A high concentration is found in the fetal cerebellum, the spinal chord and peripheral nerves (Idänpään-Heikkilä *et al.*, 1971; van der Kleijn and Wijffels, 1971). These findings may explain the hypoactivity and hypotonicity that has been reported to occur in human infants whose mothers received diazepam during labour.

C. *Phenothiazine Derivatives and Tricyclic Antidepressants*

These drugs show a binding to the fetal melanin-containing tissues (eye, inner ear and skin) and also accumulate in both the maternal and fetal

139

Figure 5.7: Quaternary compounds: Autoradiogram Showing the Head of a Mouse Fetus 4 Hours after the Injection of ^{14}C-labelled Aprobit® (a Quaternary Phenothiazine Derivative) to the Mother. Note the high accumulation in the choroid plexus. The choroid plexus may possibly act as an outwardly directed pump, clearing from the brain the quaternary compound which has leaked through the blood-brain barrier.

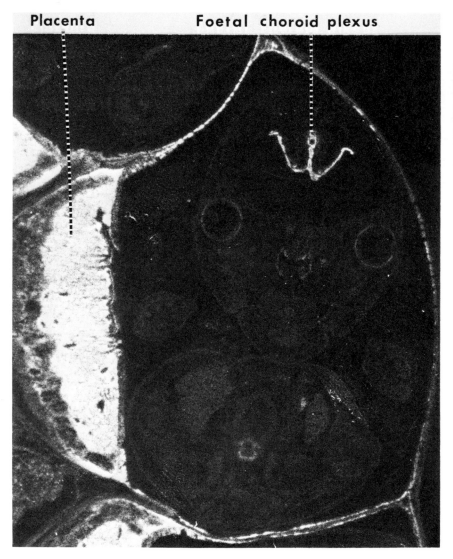

Placenta   Foetal choroid plexus

lung (Lindquist and Ullberg, 1972). The transfer of the quaternary phenothiazine derivative (Aprobit) is partially blocked by the placenta, where it
is accumulated. An interesting accumulation in the fetal choroid plexus
was found (Fig. 5.7).

D. *Non-Narcotic Analgesics*

Salicylic acid (Dencker, 1976) and paracetamol (A. Lindgren and L.
Dencker, unpublished work) reach high fetal concentrations. Interestingly,
there are differences in the distribution pattern of salicylic acid during the
various stages of gestation. Early, a high accumulation in the neuroepithelium and the developing brain can be detected. The fetal pattern at
term is characterised by a relatively high concentration in blood and
amniotic fluid. However, the concentration is low in the fetal brain.

Paracetamol is also easily transferred to the fetus in late stages of
gestation. In contrast to most other drugs studied, paracetamol shows a
much higher concentration in fetal tissues than in maternal tissues (Fig.
5.8). The distribution pattern is rather similar in maternal and fetal
tissues, although there is a greater accumulation in fetal than in maternal
liver. Human fetal liver *in vitro* has been shown to form active metabolites
of paracetamol through oxidation and also to form sulphate conjugates
(Rollins *et al.*, 1979). The hepatic accumulation possibly indicates a risk
of hepatic damage in the fetus.

E. *Narcotic Analgesics and other Drugs of Abuse*

Several drugs of abuse have been found to reach a higher concentration in
the fetal brain than in the maternal brain. This may explain the abstinence
symptoms which appear in children born to drug addicts. Studies on
morphine have shown a higher concentration in the fetal brain than in
other fetal tissues (Waddell, 1972). Methadone shows a similar distribution pattern to morphine. The concentration of methadone in the brain
of the fetus is two- to threefold greater than the concentration in the
maternal brain. The high brain concentration in the fetus is at least partly
explained by the lack of a blood-brain barrier (Peters *et al.*, 1972).

The placental transfer of mescaline in late pregnancy is limited because
of the high degree of ionisation of mescaline at physiological pH. Despite
this, radioactivity is found in the fetal brain and the concentration is more

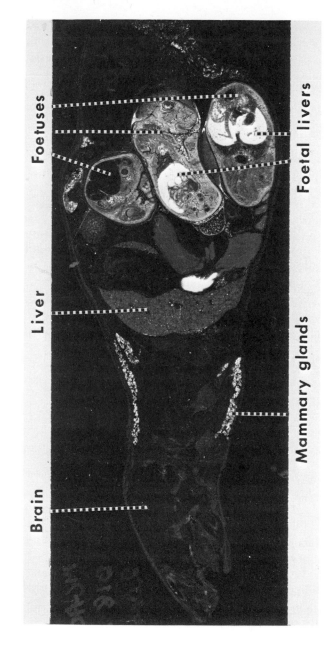

Figure 5.8: Paracetamol: Distribution in a Pregnant Mouse at Late Gestation, 2 Hours after Intravenous Injection of ^{14}C-paracetamol. The concentration in the fetal tissues, especially liver, is higher than in the maternal.

Foetuses

Foetal livers

Liver

Mammary glands

Brain

than twice that of the maternal brain. The fetal brain also shows a more rapid accumulation and a lower rate of disappearance compared with the maternal brain. Even if the transfer of the fetus appears to be restricted, the prolonged and high concentration in the fetal brain emphasises a potential hazard to the developing fetus (Shah *et al.*, 1973).

Lysergic acid diethylamide (LSD) shows uptake into the brain, the adrenals, the hypophysis and excretory organs in both the mother and the fetus. A greater amount of the radioactive dose crosses the placenta in early gestation than at later stages (Idänpään-Heikkilä and Scholar, 1969).

F. *Nicotine*

Nicotine reaches only a rather low overall concentration in the fetus, but accumulates selectively at several sites. The most accentuated accumulation in pigmented animals is in the melanin of the fetal eye where nicotine is apparently incorporated as a false precursor (cf. melanin - thiouracil below). The fetal melanin therefore reaches a much higher concentration than the adult (Dencker *et al.*, 1979; Larsson *et al.*, 1979). Nicotine is also accumulated in the adrenal medulla in both the adult and in the fetus. A rather pronounced localisation is also seen in the whole respiratory tract of the full-term fetus (bronchi, trachea, larynx, and nasal mucosa) (Tjälve *et al.*, 1968) (Fig. 5.9). The uptake in the respiratory tract, which is seen also in the adult, is apparently connected with biotransformation of nicotine in the respiratory mucosa. It should be noted that these observations concern intravenously administered nicotine.

G. *Antibiotics and Chemotherapeutics*

Benzylpenicillin (Ullberg, 1954) apparently behaves very differently in the adult and fetal body. Although it is very efficiently blocked by the adult blood-brain barrier, it is only partially prevented from crossing the placenta. In the adult animal it is concentrated in excretory organs, but in the fetus it seems to be distributed mainly in the extracellular space. In the full-term fetus, the uniformity in its distribution pattern is disturbed mainly by an increasingly effective blood-brain barrier. The lack of a specific tissue accumulation of penicillin can probably be regarded as an advantage with respect to the risks of fetal damage.

Another antibiotic, tetracycline (André, 1956; Blomquist and Hanngren,

Figure 5.9: Nicotine (^{14}C-labelled) in Mouse Fetus 30 Minutes after Injection. Note the high uptake by the whole respiratory tract (lung, trachea, and larynx), where nicotine is metabolised. Excretion has started into the intestinal lumen.

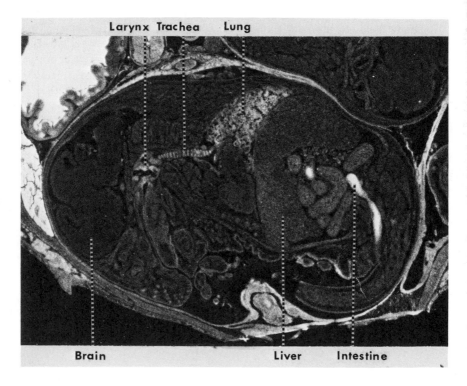

1966). behaves rather differently. In the adult organism it is firmly bound to the skeleton, where it is taken up to give a high concentration in the growth zones, but it is also temporarily accumulated in many soft tissues. In the fetus there is a very marked and persistent accumulation in the skeleton and the developing teeth, but no soft-tissue uptake is seen. This hard-tissue affinity of tetracycline probably explains the brownish fluorescent enamel spots which may appear on the teeth of children after the mother has been treated with tetracycline during pregnancy.

The transfer of dihydrostreptomycin (André, 1956) to the fetus is also partially blocked, the fetal blood concentration being only 15-25% of the maternal. Streptomycin is temporarily bound to cartilage (early fetal skeleton) and to connective tissue.

The antitubercular agent para-aminosalicylic acid (PAS) (Hanngren, 1959) accumulates in the neural tube in early gestation but is prevented from reaching the brain in the full-term fetus.

Sulphapyridine (Hanngren *et al.*, 1963) crosses freely to the fetus. The fetal concentration reaches maternal values within 20 minutes. It also rather rapidly and completely leaves the fetal body.

H. *Chlorinated Hydrocarbons*

Hexachlorophene has been considered a human teratogen and its teratogenicity in rodents has been documented. It reaches the embryo in considerable concentration when given at any stage of gestation. What makes it different from most other drugs is its long retention time in the late gestation fetal tissues as compared with maternal tissues. Thus, 24 hours after injection, the fetal serum concentration is about threefold greater than that of the maternal serum concentration. This ratio increases further with time. Even hexachlorophene, injected before gestation and stored in maternal depots, will be transferred to the fetus and reach higher concentrations than in the mother (Brandt *et al.*, 1979). As hexachlorophene is not considered to be metabolised in the fetus to more polar metabolites (compare biphenyl above), there seems to be no simple explanation for the retention in the fetus. This indicates that for some drugs the transfer back through the placenta from the fetus to the mother is retarded. A similar retention in full-term fetuses has been observed for biphenyl (Brandt, 1977) and certain polychlorinated biphenyls also redistribute from maternal fat depots and are continuously transferred to the growing fetus.

I. *Nitrosamines*

Like diethylstilboestrol, nitroso compounds are known to cause transplacental cancer. Diethylnitrosamine is enzymically degraded and labelled fragments of ^{14}C-diethylnitrosamine have been found in several organs of adult animals which are enzymically active (E. Brittebo, A. Lindgren and H. Tjälve, unpublished work). Late gestational fetal bronchi, nasal mucosa and to some extent liver also contain such fragments. This also occurs when the compound has been injected locally into fetuses *in utero*, indicating that these structures have a developed enzymic capacity for this particular metabolism in late gestation (Brittebo *et al.*, 1981).

J. *Metals: Inorganic Ions and Organic Metallic Compounds*

The occupational and environmental hazards of metal exposure are of great concern. Some metals such as cadmium, mercury, lead, chromium and nickel have profound effects on fetal development. Other metals such as zinc are essential for fetal growth and development. To complement the previous discussion on the ability of the placenta to discriminate toxic from beneficial elements, it may be interesting to compare cadmium and zinc which belong to the same group in the periodical table, but behave totally differently with respect to fetal uptake.

Cadmium, administered to the mouse and hamster during early pregnancy, can reach the embryonic gut endoderm via the yolk-sac cavity and through the vitelline duct. An accumulation can be seen in the embryonic gut wall but it is not transferred further from the gut wall into the embryo (Fig. 5.10). After the closure of the vitelline duct (around day 9 in mouse and hamster, and day 11 in rat), cadmium does not reach the embryo in any large quantities (Dencker, 1975). This may indicate that the early serious malformations caused by cadmium are due to a direct action on the embryo during organogenesis. But cadmium may cause damage even at a later fetal age, although it does not reach the fetus. Thus, there is some indication that cadmium in the placenta can act indirectly by interfering with the transport of essential nutrients to the fetus (e.g. vitamin B_{12}, see Section II(A)).

Zinc is an essential trace element and zinc deficiency is known to cause malformations in experimental animals and is believed to do so in humans. Zinc can counteract several of the toxic effects of cadmium, including the teratogenicity. Contrary to cadmium, zinc is accumulated in all embryonic structures and especially in the neuroepithelium. Zinc is, however, not particularly accumulated in the placenta at late pregnancy but is instead localised in the fetal liver and in specific areas of the brain (Dencker, 1976).

Inorganic mercury (Hg^{2+}) shows a similar distribution picture to cadmium in early pregnancy. Compared with cadmium, however, its uptake in the embryonic gut is somewhat lower. During late pregnancy mercury is accumulated mainly in the placenta, but contrary to cadmium it is transferred to the fetus only slightly. The fetal concentration is, however, much lower than the maternal (Dencker, 1976). A low penetration to the fetus as well as to the brain is also observed for the unstable organic

Figure 5.10: Cadmium: Section Plus Autoradiogram (Black Areas Represent a High Concentration in this Case). Hamster uterus 24 hours after injection of ^{109}CdCl$_2$ on day 8 of gestation. Note the high uptake by endoderm of the embryonic gut and visceral yolk-sac placenta. There is no further transfer to other embryonic tissues.

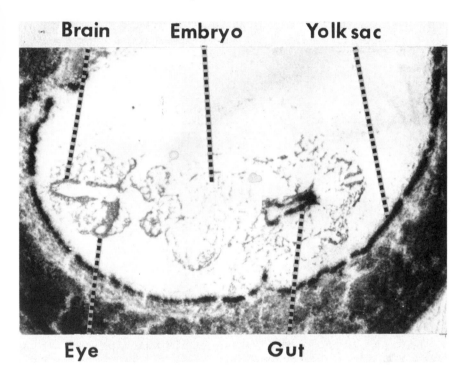

mercurials, such as phenyl- and alcoxyethyl-mercury, which are rapidly broken down in the body to inorganic mercury (Berlin and Ullberg, 1963a).

In contrast, the stable and rather fat-soluble methyl mercury will pass both to the brain (and more rapidly to nerve ganglia) and to the fetus. The fetal concentration reaches a value which is similar to the maternal after a few days. The volatile dimethyl mercury also passes to the fetus. It localises mainly in the respiratory tract, where it is probably transformed into methyl mercury (Östlund, 1969). Both methyl and dimethyl mercury are also accumulated in the fetal lens, while in the adult lens only a faint peripheral localisation is seen. When administered by inhalation, metallic mercury is very rapidly concentrated in the brain (Placidi *et al.*,

1977; Khayat, 1977), but its uptake by the fetus has to our knowledge not been studied.

If unstable organic mercury compounds (such as phenyl mercury) are given together with the chelating agent dimercaptopropanol (BAL), a mercury-BAL complex is apparently formed which penetrates rapidly to both the brain and the fetus (Berlin and Ullberg, 1963c).

For lead, the situation is similar to that for mercury in that the organic lead compounds, which are used in gasoline as antiknock agents (tri- and tetramethyl and tri- and tetraethyl lead), will reach a high concentration both in the fetus and in the brain.

IV. Fetal Organs

A. *Brain*

There are significant differences in the uptake of chemicals by the brain when the fetus, even in late gestation, and the mother are compared. This is a reflection of the fact that the brain and the blood-brain barrier, even after parturition, are continuously changing throughout development. The lack of accumulation of certain substances (e.g. glucose) in the brain even in late-gestation fetuses shows that the brain is still not functionally mature (i.e. it has a low metabolic rate). On the other hand, the fetal brain sometimes shows a greater uptake of foreign chemicals than the maternal brain. This indicates that the fetal blood-brain barrier is poorly developed.

If brain uptake is studied as a function of development, it is found to be greater chiefly in early rather than in late gestation (Dencker, 1979). This is true for nutrients like thymidine, amino acids, zinc, vitamin A, retinoic acid and nicotinamide. The accumulation may be related to the rapid growth of neuroepithelium when the gross structure of the brain is established. However, even at full term parts of the brain accumulate these compounds; e.g. thymidine is accumulated in the cell layers close to the ventricles where cell division take place. Retinoic acid shows the greatest growth-related uptake in the early brain (Fig. 5.4). Its uptake by other embryonic tissues is comparatively very low.

Also a number of foreign compounds, drugs as well as others, show a relatively high uptake by the neuroepithelium compared with other embryonic tissues early in gestation. Some examples are salicylic acid, hexachlorophene, diphenylhydantoin, nicotine, and arsenic (Dencker, 1979). These are chemically unrelated compounds, indicating that this

148

uptake by the neuroepithelium is rather non-specific, but it also shows that the risk for a potentially toxic compound to be accumulated here is significant. The high incidence of malformations of the central nervous system, experimentally as well as clinically, might be related to this tendency for accumulation. As previously noted, the uptake of drugs in the fetal brain in late gestation has been related to psychological and neurological disturbances (see also Chapter 9).

B. *Liver*

The liver has the highest uptake of thymidine of all fetal tissues from day 12 or 13 up to day 17 of gestation. This can be related not only to the massive growth of the liver itself but also to the haematopoietic role of the liver at this time. During the same period, retinol (but not retinoic acid) is also accumulated in the liver, which suggests its possible participation in some synthetic process (Dencker, 1979). However, part of its accumulation may be related to the storage function of the liver, at least late in gestation.

Foreign compounds may be accumulated in fetal liver as in the maternal organ, and this is often associated with biliary excretion into the intestine, although only during the last few days of gestation. More often, however, little or no hepatic accumulation is seen. This may sometimes be due to a low capacity of metabolic enzyme activity or for biliary excretion.

Diethylstilboestrol (A. Lindgren and L. Dencker, unpublished work) may be discussed as a model substance for drugs that do accumulate. If the developmental pattern of uptake is followed, it is found that in early gestation no significant embryonic uptake is seen. After day 12-13, transfer to the fetus is increased, but not until day 15 is an accumulation seen in the liver. When given on day 16, a minor excretion of the drug is found in the fetal intestine, an excretion which increases considerably towards the end of gestation. These results, taken together with earlier work from other laboratories (McLachlan, 1977; Lucier *et al.*, 1979), reflect the increasing ability of the liver to form conjugates, which are more easily excreted to the intestine. The formation of more polar conjugates may also be partly responsible for the sharp increase in the average fetal concentration as the polar conjugates may be less likely to cross the placenta back to the maternal serum.

A few drugs like paracetamol (acetaminophen) accumulate to a greater extent in the fetal than in the maternal liver (A. Lindgren and L. Dencker, unpublished work) (Fig. 5.8). Paracetamol is known to form reactive inter-mediates and also to be conjugated, and the high fetal liver concentration may be due to a slower excretion of conjugates than in the maternal liver.

C. *Respiratory Tract*

The mouse fetal lungs can be recognised from day 13-14 of gestation and at that time a relatively high tissue thymidine and amino acid uptake is found. Retinol (and retinyl acetate), but not retinoic acid, also shows a strong accumulation in the developing lungs at this early stage (Dencker, 1979) (Fig. 5.3). Later on, the uptake is seen mainly in the peripheral parts of the lungs, and at day 18 a thin zone of accumulation is seen which apparently corresponds to the pulmonary pleura.

Some compounds accumulate in the bronchial mucosa in relation to metabolic transformation. One of these is nicotine (Tjälve *et al.*, 1968; Lindquist and Ullberg, 1974) (Fig. 5.9), the accumulation of which in the lungs has been related to its *N*-demethylation (Szüts *et al.*, 1978).

Another group of chemicals showing a bronchial uptake in fetuses and adults are the polychlorinated biphenyls. Structural requirements are needed for this accumulation: the position of the chlorine atoms in the PCB molecule (Brandt, 1977; Bergman *et al.*, 1979). The accumulation process is slow, reflecting a continuous formation of methylsulphonyl derivatives with a high bronchial affinity.

Diethylnitrosamine accumulates in the fetal bronchial mucosa of mice in late gestation, and the fetal lungs are capable of degrading this com-pound *in vitro* (Brittebo *et al.*, 1981). This metabolic capacity may be related to the transplacental carcinogenic effect (pulmonary adenomas) of diethylnitrosamine.

Other drugs, such as chlorpromazine (Sjöstrand *et al.*, 1965) and tri-cyclic antidepressants, like imipramine (Cassano and Hansson, 1966), are taken up to some extent by the lung parenchyma of fetuses, but the concentration is lower than that of the maternal lung.

D. *Thyroid*

Iodide localises strongly in the fetal thyroid. Of the related halogens, there is a tendency for bromide and the pseudohalide thiocyanate to localise in the fetal as well as the maternal thyroid, but no specific thyroidal uptake is seen for fluoride which accumulates instead in bone (Ullberg *et al.*, 1964). The thyroid blocker thiouracil is localised very selectively in the fetal thyroid (Fig. 5.11). In albino mouse fetuses, there is a low and even distribution in the rest of the fetal body (Slanina *et al.*, 1973). The well-known drug-induced fetal goitre can thus be related to a selective uptake by the critical fetal organ. (In pigmented fetuses, there is also an incorporation into melanin; see Section IV (I).)

E. *Islets of Langerhans*

Many agents tend to localise in the adult islet tissue. One which may be of physiological significance is zinc (Dencker and Tjälve, 1979). It also shows a weak but discernible localisation in fetal islets.

The diabetogenic substances alloxan (Hammarström and Ullberg, 1966) and streptozotocin (E. Brittebo and H. Tjälve, unpublished work), both localise very selectively in adult pancreatic islets. They have not, however, been observed to concentrate in fetal islets. Alloxan did not even accumulate in the islets of newborn mice and is known not to be diabetogenic in the fetus and the newborn mouse. Another drug which localised in adult pancreatic islets but not in fetal islets is chloroquine. This is true not only for rodents but also for the Macaca monkey in late gestation (Dencker *et al.*, 1975).

F. *Adrenal*

Steroidogenesis in the fetal adrenal gland is of importance for the sexual development of the fetus, and the glucocorticoids produced probably have an influence on, for example, cellular growth. Drug accumulation in the adrenal cortex may indicate a risk of interference in steroid production.

Chemicals which do accumulate in the fetal (as well as maternal) adrenal cortex are some of the highly chlorinated and brominated biphenyls and DDT (Brandt, 1977; I. Brandt, unpublished work). Some of these are known to interfere with steroid metabolism, and the fact that only certain halogenated biphenyls are accumulated may indicate a stereospecific binding to steroidogenic enzymes. This is supported by the fact that drugs of a diphenyl alkene character, known to affect steroid production (Appelgren, 1969), are also accumulated by the fetal adrenal and have

151

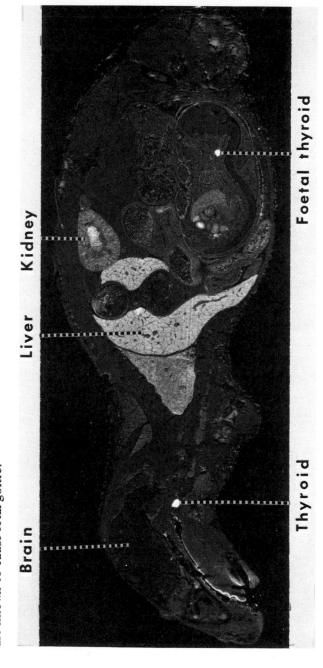

Figure 5.11: Thyroid Blockers:[14] C-thiouracil, which Blocks the Formation of Iodinated Thyroid Hormones is Accumulated at its Main Site of Action (Thyroid Gland) in Both Maternal and Fetal Mouse. Thyroid Blockers are known to cause fetal goitre.

152

been shown to inhibit Δ-5-3-β-hydroxysteroid dehydrogenase activity.

Bengtsson *et al.* (1964) studied progesterone uptake by perfused aborted fetuses and found considerable uptake by the adrenal cortex (Fig. 5.6), where it probably serves as a precursor for steroidogenesis.

Diphenylhydantoin is accumulated in the fetal as well as the maternal adrenal cortex (Waddell and Mirkin, 1972; A. Druga and L. Dencker, unpublished work). This drug is known to cause cleft lip and palate in experimental animals and in man. Although a direct effect of diphenylhydantoin on palatal growth is probable, an interference in glucocorticoid production in the fetus and/or the mother may also have to be taken into account.

Ritzén *et al.* (1965) found an accumulation of 5-hydroxytryptophan in the fetal adrenal medulla. In a monkey (Macaca) fetus in late gestation, a chloroquine analogue was found to accumulate in the adrenal medulla (Dencker *et al.*, 1975) (Fig. 5.12). After injection of ^{14}C-nicotine, accumulation was seen in both the maternal and fetal adrenal medulla (Tjälve *et al.*, 1968).

G. *Skeleton*

Before the fetal skeleton has started to mineralise, it behaves very similarly to adult cartilage in that it accumulates all compounds which are taken up by the maternal cartilage and which are also transferred to the fetus (see below).

In late gestation, after mineralisation has started, the same applies to 'bone seekers'. These agents are taken up by the fetal bone as well as by the adult (see Waddell and Marlowe, 1976). Among the bone seeking elements are calcium and other elements belonging to the same group in the periodic table: strontium and barium (Dencker *et al.*, 1976). Other physiological bone seekers are phosphate and carbonate ions. This means that organic substances which are radioactively labelled with, for example, ^{32}P may lose some of the radioactive phosphorus which could then be incorporated into the adult or fetal bone. The situation is similar for radioactive sulphur, which participates in the formation of chondroitin sulphate and becomes localised in maternal cartilage and also in cartilaginous fetal bone. Other bone-seeking elements which are also found in the fetal bone are vanadium, cobalt, zinc, sodium, and to a small extent, iron. Chronium (B. Danielsson, unpublished work) and inorganic lead (A. Lindgren and L. Dencker, unpublished work) which accumulate

Figure 5.12: Chloroquine: Moneky Fetus 72 Hours after Injection of a Chloroquine Analogue. The substance is bound to the melanin of the eye and also accumulated in the adrenal medulla.

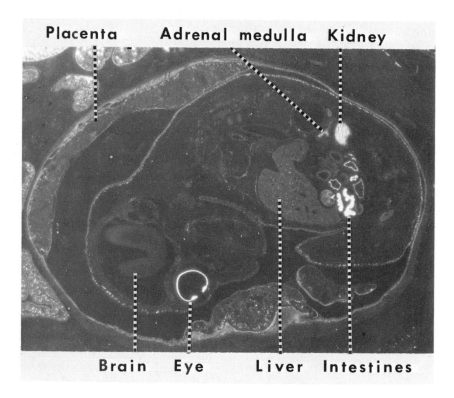

Placenta   Adrenal medulla   Kidney

Brain   Eye   Liver   Intestines

strongly in adult bone cross the placenta poorly but can be found selectively in fetal bone. Bone also accumulates most of the rare earth metals and many of these are transferred to a certain extent to the fetus.

Plutonium is hardly absorbed at all in the intestine but may be taken up to a small extent in the respiratory tract after inhalation of plutonium-containing dusts. It is concentrated in the ovarian follicles and in the maternal skeleton but does not seem to be transferred to the fetus (Ullberg *et al.*, 1962). Fluoride ions are poorly transferred to the fetus, but that amount which does is selectively accumulated by the fetal hard tissues. Chelating agents such as EDTA and NTA (Tjälve, 1972) are also accumulated by both adult and fetal bone.

Among the drugs which are taken up by the mineralising fetal skeleton, the tetracycline group is an outstanding example (André, 1956). In the adult the tetracyclines are also localised in many soft tissues, but in the fetus the skeletal localisation is remarkably selective and may be related to enamel spots on the teeth of the offspring.

As mentioned above, many elements and radioactively-labelled substances are also localised in the fetal skeleton even before calcification has started. Such agents are also generally found to accumulate in the adult cartilage. Among the elements which are incorporated into cartilage are bromide, and several cations such as nickel (Olsen and Jonsen, 1979) and caesium. Also streptomycin (André, 1956) and the other aminoglycoside antibiotics; and quaternary drugs such as pancuronium and hexamethonium (Shindo, 1972), being cations, bind to cartilage due to a cation exchange mechanism. This is also true for the herbicide paraquat (H. Tjälve, unpublished work). Streptomycin is partially prevented from reaching the fetus but can be seen in the fetal skeleton autoradiographically while the placental passage of most quaternary drugs is almost totally blocked.

A peculiar observation is that in autoradiographic experiments with the lipophilic insecticides aldrin and dieldrin (^{14}C-labelled), a localisation was found both in adult cartilage and in the fetal skeleton (Brandt and Högman, 1980). Inhibition of liver metabolism by preinjection of carbon tetrachloride did not decrease the accumulation, which possibly indicates that it is the intact substances and not their metabolites that are accumulated.

H. *Optic Lens*

The fetal lens accumulates some foreign substances which are not taken up by the maternal lens. Thus some amino acid analogues, mainly iodinated phenylalanines, are highly concentrated in the fetal lens and in the lens of the newborn but not at all in the adult lens. For some unknown reason, the catecholamine precursor dihydroxyphenylalanine (dopa) is accumulated in the fetal lens. Methyl and dimethyl mercury (Östlund, 1969) and inorganic arsenic (Lindgren and Dencker, 1980) are also accumulated strongly in the fetal lens. However, for these substances there is a tendency for uptake by the peripheral zone of the lens of the maternal eye.

Distribution of Drugs and Other Agents in the Fetus

I. *Melanin*

We have found in our autoradiographic investigations that many substances, often related to polycyclic amines, are accumulated in both adult and fetal melanin (Fig. 5.12). The uptake is due to binding, which is about equally strong for both fetal and adult melanin. As the melanin content is especially high in the eye, the eye in many cases dominates the autoradiographic distribution pattern. The uptake by the fetal eye is observed immediately after the drug has entered the fetal circulation, and the binding is very persistent. Some activity may be seen in the eyes of the offspring several months after injection of, for example, ^{14}C-chloroquine to the pregnant dam (Lindquist and Ullberg, 1972). This binding can probably be related to the drug-induced fetal eye and ear damage observed clinically (Hart and Naunton, 1964).

A theoretically more interesting finding is that some foreign compounds (e.g., the thyrostatic agent thiouracil) are incorporated as false precursors during the formation of melanin (Dencker *et al.*, 1979). Such substances are thus accumulated in the fetal but not the maternal eye (Fig. 5.13). Some other thyrostatics, and nicotine and aniline, behave similarly. The utilisation of a foreign substance as a false precursor during the rapid formation of a fetal tissue seems to be a particularly important phenomenon, and similar processes may occur during embryonic organogenesis.

J. *Visceral Yolk-Sac Placenta*

The visceral yolk-sac placenta is the only structure which mediates the transfer of nutrients and through which foreign substances can be transferred to the embryo from the time of implantation up to around day 11 in the mouse. However, it continues to mediate transfer throughout gestation. Before the fetal liver takes over, the role of haematopoiesis occurs in the yolk sac. Interference with the yolk-sac function may therefore be deleterious for embryonic nutrition (see Chapters 1 and 4).

As embryonic nutrition early in gestation comes from the secretion of the uterine epithelium, it is obvious that foreign compounds entering the uterine lumen along with this secretion will be available for accumulation by the yolk-sac placenta. It thus concentrates more foreign substances than any other fetal structure. Sometimes these substances are accumulated without any significant further transport to the embryo. This is true for many non-physiological elements like cadmium, mercury (Hg^{2+}),

Figure 5.13: False Precursors of Melanin: Some Foreign Compounds, Such as Thiouracil, are Mistakenly Incorporated as Precursors During the Formation of Melanin. They are accumulated in growing melanin but do not bind to preformed melanin. A strong accumulation is seen here in the melanin of two fetal eyes but not in the maternal eye.

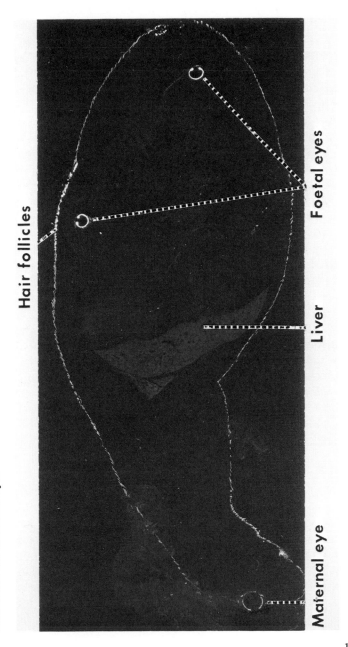

ruthenium and organic compounds like trypan blue and 2,4,5-T in early gestation. Others are transferred to the embryo with or without a simultaneous accumulation in the yolk-sac placenta. Some physiological compounds like vitamin B_{12} are highly accumulated in the embryo/fetus by the yolk-sac placenta early in gestation, as well as later by the chorio-allantoic placenta.

Generally, the yolk-sac placenta seems to be more discriminatory with regard to the transfer of foreign compounds than the chorio-allantoic placenta, as several chemicals such as 2,4,5-T, biphenyl, and diethylstilboestrol do not enter the early embryo but are transferred to the later fetus. Waddell (1972) has found that glucocorticoids are concentrated in the uterine lumen of pregnant animals, apparently followed by excretion through the vagina. He proposes this as a mechanism of drug elimination from the fetus. Brandt (1977) has observed a similar accumulation of a polychlorinated biphenyl in the uterine fluid.

The visceral yolk-sac epithelium at the earliest stages will later develop into two different structures: the visceral yolk-sac placenta and the epithelium of the fetal gastrointestinal tract. Compounds that accumulate in the more primitive yolk-sac epithelium will thus be liable to affect the development of the gastrointestinal tract and possibly other embryonic structures as a result of tissue interactions.

We have found that compounds like trypan blue, cadmium (Fig. 5.10) and mercury (Hg^{2+}) are accumulated by the intestine when administered before the closure of the vitelline duct (Dencker, 1976). This largely coincides with the period of teratogenic sensitivity, indicating that accumulation is important in the teratogenic mechanism.

V. Summary and Conclusions

A number of compounds have been found to localise selectively in the critical fetal tissue — the site of subsequent damage. There are a few such examples: thyroid-blocking agents which are known to cause fetal goitre are localised in the fetal thyroid; tetracyclines which are known to cause enamel spots are localised selectively in the fetal hard tissues and especially in the developing teeth; chloroquine which has been found to cause congenital retinal and otic lesions is accumulated in the melanin of the eye and inner ear. In early pregnancy, several agents which cause malformations of the central nervous system have been found to be localised in the neuroepithelium. Such findings support the idea that many, probably most, agents exert their adverse effects directly in the critical fetal tissues.

On the other hand, it is obvious that some compounds can be teratogenic or fetotoxic without appearing in the embryo/fetus in significant amounts. The heavy metals cadmium and mercury are examples. They are localised in the yolk-sac epithelium and in the placenta but do not come into contact with other fetal tissues, except the gut endoderm before the closure of the vitelline duct. The possibility that interference with yolk-sac function may be responsible for teratogenic effects was suggested by Beck *et al.* (1967; see also Chapters 1 and 4). Cadmium may disturb nutrition in the chorio-allantoic placenta. Preadministration of cadmium has been shown to decrease the transfer of labelled vitamin B_{12} to the fetus through the chorio-allantoic placenta. This indicates that the transport of nutrients to the fetus is a delicate process which may easily be disturbed. The deficient placental transport of an essential nutrient such as vitamin B_{12} may possibly cause fetal damage. Vitamin B_{12} is normally accumulated intensely by the placenta and then rather slowly transferred further to the fetus. It may be concentrated in the fetal tissues more than a hundredfold if a low dose is given. Many other physiological substances are also accumulated in the fetus compared with the mother. Such substances include other vitamins, the hormone oestradiol, amino acids, glucose and several microelements. The placenta apparently selects between chemically related substances and usually favours the physiologically important elements. An example is the ready transport of zinc to the fetus, but not that of cadmium.

Most nutrients are thus transferred in a one-way direction to the fetus, many by an active transport mechanism, and are more or less permanently incorporated into fetal tissues. Non-physiological drugs and environmental chemicals, on the other hand, pass from the mother through the placenta to the fetus and then back again. The degree of transfer to the fetus, however, varies greatly. High fat solubility and small molecular size generally seem to favour transfer.

Fat-soluble compounds such as the short-acting barbiturates can be detected in the fetus within a few minutes after intravenous injection into the mother. They seem to diffuse through the placenta without being accumulated and all the fetuses are exposed simultaneously to the drug. Such drugs are often accumulated both in the maternal and fetal brain, which may be a problem in obstetric anaesthesia. The fetal brain concentration, however, seldom exceeds the maternal.

Highly ionised drugs such as quaternary bases, on the other hand, are transferred very slowly and are sometimes not found in any detectable amounts in the fetus. However, they are found at a high concentration in the placenta. In addition, some toxic metals such as inorganic mercury (Hg^{2+}) and cadmium are largely prevented from reaching fetal tissues in a similar way.

The same physicochemical properties which favour transfer across the placenta usually also favour transfer across the (adult) blood-brain barrier. There are, however, many exceptions. Thus, inhibition of the transfer of quaternary drugs and some antibiotics is more efficient in the brain than in the placenta. On the other hand, some fat-soluble compounds are accumulated more in the brain than in the fetus. Thus, the difference in concentration range seems to be smaller for the fetus than for the brain.

Several of the drugs which have been studied comparatively at different stages of gestation show increased uptake by the fetus with gestational age (e.g. 2,4,5-T, biphenyl and diethylstilboestrol). A possible explanation is that they are effectively blocked by the yolk-sac placenta which is the only placental structure up to day 11-12 (mouse and rat). After this time, the chorio-allantoic placenta develops, allowing an increase in transfer. Other substances (salicylic acid, hexachlorophene) are not blocked by the yolk-sac placenta and can be found in high concentrations in the fetus irrespective of when they are administered to the mother.

The fetal distribution picture varies considerably between one substance and another. Generally the pattern is more complex the more physiological a substance is. The most even picture we have seen is that for non-metabolised ethanol, which seems to be distributed in total body water. Another rather even picture is that of benzylpenicillin, which is probably distributed in the extracellular space. In contrast to this is the differential distribution picture which is observed for many vitamins and hormones.

The fetal pattern, however, is less complex than the adult. Many sites of accumulation and transport are lacking, and a few localisation sites can be accentuated in the fetus and totally dominate the pattern. Such a localisation may be temporary or more long-lasting. Exceptionally long-lasting retentions have been observed in the skeleton (tetracyclines) and in melanin (polycyclic amines). A rather common site of accumulation is the fetal adrenal cortex.

The reason for a selective tissue accumulation and its consequences may vary greatly. It may be due to an interference with the metabolism in, for example, a gland (thyrostatics in the thyroid). It may also be due to an affinity for an enzyme because of some stereostructural resemblance to the physiological substrate of the enzyme. Some substances such an nitrosamines are localised mainly at the sites where they are metabolised.

Diethylnitrosamine is, for instance, accumulated and metabolised greatest in the nasal and bronchial mucosa; far more than in the liver. In some cases, fetal accumulation even in late pregnancy seems to be specifically growth related. Thus, a specific accumulation is found for amino acid analogues and mercurials in the fetal but not in the maternal optic lens. The observation that foreign substances can be incorporated as false precursors during the formation of fetal melanin might stimulate a search for similar phenomena during organogenesis. The risk of a mistake in the selection between physiological and foreign substances may be increased during rapid synthesis. A parallel to this may be the accumulation of amino acid analogues, such as para-iodophenylalanine, only at sites of very rapid protein synthesis (pancreas and tumours) (Blomquist, 1972). The complexity of the distribution pattern generally seems to increase with fetal age. Specific tissue localisations, a blood-brain barrier and an excretory pattern usually appear during the last few days before parturition.

The time sequence for uptake and elimination varies considerably between one compound and another. In some cases, the peak concentration in the fetus is reached after only 20 minutes while in most cases it occurs much later. Between 24 hours and 4 days, the elimination of foreign chemicals is usually complete. Exceptions include persistent chlorinated hydrocarbons, such as DDT and the PCBs, which are redistributed to the fetus if given early during pregnancy. A few substances such as hexachlorophene, biphenyl, cyclamate, and paracetamol will reach higher fetal than maternal concentrations.

It is apparent from the preceding pages that there are evident differences between various groups of compounds with respect to their uptake and distribution in the fetus. These are particularly obvious if we compare physiological and foreign substances. Within each group of substances, the similarities dominate. But there always seem to be some differences even between rather closely related agents. It is therefore only possible to a certain degree to foresee the fetal kinetics of a specific compound as assessed from its structure and chemical properties. There are also some common tendencies when early and late pregnancy are compared and between the fetal and adult patterns. Distribution studies is one approach which together with many others may finally lead to a better understanding of the influence of chemicals on fetal development.

Distribution of Drugs and Other Agents in the Fetus

Acknowledgement

Many of the investigations referred to in this chapter have been supported by the Swedish Medical Research Council, Grant No. 14X-02876.

References

André, T. (1956) *Acta Radiol.*, Suppl., *142*, 1-89
Appelgren, L.-E. (1967) *Acta Physiol. Scand.*, Suppl., *301*, 1-108
—— (1969) *J. Reprod. Fertil.*, *19*, 185-6
—— (1972) in *5th International Congress on Pharmacology*, Abstract No. 47, Volunteer Papers, San Francisco
Beck, F., Lloyd, J.B. and Griffiths, A. (1967) *Science*, *157*, 1180-2
Bengtsson, G. and Ullberg, S. (1963) *Acta Endocrinol.*, *43*, 561-70
Bengtsson, G., Ullberg, S., Wiqvist, N. and Diczfalusy, E. (1964) *Acta Endocrinol.*, *46*, 544-51
Bergman, A., Brandt, I. and Jansson, B. (1979) *Toxicol. Appl. Pharmacol.*, *48*, 213-20
Berlin, M. and Ullberg, S. (1963a) *Arch. Environ. Health*, *6*, 589-616
Berlin, M. and Ullberg, S. (1963b) *Arch. Environ. Health*, *7*, 686-93
Berlin, M. and Ullberg, S. (1963c) *Nature (London)*, *197*, 84-5
Blomquist, L. and Hanngren, A. (1966) *Biochem. Pharmacol.*, *15*, 215-19
Blomquist, L. (1972) *Acta Radiol.*, Suppl., *322*, 1-140
Brandt, I. (1977) *Acta Pharmacol. Toxicol.*, *40*, Suppl. 2, 1-108
Brandt, I. and Högman, P.-G. (1980) *Arch. Toxicol.*, *45*, 223-6
Brandt. I., Dencker, L. and Larsson, Y. (1979) *Toxicol. Appl. Pharmacol.*, *49*, 393-401
Brittebo, E., Lindgren, A. and Tjälve, H. (1981) *Acta Pharmacol. Toxicol.*, in press
Cassano, G.B. and Hansson, E. (1966) *Int. J. Neuropsychol.*, *2*, 269-78
DeLuca, L.M. (1977) *Vitam. Horm.*, *35*, 1-57
Dencker, L. (1975) *Reprod. Fertil.*, *44*, 461-71
—— (1976) *Acta Pharmacol. Toxicol.*, *39*, Suppl. 1, 1-131
—— (1979) in *Advances in the Study of Birth Defects*, Vol. 1, (Persaud, T.V.N., ed.), pp. 1-18, MTP Press Ltd., Lancaster, England
Dencker, L. and Tjälve, H. (1979) *Med. Biol.*, *57*, 391-7
Dencker, L., Larsson, B., Olander, K., Ullberg, S. and Yokota, M. (1979) *Br. J. Cancer*, *39*, 449-52
Dencker, L., Lindquist, N.G. and Ullberg, S. (1975) *Toxicology*, *5*, 225-64
Dencker, L., Nilsson, A., Rönnbäck, C. and Walinder, G. (1976) *Acta Radiol.*, *15*, 273-87
Deren, J.J., Padykula, H.A. and Wilson, T.H. (1966) *Develop. Biol.*, *13*, 349-69
Flodh, H. (1968) *Acta Radiol.*, Suppl., *284*, 1-80
Garzo, T., Hansson, E. and Ullberg, S. (1962) *Experientia*, *18*, 43-6
Hammarström, L. (1966) *Acta Physiol. Scand.*, *70*, Suppl. 289, 1-84
Hammarström, L., Neujahr, H. and Ullberg, S. (1966) *Acta Pharmacol. Toxicol.*, *24*, 24-32
Hammarström, L. and Ullberg, S. (1966) *Nature (London)*, *212*, 708-9
Hanngren, Å. (1959) *Acta Radiol.*, Suppl., *175*, 1-118
Hanngren, Å., Hansson, E., Svartz, N. and Ullberg, S. (1963) *Acta Med. Scand.*, *173*, 391-9
Hanngren, Å., Einer-Jensen, N. and Ullberg, S. (1965) *Nature (London)*, *208*, 461-2
Hansson, E. and Garzo, T. (1961) *Experientia*, *17*, 501-3
Hart, C.W. and Naunton, R.F. (1964) *Arch. Otolaryng.*, *80*, 407-12
Howell, J. McC., Thompson, J.N. and Pitt, G.A. (1964) *J. Reprod. Fertil.*, *7*, 251-8
Hurley, L.S. and Swenerton, H. (1966) *Proc. Soc. Exp. Biol.*, *123*, 692-6
Idänpään-Heikillä, J.E. and Scholar, J.C. (1969) *Science*, *164*, 1295-7
Idänpään-Heikillä, J.E., Taska, R.J., Allen, H.A. and Scholar, J.C. (1971) *J. Pharmacol. Exp. Ther.*, *176*, 752-7
Khayat, A. (1977) Master's Thesis: *Alteration of Mercury Vapour Metabolism by Ethyl Alcohol in Rat Tissues in vivo and in vitro*. The University of Rochester, New York

Kochhar, D.M. (1967) *Acta Pathol. Microbiol. Scand., 70,* 398-404
Lal, H., Barlow, C.F. and Roth, L.J. (1964) *Arch. Int. Pharmacodyn. Ther., 149,* 25-36
Larsson, B., Olsson, S., Szüts, T., Ullberg, S., Enzell, C. and Pilotti, A. (1979) *Toxicol. Lett., 4,* 199-203
Lindgren, A. and Dencker, L. (1980) *Proceedings of the International Symposium on Arsenic and Nickel,* July 8-10, 1980, Jena, GDR
Lindquist, N.G. and Ullberg, S. (1972) *Acta Pharmacol. Toxicol., 31,* Suppl. 2, 1-32
Lindquist, N.G. and Ullberg, S. (1974) *Nature (London), 248,* 600-1
Lucier, G.W., Lui, E.M.K. and Lamartinière, C.A. (1979) *Environ. Health Perspect., 29,* 7-16
McLachlan, J.A. (1977) *J. Toxicol. Environ. Health, 2,* 527-37
Olsen, I. and Jonsen, J. (1979) *Toxicology, 12,* 165-72
Östlund, K. (1969) *Acta Pharmacol. Toxicol., 27,* Suppl. 1, 1-132
Padykula, H.A., Deren, J.J. and Wilson, T.H. (1966) *Develop. Biol., 13,* 311-48
Peters, M.A., Turnbow, M. and Buchenauer, D. (1972) *J. Pharmacol. Exp. Ther., 181,* 273-8
Placidi, G.F., Cassano, G.B. and Viola, P.L. (1977) *Acta Pharmacol. Toxicol., 41,* Suppl. 1, 160-1
Ritzén, M., Hammarström, L. and Ullberg, S. (1965) *Biochem. Pharmacol., 14,* 313-21
Rollins, D.E., von Bahr, C., Glaumann, H., Moldeus, P. and Rane, A. (1979) *Science, 205,* 1414-6
Sarteschi, P., Cassano, G.B. and Placidi, G.F. (1973) *Pharmakopsychiatr., 6,* 50-8
Schechter, P.J. and Roth, L.J. (1967) *J. Pharmacol. Exp. Ther., 158,* 164-73
Shah, N.S., Nely, A.E., Shah, K.R. and Lawrence, R.S. (1973) *J. Pharmacol. Exp. Ther., 184,* 489-93
Shindo, H. (1972) *Ann. Saukyo Res. Lab., 24,* 1-72
Sjöstrand, S.E., Cassano, G.B. and Hansson, E. (1965) *Arch. Int. Pharmacodyn. Ther., 156,* 34-47
Slanina, P., Ullberg, S. and Hammarström, L. (1973) *Acta Pharmacol. Toxicol., 32,* 358-68
Szüts, T., Olsson, S., Lindquist, N.G., Ullberg, S., Pilotti, A. and Enzell, C. (1978) *Toxicology, 10,* 207-20
Takahashi, Y.I., Smith, J. and Goodman, D.S. (1977) *Am. J. Physiol., 233,* E263-E272
Tjälve, H. (1972) *Toxicol. Appl. Pharmacol., 23,* 216-21
Tjälve, H., Hansson, E. and Schmiterlöw, C.G. (1968) *Acta Pharmacol. Toxicol., 26,* 539-55
Ullberg, S. (1954) *Acta Radiol.,* Suppl., *118,* 1-110
—— (1973) in *Fetal Pharmacology* (Boréus, L.O., ed.), pp. 55-73, Raven Press, New York
—— (1977) *The Technique of Whole Body Autoradiography,* pp. 1-29, Science Tools, The LKB Instrument Journal
Ullberg, S. and Bengtsson, G. (1963) *Acta Endocrinol., 43,* 75-86
Ullberg, S. and Blomquist, L. (1968) *Acta Pharm. Suecica, 5,* 45-53
Ullberg, S., Sörbo, B. and Clemedson, C.-J. (1961) *Acta Radiol., 55,* 145-55
Ullberg, S., Appelgren, L.-E., Clemedson, C.-J., Ericsson, Y., Ewaldsson, B., Sörbo, B. and Söremark, R. (1964) *Biochem. Pharmacol., 13,* 407-12
Ullberg, S., Kristoffersson, H., Flodh, H. and Hanngren, A. (1967) *Arch. Int. Pharmacodyn. Ther., 167,* 431-49
Ullberg, S., Nelson, A., Kristoffersson, H. and Engström, A. (1962) *Acta Radiol., 58,* 459-71
Vahlquist, A., Peterson, P.A. and Wibell, L. (1973) *Europ. J. Clin. Invest., 3,* 352-62
Van der Kleijn, E. (1969) *Arch. Int. Pharmacodyn. Ther., 178,* 193-215
Van der Kleijn, E. and Wijffels, C.C.G. (1971) *Arch. Int. Pharmacodyn. Ther., 192,* 255-64
Waddell, W.J. (1971) in *Fundamentals of Drug Metabolism and Drug Disposition* (LaDu, B.N., Mandel, H.G., Way, E.L., eds.), pp. 505-14, Williams and Wilkins, Baltimore, USA
Waddell, W.J. (1972) *Fed. Proc. Fed. Am. Soc. Exp. Biol., 31,* 52-61
Waddell, W.J. and Mirkin, B.L. (1972) *Biochem. Pharmacol., 21,* 547-52
Waddell, W.J. and Marlowe, G.C. (1976) in *Perinatal Pharmacology and Therapeutics* (Mirkin, B.L., ed.), pp. 119-268, Academic Press, New York

CHAPTER SIX

THE DIFFERENTIATION OF DRUG METABOLISM IN RELATION TO DEVELOPMENTAL TOXICOLOGY
Olavi Pelkonen

CONTENTS

I. Introduction

Drugs and other chemicals foreign to the body (the so-called xenobiotics) are metabolised in the body through the catalysis of drug- or xenobiotic-metabolising enzymes and in most cases their pharmacological and toxicological actions are decreased or terminated altogether (Testa and Jenner, 1976). On this basis xenobiotic biotransformations are sometimes called detoxification reactions. However, in an ever-increasing number of cases the products of metabolism (metabolites) are agents harmful to the body and consequently these reactions are referred to as activation reactions (see Jollow *et al.*, 1977; Neubert *et al.*, 1978). It is therefore of considerable importance to know the consequences of xenobiotic metabolism to the fetus. Traditionally, the relative lack of fetal drug metabolism has been regarded as teleologically meaningful, because the back-diffusion of xenobiotics through the placenta to the mother is the most significant route for the fetus to eliminate foreign chemicals and because this diffusion is thought to be most rapid for unchanged lipid-soluble substances. If, however, the fetus should metabolise foreign substances to more water-soluble metabolites, these metabolites might accumulate on the fetal side of the placental barrier. The presence of xenobiotic metabolism in the fetus would also raise the possibility of the production of reactive metabolites with possible harmful consequences. Our current knowledge about fetal xenobiotic metabolism and its relation to toxic reactions is the topic of this chapter.

167

II. Differentiation of Xenobiotic Metabolism in Experimental Animals and Man

A. *Early Embryonic Period*

The degree and type of reaction shown by an organism depend on the developmental stage at which exposure to a foreign chemical occurs. This is one of the most basic principles of developmental toxicology. Analogously, it is conceivable that the extent and type of biotransformation reactions depend on the stage of development. Fetal organs and tissues as well as the individual as a whole are in a state of more or less rapid change. This fact makes it difficult to consider 'fetal xenobiotic metabolism' as a single concept without referring to a specified stage of development. However, our lack of relevant knowledge dictates that we must deal with biotransformation reactions mostly at a relatively advanced stage of development. This limitation is even more regrettable because most of the serious developmental toxicities, malformations, are produced relatively early during embryonic life. Data are virtually non-existent on the capacity of the early mammalian embryo to carry out biotransformations of xenobiotics. With the possible exception of aryl hydrocarbon hydroxylase activity which might be induced very early during development by appropriate inducers (Schlede and Merker, 1974, Neubert and Tapken, 1978), one may assume that embryos do not metabolize xenobiotics until the principal xenobiotic-metabolising organs such as the liver, lungs, kidneys and bowel have acquired some degree of functional competence resembling that of the adult.

B. *Species Differences*

During the last 20 years it has become increasingly clear that many laboratory animal species are deficient in microsomal xenobiotic-oxidising activity associated with the cytochrome P450-linked microsomal electron transport chain until the later stages of fetal development (Table 6.1). With few exceptions, laboratory animal species have a very low capacity to oxidise xenobiotics until after birth; adult levels of xenobiotic metabolism are not usually observed until the animal is several weeks old. Most conjugation reactions (phase II metabolism) are also poorly developed in the fetuses of any one species, but not as uniformly as oxidation (phase I)

The Differentiation of Drug Metabolism

Table 6.1: **Comparison Between Fetal/Neonatal and Adult Levels of Hepatic _N_-dealkylation Reactions in Different Species**

Species	_N_-Dealkylation reaction substrate	Fetus/Adult × 100		Reference
Human (gestation 265 days)	Aminopyrine	25	Mid-gestation	1, 2
	Ethylmorphine	40		3, 4
	Diazepam	10		5
	Prazepam	20		6
Guinea-pig (gestation 65 days)	_p_-Chloro-_N_-methyl-aniline	0	(−21)[1]	7
		1.6	(−11)	
		8.6	(− 1)	
		140	(+ 1)	
	_p_-Nitroanisole	<5	(− 8)	8
		<5	(− 4)	
		75	(+ 4)	
Rabbit (gestation 32 days)	Aminopyrine	0	(−12)	9
		50	(− 2)	
	N, _N_-Dimethylaniline	2.5	(− 4)	10
		13	(0)	
Rat (gestation 21 days)	_p_-Nitroanisole	3	(− 3)	11
		10	(0)	
	Prazepam	0.3	(− 3)	12
		5	(0)	
Swine (gestation 114 days)	_p_-Nitroanisole	<1	(− 7)	13
		9	(0)	

[1] Numbers in parentheses denote days before and after birth. Zero means newborn.

References: (1) Pelkonen _et al._, 1973; (2) Pelkonen, 1973; (3) Rane and Ackermann, 1972; (4) Thorgeirsson, 1972; (5) Ackermann and Richter, 1977; (6) Nau and Liddiard, 1978; (7) Kuenzig _et al._, 1974; (8) Ecobichon _et al._, 1978; (9) Rane _et al._, 1973; (10) Bend _et al._, 1975; (11) Bell _et al._, 1975; (12) Nau and Neubert, 1978; (13) Short and Davis, 1970.

reactions.

Livers of human and primate fetuses possess a relatively well-developed mono-oxygenase complex capable of oxidising a wide variety of foreign substances. Selected data in Table 6.1 illustrate that the difference between human and animal fetuses is very considerable and that activities in rodent fetal livers are generally an order of magnitude lower than those in human fetal liver. Other biotransformation reactions have been studied to a much lesser extent, but it seems that many hydrolytic as well as conjugative reactions are active in human fetal liver. Fetal adrenal glands also have some capability of metabolising foreign compounds. Some properties of human fetal xenobiotic-metabolising enzyme systems are compared with the corresponding adult systems in Table 6.2. It must be stressed that data in this table refer to the situation at mid-gestation, for obvious reasons; but some pharmacokinetic studies during the perinatal period indicate that the situation at that time does not differ appreciably from mid-gestation (see Neims *et al.*, 1976). It seems clear that human fetuses differ from commonly used laboratory animals in their capacity to metabolise xenobiotics.

C. *Inducibility of Fetal Enzymes*

Xenobiotic-metabolising enzymes in fetal liver and other tissues can be induced by perinatal exposure to foreign chemicals and this has been recently summarised (Pelkonen, 1980b). A vast majority of studies indicate that fetal microsomal enzyme activity can be stimulated only when the inducing compound is administered to the mother during the last few days of gestation. Moreover, the appearance of induction seems to depend on the inducer and on the substrate or the pathway studied. Generally speaking, inducers like polycyclic aromatic hydrocarbons and polychlorinated biphenyls which induce cytochrome P448 or P_1 450 (Thorgeirsson and Nebert, 1977) are the most potent inducers during the perinatal period, whereas phenobarbital and other inducers hardly induce xenobiotic metabolism at this time (see, for example, Guenthner and Mannering, 1977; Cresteil *et al.*, 1979). Synergistic effects between inducing agents have also been observed (Guenthner and Mannering, 1977). In any case, the absolute fetal enzyme activities reached after induction are much lower than they are in the neonatal or the adult liver, although the ratio between induced and basal values may be quite high because of extremely low basal values.

Table 6.2: Properties of Human Fetal Hepatic and Adrenal Gland Xenobiotic-metabolising Enzyme Systems as Compared with the Adult Hepatic Systems

Parameter	Fetal liver	Fetal adrenal gland	Adult liver
Cytochrome P450:			
In microsomal protein (mol/g)	0.2-0.4	1.7	0.4-0.8
In tissue (nmol/g)	3-11	12-38	6-15
CO peak (nm)	450[1]	446-448	450
Oxidation of xenobiotics:			
Aminopyrine	++	+	++++
Aniline	+++	+	++++
7-Ethoxycoumarin	++	+	++++
Benzo (a) pyrene	+	+++	++++
Hydrolases:			
Epoxide hydration	++	++	++++
Conjugation of xenobiotics:			
Glucuronidation	0 to +	0	++++
Sulphate conjugation	+++	++	++++
Glutathione conjugation	+++	++	++++
Glycine conjugation	+++	Not known	++++
Inducibility by:			
Phenobarbital	Possible	No	Yes
Polycyclic hydrocarbons	No	No	Yes

[1] A partially purified cytochrome gave a peak between 449 and 450 nm (Kitada and Kamataki, 1979).

Source: Original references for this table are in the following reviews: Pelkonen, 1977b; 1980a, c; Juchau, 1980.

D. *Ontogenetic Patterns*

Numerous studies have shown that enzyme activities have distinctive ontogenetic patterns (see Snell, Chapter 10; Greengard, 1977) and, indeed, this is the case for xenobiotic-metabolising enzymes. A number of experimental studies have demonstrated that the prenatal and postnatal development of different enzyme activities may follow differing time courses

171

(see Waddell and Marlowe, 1976; Short *et al.*, 1976; Klinger *et al.*, 1979). Figure 6.1 gives some schematised examples of the ontogenetic patterns of xenobiotic-metabolising enzymes in human and rodent livers. Although it is now difficult to classify enzymes of xenobiotic metabolism into definite 'clusters' with respect to ontogenetic development, some examples illustrate that this may indeed be possible in the future. For example, in a recent study Henderson (1978) found no parallels in the rate of postnatal development between the oxidative N-demethylation of N-methyl- and N, N-dimethylamphetamine in the rat liver. This finding strongly supports the concept of multiple forms of N-demethylating enzymes which develop independently of each other. Wishart and Dutton (1978) have shown that there is a developmental heterogeneity of UDP-glucuronyltransferase activity towards two groups of substrates which they classify as the 'late fetal group' and the 'neonatal group' on the basis of the time of developmental upsurge. In the neonatal rabbit aryl hydrocarbon hydroxylase activity, which in the adult is poorly inducible by polycyclic aromatic hydrocarbons, responds to treatment by 3-methylcholanthrene or 2, 3, 7, 8-tetrachlorodibenzo-*p*-dioxin (TCDD) and this induction is associated with the appearance of a specific form of cytochrome P450 (Atlas *et al.*, 1977; Norman *et al.*, 1978). A similar kind of perinatal development is also found in the rat and mouse (Guenthner and Nebert, 1978). Thus it seems probable that different forms of oxidative and conjugative enzymes develop at different times and the inducibility of different forms may also undergo changes during development.

The available evidence indicates, although in a very preliminary way, that human fetal, neonatal and placental xenobiotic-metabolising enzymes are regulated in a manner analogous to that in animals. Fetal hepatic, adrenal gland and placental mono-oxygenase systems differ from each other (see Juchau, 1980 and Chapter 7). Fetal hepatic mono-oxygenase differs from the adult counterpart in a very distinct way, namely in having polycyclic aromatic hydrocarbon inducible cytochrome(s) P450 (Pelkonen, 1977a). Neims *et al.* (1976) have given very clear evidence that mono-oxygenase activities develop postnatally in different ways depending upon the substrate and metabolic pathway. We can postulate that different forms of xenobiotic-metabolising enzymes in human tissues have specific developmental patterns and because we know that different forms have different substrate specificies and activities, an obvious implication is that the metabolism of xenobiotics at a given age is both qualitatively and quantitatively different from that at another age. If this is generally true, it creates problems in drug testing. In effect, each age class of fetuses or newborns must be regarded as 'a new species' pharmacokinetically. The consequent implications for developmental toxicology are tremendous.

Figure 6.1: **Some Schematic Patterns of Ontogenetic Development of Xenobiotic Metabolism. Curve A: Typical for several drug-metabolising enzyme activities in the rat and other common laboratory animal species (see Short *et al., * 1976). Benzo (a) pyrene hydroxylation in human fetal, and possibly neonatal, liver and related activities (Aldridge *et al., * 1979) exhibit a similar ontogenetic pattern. Curve B: The development of a number of oxidative enzyme activities in human liver usually associated with control and/or phenobarbital-inducible cytochrome P450 (see Pelkonen, 1980a). The postnatal part of the curve is inferred from pharmacokinetic studies (Neims *et al., * 1976). Curve C: Represents the so-called 'late-fetal group' of UDP-glucuronyltransferase activities in the rat described by Wishart and Dutton (1978). The upsurge of the 'neonatal group' begins after birth. Curve D: A typical representative is the development of benzo (a) pyrene hydroxylation in the perinatal guinea-pig liver (Kuenzig *et al., * 1974).**

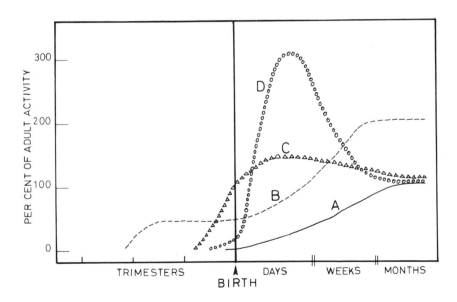

III. Dextoxification Functions of Fetal Drug Metabolism

The most important problem of metabolism of foreign substances by the fetus has to do with the functions of this ability in 'detoxification' and 'activation'. Some possible consequences of fetal xenobiotic metabolism are illustrated in Figure 6.2. If active intermediates are formed, it is relatively simple to envisage a hypothetical link with developmental toxicity and hope that future research will prove or refute this link (see Section V). On the other hand, it is much more difficult to conceptualise what is meant by detoxification during fetal life. It is generally considered in reviews and textbooks that, teleologically speaking, the fetus does not need any detoxification functions and they may even be harmful, if present, because xenobiotics are handled by the metabolic and elimination machinery of the mother. Detoxification as a concept implies *a priori* pharmocological and/or toxicological effects; but what are these effects in the fetus? Drugs exert their effects generally via specific receptors or other macromolecules. At what stage in development do these drug receptors and receptor responses develop in the fetus? Only after the development of the appropriate receptors and responses can we speak about detoxification in a classical sense, because there is no need to 'detoxify' substances which do not cause responses in the particular target, the fetus. However, this raises another problem. The fetus is certainly not an adult. The constantly changing biochemical machinery of the fetus may make it vulnerable to foreign substances in ways which are distinctly different from the responses these same substances may elicit in the adult. We know this difference well enough from experimental and clinical teratology and fetal toxicology. In this latter context we can talk about fetal detoxification functions, which we can formulate as 'the ability of the fetal xenobiotic metabolism to decrease steady-state concentrations of substances which cause pharmacological and/or toxico-logical responses in the fetus so that these responses become less pro-nounced'. The next question is obviously: is fetal xenobiotic metabolism, and at what point in time, active enough to decrease xenobiotic levels in fetal targets so that responses become less common?

On the basis of the known activity of xenobiotic-metabolising enzymes in the fetal tissues and the placenta and of the theoretical considerations of Gillette *et al.* (1973) and Gillette and Stripp (1975), the steady-state levels of foreign compounds in the fetus or in the mother are probably not appreciably affected by the activity of fetal xenobiotic-metabolising enzymes.

Figure 6.1: Some Possible Effects of Foreign Substances in the Fetus as Related to Xenobiotic Metabolism and Pharmacodynamic Maturation

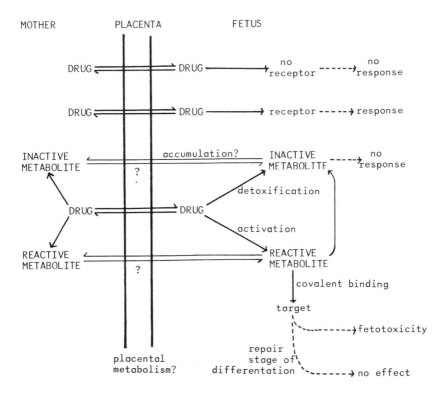

As stated earlier, the relative lack of drug metabolism in the fetus has been regarded as teleologically meaningful because of the difference assumed to exist in the relative transplacental transfer rates of xenobiotics and their metabolites. Metabolites less lipid soluble than the parent compound may transfer more slowly back to the mother and thus accumulate in the fetus. Theoretically only conjugated metabolites would be expected to accumulate significantly because they are water soluble (for discussion, see Pelkonen, 1977b). The capacity of human and animal fetuses to conjugate foreign compounds seems to vary according to the endogenous acceptor. Those conjugates which are readily formed in fetal tissues may accumulate on the fetal side. Thalidomide appears to be an illustrative example, although metabolites are not formed through metabolism but through spontaneous hydrolysis (Williams *et al.*, 1965). These products, which have comparable water solubilities to xenobiotic conjugates, accumulate in the rabbit fetus after the administration of thalidomide to the mother.

After birth, the newborn must dispose of foreign chemicals using its own metabolic and excretory machinery. If xenobiotic metabolism is deficient, a severe overdosage might develop after an exposure which in the adult would not cause any harm. There is ample clinical and experimental evidence that the newborn is more sensitive to many foreign compounds and in many instances this sensitivity is due to the immaturity of xenobiotic-metabolising enzymes (Mirkin, 1970; Yaffe and Juchau, 1974; Horning *et al.*, 1975). On the other hand, the deficiency of xenobiotic metabolism may be a protecting factor, if a compound must be activated before it can exert its toxic effects. With bromobenzene and paracetamol there is evidence that newborn animals are resistant to the hepatotoxic action of these compounds, presumably because of deficient activation reactions and/or an activation–detoxification balance favouring detoxification (Mitchell *et al.*, 1971; Hart and Timbrell, 1979).

IV. Generation of Reactive Metabolites by Fetal Tissues

A. *Animal Studies*

The role of active intermediates in the causation of tissue lesions, carcinogenesis and the other harmful effects of foreign compounds has received considerable attention in recent years and in a number of cases the relationship between metabolism and toxicity is well established (see Jollow *et al.*, 1977). The literature contains several publications which demonstrate or implicate the formation of reactive metabolites catalysed by animal fetal tissues. Numerous studies have demonstrated the presence and inducibility of aryl hydrocarbon hydroxylase in animal fetuses and neonates (for references see Pelkonen, 1980b). The activity, however, is generally extremely low in comparison with the adult. In some studies, the formation of different classes of metabolites was investigated and the formation of dihydrodiols, implicating epoxide formation, was detected (Wang *et al.*, 1975; Berry *et al.*, 1976, 1977). Nunnink *et al.* (1978) have demonstrated the presence of aryl hydrocarbon hydroxylase activity in fetal and neonatal rat nuclei. The activity was inducible by the administration of 3-methylcholanthrene and the greatest increase in nuclear enzyme activity was observed in the 1–2-day-old rat. The formation of benzo (*a*) pyrene-7,8-dihydrodiol, the putative proximate carcinogen, was also observed in neonatal nuclei (Bresnick *et al.*, 1979). However, the formation of reactive intermediates does not, in itself, prove that they can reach critical targets and cause harmful effects. It is widely thought that it is the balance between activating and detoxifying enzymes that is of the utmost importance in determining the final outcome or at least the possibility of interaction with critical targets. In this context it is interesting to speculate on the differing ontogenetic patterns of activating and detoxifying enzymes and their possible role in fetotoxicity. For example, aryl hydrocarbon hydroxylase activity, and possibly the formation of the primary reactive epoxide intermediates, is inducible by 3-methylcholanthrene in fetal rat liver, but epoxide hydratase activity (which converts epoxides to dihydrodiols) is not inducible (Oesch, 1975). Although this finding cannot be interpreted to represent an enhancement of toxicity (because of complex metabolic pathways thought to be operating in the metabolic activation of polycyclic aromatic hydrocarbons) it nevertheless demonstrates that different pathways can be affected differently. The change in the balance of enzymes may lead to an enhancement or a decrease in fetotoxicity. This area is still largely unexplored.

In some studies it has been possible to show that active intermediates produced in *in vitro* experimental systems by fetal tissues cause effects which are thought to be indicative or analogous to effects *in vivo*. Some examples are listed in Table 6.3. To select some of the more illustrative studies, Sehgal and Hutton (1977) showed that rat fetal tissues catalysed the formation of carcinogenic metabolites mutagenic to *Salmonella typhimurium* strains. Pretreatment of pregnant animals with 3-methylcholanthrene increased the mutagenic activity. Juchau *et al.* (1979) demonstrated that fetal tissues of rat and mouse were capable of converting 7, 12-dimethylbenz (*a*) anthracene, benzo (*a*) pyrene and 2-acetylaminofluorene into mutagenic metabolites. Especially interesting was the finding that the fetal brain of rats, a target for the transplacental carcinogenic action of 7,12-dimethylbenz (*a*) anthracene, display a high capacity to convert this carcinogen to metabolites mutagenic to bacteria.

B. *Human Studies*

The ability of the human fetus to oxidise xenobiotics implies that

Table 6.3: Examples of Immediate Biochemical or Biological Effects Produced by Reactive Intermediates as Catalysed by Fetal Tissue Samples *in vitro* or After Administration *in vivo*

Compound	Fetal tissue *in vitro* or target *in vivo*	Biochemical or biological effect observed	Reference
2-Aminoanthracene	Rat liver, lung, intestine, skin	Mutagenesis in Salmonella	Sengal and Hutton, 1977
Benzo (*a*) pyrene	Rat liver, lung, brain (intestine and skin negative)	Mutagenesis in Salmonella	Sehgal and Hutton, 1977; Juchau *et al.*, 1979
	Mouse liver, lung	Mutagenesis in Salmonella	Juchau *et al.*, 1979; Blake *et al.*, 1978
	Rat, guinea-pig liver	Binding to DNA	Pelkonen, unpublished
	Mouse fetus *in utero*	Binding to protein and DNA	Shum *et al.*, 1979
Cigarette smoke condensate	Rat lung, intestine (liver and skin negative)	Mutagenesis in Salmonella	Sehgal and Hutton, (1977)
7, 12-Dimethylbenzanthracene	Rat liver, brain, lung Mouse liver, lung	Mutagenesis in Salmonella	Juchau *et al.*, 1979
2-Acetylaminofluorene	Rat liver, lung Mouse liver, lung, brain	Mutagenesis in Salmonella	Juchau *et al.*, 1979
Nitrofurazone	Mouse fetal liver *in vivo*	Binding to protein	Gillette *et al.*, 1973
Phenytoin	Mouse fetus *in vivo*	Binding to protein	Blake *et al.*, 1978

potentially toxic intermediates can be formed (Pelkonen, 1977c) and, indeed, some possible candidates have been tentatively identified or postulated in the metabolism of several compounds (Table 6.4). These examples on the formation of active intermediates by fetal tissues *in vitro* do not constitute a proof that toxic reactions actually occur in the fetus. Nevertheless, the existence of these metabolic pathways is a necessary (although not sufficient) prerequisite for toxic manifestations associated with the compounds listed in Table 6.4. Another important factor is that the activity of human fetal enzymes is lower than that of adult enzymes and thus active intermediates are probably formed in smaller quantities. In this respect, however, the sensitivity of fetal tissues to exogenous influences is important. It is likely that fetal tissues and their functions differ from their adult counterparts with respect to sensitivity to exogenous influences, such as xenobiotics and their activated metabolites. The low activities of fetal enzymes do not necessarily mean that there is less likelihood of harmful effects being mediated by their metabolites.

Lipid peroxidation, the oxidative deterioration of polyunsaturated lipids promoted by cytochrome P450 and its reductase, may play a basic role in the damage of endoplasmic reticulum membranes particularly in the onset and development of liver injury by some halogenated hydrocarbons (Wills, 1969; Recknagel and Glende, 1973). Studies on human fetal (Arvela *et al.*, 1976; Nau *et al.*, 1978) and neonatal liver (Renton *et al.*, 1976) have demonstrated that lipid peroxidation occurs with the addition of several halogenated compounds to liver homogenates. Thus these studies suggest that lipid peroxidation may be induced by xenobiotics during the fetal and neonatal period of human development but the possible consequences, such as liver injury after exposure to halogenated anaesthetics, have not as yet been observed.

V. Association Between Reactive Intermediates and Fetotoxity

The observation that fetal tissues catalyse the formation of reactive metabolites is very suggestive in developmental toxicology, but does not constitute a direct proof for linking these two phenomena together. Other experimental approaches ought to be adopted, but are very difficult to find. In fact, there are no examples of fetotoxicity which have been shown unequivocally to be caused by active intermediates. However, in some cases there are strong indications of an association between reactive

Table 6.4: Potential Activation Reactions Catalysed by Human Fetal Tissues *In Vitro*.

Compound	Metabolic pathway detected	Harmful effects implicated	References
Benzo (*a*) pyrene	epoxidation, epoxide hydration	mutagenesis, carcinogenesis	(1) (2)
7, 12-Dimethylbenz (*a*) anthracene		mutagenesis, carcinogenesis	(3)
2-Acetylaminofluorene	N-hydroxylation and esterification	mutagenesis, carcinogenesis	(4) (5)
Dimethylnitrosamine	N-demethylation	mutagenesis, carcinogenesis	(6)
Aldrin	epoxidation	increased toxicity	(1)
Diphenylhydantoin	epoxidation	teratogenesis	(7)
Aniline	N-oxidation	methemoglobinemia	(8)
Carbon tetrachloride	(free radicals?)	lipid peroxidation, tissue injuries	(9)
Paracetamol	GSH-conjugation of active metabolite	liver injury	(10)

References: (1) Pelkonen and Kärki, 1975; (2) Berry *et al.*, 1977; (3) Jones *et al.*, 1977; (4) Juchau *et al.*, 1975; (5) Namkung *et al.*, 1977; (6) Ivankovic *et al.*, 1974; (7) Egger *et al.*, 1978; (8) Rane and Ackermann, 1972; (9) Nau *et al.*, 1978; (10) Rollins *et al.*, 1979.

Table 6.5: Examples of a Probable Association Between Metabolically Formed Reactive Intermediates and Fetotoxicity

Compound(s)	Fetotoxicity	Evidence for the association	References
Dimethylnitrosamine Diethylnitrosamine	Carcinogenesis	Coincidence of the development of activating enzymes and the initiation of harmful effects	Druckrey, 1973
Phenytoin	Resorptions, teratogenesis	Covalent binding of phenytoin to fetal macromolecules	Blake *et al.*, 1978
7, 12-Dimethylbenzanthracene	Stillbirths, resorptions	Mouse strains responsive to induction by polycyclic hydrocarbons more susceptible to fetotoxic effects	Lambert and Nebert, 1977
Benzo (*a*) pyrene	Stillbirths, resorptions, malformations	Genetically responsive fetuses more susceptible to fetotoxic effects than non-responsive in the same uterus	Shum *et al.*, 1979

intermediates and fetotoxicity, and some examples are listed in Table 6.5. For example, experimental studies on transplacental carcinogenesis suggest that agents requiring metabolic activation are effective only just before birth when xenobiotic-metabolising enzymes appear in fetal tissues (Napalkov, 1973; Druckrey, 1973). Perhaps the best approach thus far has been the use of the genetic model developed by Nebert and co-workers (see Thorgeirsson and Nebert, 1977). In this model, the inducibility of aryl hydrocarbon hydroxylase activity in the liver and other tissues is controlled by alleles at the so called Ah locus in a manner which obeys in many genetic crosses simple Mendelian rules. Thus, in genetic crosses between mice from C57B1/6 and DBA/2 strains the responsiveness segregates as an autosomal dominant trait and in appropriate back-crosses an association between the Ah locus and the fetotoxicity of a xenobiotic can be studied without interference by numerous non-specific effects of the compound. Because it has been shown that the induced enzyme produces more proximal carcinogens, mutagenic metabolites and DNA-bound metabolites than the control enzyme, both *in vitro* and *in vivo*, the association between this genetic trait and the biological effect caused by a foreign chemical, if demonstrated, is very probably due to reactive metabolites (Pelkonen *et al.*, 1978; Nebert *et al.*, 1979).

Recent studies from Nebert's laboratory demonstrated that there is indeed a correlation between genetic responsiveness and the incidence of fetotoxicity. Lambert and Nebert (1977) demonstrated that responsiveness at the Ah locus was associated with an increased incidence of stillbirths, resorptions and malformations induced by 3-methylcholanthrene and 7, 16-dimethylbenzanthracene. A more definitive study by Shum *et al.* (1979) showed that benzo (*a*) pyrene given at day 7 or 10 of gestation caused more toxicity and teratogenicity *in utero* in genetically responsive than in non-responsive mice. With the use of back-crosses, they showed that allelic differences at the Ah locus in the fetus can be correlated with dysmorphogenesis. Furthermore, they were able to show that the phenotype of the mother is also important. If the mother is non-responsive, the responsive genotype in the fetus is associated with more stillbirths and resorptions, decreased fetal weight, increased congenital abnormalities and enhanced covalent binding of benzo (*a*) pyrene metabolites to fetal protein and DNA, when compared with the non-responsive genotype in the fetus from the same uterus. If the mother is responsive, however, none of the above mentioned parameters can be distinguished between responsive and non-responsive individuals in the same uterus. This last observation is of particular interest because it demonstrates that

182

the mother and the father must be of a particular genotype before differences in fetotoxicity among fetuses due to their genotype are expressed. Presumably, the enhanced benzo (*a*) pyrene metabolism in the responsive mother cancels out differences between individual fetuses of different genotypes.

Although the above studies constitute the most convincing case in favour of the participation of reactive intermediates in fetotoxicity, it is still too early to regard their role as settled. In a recent study, Poland and Glover (1980) reported the association between genetic responsiveness and the incidence of cleft palate produced by 2, 3, 7, 8-tetrachlorodibenzo-*p*-dioxin (TCDD). However, as a mechanism for the toxicity of TCDD they propose the stereospecific binding of TCDD by the induction receptor and the subsequent sustained expression (or repression) of one or more genes controlled by the receptor. They propose that the induction of aryl hydrocarbon hydroxylase activity *per se*, with a consequent enhancement of production of reactive intermediates, is not directly responsible for fetotoxicity. Because in the study of Shum *et al.* (1979) the production of cleft palate was a prominent feature of fetotoxicity produced by benzo (*a*) pyrene, one might argue that this specific effect is related to the association of benzo (*a*) pyrene with the induction receptor and not to reactive intermediates. The answer apparently must await further research.

VI. Conclusions and Perspectives

This short review shows that although the importance of xenobiotic metabolism in detoxification and activation of foreign compounds in the adult organism is firmly established, its overall significance and the relation to fetotoxicity during the fetal and perinatal periods is still largely a matter of conjecture and speculation. Differences between species in fetal xenobiotic metabolism are large, especially between experimental animals and man. Although there are differences in ontogenetic development between different enzymes, easily recognisable 'clusters' have yet to be identified in all cases, and even the existence of specific 'clusters' may depend on species.

Nevertheless, many studies have demonstrated the production of reactive metabolites by animal and human fetal tissues and in some cases this production has been shown to result in biological consequences; for example, mutagenesis in bacteria. In almost all cases direct proof is lacking but indirect evidence strongly suggests that fetotoxic, teratogenic and carcinogenic effects of some polycyclic aromatic hydrocarbons and nitrosamines are due to the formation of reactive intermediates.

The metabolism of most substances is catalysed by many different enzymes which may be under different temporal regulation. Consequently, it will not be easy to predict the metabolic fate of a given compound at a given age. Furthermore, the balance between different enzymes can be perturbed at any age by numerous factors: induction, inhibition, disease, and so on. The elucidation of these complex interplays between chemical substances and development is bound to be a formidable task, but it is also a very important one, because permanent interference with early development by chemicals may lead to extreme human suffering, as illustrated by the thalidomide tragedy.

Acknowledgement

The secretarial assistance of Leena Pyykkö is gratefully acknowledged.

References

Ackerman, E. and Richter, K. (1977) *Eur. J. Clin. Pharmacol., 11*, 43-9
Aldridge, A., Aranda, J.V. and Neims, A.H. (1979) *Clin. Pharmacol. Ther., 25*, 447-53
Arvela, P., Kärki, N.T. and Pelkonen, O. (1976) *Experientia, 32*, 1311-13
Atlas, S.A., Boobis, A.R., Felton, J.S., Thorgeirsson, S.S. and Nebert, D.W. (1977) *J. Biol. Chem. 252*, 4712-21
Bell, J.U., Hansell, M.M. and Ecobichon, D.J. (1975) *Can. J. Physiol. Pharmacol., 53*, 1147-57
Bend, J.R., James, M.O., Devereux, T.R. and Fouts, J.R. (1975) in *Basic and Therapeutic Aspects of Perinatal Pharmacology* (Morselli, P.L., Garattini, S. and Sereni, F., eds.), pp. 229-43, Raven Press, New York
Berry, D.L., Slaga, T.J., Wilson, N.M., Zachariah, P.K., Namkung, M.J., Bracken, W.M. and Juchau, M.R. (1977) *Biochem. Pharmacol., 26*, 1383-8
Berry, D.L., Zachariah, P.K., Namkung, M.J. and Juchau, M.R. (1976) *Toxicol. Appl. Pharmacol., 36*, 569-84
Berry, D.L., Zachariah, P.K., Slaga, T.J. and Juchau, M.R. (1977) *Europ. J. Cancer, 13*, 667-75
Blake, D.A., Martz, F., Failinger, III, C. and Gery-Martz, A.M. (1978) in *Carcinogenesis* (Jones, P.W. and Freudenthal, R.I., eds.), Vol. 3, pp. 401-11, Raven Press, New York
Bresnick, E., Chuang, A.H.L. and Bornstein, W.A. (1979) *Chem.-Biol. Interact., 24*, 111-15
Cresteil, T., Flinois, J.P., Pfister, A. and Leroux, J.P. (1979) *Biochem. Pharmacol., 28*, 2057-63
Druckrey, H. (1973) *Xenobiotica, 3*, 271-303
Ecobichon, D.J., Dykeman, R.W. and Hansell, M.M. (1978) *Can. J. Biochem., 56*, 738-45
Egger, H. -J., Wittfoht, W. and Nau, H. (1978) in *Role of Pharmacokinetics in Prenatal and Perinatal Toxicology* (Neubert, D., Merker, H. -J., Nau, H. and Langman, J., eds.), pp. 109-21, Georg Thieme, Stuttgart
Gillette, J.R. and Stripp, B. (1975) *Fed. Proc. Fed. Am. Soc. Exp. Biol., 34*, 172-8
Gillette, J.R., Menard, R.H. and Stripp, B. (1973) *Clin. Pharmacol. 14*, 680-92

Greengard, O. (1977) *Pediatr. Res. 11*, 669-76
Guenthner, T.M. and Mannering, G.J. (1977) *Biochem. Pharmacol., 26*, 567-75
Guenthner, T.M. and Nebert, D.W. (1978) *Eur. J. Biochem., 91*, 449-56
Hart, J. and Timbrell, J.A. (1979) *Biochem. Pharmacol., 28*, 3015-17
Henderson, P.T. (1978) *Gen. Pharmac., 9*, 59-63
Horning, M.G., Butler, C.M. and Hill, R.M. (1975) *Life Sci., 16*, 651-72
Ivankovic, S., Schmähl, D. and Zeller, W.J. (1974) *Gewebe. Z. Krebsforsch., 81*, 269-72
Jollow, D.J., Kocsis, J.J., Snyder, R. and Vainio, H. (eds.) (1977) *Biological Intermediates*, Plenum Press, New York
Jones, A.H., Fantel, A.G., Kocan, R.A. and Juchau, M.R. (1977) *Life Sci., 21*, 1831-6
Juchau, M.R. (1980) *Pharmac. Ther., 8*, 501-24
Juchau, M.R., DiGiovanni, J., Namkung, M.J. and Jones, A.H. (1979) *Toxicol. Appl. Pharmacol., 49*, 171-8
Juchau, M.R., Namkung, M.J., Berry, D.L. and Zachariah, P.K. (1975) *Drug Metab. Disp., 3*, 494-502
Kitada, M. and Kamataki, T. (1979) *Biochem. Pharmacol., 28*, 793-7
Klinger, W., Mueller, D. and Kleeberg, U. (1979) in *The Induction of Drug Metabolism* (Estabrook, R.W. and Lindenlaub, E., eds.), pp. 517-44, Schattauer Verlag, Stuttgart
Kuenzig, W., Kamm, J.J., Boublik, M., Jenkins, F. and Burns, J.J. (1974) *J. Pharmacol. Exp. Ther., 191*, 32-44
Lambert, G.H. and Nebert, D.W. (1977) *Teratology, 16*, 147-54
Mirkin, B.L. (1970) *Ann. Rev. Pharmacol., 10*, 255-72
Mitchell, J.R., Reid, W.D., Christie, B., Moskowitz, J., Krishna, G. and Brodie, B.B. (1971) *Res. Commun. Chem. Pathol. Pharmacol., 2*, 877-88
Namkung, M.J., Zachariah, P.K. and Juchau, M.R. (1977) *Drug Metab. Disp. 5*, 288-94
Napalkov, N.P. (1973) in *Transplacental Carcinogenesis* (Tomatis, L. and Mohr, U., eds.), pp. 1-13, IARC, Lyon
Nau, H. and Liddiard, C. (1978) in *Role of Pharmacokinetics in Prenatal and Perinatal Toxicology* (Neubert, D., Merker, H. -J., Nau, H. and Langman, J., eds.), pp. 77-90, Georg Thieme, Stuttgart
Nau, H. and Nebert, D. (1978) in *Role of Pharmacokinetics in Prenatal and Perinatal Toxicology* (Neubert, D., Merker, H. -J., Nau, H. and Langman, J., eds.), pp. 13-44, Georg Thieme, Stuttgart
Nau, H., Liddiard, C., Egger, H. -J., and Wittfoht, W. (1978a) in *Advances in Pharmacology and Therapeutics* (Olive, G., ed.), Vol. 8, Pergamon Press, Oxford
Nebert, D.W., Levitt, R.C. and Pelkonen, O. (1979) in *Carcinogens: Identification and Mechanisms of Action* (Griffin, A.D. and Shaw, C.R., eds.), pp. 157-85, Raven Press, New York
Neims, A.H., Warner, M., Loughnan, P.M. and Aranda, J.V. (1976) *Ann. Rev. Pharmacol. Toxicol., 16*, 427-45
Neubert, D. and Tapken, S. (1978) in *Role of Pharmacokinetics in Prenatal and Perinatal Toxicology* (Neubert, D., Merker, H. -J., Nau, H. and Langman, J., eds.), pp. 69-76, Georg Thieme, Stuttgart
Neubert, D., Merker, H. -J., Nau, H. and Langman, J. (eds.) (1978) *Role of Pharmacokinetics in Prenatal and Perinatal Toxicology*, Georg Thieme, Stuttgart
Norman, R.L., Johnson, E.F. and Müller-Eberhard, U. (1978) *J. Biol. Chem., 253*, 8640-7
Nunnink, J.C., Chuang, A.H.L. and Bresnick, E. (1978) *Chem. -Biol. Interact., 22*, 225-30
Oesch, F. (1975) *FEBS Lett., 53*, 205-10
Pelkonen, O. (1973) *Studies on Drug Metabolizing Enzymes in the Human Fetus*. Academic thesis, The University of Oulu, Oulu
—— (1977a) *Acta Pharmacol. Toxicol., 41*, 306-16
—— (1977b) in *Progress in Drug Metabolism* (Bridges, J.W. and Chasseaud, L.F., eds.), Vol. 2, pp. 119-61, Wiley, London
—— (1977c) in *Biological Reactive Intermediates* (Jollow, D.J., Kocsis, J.J., Snyder, R. and Vainio, H., eds.), pp. 148-59, Plenum, New York
—— (1980a) in *Concepts in Drug Metabolism* (Jenner, P. and Testa, B., eds.), pp. 285-309, Marcel Dekker, New York
—— (1980b) *Eur. J. Clin. Pharmacol., 18*, 17-24
—— (1980c) *Pharmacol. Ther., 10*, 261-81
Pelkonen, O. and Kärki, N.T. (1975) *Biochem. Pharmacol., 24*, 1445-6

Pelkonen, O., Boobis, A.R. and Nebert, D.W. (1978) in *Carcinogenesis — A Comprehensive Survey* (Jones, P.W. and Freudenthal, R.I., eds.), Vol. 3, pp. 383-400, Raven Press, New York

Pelkonen, O., Kaltiala, E.H., Larmi, T.K.I. and Kärki, N.T. (1973) *Clin. Pharmacol. Ther., 14,* 840-6

Poland, A. and Glover, E. (1980) *Molec. Pharmacol., 17,* 86-94

Rane, A. and Ackermann, E. (1972) *Clin. Pharmacol. Ther., 13,* 663-70

Rane, A., Bergren, M., Yaffe, S. and Ericsson, J.L.E. (1973) *Xenobiotica, 3,* 37-48

Recknagel, R.O. and Glende, E.A. (1973) *CRC Crit. Rev. Toxicol., 2,* 263-97

Renton, K.W., Aranda, J.V. and Eade, N.R. (1976) *Can. J. Physiol. Pharmacol., 54,* 116-22

Rollins, D.E., von Bahr, C., Glaumann, H., Moldéus, P. and Rane, A. (1979) *Science, 205,* 1414-16

Schlede, E. and Merker, H. -J. (1974) *Arch. Pharmacol., 282,* 59-73

Sehgal, C.B. and Hutton, J.J. (1977) *Mutat. Res., 46,* 325-44

Short, C.R. and Davis, L.E. (1970) *J. Pharmacol. Exp. Ther., 174,* 185-96

Short, C.R., Kinden, D.A. and Stith, R. (1976) *Drug Metab. Rev., 5,* 1-42

Shum, S., Jensen, N.M. and Nebert, D.W. (1979) *Teratology, 20,* 365-76

Testa, V.B. and Jenner, P. (1976) in *Drug Metabolism: Chemical and Biochemical Aspects,* Marcel Dekker, New York

Thorgeirsson, S.S. (1972) in *Mechanism of Hepatic Drug Oxidation and Its Relationship to Individual Differences in Rates of Oxidation in Man,* PhD Thesis, University of London

Thorgeirsson, S.S. and Nebert, D.W. (1977) *Adv. Cancer Res., 25,* 149-93

Waddell, W.J. and Marlowe, G.C. (1976) in *Perinatal Pharmacology and Therapeutics* (Mirkin, B., ed.), pp. 119-268, Academic Press, New York

Wang, I.Y., Rasmussen, R.E. and Crocker, T.T. (1974) *Life Sci., 15,* 1291-1300

Williams, R.T., Schumacher, H., Tabro, S. and Smith, R.L. (1965) in *Embryopathic Activity of Drugs* (Robson, J.M., Sullivan, F.M. and Smith, R.L., eds.), pp. 167-82, J. and A. Churchill, London

Wills, E.D. (1969) *Biochem. J., 113,* 315-24

Wishart, G.J. and Dutton, G.J. (1978) in *Role of Pharmacokinetics in Prenatal and Perinatal Toxicology* (Neubert, D., Merker, H. -J., Nau, H. and Langman, J., eds.), pp. 215-24, Georg Thieme, Stuttgart

Yaffe, S.J. and Juchau, M.R. (1974) *Ann. Rev. Pharmacol., 14,* 219-38

CHAPTER SEVEN

THE ROLE OF THE PLACENTA IN DEVELOPMENTAL TOXICOLOGY
Mont R. Juchau

CONTENTS

I. Introduction

Recent years have witnessed a steadily increasing interest in the placenta as a determining factor in the toxicological effects of various chemicals on the developing conceptus. A major reason for this increased interest has been the recognition that various drugs (e.g. thalidomide, methotrexate, diethylstilboestrol, ethanol, androgens, etc.) are capable of eliciting deleterious effects on the offspring of mothers exposed to doses within the ranges regularly used in medical practice. In addition, it has been recognised that a number of fairly common chemical contaminants in the environment (e.g. polyhalogenated biphenyls, methyl mercury, cigarette smoke, dioxins, etc.) likewise appear to be harmful to human embryos and fetuses. This recognition has also been a major factor in the increased attention to placental toxicology.

An element not often considered in placental toxicology is the differential response of pregnant and non-pregnant females to toxic results. During pregnancy, the placenta synthesises substances that may interact with toxic chemicals to produce greater, lesser or unexpected untoward reactions. The most obvious example is the high rate of synthesis of progestins and oestrogens by human placental enzyme systems coupled with the inhibitory effects of these hormonal steroids and their metabolites on hepatic drug-metabolising enzymes. Less often considered is the potential for placentally-synthesised oestrogens to act as tumour promoters or co-carcinogens after exposure to chemical carcinogenic initiating agents.

Considerations of the role of the placenta in developmental toxicology demand attention to at least four separate aspects of interactions of toxic chemicals with placental function. Firstly, the many and varied important physiological capacities of the placenta may be impaired to greater or lesser extents by toxicological insults, resulting in secondary damage to the conceptus, the maternal organism or both. As an example, an impaired capacity of the placenta to synthesise progesterone could result in a decreased ability to carry the conceptus to term.

Secondly, one must consider the physiological alterations in the female that occur as a result of the presence of a normally functioning placenta, the kinds of toxic effects that agents may produce as a result of such alterations and the interactive effects of the products of placental syntheses and toxic chemicals.

Thirdly, it is increasingly recognised that the placenta plays an important role as a determinant of the accessibility of chemicals to the developing embryo/fetus. Both anatomical (e.g. vascular) and biochemical aspects require consideration in this regard. A recent example of the importance of biochemical considerations has been provided by studies published by Levitz *et al.* (1978) who showed that the biotransformation of corticosteroids in placental tissues was sufficiently rapid to constitute a significant 'metabolic barrier' in the transfer of steroids to the fetus.

Fourthly, the acknowledged, extensive biochemical capabilities of the placenta raise the possibility that placental enzymes may be capable of converting exogenous or endogenous chemicals to reactive intermediates that could be harmful to the developing embryo or fetus or possibly even to the maternal organism. Little documentation for the biological significance of this last consideration is currently available, but investigations of this possibility have only just begun. This chapter will deal briefly with considerations of these four aspects of potential interactions of toxic chemicals with placental functions. Because of the burgeoning literature on these topics, however, considerations of each of the four aspects will be limited to a few recent and pertinent examples.

II. Effects of Toxic Agents on Placental Functions

Placental functions are divisible into two categories — those that are essential for the continued existence of placental cells (and are common to virtually all mammalian cells) and those that may be regarded as 'specialised' functions of placental tissues. With regard to the first category, we may expect as a first approximation that toxic agents would exert the same effects on placental cells as on other cells in the body, e.g.

the effects of cyanide on cytochrome oxidase in placental cells probably would not differ significantly from its effects in hepatic or renal cells. However, to what extent this generalization may be extended is presently uncertain, since dispositional factors conceivably could play a definitive role depending upon the agent under consideration. Also, subtle differences may exist even where cellular functions appear identical in cells of various tissues. Furthermore, even though certain toxic effects may be virtually identical at the cellular or subcellular level — the effects on placental tissues could be much more (or less) biologically significant because of the importance of the affected parameter to gestation-related functions and to the unborn individual.

Recognition of the specialised functions of the placenta and of the effects of toxic chemicals upon those functions represents a topic of much greater interest currently. Most tabulations of specialised placental functions would probably include the following:

(1) Synthesis of oestrogens.
(2) Synthesis of progesterone.
(3) Synthesis of human chorionic gonadotropin (HCG).
(4) Synthesis of human placental prolactin (HPL), also referred to as human chorionic somatomammotropin (HCS) and chorionic growth hormone.
(5) Active transport of various nutrients.
(6) Facilitated diffusion of various nutrients and gases.
(7) Glycogen synthesis, storage and breakdown.

Studies reported in the literature during the past few years have greatly illuminated the mechanisms by which placental cells synthesise oestrogenic substances, although much remains to be elucidated. Upon finding cytochrome P450 associated with placental microsomes, Meigs and Ryan (1968) originally postulated that placental microsomal P450 functioned in the conversion of endogenous androgens to oestrogens. However, upon finding that carbon monoxide did not inhibit the conversion of androstenedione to oestrone (Meigs and Ryan, 1971), even under conditions of limiting oxygen concentrations and *excess* NADPH, these investigators concluded that P450 was not involved in the aromatisation reaction. In 1973, Symms and Juchau (1973) and Thompson and Siiteri (1973) reported that androgenic substances bound human placental microsomal cytochrome P450 with a high degree of specificity. Again it was suggested that placental cytochrome P450 catalysed oestrogen biosynthesis even though the lack of inhibition by carbon monoxide remained unexplained. (An attempt to explain lack of inhibition in terms of occurrence of a rate-limiting step before formation of the oxygenated intermediate (Thompson and Siiteri, 1973, 1974) was clearly untenable because restriction of O_2 tensions could be made to limit the reaction rate and CO did not inhibit the reaction under those conditions.) Furthermore, it was still uncertain as to whether the cytochrome P450 detected in placental microsomal fractions represented a mitochondrial contaminant or was a bona fide component of the endoplasmic reticulum of placental cells.

An additional reservation was provided by observations (Juchau, 1971; Meigs and Ryan, 1971) that carbon monoxide would effectively inhibit the monoxygenation of foreign organic compounds such as benzo (*a*)-pyrene and 19-norn-steroids. Thus, evidence from studies with the classical inhibitor of P450-dependent monoxygenation reactions, CO, suggested that the microsomal cytochrome functioned in the biotransformation of foreign organic chemicals, whereas evidence from studies of substrate binding suggested that its function was catalysis of the conversion of endogenous androgens to oestrogens. Several lines of evidence strongly suggested that the two functions were not mediated by the same cytochrome (Zachariah and Juchau, 1977). The question of association with membranes of the endoplasmic reticulum was resolved when it was shown that placental cytochrome P450 was present both in the mitochondria and endoplasmic reticulum (Juchau *et al.*, 1974). The question of participation of placental P450 in the conversion of androstenedione to oestrone was resolved in a series of experiments in which it was first shown that androstenedione, 19-hydroxyandrostenedione and 19-oxoandrostenedione each could displace bound carbon monoxide and other haem-binding ligands from the microsomal cytochrome (Juchau and Zachariah, 1975; Zachariah and Juchau, 1975; Hodgson and Juchau, 1977). Various 19-nor-steroids, (e.g. 19-nortestosterone, 19-norandrostenedione) the aromatisation of which are inhibited by carbon monoxide, not only did not displace carbon monoxide from binding but facilitated its binding to the microsomal cytochrome (Juchau *et al.*, 1976a). This facilitation of CO binding by 19-nor-steroids provided the final piece in the puzzle of the involvement of cytochrome P450 in placental oestrogen synthesis when it was shown that CO would inhibit the aromatisation of androstenedione in the presence of 19-nor-steroids (Lee *et al.*, 1975) and that the reversal of inhibition by CO with monochromatic light was optimal at a wavelength of 450 nm (Zachariah and Juchau, 1977). The latter observation is generally regarded as the requisite definitive proof for cytochrome P450 participation in any mixed-function oxygenation reaction.

From the studies cited above, some of the characteristics of the aromatising cytochrome are already known. It binds substrates with a very high specificity; androstenedione exhibits an apparent dissociation constant of approximately $10^{-9} - 10^{-10}$ mol/l in intact microsomes, wheras testosterone binds with an apparent affinity that is 2–3 orders of magnitude lower than that of androstenedione. The binding of most foreign organic chemicals, with the exception of close structural relatives of androstenedione, cannot be demonstrated with conventional difference spectroscopy. Contrastingly, androstenedione elicits extremely intense binding spectra. Cytochrome P450 concentrations in placental tissues is 1–2 orders of magnitude lower than the total concentrations of P450 cytochromes in hepatic tissues. It is not inducible by methylcholanthrene- or phenobarbital-type inducing agents but its concentration can be increased with dibutyryl cyclic AMP (Bellino and Hussa, 1978). The cytochrome thus far has resisted attempts at purification (Symms and Juchau, 1973; Thompson and Siiteri, 1976; Bellino and Osawa, 1978; Bellino, 1980; Osawa and Higashiyama, 1980) although solubilisation, partial purification and reconstitution have been accomplished. Experiments with androstenedione and 19-norandrostenedione, demonstrating their respective capacities to inhibit and facilitate the binding of CO to human placental microsomal cytochrome P450, have also indicated that the cytochrome that functions in the aromatisation of androgens is the only spectrally observable microsomal cytochrome in the placenta. This may provide an exceptional challenge for investigations attempting to purify placental microsomal P450, since several lines of evidence suggest strongly that multiple P450 species exist in human placental microsomes (Juchau, 1980a, b). Nevertheless, further understanding of oestrogen biosynthesis in placental (or other) tissues appears to depend in large measure upon the successful isolation and purification of the components of the aromatase system. With further understanding, one may expect a fuller comprehension of the mechanisms by which toxic chemicals may affect the system and, hopefully, allow an assessment of which effects may be important clinically.

The human placenta at term can synthesise in excess of 300mg of progesterone daily (Pearlman, 1957; Lin *et al.*, 1972), yet the factors which control the rate of synthesis are not well understood. In contrast to oestrogen biosynthesis, the synthesis of progesterone from cholesterol occurs in the mitochondria. Hydroxylations at carbons 20 and 22 followed by cleavage (cholesterol side-chain cleavage) between the two carbons represent the important, rate-limiting steps in the reaction sequence which leads first to pregnenolone formation. Evidence to date indicates that cholesterol side-chain cleavage in the human placenta requires mitochondrial cytochrome P450, an NADPH-dependent flavoprotein and an iron–sulphur protein (Mason and Boyd, 1971) analogous to the side-chain cleavage system in adrenal cortex mitochondria. In the adrenals, the action of ACTH results in the conversion of $P450_{SCC}$ to a high-spin state (perhaps as the result of facilitated binding of substrate to the cytochrome) and thereby renders the cytochrome more readily reducible by electrons coming through the electron transport chain. Whether or not progesterone synthesis in the placenta is driven by a tropic stimulus such as placental HCG is not firmly established at present. Simpson and Miller (1978) have proposed that the placental mitochondrial cholesterol side-chain cleavage system may be under tonic–tropic stimulation and that the rate of progesterone biosynthesis in the placenta may be determined by the rate of uptake of maternal plasma lipoproteins (principal source of cholesterol) by the trophoblast. An interesting observation regarding the control of progesterone synthesis was made by Simpson and Miller (1978). Addition of either $100\mu mol/l$ cholesterol or $1 mmol/l$ calcium chloride to rat adrenal cortex mitochondria resulted in a modest stimulation of pregnenolone formation. Addition of both together caused a very large stimulation. Addition of cholesterol to human placental mitochondria caused a slight increase in pregnenolone formation but addition of calcium alone or together with cholesterol produced no further increase. The reason for the difference in behaviour between adrenal and placental mitochondria was not apparent but again indicated differing modes of regulation for the two systems. It will indeed be interesting to ascertain the mechanism (or mechanisms) that accounts for the difference between the adrenal and placental systems.

A number of drugs and chemicals are known to be capable of influencing rates of progesterone synthesis. Various cholesterol analogues are known to inhibit the side-chain cleavage system (Kobayashi and Ichii, 1969). The most potent of these analogues appears to be 22-azacholesterol (Counsell *et al.*, 1971), suggesting that hydroxylation at carbon 22 is rate limiting for the reaction sequence. Carbon monoxide inhibits the reaction by virtue of its interaction with cytochrome P450 at the haem site. Aminoglutethimide is one of the most widely known inhibitors of this reaction but side effects, including virilism and sexual precocity (Telegdy, 1973), suggest that inhibition of the aromatase system may be of greater importance *in vivo*. The placental synthesising system probably is not inducible by phenobarbital and may be somewhat repressed after chronic exposure to polycyclic aromatic hydrocarbons (Juchau *et al.*, 1972, 1974). As with oestrogens, the possibilities for modulation of rates of progesterone synthesis by toxic chemicals are numerous but much remains to be learned in this area. In view of the extreme importance of placentally synthesised progesterone for optimal maintenance of pregnancy and the increasing exposure of pregnant women to toxic substances, systematic investigations would seem to be merited.

At present, few positive statements can be made on the effects of noxious substances on other placental functions, because to my knowledge no systematic investigations have been undertaken. It would seem that it is time to begin.

A review of articles written on aspects of placental function and published in 1978 and 1979 revealed that, with the exception of articles dealing with effects of chemical agents on blood flow through the placenta (by no means unimportant), virtually no original research was published on the effects of drugs and other exogenous agents on the placenta and its specialised functions.

III. Interactions of Toxic Substances with Products of Placental Metabolism: Effects on the Maternal Organism

The human placenta produces large quantities of oestrogens and progesterone, particularly during the latter part of gestation. These substances and some of their metabolites are relatively potent competitive inhibitors of the cytochrome P450-dependent mono-oxygenases that function in the oxidative degradation of foreign organic chemicals (Soyka and Deckert, 1974; Feuer *et al.*, 1977; Kramer *et al.*, 1978) and are therefore prime candidates for placental-mediated, pregnancy-specific toxicological responses of the maternal organism to chemicals. Growth hormone (STH) also is capable of reducing rates of hepatic drug-metabolising reactions (Wilson, 1973; Kramer *et al.*, 1978) and, in view of the similarities of STH to HPL, HPL has also been implicated as a possible potentiator of drug effects during pregnancy. Of interest in this regard is the recent report indicating that human prolactin passes through human placental membranes at extremely slow or negligible rates (Schenker *et al.*, 1979).

At present, other products of placental metabolism appear not to have been implicated in adverse responses to toxic chemicals. It should be emphasised, however, that this lack of incrimination is not due to results obtained from extensive investigations. In addition, interactions with xenobiotic biotransforming systems represent only one of many possible modes of modification of toxic effects by products of placental metabolism, yet appears to be the only mode to have attracted much attention to date.

Studies *in vitro* indicate that, when expressed in units of hepatic microsomal protein or wet weight of hepatic tissue, rates of monooxygenation of most foreign organic chemicals are slightly to moderately decreased during pregnancy (Feuer, 1979). However, the increase in liver size that accompanies pregnancy is thought by many investigators to offset decreased rates of drug oxidation. Rates of glucuronidation, likewise, appear to decrease during pregnancy (when rates are expressed per unit of tissue weight) but are also probably offset by the increased mass of hepatic tissue. In pharmacokinetic studies in human patients, Morgan *et al.* (1977, 1978) found little or no differences in total clearances of flow-limited drugs (pethidine and etidocaine) during pregnancy. Moore and McBride (1978) obtained similar results in studies with diazepam. Kuhnert *et al.* (1979) reported that the clearance of meperidine from plasma did not appear to be altered significantly by pregnancy. However, Eadie *et al.* (1977) obtained results suggesting that the biotransformation of phenytoin and other anticonvulsants increases markedly during pregnancy but decreases again at the puerperium. By contrast, other earlier studies provided evidence for a net decrease in the overall rates of metabolism during pregnancy (Crawford and Rudofsky, 1966; Neale and Parke, 1973; Devereux and Fouts, 1975; Feuer and Kardish, 1975; Guenther and Mannering, 1977). Data obtained from studies in experimental animals suggested that decreases in mixed-function oxygenase activities during pregnancy were observable primarily during the latter stages of gestation but that such decreases appeared to result from decreased levels of enzymes rather than inhibition by increased circulating oestrogens and progestins, since V_{max} values were lower and no significant changes in K_m values could be observed (Guarino *et al.*, 1969).

Studies by Schlede and Borowski (1974) and by Guenther and Mannering (1977) indicated that pregnant rats were less susceptible to induction of hepatic cytochrome P450-dependent enzyme systems by phenobarbital (but not 3-methylcholanthrene) than non-pregnant females. Likewise, Vaisman *et al.* (1976) reported that administration of phenobarbital stimulated a smaller increase in UDP-glucuronyl transferase in late gestation than it did in early gestation or in the non-pregnant female rat. The progressive decrease in response to the inducing properties of phenobarbital could be due to any of several possibilities; nevertheless, it serves to illustrate how metabolism and enzyme induction can be altered by pregnancy.

A general survey of the literature on this topic leaves the impression that overall rates of xenobiotic biotransformation may be slightly decreased during late pregnancy but that such decreases may be of little pharmacokinetic consequence *in vivo*. The effects of pregnancy on bioactivation of chemicals, however, has not been investigated rigorously and appears to represent an important future research area.

Other modes of possible (largely undocumented) interactions are numerous indeed. One need only consider the multiple biological effects produced by oestrogens and progestins and the ways in which such effects could ameliorate or exacerbate the effects of noxious chemicals.

IV. Role of the Placenta in Transplacental Movement of Toxic Chemicals

This topic has been reviewed on numerous occasions; a recent, thorough review has been provided by Waddell and Marlowe (1981). Therefore only a summary of the pertinent information will be provided here. Chemicals are known to pass across membranes via five processes: simple diffusion, filtration, facilitated diffusion, active transport and pinocytosis. For most foreign toxic substances, simple diffusion represents the primary process for passage across biological membranes, including those of the placenta. Highly water soluble compounds traverse placental membranes with considerably less facility than lipid-soluble, unionized chemicals. Filtration appears to be important only for very small molecules, at least until the later stages of gestation. In general, the placenta behaves like a lipid membrane towards foreign toxic chemicals; most of these substances pass from the maternal to fetal circulation in accordance with their concentration gradient, lipid solubility and degree of ionization. Other factors that can play a significant role in individual cases, however, include: differential binding of chemicals to proteins (or other macromolecules) present in maternal plasma, fetal plasma or the placental tissue *per se*; molecular weight and size; and active transport or facilitated diffusion for molecules with chemical structures closely similar to nutrient chemicals that undergo these same processes. Certain drugs may also cross by pinocytosis; this would normally be of physiological importance only for the transfer of macromolecules with potent biological actions. Finally, it is increasingly evident that the question as to whether placental cells may biotransform toxic substances during transplacental passage is one that needs to be addressed. Again, it would appear that for the large majority of foreign organic chemicals, placental biotransformation would play only a minor role as a determinant of rates of transplacental transfer. This topic has been reviewed on numerous occasions by the author; the most recent reviews appeared in 1980 (Juchau, 1980a; Juchau, 1980b).

Many toxic chemicals, however, possess structures that are very similar to those of endogenous substrates for placental enzymes. For these, the likelihood that placental biotransformation could play a highly significant role in transfer rates is considerably greater. Evidence has been presented (Hensleigh *et al.*, 1975) that women with greatly increased serum testosterone concentrations will deliver female newborns without virilized external genitalia because the placenta protects the fetus from endogenous androgens through the highly efficient conversion to oestrogens. Thus, comparison of rates of placental biotransformation of clinically-utilised substances with androgenic or virilising activity would appear to be useful, even though such compounds would only rarely be taken by pregnant women. Levitz *et al.* (1978) showed that corticosteroids were metabolised so rapidly by placental tissues that the transfer of steroids from the maternal to fetal circulation was impeded and that the placenta, in this case at least, could be regarded as a 'metabolic barrier'. Again, studies on the placental biotransformation of synthetic corticosteroids would provide needed basic information for cases in which steroid administration during pregnancy is necessary or desirable (e.g., in conjuction with the respiratory distress syndrome). Indeed, some studies along these lines have already been reported in the literature (Blanford and Murphy, 1977; Levitz *et al.*, 1978).

Another example of the 'metabolic barrier' function of the placenta that may be cited pertains to the evidence for a role for placental catechol-*O*-methyl-transferase and monoamine oxidase in restricting the transfer to the fetus of catecholamines from the maternal circulation (Morgan *et al.*, 1972; Chen *et al.*, 1976; Burba, 1979). Furthermore, Gillette *et al.* (1973) calculated that the activities of enzymes that catalyse the mixed-function oxidation of desipramine and benzo (*a*) pyrene in human placentas and fetuses may be sufficiently high to produce decreased concentrations of these agents on the fetal side (as compared with the maternal side) at steady state.

According to Dawes (1973), the time-constant for fetal-maternal plasma drug equilibration is three times that which would be obtained if the fetal tissues were supplied directly by maternal blood. This calculation was based upon geometric considerations and would appear to apply only in an approximate fashion to drugs or other chemicals showing the following characteristics:

(1) Unionised at the pH of the exchange surfaces (approximately 7.4).
(2) A very high lipid/water partition coefficient in the unionised form.
(3) A molecular weight of less than 600.
(4) Not subject to active transport, facilitated diffusion or pinocytosis in either the maternal-to-fetal or fetal-to-maternal directions.
(5) Bind equivalently to macromolecular constituents of the maternal and fetal blood.
(6) Do not bind significantly to placental macromolecules.
(7) Are not subject to biotransformation or conjugation in placental tissues.

Each of the above characteristics is dependent upon the presence of placental tissues intervening between the maternal and fetal circulations. Although some toxic chemicals may display each of the above properties, many others do not, thus precluding generalisations on the transplacental movement of toxic chemicals.

A crucial question in fetal toxicity is not *whether* a potentially toxic chemical will 'cross the placenta' (regardless of the compound studied, a certain number of molecules will appear in the fetal blood-stream almost immediately after maternal administration and the 'appearance' will be limited only by the circulation time if the method for assaying the chemical is sufficiently sensitive) but at what *rate* will the transfer occur? Even only small and seemingly unimportant restrictions in placental transfer could mean the difference between potentially reversible (embryotoxic/ fetotoxic) and irreversible (teratogenic) effects of noxious chemicals.

In summary, a number of properties of placental tissues may serve to restrict (or in some cases facilitate) the transfer of drugs from the maternal to fetal circulations. These are:

(1) Physical separation of maternal and fetal circulations.
(2) Geometric aspects of the placental circulation.
(3) Physical presence of placental macromolecules.
(4) Filtration characteristics of placental membranes.
(5) Lipid-barrier function of placental membranes.
(6) Active transport, facilitated diffusion and pinocytotic functions of placental cells.
(7) Capacity of placental enzymes to catalyse the biotransformation/ conjugation of toxic chemicals.

V. Bioactivation in Placental Tissues

The placenta is increasingly recognised not simply as a relatively inert membrane system that serves to separate the fetal from the maternal circulation and mediate the transfer of nutrients and gases between the two, but rather as containing a rich variety of enzyme systems and as being extremely active metabolically. Research performed during the past decade has demonstrated amply that placental tissues also contain enzyme systems that attack foreign organic chemicals as substrates and this topic has been reviewed on numerous occasions as previously indicated. Initially, studies of this phenomenon were of interest because of the possible role of placental biotransformation in the regulation of transplacental drug movement. That, for certain cases, this role can be important has indeed been documented (Section IV). However, the weight of evidence soon favoured the view that, for most drugs and toxic chemicals, biotransformation in placental tissues would occur at sufficiently low rates to make little difference to rates of transplacental movement of foreign organic chemicals. In terms of the metabolic clearance of such chemicals from the maternal or fetal circulation, studies suggested that the placenta would also be quite inefficient for most agents. As studies of placental drug biotransformation progressed, however, it was striking that many of the foreign organic substances that acted as substrates for placental mono-oxygenase systems were promutagens and procarcinogens whose rates of metabolism were markedly increased by pre-exposure to environmental (methylcholanthrene-type) inducing agents. Examples are benzo-(a) pyrene and 3'-methyl-4-monomethylaminoazobenzene (Welch *et al.*, 1969), N-2-fluorenylacetamide (Juchau *et al.*, 1975), 3-methylcholanthrene (Guibbert *et al.*, 1972) and 7,12-dimethylbenz (a) anthracene (Juchau *et al.*, 1978a, b). For these reasons interest shifted from attention to pharmacokinetic considerations to the possibility that enzyme systems in human placental tissues might convert environmental chemicals to reactive intermediates.

This shift in interest paralleled a growing general effort in research pertaining to the biochemical generation of reactive intermediates. These intermediates are currently implicated in the aetiology of a very large number of pathological processes including cellular and tissue necrosis (Nelson *et al.*, 1977), allergic reactions, methaemoglobinaemia, porphyria, bone-marrow aplasia (Gillette *et al.*, 1974), somatic cell mutagenesis (Huberman and Sachs, 1976; Umeda and Saito, 1975) germ cell mutagenesis (Epstein *et al.*, 1972; Heinrichs and Juchau, 1980), carcinogenesis

(Heidelberger, 1975), atherogenesis (Bond *et al.*, 1979, 1980; Juchau *et al.*, 1979), teratogenesis (Manson and Smith, 1977; Fantel *et al.*, 1979), increased rates of ageing (Schwartz and Moore, 1979) and immuno-suppression (Brock and Hohorst, 1963; Brock *et al.*, 1973). These pathological effects show that the generation of reactive intermediates in the placenta has the potential to produce profound effects on the highly susceptible developing embryo or fetus.

Thus far, evidence for the placental generation of toxic metabolites rests on studies performed *in vitro* with tissue homogenates or homogenate subfractions. Earlier studies demonstrating that placental tissues contain mono-oxygenase systems that catalyse the mixed-function oxidation of various procarcinogens (listed above) already alert one to the possibility of bioactivation since it is now well established that cytochrome P450-mediated oxygenations of such substrates play a major role in their conversion to proximate and/or ultimate mutagens and carcinogens.

Most of the foreign organic procarcinogens and promutagens that act as substrates for placental mono-oxygenases are polynuclear aromatic hydrocarbons (PAH). Two reviews dealing specifically with the placental metabolism of these environmentally ubiquitous substances have appeared recently (Pelkonen *et al.*, 1979; Juchau *et al.*, 1981). Even though studies are not extensive, more information is available on the placental metabolism of PAH (particularly benzo (*a*) pyrene) than of any other foreign organic substrates for placental mono-oxygenases. Recently we have demonstrated that benzo (*e*) pyrene, chrysene, dibenz (*a,h*) anthracene and benz (*a*) anthracene are likewise substrates for placental mono-oxygenases and that placental mono-oxygenase systems that catalyse the hydroxylation of these chemicals appear to be the same or similar to those that catalyse the aromatic ring hydroxylations of benzo (*a*) pyrene, *N*-2-fluorenylacetamide or 7,12-dimethylbenz (*a*) anthracene (Juchau *et al.*, 1981). These mono-oxygenation reactions occur at particularly high rates in human placental tissues of cigarette smokers at full term or in placentas of experimental animals pretreated with methylcholanthrene-type inducing agents. The mono-oxygenase activities are low to negligible in human placental tissues obtained before the end of the first trimester of pregnancy (Juchau, 1971; Pelkonen *et al.*, 1972), even if the placental donor is a heavy smoker. This would seem to allay concern for possible teratogenic effects of PAH since the principal danger period for chemical teratogens is during the first trimester. Transplacental carcinogenesis, however, may be more important at later stages of gestation (Rice *et al.*, 1978; see also Kleihues, Chapter 8).

One cause for concern in terms of placental generation of reactive intermediates is that currently available information indicates that the activity of at least some of the placental enzymes that catalyse the conversion of reactive chemicals to inactive metabolites via glucuronidation, epoxide hydration, sulphation, etc. are very low or non-existent in placental tissues (Juchau, 1980a, b). Under such conditions, there would seem to be an increased likelihood that a toxic metabolite generated in the placenta via mono-oxygenation would be translocated subsequently to sensitive fetal tissues. Lack of extensive investigations on placental deactivating enzymes, however, precludes any broad generalisations at present. Also, whether activation or deactivation predominates in any given tissue depends upon a host of factors including the specific substrate attacked, specific metabolic products formed, rates of subsequent degradation of generated reactive metabolites and relative rates of activation and deactivation. The half-life of the reactive species at the site of action is, of course, a most critical determinant of biological activity.

In addition to the several studies that have firmly established that placental tissues contain enzyme systems which catalyse the mono-oxygenation of promutagen/procarcinogens, recent studies have demonstrated more directly that such enzyme systems do, indeed, catalyse the conversion of PAH to reactive intermediates. Berry *et al.* (1977) reported that enzymes present in placental tissues catalysed the conversion of benzo (*a*) pyrene to metabolites that bound covalently to DNA. The placenta with the highest aryl hydrocarbon hydroxylase activity likewise showed the greatest capacity to catalyse covalent binding to DNA. This implied that exposure to environmental inducing agents of the type present in cigarette smoke would increase the bioactivation/deactivation ratio for benzo (*a*) pyrene. Further evidence for this suggestion was provided in a series of experiments with *Salmonella typhimurium* auxotrophs. Jones *et al.* (1977) and Juchau *et al.* (1978a, b) demonstrated that microsomal fractions isolated from human placental tissues with high aryl hydrocarbon hydroxylase activity would catalyse the conversion of benzo-(*a*) pyrene, 7,12-dimethylbenz (*a*) anthracene and *N*-2-fluorenylacetamide to oxidised intermediates capable of reverting the bacteria to prototrophy. Tester strains TA-98, TA-100 and TA-1538 were used in the experiments; strain TA-98 appeared to be the most susceptible to placentally catalysed conversion of PAH to mutagenic intermediates. Placentas from five nonsmokers (each of which showed very low or negligible aryl hydrocarbon hydroxylase activity) displayed no capacity to catalyse conversion of PAH to mutagens. Again, the placental tissues with the highest mono-oxygenase activities likewise showed the greatest capacity to catalyse the bioactivating reactions (mutagenesis).

Several laboratories (Pelkonen and Kärki, 1975; Wang *et al.*, 1977; Vaught *et al.*, 1979) including our own (Juchau *et al.*, 1976b; Berry *et al.*, 1977; Juchau *et al.*, 1978a, b) investigated the biotransformation of benzo (*a*) pyrene in microsomal fractions of human placental homogenates with methods that could separate several of the organic-phase-soluble metabolites into phenolic, quinone and diol fractions. High-pressure liquid chromatography and thin-layer chromatography were used to separate the metabolites. In our studies, the results indicated that considerable quantities of phenolic metabolites were formed in placentas obtained from smokers but that only very small quantities of dihydrodiols were formed in experiments with the same placental tissue, even though readily detectable quantities of diols were generated in flasks containing rat-liver microsomes as the source of enzymes.

However, other investigators had obtained contrasting results indicating that placental mono-oxygenases/epoxide hydratases catalysed the formation of very substantial quantities of diols, including the important 7, 8-diol. Since the 7, 8-diol has been implicated very heavily as a proximate mutagen/carcinogen by numerous investigators during the past decade, we investigated the source of the apparent discrepancy (Namkung and Juchau, 1980). The investigation showed that the use of high substrate concentrations in reaction vessels resulted in concentration-dependent increases in ratios of phenols/diols formed in reaction flasks. Since we had used very high substrate concentrations (200 μmol/l) in our previous experiments to assure attainment of $V_{\max}$ for the formation of phenols, quantities of diols appearing in the metabolite profiles were minimal. Other investgators had used much lower substrate concentrations (2.7–63 μmol/l), thus accounting for the appearance of relatively high quantities of diols in their profiles. The observations were interesting but, more importantly, pointed out the likelihood that comparatively high concentrations of a proximate mutagen/carcinogen could be generated from the ubiquitous benzo (*a*)-pyrene in placentas of women who smoke. Since this metabolite is comparatively stable, it could be carried in the umbilical circulation to fetal tissues. Cytochrome P450-dependent and arachidonate-dependent (cyclooxygenase) systems could then convert the diol to the highly reactive diolepoxide in fetal tissues.

Most recently, studies of the conversion of oestrogens to catechol oestrogens in placental tissues have attracted attention. Earlier studies on hepatic tissues had demonstrated that the conversion of oestrogens to catechol oestrogens was a cytochrome P450-dependent reaction (Sasame *et al.*, 1977; Paul *et al.*, 1977; Nelson *et al.*, 1976; Numazawa *et al.*, 1979) and also that human placental tissues contained the necessary enzymes for catalysis of the aromatic hydroxylation of oestrogens (Fishman and Dixon, 1967; Smith and Axelrod, 1969). It was therefore of interest to attempt to ascertain what interrelationships might exist between the placental catechol oestrogen-forming system and other placental cytochrome P450-dependent enzyme systems such as the aromatising system and placental aryl hydrocarbon hydroxylase. Heightened interest was provided by observations that catechol oestrogens are not inactive metabolites but possess potent biological and endocrine activities. Included in these activities are the capacity to decrease plasma concentrations of luteinising hormone (Parvizi and Ellendorff, 1975), strong inhibition of the *O*-methylation of catecholamines (Ball *et al.*, 1972), inhibition of lipid peroxidation and the *O*-demethylation of mestranol (Bolt and Kappus, 1976). In studies with rat hepatic microsomes, both natural and synthetic oestrogens are metabolised through catechol formation and bind to proteins (Helton and Goldzieher, 1977; Tsibris and McGuire, 1977). Tsibris and McGuire (1977) also proposed that the polycyclic aromatic hydrocarbon-inducible cytochrome P448 could catalyse the conversion of oestrogens to intermediate arene oxides that could bind covalently to nucleic acids and proteins. In view of the profound induction of placental aryl hydrocarbon hydroxylase by polycyclic aromatic hydrocarbons, this proposal assumes particular importance for the placental generation of reactive intermediates.

Studies in our laboratory (Chao and Juchau, 1980) demonstrated that oestrone, β-oestradiol and oestriol each interacted with human placental microsomal cytochrome P450 to produce the classical type I binding spectra. The maximal intensities of the spectral changes produced (as well as the apparent affinities of the oestrogens for the cytochrome) were extremely variable and in some placentas could not be detected at all. Attempts to correlate maximal intensities of steroid binding spectra to concentrations of the cytochrome as assessed by CO-difference spectra showed that the intensities of the spectra produced both by CO and β-oestradiol were highly correlated with intensities of androstenedione-binding spectra at saturating ligand concentrations. In general, β-oestradiol produced the most intense binding spectra of the oestrogens tested but androstenedione produced much more (approximately threefold) intense binding spectra than β-oestradiol and also showed a much higher apparent affinity for the cytochrome. Aryl hydrocarbon hydroxylase activities were not correlated with the intensities of difference spectra produced by androstenedione, β-oestradiol or CO. The capacity of oestrogens to bind to placental cytochrome P450 did not appear to be related to their effectiveness in inhibition of the aromatase reaction despite the correlated binding parameters.

To determine whether any relationships existed between placental aryl hydrocarbon hydroxylase and the placental catechol oestrogen-forming system, we examined the effects of a number of inducers and activators of the former system on the latter system (Omiecinski *et al.*, 1980a; Chao *et al.*, 1980). Inducers used in studies with experimental animals were 3-methylcholanthrene, Aroclor 1254 (a mixture of polychlorinated biphenyls with both methylcholanthrene-type and phenobarbital-type inducing properties) and phenobarbital. Activators studied were α-naphthoflavone and hematin, both of which activate aryl hydrocarbon hydroxylase. Hematin is particularly effective in extrahepatic tissues (Omiecinski *et al.*, 1978; Omiecinski *et al.*, 1980b; Omiecinski and Juchau, 1980a, b) including the placenta (Omiecinski *et al.*, 1980a). Initial results suggested that the same or very similar placental enzyme systems catalysed the aromatic hydroxylations of β-oestradiol and benzo (*a*) pyrene, since both were induced by methylcholanthrene (in rats) and Aroclor 1254 and both were activated by hematin. Human placentas obtained from smokers also exhibited enhanced catechol oestrogen formation, and this activity was well correlated ($r=0.946$) with hydroxylation of benzo (*a*) pyrene in the same human placentas. A closer analysis of this problem, however, revealed that a number of important differences could also be discerned. For example, phenobarbital pretreatment of pregnant rats resulted in increased catechol oestrogen formation but no change in benzo (*a*) pyrene hydroxylation. Also the effects of hematin addition were quantitatively dissimilar. It would appear, however, that certain similarities between the two systems do exist and determination of the extent of the similarities presents a highly interesting and challenging problem for future investigations.

VI. Summary and Conclusions

A consideration of the role of the placenta in developmental toxicology suggests that four aspects of placental function require consideration. These are:

(1) The effects of toxic chemicals on the important reproductive functions of the placenta.

(2) The interactions of toxic chemicals with the products of placental metabolism in terms of effects on maternal and fetal organisms.

(3) The capacity of the placenta to act as a regulator of the transfer of toxic chemicals from the maternal to fetal circulation.

(4) The capacity of placental enzyme systems to catalyse the generation of reactive toxic intermediates.

Clearly, except for the third aspect, investigations have so far been only superficial. It is equally clear that the potential for any given toxic chemical to produce temporary or permanent structural or functional damage to the developing embryo or fetus or to the maternal organism may be a function of any one or a combination of these aspects. Future studies of reproductive toxicology should focus upon these four considerations of placental function, each of which has been dealt with here in only a very cursory fashion. Hopefully, however, the discussion will serve to focus and direct future research in this highly important area.

Acknowledgements

I thank Fifi Durr, who typed the manuscript. Original research was supported by NICHD grant HD-04839.

References

Ball, P., Knuppen, R., Haupt, M. and Breuer, H. (1972) *J. Clin. Endocrinol., 34*, 736-42

Bellino, F.L. (1980) *Fed. Proc. Fed. Am. Soc. Exp. Biol., 39*, 2052

Bellino, F.L. and Hussa, R.O. (1978) *Biochem. Biophys. Res. Commun., 85*, 1588-95

Bellino, F.L. and Osawa, Y. (1978) *J. Steroid Biochem., 9*, 216-9

Berry, D.L., Zachariah, P.K., Slaga, T.J. and Juchau, M.R. (1977) *Europ. J. Cancer, 13*, 667-75

Blanford, A.T. and Murphy, B.E.P. (1977) *Am. J. Obstet. Gynecol., 127*, 264-70

Bolt, H.M. and Kappus, H. (1976) *J. Steroid Biochem., 7*, 311-18

Bond, J.A., Omiecinski, C.J. and Juchau, M.R. (1979) *Biochem. Pharmacol., 28*, 305-12

Bond, J.A., Yang, H.L., Majesky, M.W., Benditt, E.P. and Juchau, M.R. (1980) *Toxicol. Appl. Pharmacol., 52*, 323-35

Brock, N. and Hohorst, H.J. (1963) *Arzneimittel Forsch., 13*, 1021-31

Brock, N., Hoefer-Janker, H., Hohorst, H.J., Scheef, W., Schneider, B. and Wolf, H.C. (1973) *Arzneimittel Forsch., 23*, 1-14

Burba, J.V. (1979) *Can. J. Physiol. Pharmacol., 57*, 213-16

Chao, S.T. and Juchau, M.R. (1980) *J. Steroid Biochem., 13*, 127-33

Chao, S.T., Omiecinski, C.J., Namkung, M.J., Nelson, S.D., Dvorchik, B.H. and Juchau, M.R. (1981) *Develop. Pharmacol. Ther., 1*, (in press)

The Role of the Placenta In Developmental Toxicology

Chen, C.H., Klein, D.C. and Robinson, J.C. (1976) *J. Reprod. Fertil., 46*, 477-9
Counsell, R.E., Lu, M.C., Marsy, S.E. and Weinhold, P.A. (1971) *Biochem. Pharmacol., 20*, 2912-19
Crawford, J.S. and Rudofsky, S. (1966) *Br. J. Anaesthesiol., 38*, 446-51
Dawes, G.S. (1973) in *Fetal Pharmacology* (Boreus, L., ed.), pp. 381-400, Raven Press, New York
Devereux, T.R. and Fouts, J.R. (1975) *Drug Metab. Dispos. 3*, 254-8
Eadie, M.J., Lander, C.M. and Tyrer, H.H. (1977) *Clin. Pharmacokinet., 2*, 427-36
Epstein, S., Arnold, E., Andrea, J., Bass, W. and Bishop, Y. (1972) *Toxicol. Appl. Pharmacol., 23*, 288-325
Fantel, A.G., Greenaway, J.C., Juchau, M.R. and Shepard, T.H. (1979) *Life Sci., 25*, 67-72
Feuer, G. (1979) *Drug Metab. Rev., 9*, 147-69
Feuer, G. and Kardish, R. (1975) *Int. J. Clin. Pharmacol., 11*, 366-70
Feuer, G., Kardish, R. and Farkas, R. (1977) *Biochem. Pharmacol., 26*, 1495-9
Fishman, J. and Dixon, D. (1967) *Biochemistry, 6*, 1683-90
Gillette, J.R., Menard, R.H. and Stripp, B. (1973) *Clin. Pharmacol. Therap., 14*, 680-92
Gillette, J.R., Mitchell, J.R. and Brodie, B.B. (1974) *Ann. Rev. Pharmacol., 14*, 271-88
Guarino, A.M., Gram, T.E., Schroeder, D.H., Call, J.B. and Gillette, J.R. (1969) *J. Pharmacol. Exp. Therap., 168*, 224-8
Guenther, T.M. and Mannering, G.J. (1977) *Biochem. Pharmacol., 26*, 577-84
Guibbert, D., Duperray, B., Pacheco, H., Tomatis, L. and Turusov, V. (1972) *Therapie, XXVII*, 907-18
Heidelberger, C. (1975) *Ann. Rev. Biochem., 44*, 79-121
Heinrichs, W.L. and Juchau, M.R. (1980) in *Extrahepatic Metabolism of Drugs and Other Foreign Compounds* (Gram, T.E., ed.), pp. 319-33, Spectrum Publications, Jamaica, New York
Helton, E.D. and Goldzieher, J.W. (1977) *J. Toxicol. Env. Hlth., 3*, 213-19
Hensleigh, P.A., Carter, R.P. and Grotjan, H.E. (1975) *J. Clin. Endocrinol. Metab., 40*, 816-23
Hodgson, E. and Juchau, M.R. (1977) *J. Steroid Biochem., 8*, 669-77
Huberman, E. and Sachs, M. (1976) *Proc. Natl. Acad. Sci. U.S.A., 73*, 188-92
Jones, A.H., Fantel, A.G., Kocan, R.A. and Juchau, M.R. (1977) *Life Sci., 21*, 1831-7
Juchau, M.R. (1971) *Toxicol. Appl. Pharmacol., 18*, 665-75
—— (1980a) in *Extrahepatic Metabolism of Drugs and Other Foreign Compounds* (Gram, T.E., ed.), pp. 732-51, Spectrum Publications, Holliswood, New York
—— (1980b) *Pharmacol. Ther., 8*, 501-24
Juchau, M.R. and Zachariah, P.K. (1975) *Biochem, Biophys. Res. Commun., 65*, 1026-32
Juchau, M.R., Berry, D.L., Zachariah, P.K., Namkung, M.J. and Slaga, T.J. (1976b) in *Carcinogenesis: A Comprehensive Survey* (Freudenthal, R. and Jones, P.W., eds.), Vol. 1, pp. 23-34, Raven Press, New York
Juchau, M.R., Bond, J.A., Kocan, R.A. and Benditt, E.P. (1979) in *Polynuclear Aromatic Hydrocarbons* (Jones, P.W. and Leber, P., eds.), pp. 639-52, Ann Arbor Science, Ann Arbor, Michigan
Juchau, M.R., Chao, S.T. and Namkung, M.J. (1981) in *Biological Reactive Intermediates* (Jollow, D.J., Parke, D.V. and Snyder, R., eds.), Vol. 2, (in press), Plenum Press, New York
Juchau, M.R., Jones, A.H., Namkung, M.J. and DiGiovanni, J. (1978b) in *Carcinogenesis: A Comprehensive Survey* (Jones, P.W. and Freudenthal, R., eds.), Vol. 3, pp. 361-70, Raven Press, New York
Juchau, M.R., Lee, Q.H. and Blake, P.H. (1972) *Life Sci., 11*, 949-55
Juchau, M.R., Mirkin, D.L. and Zachariah, P.K. (1976a) *Chem. -Biol. Interact., 15*, 337-47
Juchau, M.R., Namkung, M.J., Berry, D.L. and Zachariah, P.K. (1975) *Drug Metab. Dispos., 3*, 494-502
Juchau, M.R., Namkung, M.J., Jones, A.H. and DiGiovanni, J. (1978a) *Drug Metab. Dispos., 6*, 273-81
Juchau, M.R., Zachariah, P.K., Colson, J., Symms, K.G., Krasner, J. and Yaffe, S.J. (1974) *Drug Metab. Dispos., 2*, 79-86
Kobayashi, S. and Ichii, S. (1969) *J. Biochem. (Tokyo), 66*, 51-9
Kramer, R.E., Greiner, J.W., Rumbaugh, R.C., Sweeney, T.D. and Colby, H.D. (1978) *J. Pharmacol. Exp. Ther., 204*, 247-54
Kuhnert, B.R., Kuhnert, P.M., Tu, A.L., Lin, D.C. and Foltz, R.L. (1979) *Am. J. Obstet. Gynecol., 133*, 904-8
Lee, Q.P., Zachariah, P.K. and Juchau, M.R. (1975) *Steroids, 26*, 571-9

The Role of the Placenta in Developmental Toxicology

Levitz, M., Jansen, V. and Dancis, J. (1978) *Am. J. Obstet. Gynecol., 132*, 363-6
Lin, T.J., Lin, S.L., Erlenmeyer, F., Kline, I.T., Underwood, R., Billiar, R.B. and Little, B. (1972) *J. Clin. Endocrinol. Metab., 34*, 287-97
Manson, J.M. and Smith, C.C. (1977) *Teratology, 15*, 291-300
Mason, J.I. and Boyd, G.S. (1971) *Eur. J. Biochem., 21*, 308-21
Meigs, R.A. and Ryan, K.J. (1968) *Biochem. Biophys. Acta, 165*, 476-82
Meigs, R.A. and Ryan, K.J. (1971) *J. Biol. Chem., 246*, 83-9
Moore, R.G. and McBride, W.G. (1978) *Eur. J. Clin. Pharmacol., 13*, 275-81
Morgan, C.D., Sandler, M. and Panigel, M. (1972) *Am. J. Obstet. Gynecol., 112*, 1068-74
Morgan, D.J., Cousins, M.J., McQuillon, D. and Thomas, J. (1977) *Eur. J. Clin. Pharmacol., 12*, 359-67
Morgan, D.J., Thomas, J. and Triggs, E.J. (1978) *Clin. Pharmacol. Therap., 23*, 288-93
Namkung, M.J. and Juchau, M.R. (1980) *Toxicol. Appl. Pharmacol., 55*, 253-9
Neale, M.G. and Parke, D.V. (1973) *Biochem. Pharmacol., 22*, 1451-61
Nelson, S.D., Boyd, M.R. and Mitchell, J.R. (1977) in *Drug Metabolism Concepts* (Jerina, D.M., ed.) pp. 155-88, ACS Symposium Series, Washington, DC
Nelson, S.D., Mitchell, J.R., Dybing, E. and Sasame, A.H. (1976) *Biochem. Biophys. Res. Commun., 70*, 1157-64
Numazawa, M., Soede, N., Kuyono, Y. and Nambara, R. (1979) *J. Steroid Biochem., 10*, 227-35
Omiecinski, C.J., Bond, J.A. and Juchau, M.R. (1978) *Biochem. Biophys. Res. Commun., 83*, 1004-11
Omiecinski, C.J., Chao, S.T. and Juchau, M.R. (1980a) *Develop. Pharmacol. Ther., 1*, 90-100
Omiecinski, C.J., Namkung, M.J. and Juchau, M.R. (1980b) *Molec. Pharmacol., 17*, 225-32
Omiecinski, C.J. and Juchau, M.R. (1980a) in *Polynuclear Aromatic Hydrocarbons: Chemistry and Biological Effects* (Bjorseth, A. and Dennis, A.J. eds.), pp. 498-514, Battelle Press, Columbus, Ohio
Omiecinski, C.J. and Juchau, M.R. (1980b) in *Microsomes, Drug Oxidations and Chemical Carcinogenesis* (Coon, M.J., ed.), pp. 969-72, Academic Press, New York
Osawa, Y. and Higashiyama, T. (1980) *Fed. Proc. Fed. Am. Soc. Exp. Biol., 39*, 2052
Parvizi, N. and Ellendorff, F. (1975) *Nature (London), 256*, 59-62
Paul, S.M., Axelrod, J. and Diliberto, E.J. (1977) *Endocrinol., 101*, 1604-11
Pearlman, W.H. (1957) *Biochem. J., 67*, 1-5
Pelkonen, O., Jouppila, P. and Kärki, N.T. (1972) *Toxicol. Appl. Pharmacol., 23*, 399-407
Pelkonen, O. and Kärki, N.T. (1975) *Biochem. Pharmacol., 24*, 1445-8
Pelkonen, O., Kärki, N.T., Korhonen, P., Koivisto, M., Tuimala, R. and Kauppila, A. (1979) in *Polynuclear Aromatic Hydrocarbons* (Jones, P.W. and Leber, P., eds.), pp. 765-78, Ann Arbor Science, Ann Arbor, Michigan
Rice, J.M., Joshi, S.R., Shenfelt, R.E. and Wenk, M.L. (1978) in *Carcinogenesis: A Comprehensive Survey* (Jones, P.W. and Freudenthal, R.I., eds.), Vol. 3, pp. 413-22, Raven Press, New York
Sasame, H.A., Ames, M.A. and Nelson, S.D. (1977) *Biochem. Biophys. Res. Commun., 78*, 919-24
Schenker, J.G., Ben-David, M. and Albin, D. (1979) *Gynecol. Obstet. Invest., 10*, 311-16
Schlede, E. and Borowski, R. (1974) *Naunyn-Schmiedeberg's Arch. Pharmacol., 281*, 341-55
Schwartz, A.G. and Moore, C.J. (1979) *Fed. Proc. Fed. Am Soc. Exp. Biol., 28*, 1989-93
Simpson, E.R. and Miller, D.A. (1978) *Arch. Biochem. Biophys., 190*, 800-8
Smith, S.W. and Axelrod, L.R. (1969) *J. Clin. Endocrinol., 29*, 1182-9
Soyka, L.F. and Deckert, F.W. (1974) *Biochem. Pharmacol., 23*, 1629-39
Symms, K.G. and Juchau, M.R. (1973) *Life Sci., 13*, 1221-30
Telegdy, G. (1973) in *Fetal Pharmacology* (Borens, L., ed.), pp. 335-54, Raven Press, New York
Thompson, E.A. and Siiteri, P.K. (1973) *Ann. N.Y. Acad. Sci., 212*, 378-91
Thompson, E.A. and Siiteri, P.K. (1974) *J. Biol. Chem., 249*, 5373-8
Thompson, E.A. and Siiteri, P.K. (1976) *J. Steroid Biochem., 7*, 635-41
Tsibris, J.C.M. and McGuire, P.M. (1977) *Biochem. Biophys. Res. Commun., 78*, 411-17
Umeda, M. and Saito, M. (1975) *Mutat. Res., 30*, 249-54
Vaisman, S.L., Lee, K. and Gartner, L.M. (1976) *Biol. Neonate, 28*, 287-96
Vaught, J.B., Gurtoo, H.L., Parker, N.B., Le Boeuf, R. and Doctor, G. (1979) *Cancer Res., 39*, 3177-83
Waddell, W.J. and Marlowe, C. (1981) in *The Biochemical Basis of Teratogenesis* (Juchau, M.R.,

ed.), Elsevier Press, New York, in press

Wang, I.Y., Rasmussen, R.E., Creasey, R. and Crocker, T.T. (1977) *Life Sci., 20*, 1265-72

Welch, R.M., Harrison, Y.F., Gomni, B.W., Poppers, P.J., Finster, M. and Conney, A.H. (1969) *Clin. Pharmacol. Therap., 100*, 1969-75

Wilson, J.T. (1973) *Biochem. Pharmacol., 22*, 1717-28

Zachariah, P.K. and Juchau, M.R. (1975) *Life Sci., 16*, 1689-92

Zachariah, P.K. and Juchau, M.R. (1977) *J. Steroid Biochem., 8*, 221-8

CHAPTER EIGHT

DEVELOPMENTAL CARCINOGENICITY
Paul Kleihues

CONTENTS

I. Introduction

Evidence has accumulated from observations both in humans and experimental animals that the adverse effects of toxic compounds on fetal and postnatal development are not restricted to the causation of malformations. Exposure to chemical carcinogens may, in addition to cytotoxic effects, lead to the initiation of malignant transformation at very early stages of organogenesis. The first report on transplacental tumour induction in experimental animals was by Larsen (1947) who observed a high incidence of lung adenomas in the offspring of mice treated with urethan (ethyl carbamate) during the last three days of gestation. Surprisingly, this observation remained largely neglected during the following two decades. In 1964, Mohr and Althoff reported an increased incidence of respiratory tract tumours in Syrian Golden hamsters after transplacental administration of diethylnitrosamine. At about the same time, the powerful perinatal carcinogenicity of ethylnitrosourea was discovered by Druckrey et al. (1966). Since then, a great number of chemical carcinogens has been found to be similarly effective in a variety of experimental animals (Table 8.1).

Research into the susceptibility of fetal tissues for malignant transformation was greatly stimulated by the observation by Herbst et al. (1971) and Greenwald et al. (1971) of vaginal adenocarcinoma in young women after maternal treatment with diethylstilboestrol (DES). Although DES has, until now, remained the only agent known to induce tumours transplacentally in humans, some aspects of developmental carcinogenesis have caused much concern and represent special problems in the safety evaluation of drugs and environmental contaminants:

213

(1) For most transplacental carcinogens, the dose required for malignant transformation is considerably lower in fetuses than in adults. Often, adverse biological effects are hardly detectable in maternal tissues.

(2) Perinatal tumour induction is often but not necessarily associated with teratogenic effects. In several animal models a significant tumour incidence can be produced with doses that cause no detectable malformations.

(3) Interference of chemical carcinogens with germ cells during maturation may cause an increased tumour risk in subsequent generations.

The present overview summarises some characteristic features of developmental carcinogenesis in humans and experimental animals. In addition to long-term carcinogenicity studies, special emphasis has been given to the mechanism of action of perinatal carcinogens and the biochemical basis of the organ specificity. This subject has previously been reviewed by Rice (1973), Druckrey (1973b), Ivankovic (1975), and Mohr *et al.* (1980). Many valuable data have been made accessible in congress reports (Tomatis and Mohr, 1973; Rice, 1979) and in a special abstract service of the U.S. National Cancer Institute (Anderson, 1980).

II. Developmental Carcinogenesis in Humans: Transplacental Effects of Diethylstilboestrol (DES)

DES (4, 4'-dihydroxy-α, β-diethylstilbene) is a very potent synthetic oestrogen that has been widely used both as a therapeutic drug in humans and as a growth-promoting agent in livestock. First synthesised in 1938, its widespread use was mainly due to its low price and effectiveness after oral administration (in humans) or local implantation (in animals).

Therapeutic use of DES was introduced in 1946 as a treatment for threatened abortion in women. Although a later double-blind study questioned the capacity of DES to reduce the incidence of abortion, it has been estimated that 500 000 to 3 million women were treated between 1945 and 1955 and that approximately 33 000–100 000 children were exposed to DES *in utero* during the period 1960–70 (for review see Bibbo, 1979; McLachlan and Dixon, 1976). Daily oral doses ranged from 1.5 to 125 mg, often in stepwise increments. Duration of treatment varied from 12 days in the first trimester to continuous application until the 35th week or even throughout pregnancy. The total dose administered ranged between 0.175 and 46.6 g. When taken immediately after intercourse (25 mg twice daily for 5 days), DES is a strong contraceptive. The extent of its use for this purpose is difficult to estimate. DES has also been used for hormone replacement in young women with a gonadal dysgenesis and in post-menopausal women. To some extent, it has further been used for the treatment of breast cancer.

Non-therapeutic use of DES as growth-promoter in sheep and cattle breeding is still widespread although this application is now illegal in most Western countries. DES residues in beef and veal have often been detected, although at very low concentrations when compared with medicinal application (for review see McLachlan and Dixon, 1976).

A. *Carcinogenic and Teratogenic Effects in Children and Young Women after Maternal DES Therapy*

Since publication of the initial reports by Herbst *et al.* (1971) and Green-wald *et al.* (1971), the causal relationship between prenatal DES exposure and subsequent occurrence of *clear-cell adenocarcinoma* of vagina and cervix has been confirmed in numerous studies (for review see Herbst *et al.*, 1977, 1978). Among 262 registry cases with clear-cell carcinoma, 66% had been exposed prenatally to DES or related non-steroidal hormones (dienoestrol, hexoestrol). Maximum daily doses ranged from 1.5 to 150 mg, total doses from 135 mg to 18.2 g. Adenocarcinoma of the vagina or cervix appeared 7-27 years after intrauterine exposure, with a sharp rise in the incidence curve at 14 years, a peak at 19 years, and a sharp decline until 22 years. Among exposed women aged up to 24 years, the overall risk of developing clear-cell adenocarcinoma ranged from 0.14 to 1.4/1 000 (Herbst *et al.*, 1978).

Non-neoplastic abnormalities of the female genital tract are considerably more common. Most common are vaginal adenosis, i.e. in the columnar epithelium lining the vaginal surface, or glands in the lamina propria (35–90% incidence) and cervicovaginal ridges (22–58% incidence). The latter include transverse ridges, collars, deformities and hypoplasia of the cervix. There is increasing evidence that DES-induced clear-cell carcinomas are derived from persistent epithelium of the embryonic Müllerian ducts, since these tumours originate from superficial layers of cervix and vagina where Müllerian-type epithelium is found in over 90% of women with cervical ectropion and vaginal adenosis. More recently, transplacental effects of DES were also discovered in male offspring (for review see

Bibbo, 1979). They manifest as an increased incidence of anatomical abnormalities (epididymal cysts, undescended and hypoplastic testes) and functional deficiency (abnormal semen). However, no increased tumour risk has so far been observed in DES-exposed males.

B. *Transplacental Effects of DES in Experimental Animals*

As with humans, experimental animals perinatally exposed to DES show both benign abnormalities and – less commonly – malignant transformation.

Female mice treated with DES *in utero* during days 9–16 of gestation showed a dose-related decrease in reproductive capacity, cystic endometrial hyperplasia and uterine adenocarcinoma (McLachlan, 1977). Treatment during days 15–19 resulted in the induction of persistent urogenital sinus and hypertrophy of the portio vaginalis (Nomura and Kanzaki, 1977). In male offspring, similar treatment resulted in nodular enlargements of seminal vesicle and/or prostate (day 9–16) and undescended testes and testicular hypogenesis (days 15–19). Müllerian duct tissue appeared to be the target for transplacental toxicity of DES both in the female and male fetus (McLachlan, 1977).

Transplacental and transmammary exposure of rats to DES resulted in abnormalities in the development of the urogenital sinus in both females and males (e.g., hypospadias, phallic hypoplasia, urethro-vaginal cloacal formation). In addition, female offspring developed vaginal adenosis and two genital malignancies (Vorherr *et al.*, 1976). DES-induced genital tract tumours in female offspring were also observed by Napalkov and Anisimov (1979).

The transplacental effects of DES of the Syrian Golden hamster were investigated by Rustia and Shubik (1976). Female progeny showed hypoplastic and neoplastic lesions of the reproductive system and a high incidence of continuous oestrogenic stimulation. Most of the male offspring developed spermatic granulomas of the epididymis and testes.

C. *Metabolism and Mechanism of Tumour Induction*

Investigations on the pharmacokinetics of DES have been largely restricted to mice (see McLachlan and Dixon, 1976). After intravenous injection of ^{14}C-DES in pregnant mice (day 16), the decay curve in plasma could be resolved into four major components with half-lives of approximately 4 seconds, 1 minute, 13 minutes, and 14 hours. There was a rapid uptake of DES by all maternal tissues examined but passage into fetuses was obviously delayed. However, after 30 minutes DES concentrations in the fetal genetical tract were approximately four times higher than in fetal plasma.

The mechanism of tumour induction by DES is not yet resolved and this is also true for the basic question of whether DES is a genotoxic or epigenetic carcinogen. Genotoxic carcinogens or their ultimate electrophilic intermediates react covalently with DNA, thereby causing mutations both in bacteria and mammalian cells. Epigenetic carcinogens, on the other hand, do not attack DNA, have no mutagenic metabolites and cause an increased incidence of tumours by mechanisms such as chronic tissue injury, immunosuppression, promotional activity or hormonal imbalance (Williams, 1981). The possibility that DES exerts its adverse effects solely by hormonal mechanisms cannot be ruled out, although in adult animals a very high incidence of malignant tumours is observed in extragenital tissues. Extensive oxidative metabolism of DES occurs in various species, including non-human primates and man (Metzler, 1976; Metzler and McLachlan, 1978a, Gottschlich and Metzler, 1980). Several reactive metabolites are formed by oxidation of the stilbene molecule and hydroxylation of the aliphatic and aromatic moiety. Neither DES nor any of its known metabolites yield positive results in the *Salmonella*/microsome or cell-transformation test.

However, Rüdiger *et al.* (1979) have recently shown that DES and two of its major urinary metabolites, β-dienestrol and DES-α,β-oxide, induce sister-chromatid exchange in cultured human fibroblasts. Their structural formulae are given below:

| DES | DES α, β-oxide | β-dienestrol |

Most effective was β-dienestrol, which may be formed *in vivo* from DES in a reaction catalysed by the enzyme peroxidase (Metzler and McLachlan, 1978b). A high activity of this enzyme has been found in tissues known to be targets for the carcinogenic effects of DES (McLachlan *et al.*, 1980).

The peroxidase-mediated oxidation of DES has recently been found to yield intermediates which react with DNA *in vitro* (Metzler and McLachlan, 1980).

III. Developmental Carcinogens in Experimental Animals: Biological Effects and Mode of Action

More than 40 compounds are known to cause an increased tumour risk in experimental animals if administered during fetal or early postnatal development. Table 8.1 summarises the carcinogenic effects of 33 agents which were shown to produce a tumour incidence in the offspring of at least 10%. From these data it becomes evident that the principal site of tumour induction varies considerably in different species. In rats, the most commonly induced neoplasms are malignant gliomas of the central nervous system (CNS), malignant neurinomas of the peripheral nervous system (PNS) and, less common, nephroblastomas. In contrast, mice show a general tendency to respond with an increased incidence of benign tumours of the respiratory tract (adenomas) and the liver (hepatomas). Among the different classes of chemical carcinogens, *N*-nitrosamides, aryldialkyltriazenes, hydrazine derivatives, and the polycyclic hydrocarbon 7, 12-dimethylbenz (*a*) anthracene have to be classified as the most potent perinatal carcinogens. They induce a high incidence of malignant tumours in rats and other laboratory animals and tumours in mice. Their biological effects and mode of action will be reviewed below in more detail. The remaining compounds, including most of the polycyclic hydrocarbons, *N*-nitrosamines and aromatic amines, rarely induce malignant tumours but may cause a considerable increase in the incidence of benign murine neoplasms.

A. *Monofunctional Alkylating Agents*

After spontaneous or enzymic decomposition *in vivo*, most of the potent developmental carcinogens listed in Table 8.1 yield a common monofunctional alkylating species (usually methyl or ethyl diazonium ion) as the ultimate reactive intermediate. Accordingly, it can be assumed that the initiation of malignant transformation by these agents proceeds by identical molecular and cellular mechanisms.

Table 8.1: Developmental Carcinogenesis in Experimental Animals[1]

Carcinogen	Species	Developmental stage at treatment (day)	Main target organ	Max. tumour incidence[2] %	Reference
		Alkylnitrosoureas and related N-nitrosamides			
N-Methyl-N-nitrosourea	Rat	Prenatal (21/22)	Nervous system	≈50	Wechsler (1973), Napalkov (1973)
		Newborn	Nervous system	≈50	Warzok et al. (1972)
	Rabbit	Prenatal (25/26)	Kidney	22	Dimant and Beniashvili (1978)
N-Ethyl-N-nitrosourea	Rat	Prenatal (11–23)	Nervous system	100	Ivankovic and Druckrey (1968)
		Postnatal (1–30)	Nervous system	>90	Druckrey et al. (1970a)
	Mouse	Prenatal (14–21)	Lung[3]	>80	Rice (1969), Vesselinovitch (1973)
		Prenatal (19)	Nervous system	32	Denlinger et al. (1974)
	Hamster[4]	Prenatal (11–15)	Nervous system	≈60	Ivankovic and Druckrey (1968); Mennel Züelch (1972)
	Gerbil	Postnatal (7/20)	Skin (melanomas)[3]	43	Kleihues et al. (1978)
	Opossum	Postnatal	Nervous system, eye, jaw, various tissues	54	Jurgelski et al. (1976)

Table 8.1: continued

Compound	Species	Timing		Target tissue	%	Reference
	Rabbit	Prenatal	(8–10)	Nervous system	67	Stavrou et al. (1977)
	Rabbit	Prenatal	(18–31)	Kidney	75	Stavrou et al. (1975), Fox et al. (1975)
	Dog	Prenatal		Thyroid gland, ovary	50	Warzok et al. (1977)
	Pig	Prenatal	(20–31)	Skin, sweat gland[3]	76	Kupfer et al. (1969)
	Monkey[5]	Prenatal	(30–165)	Various tissues		Rice et al. (1977)
N-n-Propyl-N-nitrosourea	Rat	Prenatal	(19)	Nervous system	50	Ivankovic and Zeller (1972)
N-n-Butyl-N-nitrosourea	Rat	Prenatal	(22)	Nervous system	50	Zeller et al. (1978)
		Newborn		Nervous system	85	Zeller et al. (1978)
		Postnatal	(10)	Nervous system	>95	Zeller et al. (1978)
N-Ethyl-N-nitrosobiuret	Rat	Prenatal	(15/22)	Nervous system	90	Druckrey and Landschütz (1971)
	Rat	Postnatal	(10)	Nervous system	100	
N-Methyl-N-nitrosourethane	Rat	Prenatal	(18)	Nervous system, kidney	19	Tanaka (1973)
	Mouse	Prenatal	(9–17)	Lung[3]	45	Nomura et al. (1974)
Hydrazines, azo and azoxy compounds						
1,2-Diethylhydrazine	Rat	Prenatal	(15)	Nervous system	>90	Druckrey et al. (1968)
1-Methyl-2-benzylhydrazine	Rat	Prenatal	(15/21)	Nervous system, kidney	>50	Druckrey (1973a)
Procarbazine	Rat	Prenatal	(22)	Nervous system	54	Ivankovic (1972)

Table 8.1: continued

Azoethane	Rat	Prenatal	(15)	Nervous system	>95	Druckrey *et al.* (1968)
Azoxyethane	Rat	Prenatal	(15)	Nervous system	>80	Druckrey *et al.* (1968)
Azoxymethane	Rat	Prenatal	(22)	Kidney, nervous system	≈ 20	Druckrey (1973a)
Cycad meal	Rat	Prenatal		Various tissues	≈ 25	Spatz and Laqueur (1967)
Dialkylaryltriazenes						
3,3-Dimethyl-1-phenyltriazene	Rat	Prenatal	(23)	Nervous system	42	Druckrey (1973a)
3,3-Diethyl-1-phenyltriazene	Rat	Prenatal	(15)	Nervous system	92	Druckrey (1973a)
3,3-Diethyl-1-pyridyltriazene	Rat	Prenatal	(15)	Nervous system	90	Druckrey (1973a)
Alkylmethanesulphonates						
Methyl methanesulphonate	Rat	Prenatal	(15/21)	Nervous system	32	Kleihues *et al.* (1972), Schneider *et al.* (1978)
Ethyl methanesulphonate	Rat	Prenatal	(21)	Nervous system	16	Schneider *et al.* (1978)

Table 8.1 : continued

Dialkylsulphates

Compound	Species			Target	%	Reference
Dimethylsulphate	Rat	Prenatal	(15)	Nervous system	10	Druckrey (1973a)
Diethylsulphate	Rat	Prenatal	(15)	Nervous system	10	Druckrey (1973a)
N-Nitrosamines						
N-Nitrosodiethylamine	Rat	Prenatal		Various tissues	≈45	Thomas and Bollman (1968)
		Prenatal	(22)	Liver	61	Ivankovic (1973)
	Mouse	Prenatal		Lung, liver[3]	82	Mohr and Althoff (1965), Likhachev (1971)
	Hamster	Prenatal	(8–16)	Respiratory tract[3]	42	Mohr et al. (1965)
	Hamster[6]	Prenatal	(13–16)	Lung[3]	76	Thust and Warzok (1977)
N-nitrosohexa-methyleneimine	Hamster	Prenatal	(8–16)	Respiratory tract[3]	10	Althoff et al. (1972)
Polycyclic aromatic hydroxarbons						
Benzo(a)pyrene	Mouse	Prenatal	(11–15)	Lung[3]	62	Bulay and Wattenberg (1971)
7,12-Dimethylbenz(a)-anthracene	Rat	Prenatal	(21)	Nervous system, kidney	75	Napalkov and Alexandrov (1974)

Table 8.1: continued

Compound	Species	Timing (days)		Tissues affected	Number (%)	Reference
7,12-Dimethylbenz(a)-anthracene	Mouse	Prenatal	(11–15)	Lung, ovary[3]	98	Bulay and Wattenberg (1971)
	Hamster[4]	Prenatal	(8–15)	Various tissues	90	Rustia (1977)
3-Methylcholanthrene	Mouse	Prenatal	(18–21)	Lung, liver[3]	98	Turusov et al. (1973)
Aromatic amines						
o-Aminoazotoluene	Mouse	Prenatal and postnatal		Liver[3] Lung[3]	64 29	Gel'shtein (1961)
4-Dimethylaminoazo-benzol	Mouse	Prenatal	(15–21)	Mammary gland, lung, liver[3]	58	Golub et al. (1974)
o-Toluidine	Mouse	Prenatal	(15–21)	Mammary gland, lung[3]	50	Golub et al. (1974)
3,3'-Dichlorobenzidine	Mouse	Prenatal	(15–21)	Lung, mammary gland[3]	54	Golub et al. (1974)
Miscellaneous compounds						
Urethan	Mouse	Prenatal	(20)	Lung[3]	100	Larsen (1947)
		Prenatal	(11–21)	Liver[3] Ovary[3] Lung[3]	92 71 25	Vesselinovitch et al. (1967)
Aflatoxin-B$_1$	Rat	Prenatal and postnatal		Various tissues	40	Goerttler et al. (1980)
Carcinolipin	Mouse	Prenatal	(14–21)	Lung[3]	47	Shabad et al. (1973b)

Table 8.1: continued

Propane sulphate	Rat	Prenatal	(15)	Nervous system	18	Druckrey *et al.* (1970b)
Furylfuramide	Mouse	Prenatal	(13–17)	Lung[3]	17	Nomura (1975)

[1] Not included are carcinogens which produced a tumour incidence of less than 10% in the offspring.
[2] Defined as tumour-bearing animals/total number of experimental animals × 100.
[3] Predominantly or exclusively benign tumours (adenomas, hepatomas, papillomas respectively).
[4] Syrian Golden hamster.
[5] Patas monkey (*Erythrocebus patas*), preliminary report.
[6] Dzungarian hamster.

(i) Biological Effects on Developing Tissues; Occurrence and Metabolism.
Pre- and postnatal tumour induction by this class of compounds has been
extensively investigated. In rats they induce a high incidence of malignant
tumours of the central and peripheral nervous system. The location of
these neoplasms, their histopathological classification, biology, and
growth characteristics have been reviewed elsewhere (Wechsler *et al.*,
1969; Ivankovic, 1975; Kleihues *et al.*, 1976; Jänisch and Schreiber,
1977).

(a) Alkylnitrosoureas and Related N-Nitrosamides. In 1965, Druckrey *et
al.* found that methylnitrosourea, given to adult BD-IX rats in weekly
intravenous doses of 5–10 mg/kg body weight, led to the development of
malignant tumours of the brain and spinal chord in more than 90% of
experimental animals. Since this report, various methylating, ethylating
and related aliphatic acylalkylnitrosamides have been found to be similarly
effective (Druckrey *et al.*, 1967a). Druckrey and his co-workers were
also the first to demonstrate that the neuro-oncogenic effect of these
agents is greatly enhanced if the carcinogen is administered transplacentally. Prenatal application of methylnitrosourea is limited by its strong
cytotoxic effects but ethylnitrosourea, given to rats as a single intravenous
dose of 40–80 mg/kg body weight on day 15 or 21 of gestation, induced
malignant tumours of the nervous system in 98–100% of the offspring.
The mean postnatal survival time ranged from approximately 180 to 210
days (Ivankovic and Druckrey, 1968). Administration of ethylnitrosourea
to pregnant rats before day 12 of the gestation period did not produce
tumours in the offspring. The developmental oncogenicity of ethylnitrosourea, when expressed as number of neurogenic tumours per animal or
as Iball index (Fig. 8.1), is highest during the last week of gestation and
in newborn rats. During postnatal growth, the oncogenic effect gradually
declines, with lower tumour incidence and increasing survival time.

In rats, the nervous system is the principal target organ, irrespective of
the developmental stage at treatment. However, administration around
birth or shortly thereafter will also induce some nephroblastomas. Stavrou
and co-workers (1975, 1977) have shown that in rabbits there are distinct
gestational periods for the induction of neural (day 8–10) and renal (day
18–31) neoplasms. In hamsters and mice, ethylnitrosourea induces a lower
incidence of neural tumours and postnatal administration to Mongolian
gerbils produced no tumours of the central or peripheral nervous system;
however, 43% of the animals developed benign neural crest-derived
cutaneous melanomas (Kleihues *et al.*, 1978). In Rhesus monkeys prenatal

Figure 8.1: Susceptibility of BD-IX Rats to the Induction of Neural Tumours by *N*-Ethyl-*N*-Nitrosourea (ENU) During Fetus and Postnatal Development.

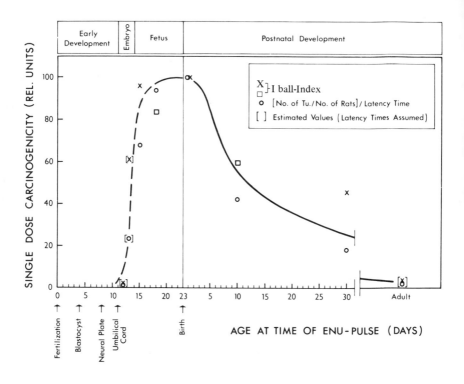

Source: Compiled from experiments by Druckrey *et al.* (1970a) (X; 60–80 mg/kg) and Rajewsky and co-workers (Goth and Rajewsky, 1974) (□; 75 mg/kg).

ethylnitrosourea was ineffective (Warzok *et al.,* 1977) but in Patas monkeys tumours were induced in different tissues, including the nervous system (J.M. Rice, personal communication).

The developmental carcinogenicity of ethylnitrosobiuret is largely identical with that of ethylnitrosourea, whereas the remainder of the *N*-nitrosamides (Table 8.1) are less effective, with the exception of butyl-nitrosourea, which is very potent when given postnatally. Depending on dose and developmental stage, alkyl/acylnitrosamides also cause a variety of teratogenic effects (for review see Wechsler, 1973). Dose–response relationships for the induction by ethylnitrosourea of neural tumours and malformations of the legs (ectro- , oligo- and syndactyly) in rats on day 15 of gestation are shown in Figure 8.2. These data show that the dose required to produce macroscopically detectable malformations was considerably lower than that needed for malignant transformation.

Figure 8.2: Dose–Response Relationship for the Carcinogenic (Incidence of Nervous System Tumours, triangles) and Teratogenic Effects (Hind- and Foreleg Malformations, circles) of N-ethyl-N-Nitrosourea in BD-IX Rats. The carcinogen was administered as a single intravenous injection on day 15 of gestation.

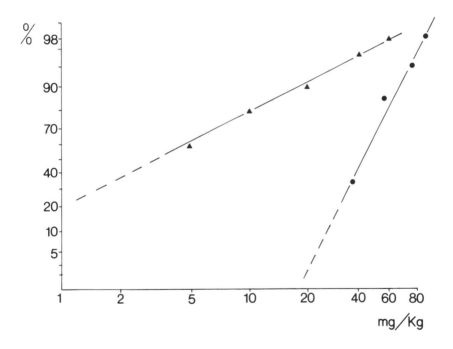

Source: Redrawn from figures published by Ivankovic and Druckrey (1968).

N-Nitroso compounds are widely distributed in the environment, including food, and nitrosamines and nitrosamides can be formed non-enzymatically in the body from their chemical precursors, i.e. amines and nitrites (for review see Mirvish, 1975). Ivankovic and Preussmann (1970) showed that feeding of ethylurea and sodium nitrite to pregnant rats (day 13–23) induced neural tumours in more than 80% of the offspring. Similar experiments have been successfully carried out in hamsters (Rustia, 1975) and with sodium nitrite plus *n*-butylurea (Maekawa *et al.*, 1977) and related chemical precursors (for review see Mohr *et al.*, 1980). Nitrosable substrates include various food components and therapeutic drugs. Nitrite is, in addition to exogenous sources, present in human saliva. However, at present the evidence for a role for *N*-nitroso compounds in the aetiology of human cancer is circumstantial. So far, no epidemiological proof for an increased cancer risk after exposure to this class of carcinogens has been put forward.

After systemic administration, methylnitrosourea and related *N*-nitrosamides are rapidly distributed throughout the body, including placenta and fetuses. They easily cross the blood-brain-barrier and there is no evidence for selective uptake in specific areas of the CNS (Kleihues and Patzschke, 1971). Under physiological conditions, their breakdown proceeds spontaneously through base-catalysed hydrolysis at a rate which depends primarily on the pH and the type of acyl and alkyl residues.

The mode of decomposition of *N*-ethyl-*N*-nitrosourea is given below:

$$O=N-N\begin{smallmatrix} C_2H_5 \\ \\ C-NH_2 \\ \| \\ O \end{smallmatrix} \longrightarrow [C_2H_5-NH-N=O] \longleftrightarrow [C_2H_5-N=N-OH]$$

$$\downarrow +H^+$$

$$[C_2H_5\ N_2^+] + H_2O$$

$$\downarrow$$

$$[C_2H_5^+] + N_2$$

Hydrolytic cleavage of the urea residue leads to the formation of *N*-nitrosoethylamine or, by proton shift, to the corresponding diazo acid, ethyl diazoniumhydroxide. The latter is unstable and rapidly converted into the diazonium ion which itself eliminates nitrogen to yield a carbonium ion as the ultimate carcinogen.

Both methyl- and ethylnitrosourea have been shown to decompose in the intact animal with a half-life of less than 10 minutes.

(b) Dialkylaryltriazenes. This class of compounds has become a valuable

tool in experimental cancer research since the initial report of Druckrey *et al.* (1967b) on the neuro-oncogenic effect of 3,3-dimethyl-1-phenyltriazene (DMPT). Systematic structure–activity studies by Preussmann *et al.* (1974) have shown that several other triazenes also induce nervous-system tumours. After perinatal application, the ethyl analogues of DMPT, 3, 3-diethyl-1-pyridyltriazene and 3,3-diethyl-1-phenyltriazene are particularly effective (Ivankovic *et al.*, 1976). Environmental or occupational exposure of humans is, to our present knowledge, negligible. Some dialkyl-aryltriazenes have cytostatic effects and of these, 5(3,3-dimethyl-1-triazeno)imidazole-4-carboxamide (DTIC) has been used as a cancer chemotherapeutic agent.

A tentative scheme of the bioactivation of 3,3-dimethyl-1-phenyltriazene (DMPT) is given below:

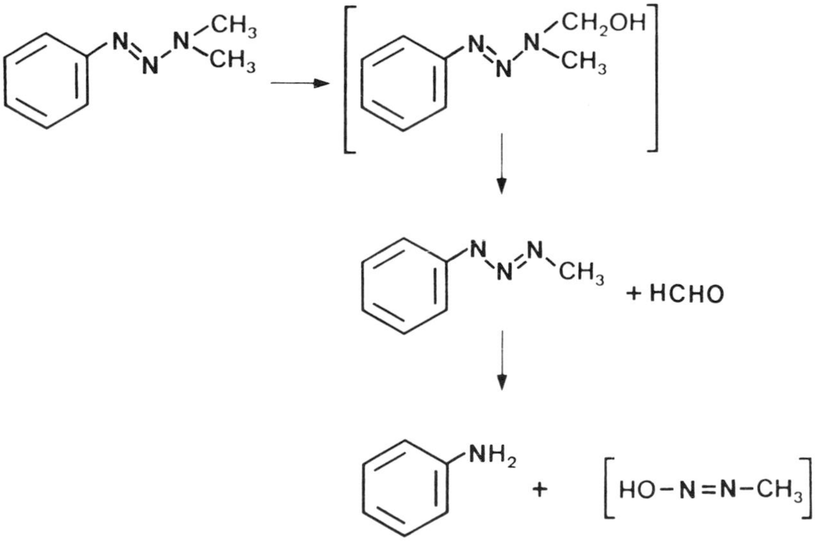

The initial step in the formation of an alkylating intermediate is the enzymic hydroxylation of one of the methyl groups which leads to the production of formaldehyde and 3-methyl-1-phenyltriazene (MPT). The latter has been postulated to be the proximate carcinogen of DMPT which, after hydrolytic fission, yields aniline and methyldiazonium hydroxide. As in the case of alkylnitrosoureas, this highly unstable product (or the released carbonium ion) is thought to methylate nucleophilic groups in cellular macromolecules. *In vitro* studies using microsomal fractions from various animal tissues (Preussmann *et al.*, 1969) indicate that the nervous system, as the principal target tissue in the carcinogenicity of DMPT and related triazenes, is itself unable to metabolise DMPT. However, the half-life of MPT is sufficiently long (> 20 seconds) to allow systemic distribution via the blood after its formation by hepatic microsomal enzymes. Furthermore, MPT is itself carcinogenic and methylates cellular DNA in the absence of drug-metabolising enzymes (Margison *et al.*, 1979).

Owing to the inability of the CNS to metabolise dialkylaryltriazenes, the extent of DNA alkylation is considerably lower in the principal target organ (brain) than in liver and kidney. In fetuses no such differences exist, indicating that during prenatal development both liver and brain (and other tissues) are transplacentally methylated by a proximate carcinogen produced in maternal organs (Fig. 8.3). After birth the rapid increase in the methylation of hepatic DNA reflects the maturation of the hepatic drug-metabolising enzyme system (Kleihues *et al.*, 1979a).

(c) Hydrazines and Related Carcinogens. 1,2-Diethylhydrazine (DEH) is a very potent neuro-oncogenic agent when given transplacentally to rats (Druckrey *et al.*, 1968). Prenatal administration of its methyl analogue, 1,2-dimethylhydrazine (DMH) is less effective but this compound is a very powerful colon carcinogen in adult rats and mice. Human exposure to either of these carcinogens is not known to occur. Hydrazines require microsomal enzymes to be converted into their biologically active intermediates.

The sequence of reactions causing the bioactivation of 1,2-diethylhydrazine is thought to start with two oxidation steps, giving rise to azoethane and azoxyethane (see scheme opposite). Both azoethane and azoxyethane are as effective as the parent carcinogen in the induction of neural tumours after prenatal administration (Druckrey *et al.*, 1968). Procarbazine (Natulan) is a derivative of methylbenzylhydrazine and is widely used in the chemotherapy of human cancer, including brain tumours. It is itself a potent neuro-oncogenic agent when administered transplacentally to rats (Ivankovic, 1972).

230

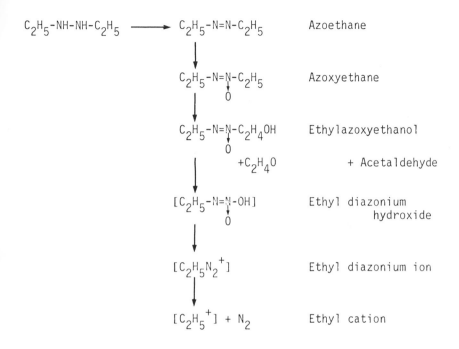

$C_2H_5-NH-NH-C_2H_5 \longrightarrow C_2H_5-N=N-C_2H_5$ Azoethane

$C_2H_5-N=N-C_2H_5$
        O Azoxyethane

$C_2H_5-N=N-C_2H_4OH$
        O Ethylazoxyethanol
    $+C_2H_4O$ + Acetaldehyde

$[C_2H_5-N=N-OH]$
        O Ethyl diazonium hydroxide

$[C_2H_5N_2^+]$ Ethyl diazonium ion

$[C_2H_5^+] + N_2$ Ethyl cation

(d) N-Nitrosamines. In contrast to alkyl-acylnitrosamides, dialkyl-nitrosamines require metabolic activation, which is usually initiated by α-C hydroxylation at one of the alkyl groups (see Druckrey *et al.*, 1967a). The resulting proximate carcinogen (alkyl-hydroxyalkylnitrosamine) is highly unstable. Accordingly, its systemic distribution through the bloodstream is limited and tumour induction is usually restricted to tissues capable of enzyme activation. During development, cytochrome P450 enzymes responsible for α-C hydroxylation of *N*-nitrosamines are largely absent in fetal tissues and these agents do not, therefore, cause teratogenic and transplacental carcinogenic effects during most of the gestational period. In rats and mice, maturation of this enzyme system starts around birth and proceeds rapidly during postnatal growth. Transplacental administration of nitrosamines at the end of gestation usually induces a low incidence of tumours in the offspring (Druckrey, 1973a; Mohr *et al.*, 1980). Of the various *N*-nitrosamines tested, diethylnitrosamine was the most effective (Table 8.1).

(ii) Reaction with Cellular DNA. Chemical carcinogens or their electrophilic metabolites (ultimate carcinogens) react with various cell constituents, including nucleic acids and proteins. During the last decade evidence has accumulated that nuclear DNA is the relevant target molecule and that malignant transformation is initiated by a change in gene structure rather than in gene expression. The hypothesis that tumours arise from somatic mutation, i.e. a heritable change in the nucleotide sequence of DNA, is strongly supported by the finding that most, if not all (genotoxic) carcinogens react covalently with DNA and thereby cause mutations both in bacteria and mammalian cells.

Monofunctional alipnatic alkylating agents react at all available nucleophilic sites in DNA bases but the relative extent of reaction at these sites varies considerably and depends primarily on the reaction type of the respective alkylating agent. Comparative studies on the *in vitro* alkylation of DNA by various compounds have revealed that agents which react predominantly at ring nitrogen atoms in DNA bases are usually weak carcinogens (e.g. diazoalkanes, alkylmethanesulphonates), whereas agents which lead preferentially to *O*-alkylation (e.g. alkylnitrosoureas) usually exhibit a strong carcinogenic activity (for review see Margison and O'Connor, 1979). The relative extent of O^6- and 7-alkylation of guanine by a series of alkylating carcinogens is shown in Table 8.2. Comparison with the bioassay data (Table 8.1) reveals that for some agents the O^6-/7-methylguanine ratio closely parallels their carcinogenicity in rats. The initial pattern of reaction products is (at physiological pH) not influenced by the cellular environment and therefore identical *in vitro* and *in vivo* (Singer *et al.*, 1978). Strandedness of DNA may effect the extent of alkylation at base-paired nitrogens (e.g. 1-alkyladenine and 3-alkylcytosine) but tne reactivity of oxygen atoms, although similarly included in hydrogen bond formation, is not a function of strandedness (Singer, 1979).

Alkylation of DNA bases can be mutagenic if the tautomeric equilibrium is changed and the modified base acquires the base-pairing properties of another base. *In vitro* studies using DNA polymerase and alkylated polydeoxyribonucleotides as templates have shown that mispairing during transcription is likely to result from substitution of O^6 of guanine, O^2 of cytosine and O^2 and O^4 of thymine, due to interference with hydrogen bonding between complementary DNA strands. Studies using RNA polymerase indicate that alkylation at the N-3 position of cytosine may also constitute a promutagenic lesion. Alkylation at these sites may cause point mutations, in contrast to bulky adducts resulting from reaction with carcinogens sucn as benzo (*a*) pyrene which may cause base displacement

Table 8.2: Reaction of Alkylating Agents with DNA *In Vitro*

Compound	Ratio O^6-alkylguanine/7-alkylguanine
Dimethyl sulphate	0.0005
Diethyl sulphate	0.003
Methyl methanesulphonate	0.004
Ethyl methanesulphonate	0.03
N-Methyl-N-nitrosourea	0.10
N-Methyl-N'-nitro-N-nitrosoguanidine	0.11
3-Methyl-1-phenyltriazene	0.11
Methyl(acetoxymethyl)nitrosamine	0.11
Isopropyl methanesulphonate	0.3
N-Ethyl-N-nitrosourea	0.68
N-n-Butyl-N-nitrosourea	0.69

Source: Kleihues *et al.* (1979a).

and frame-shift mutations.

If alkylation of DNA is a crucial event in the initiation of malignant transformation, one may expect that the extent of this reaction in different organs correlates with the location of tumours. However, no such correlation seems to exist for neuro-oncogenic agents. After systemic administration, alkylnitrosoureas are rapidly distributed throughout the animal, including the nervous system, and no accumulation occurs at sites of preferential tumour induction. Since enzymes do not affect their decomposition, levels of DNA alkylation by methylnitrosourea are similar in brain, liver, kidney, intestines and other tissues (Kleihues and Magee, 1973). Similarly, transplacental administration of ethylnitrosourea (Goth and Rajewsky, 1972) and methylmethanesulphonate (Kleihues *et al.*, 1974) did not show significant differences between target and non-target tissues. Prenatally, this is also true for 3,3-dimethyl-1-phenyltriazene (Fig. 8.3).

(iii) Possible Role of DNA Repair in the Perinatal Induction of Nervous System Tumours. Chemically induced promutagenic DNA modifications may lead to a permanent alteration of the genetic information of the daughter cells unless the lesion is removed before DNA replication. Since deficient DNA repair appears to be the cause of tumour formation in the human disease *Xeroderma pigmentosum*, numerous attempts have been

Figure 8.3: Methylation by 3,3-[^{14}C] Dimethyl-1-phenyltriazene of Liver and Brain DNA at Various Stages of Development. The carcinogen was injected subcutaneously (100 mg/kg body weight) into pregnant (21 days' gestation) or into 2-, 10- and 30-day-old rats. Animals were killed 15 hours later and 7-methylguanine (7-meG) concentrations were determined (as molar % of guanine (G)) in DNA isolated from the pooled organs of 3 (30-day-old) to 16 (fetuses) animals. The arrow indicates the time of birth.

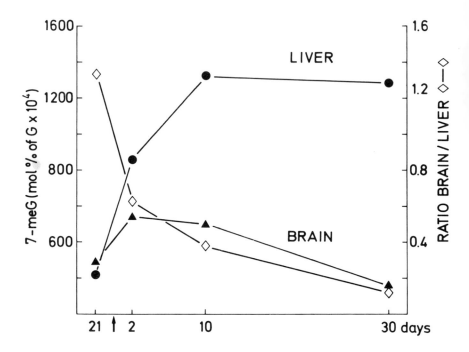

Source: Kleihues *et al.* (1979a).

made to correlate organ-specific tumour induction by chemical carcinogens with DNA repair capacities of the respective target tissue (for reviews see Singer, 1979; Kleihues *et al.*, 1979b; Margison and O'Connor, 1979).

Of the various products resulting from the reaction of aliphatic alkylating carcinogens with DNA bases, 3- and 7-alkyl purines are lost from DNA by chemical (non-enzymic) depurination, owing to the great lability of their glycosyl bonds. Depurination follows first-order kinetics with half-lives ranging from approximately 26 hours (3-alkyladenine) to 155 hours (7-alkylguanine). In addition to spontaneous glycosyl bond cleavage, 3-alkyladenine is enzymically removed by specific glycosylases (Lindahl, 1976). In any case, the loss of alkylated bases will lead to the formation of apurinic (or apyrimidinic) sites which, either directly or by subsequent endonuclease-mediated production of strand breaks, contribute to the cytostatic and teratogenic effects of alkylating agents.

Promutagenic O-alkylated bases are, under physiological conditions, chemically stable but can be enzymically removed by a repair process, which has not yet been fully elucidated. Evidence for a differential repair capacity of various organs was first demonstrated for the neuro-oncogenic alkylnitrosureas. O^6-Ethylguanine produced by a single injection of ethylnitrosourea into 10-day-old rats was found to be removed from DNA of the brain, which is the principal target organ, at a much slower rate than from that of liver, a non-target organ in this animal model (Goth and Rajewsky, 1974). Similarly, O^6-methylguanine produced by a single dose of methylnitrosourea to adult (Kleihues and Margison, 1974) or 10-day-old rats (Kleihues et al., 1979a) persisted considerably longer in brain DNA than in that of other rat organs. Within one week after the administration of alkylnitrosoureas to 10-day-old rats, the amounts of O^6-alkylguanine present in cerebral DNA were about twenty times (ethylnitrosourea) and 90 times (methylnitrosourea) higher than in hepatic DNA (Fig. 8.4).

In adult animals, the selective induction of nervous system tumours is possible only by repeated administration of small doses of neuro-oncogenic alkylating agents. When methylnitrosourea was given weekly over a period of five weeks, O^6-methylguanine was found to accumulate in brain DNA to an extent which greatly exceeded that in kidney, spleen and intestine (Margison and Kleihues, 1975). Similarly, a preferential accumulation of O^6-methylguanine in cerebral DNA was observed after multiple doses of 3,3-dimethyl-1-phenyltriazene (Cooper et al., 1978). This seemed to indicate that nervous-system specific carcinogenesis by aliphatic alkylating agents results from a deficient DNA repair capacity in the target tissues. However, comparative studies in mice showed a less consistent correlation (Kleihues et al., 1979b).

In gerbils (*Meriones unguiculatus*) the repair capacity for O^6-methyl-guanine was even less than in rat brain, although this species is apparently not susceptible to the neuro-oncogenic effect of methylnitrosourea and related agents (Kleihues et al., 1980a). In conclusion, these data indicate that the formation and persistence of O^6-alkylguanine (and other O-alkylated bases) may constitute a necessary although not sufficient event

235

Figure 8.4: Ratio of the Brain and Liver Concentrations of O^6- and 7-alkylguanine after a Single Intraperitoneal Injection of N-[^{3} H] -methyl-N-nitrosourea (10 mg/kg; Closed Symbols) or N-[^{14} C] -ethyl-N-nitrosourea (75 mg/kg; Open Symbols) in 10-day-old BD-IX Rats. Ethylnitrosourea data are taken from Goth and Rajewsky (1974).

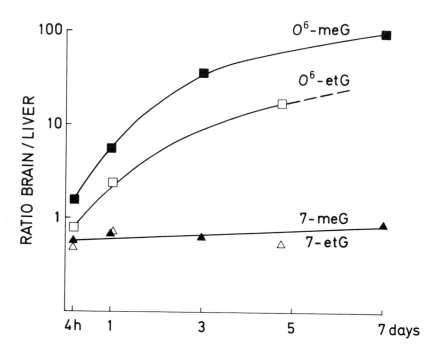

Source: Kleihues *et al.* (1979a).

for the initiation of organ-specific carcinogenesis by monofunctional alkylating agents.

B. *Polycyclic Aromatic Hydrocarbons*

Polycyclic aromatic hydrocarbons (PAH) are formed by free-radical conjugation during the incomplete combustion of fossil fuels and are, therefore, the most widely distributed carcinogenic contaminants of air, water and soil. Their part in the pathogenesis of human cancer is difficult to estimate, since they are usually present in complex mixtures of organic material (e.g. coal tar, cigarette smoke condensate) which may also contain other classes of chemical carcinogens. So far, no single PAH has been identified as a cause of increased cancer risk in man.

(i) Benzo (a) pyrene (BP). So far, the developmental carcinogenicity of BP has been investigated only in mice. As with other carcinogens, prenatal treatment resulted mainly in an increased incidence (62%) of lung adenomas. In addition, cutaneous adenomas (23% incidence) were also observed in the F_1 generation (Bulay and Wattenberg, 1970).

There is increasing evidence that the reaction of PAH with DNA occurs through the intermediate formation of diol-epoxides. In the case of BP the ultimate carcinogen has been identified as 7,8-dihydroxy-9,10-epoxy-7,8,9,10-tetrahydrobenzo (a) pyrene (for review see Brookes, 1977). It exists as a pair of diastereomers in which the 7-hydroxyl group is either *syn* (syn-BP diol epoxide) or *anti* (anti-BP diol epoxide) to the 9,10-epoxide. The (+)enantiomer of the anti-BP diol epoxide seems to be the biologically most active isomer. It is an exceptionally potent mutagen and its carcinogenicity greatly exceeds that of the parent carcinogen. It binds stereoselectively to guanine in double-stranded DNA and seems to account for the formation of the major reaction products with DNA bases. Principle sites of reaction are the exocyclic amino groups of guanine (N-2) and adenine (N-6). Experiments from several laboratories suggest that the transplacental effects of BP and related carcinogenic hydrocarbons may be mediated (a) by ultimate carcinogens (diol epoxides) produced by fetal tissues *in utero* or (b) by metabolites generated in maternal organs.

P450 cytochromes involved in the bioactivation of PAH are present in rat and mice fetuses at least during the second half of gestation. In mice, these enzymes are under regulatory control by the Ah^b allele. Shum *et al.* (1979) have shown that *in utero* toxicity and teratogenicity of BP were more pronounced in genetically 'responsive' C57B1/6 than in 'non-responsive' AKR mice. With the use of back-crosses, it could be demonstrated that allelic differences in the fetal *Ah* locus correlates with increased dysmorphogenesis, the Ah^b/Ah^d genotype suffering from more *in utero* toxicity, congenital abnormalities and a higher extent of BP binding to fetal DNA than the (non-responsive) Ah^d/Ah^d fetus from the same uterus. However, these differences were present only when the pregnant female was 'non-responsive'. The authors assume that in 'responsive' mothers enhanced metabolism in maternal tissues and placenta cancels out the differences between individual fetuses.

(ii) 7,12-Dimethylbenz(a)anthracene (DMBA). Systemic administration of DMBA in young female rats produces an almost 100% incidence of malignant mammary tumours. Prenatal exposure on day 5 of gestation was ineffective (Kellen, 1972) but intravenous injection (15 mg/kg body weight) on day 21 induced tumours of the nervous system (67% incidence) and the kidney (38% incidence) in the offspring (Napalkov and Alexandrov, 1974). After subcutaneous injection on day 20, Rice *et al.* (1978) also found neural and renal tumours in the F_1 generation, in addition to tumours in various other organs. Both DMBA and one of its metabolites (7-hydroxymethyl-12-methylbenz *(a)* anthracene) are embryotoxic and teratogenic (Currie *et al.*, 1973; Kellen *et al.*, 1976). In mice, prenatal exposure to DMBA causes an increased incidence of benign tumours of the lung and the skin. Postnatal topical administration of croton oil greatly increased the effect of transplacental (DMBA) administration (Bulay and Wattenberg, 1971; Goerttler and Loehrke, 1976). In Syrian Golden hamsters, prenatal treatment with DMBA caused a tumour incidence of 45–90% in the offspring, with skin (melanomas), kidney, ovary, thyroid gland and nervous system being most often affected (Rustia, 1977).

According to the 'bay region hypothesis' of hydrocarbon activation (Jerina and Daly, 1976) the carcinogenicity of benz (*a*) anthracene and its analogues should result from the formation of diol epoxides in the 1,2,3,4-positions of the molecule. Accordingly, 3,4-diol-1,2-epoxides would be expected to represent the ultimate carcinogens of DMBA and this view is supported by several reports on the mutagenicity of DMBA 3,4-dihydrodiols. In addition, diol-epoxides may be formed from the various hydroxymethyl derivatives of DMBA. As in the case of BP, the ultimate carcinogen and the adducts formed with DNA bases seem to exist in two diastereomeric forms (for review see DiGiovanni and Juchau, 1980).

In one experiment the reaction of ^{3}H-DMBA with DNA of maternal and fetal rat tissues was investigated (Doerjer *et al.*, 1978). After a single intravenous injection (15 mg/kg body weight) on day 21 of gestation, separation of enzymic DNA digests showed a chromatographic profile that was similar in all organs investigated. The major reaction product of DMBA with deoxyribonucleosides eluted at a methanol concentration of approximately 60% (fractions 73-80 in Fig. 8.5). This peak amounted to 35–45% of the total radioactivity present and was preceded and followed by minor radioactive peaks.

Among the maternal organs the extent of adduct formation was highest in intestine, followed by liver, lung, spleen, kidney and brain. In intestinal

Figure 8.5: Reaction of 7,12-Dimethylbenz *(a)* anthracene (DMBA) with Fetal Rat-Brain DNA. ^{3}H-DMBA was administered intravenously to the pregnant female (15 mg/kg) or directly into the amniotic fluid (4 μg/ fetus). After 12 hours animals were killed. DNA was isolated, enzymically hydrolysed and separated on Sephadex LH-20 columns eluted with 20–100% aqueous methanol. Radioactivity of each fraction is expressed as percentage of the total radioactivity present. DMBA-DNA adducts elute between fractions 60 and 90. dA, deoxyadenosine; circles, pregnant female; triangles, amniotic fluid.

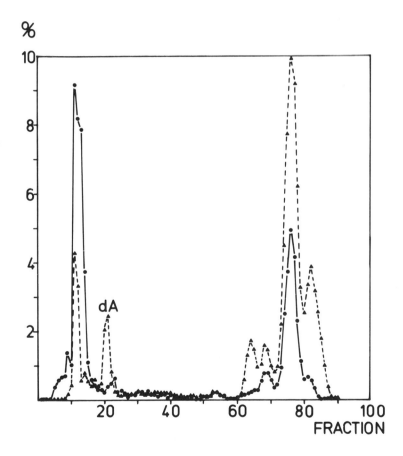

Source: Kleihues *et al.* (1981).

239

DNA, adduct concentration was almost 15 times higher than in cerebral DNA. In fetal intestine and liver, concentrations were 34% and 16% lower than in the respective maternal organs. In contrast, the concentrations of the major reaction product in fetal brain was 2.5 times higher than in maternal brain DNA.

In a further experiment ^{3}H-DMBA was directly injected into the amniotic fluid of 21-day-old rat fetuses (Kleihues *et al.*, 1980b). Superimposed radiochromatographs of DNA hydrolysates from fetal brain after intravenous and intra-amniotic injection of ^{3}H-DMBA are shown in Figure 8.5. In both conditions, the major product elutes at a similar position. However, the fraction of radioactivity present in the satellite peaks was considerably higher after intra-amniotic injection. This was also true for the incorporation of tritium into deoxyadenosine. Of all maternal organs investigated, only liver DNA contained measurable amounts of DMBA-DNA adducts (less than 10% of that in fetal DNA) after intra-amniotic injection. The observation that the chromatographic profile differs considerably depending on the route of application suggests that bioactivation responsible for DMBA binding to fetal DNA may occur both in the fetus itself and in maternal organs. Autoradiographic studies (Kleihues *et al.*, 1981) indicate that DMBA crosses the placenta rather late. At 3.5 minutes after intravenous injection of ^{14}C-DMBA there is, in contrast to most maternal organs, no detectable labelling of fetuses and even after 12 minutes they appear only moderately exposed. The possibility exists, therefore, that despite the capacity of fetuses to metabolise DMBA, proximate carcinogens produced by maternal organs may be included in the binding of DMBA to fetal DNA.

IV. Developmental Carcinogenesis Versus Tumour Induction in Adults: Comparative Aspects

Observations both in humans and experimental animals indicate that the interaction of carcinogens with developing tissues is followed by biological effects which greatly differ from the response of post-developmental organs.

A. *Dose-Response Relationship*

Several of the potent developmental carcinogens listed in Table 8.1 exert their adverse biological effects on fetuses at concentrations which produce little or no effects in the pregnant female. This is particularly true for ethylnitrosourea. When given transplacentally on day 15 of gestation, a dose of 3.2 mg/kg body weight (related to the pregnant female) is sufficient to induce a 50% incidence of malignant tumours of the nervous system in the offspring (Ivankovic and Druckrey, 1968). Even a dose of only 1 mg/kg, corresponding to 0.4% of the LD_{50} in adult rats, induces a tumour incidence of approximately 16% (Ivankovic, 1975). In adult rats, ethylnitrosourea is also a potent carcinogen but the dose required for the induction of neural tumours in 50% of experimental animals is 160 mg/kg, i.e. approximately 50 times higher than that transplacentally. An exceptionally high susceptibility of the rat nervous system during development has similarly been demonstrated for other ethylating agents, including 3,3-diethyl-l-pyridyltriazene and hydrazine derivatives.

For some agents (e.g. furylfuramide, alkyl-methanesulphonates) a significant carcinogenic effect could only be proved by prenatal administration. This is also true for the medicinal use of DES by women: carcinogenic effects have, so far, been observed only in the offspring. Association with an increased risk for breast tumour development in DES-exposed women has been suggested but is not yet proved (see Bibbo, 1979). These data lead to the conclusion that special care is necessary in the prevention of exposure to suspected cancerous agents during pregnancy.

B. *Influence of the Developmental Stage on Tumour Incidence and Organ-Specificity of Chemical Carcinogens*

In rats, the transplacental induction of neurogenic tumours is only possible after 11 days' gestation (Fig. 8.1). This is not due to a deficient passage of the carcinogen into fetal tissues, since embryotoxic and teratogenic effects have been observed after administration at earlier stages of pregnancy. The biological basis of this phenomenon, which may also be present in other species, is not yet understood. In the rat, the nervous system is apparently the target tissue for any carcinogen which reaches the fetuses between 11 and 21 days' gestation. Administration of alkylnitrosourea around birth produces, in addition, some nephroblastomas. In rabbits, on the other hand, exposure of fetuses to ethylnitrosourea during early stages of gestation leads to the induction of neurogenic tumours, whereas in later stages the same carcinogen causes a selective induction of renal neoplasms (see Section III(A)). Considerable differences have been observed in the organ-specificity of carcinogens administered prenatally or after maturation. One of the most noticeable examples is DES, which in adult hamsters produces an almost 100% incidence of malignant kidney tumours (Kirkman and Bacon, 1952) whereas the transplacental carcinogenicity of DES in hamsters is restricted to the genital tract (see Section I(B)). 1,2-Dimethylhydrazine (DMH) induces a low incidence of nervous system tumours perinatally; in adult rats it is a very powerful colon carcinogen. The ethyl analogue 1,2-diethylhydrazine is a very potent neuro-oncogenic agent when given prenatally; in adult rats, this compound induces a significant incidence of aesthesio-neuroepitheliomas (Druckrey, 1973a; Ivankovic, 1975). DBMA induces predominantly neurogenic and renal neoplasmas transplacentally; in young female rats it causes a very high incidence of mammary tumours. These and other examples demonstrate that the susceptibility of various organs changes during development, and that carcinogenicity studies in adults do not allow any conclusions regarding the response of fetal tissues of the same species.

C. *Carcinogenesis and Teratogenesis*

The relationship between developmental carcinogenesis and teratogenesis has been widely discussed (for review see Wechsler, 1973; Ivankovic, 1975; Kleihues *et al.*, 1976) and may be summarised in the statement that all developmental carcinogens are teratogenic, but only a few teratogens are carcinogenic.

The teratogenicity of perinatal carcinogens is based mainly on their cytotoxic effect on proliferating cells, e.g. the periventricular matrix cell layers of the brain. Since malignant transformation is also restricted to proliferating cell populations, a strong cytotoxic effect may reduce the target-cell population for tumourigenesis to such an extent that the tumour incidence in the offspring is greatly decreased. Methylating and ethylating carcinogens are similarly effective in adult rats. Transplacentally, however, ethylating agents are much more effective (Table 8.1). This has been shown for ethylnitrosourea versus methylnitrosourea, 3,3-diethyl-1-phenyltriazene versus 3,3-dimethyl-1-phenyltriazene and 1,2-diethylhydrazine versus 1,2-dimethylhydrazine. This phenomenon can be explained by the relatively high toxicity of methylating agents, which react predominantly at nitrogen atoms in DNA bases (Table 8.2). Ethylating carcinogens react more extensively at oxygen atoms and produce less cytotoxic effects, i.e. their balance between teratogenic and carcinogenic

242

effects is very much in favour of carcinogenicity (Fig. 5.2). Alexandrov and Napalkov (1976) have elegantly demonstrated that pretreatment with methylnitrosoura significantly reduces the incidence of tumours produced by a subsequent dose of ethylnitrosourea. Pretreatment with X-rays is similarly effective (Warkany *et al.*, 1976).

In contrast to ethylnitrosourea and related agents, diethylstilboestrol (DES) causes malformations in most of the offspring whereas tumour induction is a rare event, occurring in less than 1.4 out of 1 000 girls or young women exposed *in utero*.

D. *Multigenerational Effects of Developmental Carcinogens*

Animal experiments from several laboratories indicate that prenatal exposure to chemical carcinogens may not only induce a high incidence of tumours in the offspring (F_1 generation) but also cause an increased tumour risk in subsequent (F_2/F_3) generations. This subject has been extensively reviewed by Tomatis (1979). A persistent tumour risk in several generations of rats was observed after prenatal exposure to methylnitrosourea (Tomatis *et al.*, 1975), ethylnitrosourea (Tomatis *et al.*, 1977) and 7,12-dimethylbenz (*a*) anthracene (Tomatis, 1979). In mice, an increased incidence of lung adenomas in subsequent generations was observed after prenatal treatment with DDT but the incidence in control animals was so high that a physiological fluctuation could not be excluded (Shabad *et al.*, 1973a). Multi-generational carcinogen effects are probably due to carcinogen–DNA interactions in premature germ cells but the biological basis of this phenomenon is not yet fully understood.

References

Alexandrov, V.A. and Napalkov, N.P. (1976) *Cancer Letts., 1*, 345-50
Althoff, J., Pour, P., Cardesa, A. and Mohr, U. (1972) *Z. Krebsforsch., 78*, 78-81
Anderson, L.M. (ed.) (1980) *Selected Abstracts on Transplacental Carcinogenesis*, National Cancer Institute/International Cancer Research Data Bank, Washington
Bibbo, M. (1979) in *Perinatal Pathology* (Grundmann, E., ed.), *Current Topics in Pathology*, Vol. 66, pp. 191-212, Springer-Verlag, Berlin-Heidelberg-New York
Brookes, P. (1977) *Mutat. Res., 39*, 257-84
Bulay, O.M. and Wattenberg, L.W. (1970) *Proc. Soc. Exp. Biol. Med., 135*, 84-6
Bulay, O.M. and Wattenberg, L.W. (1971) *J. Natl. Cancer Inst., 46*, 397-402
Cooper, H.K., Hauenstein, E., Kolar, G.F. and Kleihues P. (1978) *Acta Neuropathol. (Berlin), 43*, 105-9
Currie, A.R., Crawford, A.M. and Bird, C.C. (1973) in *Transplacental Carcinogenesis* (Tomatis, L., and Mohr, U., eds.), pp. 149-53, IARC Scientific Publications No. 4, IARC, Lyon

Denlinger, R.H., Koestner, A. and Wechsler, W. (1974) *Int. J. Cancer, 13*, 559-71
DiGiovanni, J. and Juchau, M.R. (1980) *Drug. Metab. Rev., 11*, 61-101
Dimant, I.N. and Beniashvili, D.Sh. (1978) *Biull. Eksp. Biol. Med., 85*, 343-6
Doerjer, G., Diessner, H., Bücheler, J. and Kleihues, P. (1978) *Int. J. Cancer, 22*, 288-91
Druckrey, H. (1973a) *Xenobiotica*, 3, 271-303
—— (1973b) in *Transplacental Carcinogenesis* (Tomatis, L. and Mohr, U., eds.), IARC Scientific Publications No. 4, pp. 45-58, IARC, Lyon
Druckrey, H. and Landschütz, Ch. (1971) *Z. Krebsforsch., 76*, 45-58
Druckrey, H., Ivankovic, S. and Preussman, R. (1965) *Z. Krebsforsch., 66*, 389-408
Druckrey, H., Ivankovic, S. and Preussman, R. (1966) *Nature (London) 210*, 1378-9
Druckrey, H., Ivankovic, S. and Preussmann, R. (1967b) *Naturwissenschaften, 54*, 1971
Druckrey, H., Ivankovic, S., Preussmann, R., Landschütz, C., Stekar, J., Brunner, U. and Schagen, B. (1968) *Experientia, 24*, 561-2
Druckrey, H., Kruse, H., Preussmann, R., Ivankovic, S., Landschütz, Ch. and Gimmy, J. (1970b) *Z. Krebsforsch., 75*, 69-84
Druckrey, H., Preussmann, R., Ivankovic, S. and Schmähl, D. (1967a) *Z. Krebsforsch., 69*, 103-201
Druckrey, H., Schagen, B. and Ivankovic, S. (1970a) *Z. Krebsforsch., 74*, 141-61
Fox, R.R., Diwan, B.A. and Meier, H. (1975) *J. Natl. Cancer Inst., 54*, 1439-48
Gel'shtein, V.I. (1961) *Voprosy Onkologii* (English translation), 7, 1453-61
Goerttler, K. and Loehrke, H. (1976) *Virchows Archiv. A. Pathology, Anatomy and Histology, 372*, 29-38
Goerttler, K., Löhrke, H., Schweizer, H.J. and Hesse, B. (1980) *J. Natl. Cancer Inst., 64*, 1349-54
Golub, N.I., Kolesnichenko, T.S. and Shabad, L.M. (1974) *Biull. Eksp. Biol. Med., 78*, 62-5
Goth, R. and Rajewsky, M.F. (1972) *Cancer Res., 32*, 1501-5
Goth, R. and Rajewsky, M.F. (1974) *Z. Krebsforsch., 82*, 37-64
Gottschlich, R. and Metzler, M. (1980) *Xenobiotica, 10*, 317-27
Greenwald, P., Barlow, J.J., Nasca, P.C. and Burnett, W.S. (1971) *N. Engl. J. Med., 285*, 390-2
Herbst, A.L., Ulfelder, H. and Poskanzer, D.C. (1971) *N. Engl. J. Med., 284*, 878-81
Herbst, A.L., Scully, R.E., Robboy, S.J., Welch, W.R. and Cole, P. (1977) in *Incidence of Cancer in Humans, Proceedings Cold Spring Harbor Conference on Cell Proliferation*, Vol. 4 (Hiatt, H.H., Watson, J.D. and Winsten, J.A., eds.), pp. 399-412, Cold Spring Harbor Laboratory, Cold Spring Harbor
Herbst, A.L., Scully, R.E., Robboy, S.J. and Welch, W.R. (1978) *Pediatrics, 62*, 1151-9
Ivankovic, S. (1972) *Arzneim. Forsch., 22*, 905-7
—— (1973) in *Transplacental Carcinogenesis* (Tomatis, L., and Mohr, R., eds.), pp. 92-9, IARC Scientific Publications No. 4, IARC, Lyon
—— (1975) in *Handbuch der allgem. Pathologie* (Altmann, H.W., Büchner, F., Cottier, H., eds.), pp. 941-1002, Springer-Verlag, Berlin and New York
Ivankovic, S. and Druckrey, H. (1968) *Z. Krebsforsch., 71*, 320-60
Ivankovic, S. and Preussmann, R. (1970) *Naturwissenschaften, 57*, 460
Ivankovic, S. and Zeller, W.J. (1972) *Arch. Geschwulstforsch., 40*, 99-102
Ivankovic, S., Port, R., and Preussmann, R. (1976) *Z. Krebsforsch., 86*, 307-13
Jänisch, W. and Schreiber, D. (1977) *Experimental Tumors of the Central Nervous System* (Bigner, D.D. and Swenberg, J.A., eds.), The Upjohn Company, Kalamazoo
Jerina, D.M. and Daly, J.W. (1976) in *Drug Metabolism: From Microbe to Man* (Parke, D.V. and Smith, R.L., eds.), pp. 13-32, Taylor and Francis Ltd., London
Jurgelski, W., Hudson, P.M., Falk, H.L. and Kotin, P. (1976) *Science, 193*, 328-32
Kellen, J.A. (1972) *Res. Commun. Chem. Pathol. Pharmacol., 4*, 135-40
Kellen, J.A., Kolin, A. and Fletch, A.L. (1976) *J. Natl. Cancer Inst., 56*, 1063-7
Kirkmann, H. and Bacon, R.L. (1952) *J. Natl. Cancer Inst., 13*, 745-52
Kleihues, P. and Magee, P.N. (1973) *J. Neurochem., 20*, 595-606
Kleihues, P. and Margison, G.P. (1974) *J. Natl. Cancer Inst., 53*, 1839-42
Kleihues, P. and Patzschke, K. (1971) *Z. Krebsforsch., 75*, 193-200
Kleihues, P., Bamborschke, S., and Doerjer, G. (1980a) *Carcinogenesis, 1*, 111-13
Kleihues, P., Bücheler, J., and Riede, U.N. (1978) *J. Natl. Cancer Inst., 61*, 859-63
Kleihues, P., Cooper, H.K., Buecheler, J., Kolar, G.F., and Diessner, H. (1979a) *Natl. Cancer Inst. Monogr., 51*, 227-31

Developmental Carcinogenicity

Kleihues, P., Doerjer, G., Ehret, M., and Guzman, J. (1980b) *Arch. Toxicol.*, Suppl., *3*, 237-46
Kleihues, P., Doerjer, G., Swenberg, J.A., Hauenstein, E., Buecheler, J., and Cooper, H.K. (1979b) *Arch. Toxicol.*, Suppl., *2*, 253-61
Kleihues, P., Lantos, P.L. and Magee, P.N. (1976) *Int. Rev. Exp. Pathol.*, *15*, 153-232
Kleihues, P., Mende, C. and Reucher, W. (1972) *Eur. J. Cancer*, *8*, 641-5
Kleihues, P., Patzschke, K., and Doerjer, G. (1981) *Ann. N.Y. Acad. Sci.* (in press)
Kleihues, P., Patzschke, K., Margison, G.P., Wegner, L.A. and Mende C. (1974) *Z. Krebsforsch.*, *81*, 273-83
Kupfer, M., Kupfer, G., Zintzsch, I., Juhls, H., and Ehrentraut, W. (1969) *Arch. Geschwulstforsch.*, *34*, 25-33
Larsen, C.D. (1947) *J. Natl. Cancer Inst.*, *8*, 63-9
Likhachev, A.Y. (1971) *Vopr. Onkol.*, *17*, 45-50
Lindahl, T. (1976) *Nature (London)*, *259*, 64-6
McLachlan, J.A. (1977) *J. Toxicol. Environ. Hlth.*, *2*, 527-37
McLachlan, J.A. and Dixon, R.L. (1976) in *Advances in Modern Toxicology*, Vol. 1, Part 1 (Mehlman, M.A., Shapiro, R.E. and Blumenthal, H., eds.), pp. 423-48, Hemisphere Publishing, Washington DC
McLachlan, J.A., Metzler, M. and Lamb, J.C. (1980) *Life Sci.*, *27*, 2320-6
Maekawa, A., Ishiwata, H., and Odashima, S. (1977) *Gann*, *68*, 81-7
Margison, G.P. and Kleihues, P. (1975) *Biochem. J.*, *148*, 521-5
Margison, G.P. and O'Connor, P.J. (1979) in *Chemical Carcinogens and DNA* (Grover, P.L., ed.), Vol. I, pp. 111-60, CRC Press, Boca Raton (Florida)
Margison, G.P., Likhachev, A.J. and Kolar, G.F. (1979) *Chem. -Biol. Interact.*, *25*, 345-53
Mennel, H.D. and Züelch, K.J. (1972) *Acta Neuropathol. (Berlin)*, *21*, 194-203
Metzler, M. (1976) *J. Toxicol. Environ. Hlth.*, Suppl., *1*, 21-35
Metzler, M. and McLachlan, J.A. (1978a) *Biochem. Pharmacol.*, *27*, 1087-94
Metzler, M. and McLachlan, J.A. (1978b) *J. Environ. Pathol. Toxicol.*, *1*, 531-3
Metzler, M. and McLachlan, J.A. (1980) *Arch. Toxicol.*, Suppl., *3*
Mirvish, S. (1975) *Toxicol. Appl. Pharmacol.*, *31*, 325-51
Mohr, U. and Althoff, J. (1964) *Naturwissenschaften*, *51*, 515
Mohr, U. and Althoff, J. (1965) *Z. Krebsforsch.*, *67*, 152-5
Mohr, U., Althoff, J., and Wrba, H. (1965) *Z. Krebsforsch.*, *66*, 536-40
Mohr, U., Emura, M., and Richter-Reichhelm, H. -B. (1980) *Invest. Cell Pathol.*, *3*, 209-29
Napalkov, N.P. (1973) in *Transplacental Carcinogenesis* (Tomatis, L., and Mohr, U., eds.), IARC Publications No. 4, pp. 1-13, IARC, Lyon
Napalkov, N.P. and Alexandrov, V.A. (1974) *J. Natl. Cancer Inst.*, *52*, 1365-6
Napalkov, N.P., and Anisimov, V.N. (1979) *Cancer Letts.*, *6*, 107-14
Nomura, T. (1975) *Nature (London)*, *258*, 610-11
Nomura, T. and Kanzaki, T. (1977) *Cancer Res.*, *37*, 1099-1104
Nomura, T., Okamoto, E., Tateishi, N., Kimura, S., Isa, Y., Manabe, H., and Sakamoto, Y. (1974) *Cancer Res.*, *34*, 3373-8
Preussmann, R., Ivankovic, S., Landschütz, C., Gimmy, H., Flohr, E. and Griesbach, U. (1974) *Z. Krebsforsch.*, *81*, 285-310
Preussman, R., von Hodenberg, A., and Hengy, H. (1969) *Biochem. Pharmacol.*, *18*, 1-13
Rice, J.M. (1969) *Ann. N.Y. Acad. Sci.*, *163*, 813-27
—— (1973) *Teratology*, *8*, 113-26
—— (ed.) (1979) *Natl. Cancer Inst. Monogr.*, *51*
Rice, J.M., Joshi, S.R., Shenefelt, R.E. and Wenk, M.L. (1978) in *Polynuclear Aromatic Hydrocarbons*, Vol. 3, (Jones, P.W. and Freudenthal, R.I., eds.), pp. 413-22, Raven Press, New York
Rice, J.M., London, W.T., Palmer, A.E., Sly, D.L. and Williams, G.M. (1977) *Proc. Am. Assoc. Cancer Res.*, *18*, 53
Rüdiger, H.W., Haenisch, F., Metzler, M., Oesch, F. and Glatt, H.R. (1979) *Nature (London)*, *281*, 392-4
Rustia, M. (1975) *J. Natl. Cancer Inst.*, *55*, 1389-94
—— (1977) *Proc. Am. Assoc. Cancer Res.*, *18*, 1
Rustia, M. and Shubik, P. (1976) *Cancer Letts.*, *1*, 139-46
Schneider, J., Warzok, R., Schreiber, D., and Heiderstadt, R. (1978) *Exp. Pathol. (Jena)*, *16*, 157-67

Developmental Carcinogenicity

Shabad, L.M., Kolesnichenko, T.S., and Nikonova, T.V. (1973a) *Int. J. Cancer, 11*, 688-93
Shabad, L.M., Kolesnichenko, T.S. and Savluchinskaya, L.A. (1973b) *Neoplasma, 20*, 347-8
Shum, S., Jensen, N.M., and Nebert, D.W. (1979) *Teratology, 20*, 365-7
Singer, B. (1979) *J. Natl. Cancer Inst., 62*, 1329-39
Singer, B., Bodell, W.J., Cleaver, J.E., Thomas, G.H., and Rajewsky, M.F. (1978) *Nature (London) 276*, 85-8
Spatz, M. and Laqueur, G.L. (1967) *J. Natl. Cancer Inst., 38*, 233-45
Stavrou, D., Hanichen, T., and Wriedt-Lübbe, I. (1975) *Z. Krebsforsch., 84*, 207-15
Stavrou, D., Dahme, E., and Schröder B. (1977) *Z. Krebsforsch., 89*, 331-9
Tanaka, T. (1973) in *Transplacental Carcinogenesis*, (Tomatis, L., Mohr, U., eds.), IARC Scientific Publications No. 4, pp. 100-11, Int. Agency for Research on Cancer, Lyon
Thomas, C. and Bollmann, R. (1968) *Z. Krebsforsch., 71*, 129-34
Thust, R. and Warzok, R. (1977) *Zentralbl. Allg. Pathol., 121*, 82-6
Tomatis, L. (1979) *Natl. Cancer Inst. Mongr., 51*, 159-84
Tomatis, L., and Mohr, U. (eds.) (1973) *Transplacental Carcinogenesis*. IARC Scientific Publications No. 4, IARC, Lyon
Tomatis, L., Hilfrich, J., and Turusov, V. (1975) *Int. J. Cancer, 15*, 385-90
Tomatis, L., Ponomarkov, V., and Turusov, V. (1977) *Int. J. Cancer, 19*, 240-8
Turusov, V., Tomatis, L., Guibbert, D., *et al.* (1973) in *Transplacental Carcinogenesis*, (Tomatis, L., Mohr, U., eds.), IARC Scientific Publications No. 4, pp. 84-91, IARC, Lyon
Vesselinovitch, S.D. (1973) in *Transplacental Carcinogenesis*. (Tomatis, L., Mohr, U., eds.), IARC Publications No. 4, pp. 14-22, Int. Agency for Research on Cancer, Lyon
Vesselinovitch, S.D., Mihailovich, N. and Pietra, G. (1967) *Cancer Res., 27*, 2333-7
Vorherr, H., Messer, R.H., Vorherr, U.F., Jordan, S.W. and Kornfeld, M. (1976) *Fed. Proc. Fed. Am. Soc. Exp. Biol., 35*, 567
Warkany, J., Mandybur, T.I. and Kalter, H. (1976) *J. Natl. Cancer Inst., 56*, 59-64
Warzok, R., Pötzsch, D., Henning, F. and Heiderstädt, R. (1972) *Zbl. Allg. Pathol., 116*, 551-5
Warzok, R., Schneider, J., Thust, R., Scholtze, P., and Pötzsch, H. -D. (1977) *Zbl. Allg. Pathol., 121*, 54-60
Wechsler, W. (1973) in *Transplacental Carcinogenesis* (Tomatis, L. and Mohr, U., eds.), pp. 127-42, IARC Scientific Publications No. 4, IARC, Lyon
Wechsler, W., Kleihues, P., Matsumoto, S., Zülch, K.J., Ivankovic, S., Preussmann, R. and Druckrey, H. (1969) *Ann. N.Y. Acad. Sci., 159*, 360-408
Williams, G.M. (1981) *Ann. N.Y. Acad. Sci.* (in press)
Zeller, W.J., Ivankovic, S., and Zeller, J. (1978) *Arch. Geschwulstforsch., 48*, 9-16

CHAPTER NINE

BEHAVIOURAL TERATOGENICITY
Charles V. Vorhees and Richard E. Butcher

CONTENTS

I. Introduction

The emergence of behavioural teratology as a distinct and recognised field of study is a recent phenomenon, even though it is possible to trace its origins back as far as the early 1960s. Originally behavioural teratology grew out of a more general interest in 'prenatal determinants of behaviour', the title of Joffe's 1969 summarisation and critique of the early research in this area. The real impetus, however, that pressed behavioural teratology forward did not arise from the broad, basic research interests of prenatal psychobiology but was forged by a small group of scientists interested in the 'prenatal environmental determinants of abnormal behaviour'. This interest was both more specific and more applied in its aims and has drawn heavily upon the fields of teratology and toxicology in addition to the behavioural sciences. Modern behavioural teratology, therefore, is truly one of the interdisciplinary sciences, and has as its goals the understanding of causes of abnormal behavioural development and the creation of methods that may be useful in safety assessment settings to prevent potentially hazardous agents from reaching human populations.

Behavioural teratology has clearly benefited from the general growth of interest in, and concern about, environmental health and science. Teratogenesis, mutagenesis, carcinogenesis and the related toxicological sciences have grown dramatically as a result of concerns surrounding ecological contamination. Such concerns have been accentuated by the occurrence of several environmental accidents and the ensuing responses of governments throughout the world, usually in the form of the adoption of new and more rigorous safety assessment regulations. Examples of disasters that have special relevence to behavioural teratology include the revelations of methylmercury poisoning in Minimata disease (Takeuchi *et al.*, 1979; Reuhl and Chang, 1979), the widespread occurrence of alcohol abuse during pregnancy in the fetal alcohol syndrome (Clarren and Smith, 1978), the special risks for epileptic mothers from the various fetal anticonvulsant syndromes (Smith, 1977; Hanson and Smith, 1975; Feldman *et al.*, 1977), and the problem of both short and long-term risks to infants born to narcotic users in the fetal narcotic syndromes (Kandall, 1977; Lodge, 1977, Wilson *et al.*, 1979).

II. Risk Assessment and Regulations for Behavioural Teratogenesis

Perhaps because of the revelations of Minimata disease, Japan was the first country to formally require behavioural evaluation in animals as part of their teratology and reproduction safety assessment guidelines for new drugs. The guidelines do not specify exact tests, but merely require that testing for 'locomotion, learning, sensory functions and emotionality' be conducted.

The behavioural teratology guidelines for Britain are similar in that they define general categories of functional capacity that must be assessed but do not require any specific test. The British guidelines require testing for 'auditory, visual and behavioural impairment'. This guideline has also been adopted by France, so that at present there are really only two general sets of guidelines, the Japanese and the British/French. The Japanese and British/French guidelines also differ in another important respect; they require behavioural evaluations in different phases of the reproductive assessment process. The United States, Japan and the European nations have all divided their reproductive guidelines into three fairly standard phases. Phase I is often called the fertility study because it requires drug exposure before conception and throughout gestation. Phase II is often called the teratology study because it requires drug exposure during the period of embryonic development, when the conceptus is most susceptable to malformation; i.e. the period of organogenesis. Phase III may be called the perinatal study; it requires drug exposure from post-organogenesis to lactation. Japan requires behavioural testing on animals derived from phases II and III, while Britain and France require their behavioural testing on animals derived from phases I and III.

The USA has not yet set any behavioural assessment guidelines. Current

U.S. Food and Drug Administration (USFDA) guidelines state only that behavioural assessments 'may have' to be done on 'some' drugs. This wording may be strengthened slightly in the newly proposed USFDA guidelines which would state that 'some of the offspring should be raised to adulthood and tested by neurobehavioural tests' (Collins, 1978). The regulatory mood in the USA has been summarised by the United States National Toxicology Advisory Committee's Reproduction Panel as follows: 'At present . . . standardization and validation for reliability, sensitivity, and applicability of tests for neurobehavioural toxicity appear to be only beginning, and the imposition of a specific battery of tests may be premature' (Collins, 1978). The USA recommendation for behavioural testing is thus far limited only to testing of animals in phase III studies.

It is difficult at this point to determine which phase of testing is optimal for the detection of behavioural deficits, but one working principle that has emerged from behavioural teratology in recent years does provide some insight. The period of greatest vulnerability to malformations of the central nervous system (CNS) is also the period of greatest vulnerability to behavioural abnormalities (Vorhees *et al.*, 1978; Vorhees *et al.*, 1979a). Since this period is during the early part of organogenesis, these data suggest that phase II behavioural studies should be conducted. Unfortunately, this sounds easier than it is, since in phase II testing as traditionally done, the fetuses are usually harvested on days 18-20 of gestation in the rat and are never allowed to come to term. To include behavioural testing in phase II guidelines some restructuring of these guidelines would clearly be required. Several options are available, none being completely satisfactory. The options include:

(1) Randomly allowing half the animals to deliver and rearing their progeny for behavioural testing, and interrupting pregnancy in the other half for morphological examinations of the fetuses.
(2) Surgically removing at random one complete uterine horn from each gravid animal before parturition for morphological examination and allowing the remainder to proceed for postnatal behavioural assessment.
(3) Subdivide phase II into two entirely separate experiments, one for morphology and one for behaviour.

Solution (1) is troublesome, because the manifestation of terata is quite variable and it might be argued that the chances are too high for a truly random assignment of litters to the subgroups not to be obtained.

251

Solution (2) would probably be less prone to the distributive problems that might affect solution (1), but solution (2) is clearly more complex and possesses the attendant risk of bias related to postoperative uterine infections, potential test compound interactions with the anaesthetic agent and the unknown influences of laparotomy surgery on maternal and neonatal behaviour. Solution (3) presents the problem that, since no two replications of any drug experiment in a biological system ever produce identical results, the results from two separate experiments might not be concordant. The latter problem is classically minimised by the simple, though problematic, maneouvre of increasing group sizes to a point where uncontrolled vagaries are randomised. This stratagem would apply to all three solutions, but on balance solution (3) would appear to be the best compromise. Therefore, it appears that in the future behavioural guidelines should include phase II studies.

Whether behavioural testing should also be done on animals in phase I or phase III studies is more difficult to determine. Phase III covers more of the final development of the CNS, when neurotransmitter and other factors for functional organisation are presumably predominant, by extending exposure postnatally, but phase I covers more of total CNS development by including all of prenatal growth, when the overwhelming majority of neurone formation and organisation occurs. Considering the importance of these issues, it is curious that not a single study exists in the literature in which a behavioural teratogen has been given to groups of animals in all three phases of testing and the behavioural outcomes compared. This is a clear and major gap in our existing knowledge.

Another aspect of current government reproductive guidelines that warrants examination is that all require testing in at least two separate species. Most commonly this requirement is met by using rabbits and mice or rats. This requirement is going to present some problems for the behavioural guidelines because laboratory animal behaviour has only been thoroughly documented in rats, mice, pigeons and primates. Rabbits, guinea-pigs, hamsters, gerbils, cats and dogs have been much less thoroughly studied behaviourally. Cats, dogs and primates also require fairly complex and expensive behavioural testing installations. Rabbits seem more amenable to large-scale testing, but there is a real paucity of data on test methods for these animals. In the long-term, however, it might be more efficient to develop behavioural methods for rabbits than to move up to the more intricate requirements of cats, dogs and primates. Ferrets have also been used on a limited basis for both behavioural and morphological teratological examinations and might be an alternative to rabbits (Haddad *et al.*, 1979), though the wealth of morphological data and experience with rabbits argues heavily in their favour at present (Wilson *et al.*, 1978).

Before leaving the issue of government regulations it is necessary to discuss the functional categories first mentioned. The central issue revolves around what functions should actually be tested and how. The issue of how the functions are to be assessed has been left to the discretion of the manufacturer, apparently for two reasons. Firstly, there is the impression of most regulatory agencies that behavioural methodologies are not sufficiently well developed that any particular test can be singled out to represent the best that is available of its type or can even be said to be typical of a given class of tests. Secondly, there is the apparent reservation that specifying tests might inhibit the diversity that would otherwise operate to allow the best methods to rise to the top by a process akin to natural selection. The merit of a set of guidelines that would accomplish these two goals is unequivocal. The problem is that it is not clear that this intent will be realised. What stands between the intent and the reality is a concept in behavioural teratology called apical testing (Grant, 1976). Conceptually there may be nothing wrong with the idea of apical testing, but it should be understood that this concept is not yet well supported by evidence and it is a concept that could be invoked to subtly evade the intent of behavioural teratology guidelines.

The concept of apical testing in behavioural teratology has been discussed previously (Grant, 1976; Butcher, 1976) and simply stated it is the idea that in order to perform a particular test satisfactorily the animal must draw upon several functions, one or more sensory modalities plus cognitive and/or motor capacities. This approach further assumes that if any one or more of the systems required to perform the task is deficient then the animal's ultimate performance will be impaired. Clearly the detection of a deficit using this test approach does not enable the experimenter to specify the exact function that is affected; he knows only what group of functions might be impaired if he cares to sort them out with subsequent, more specific tests. There is, however, a potentially significant problem with the apical test strategy that has not been adequately discussed: the adequacy of the apical test approach for detecting hazardous agents is largely unknown. The answer to the question of adequacy is fundamentally an empirical one and at present there is not enough pertinent data to provide an answer. On theoretical grounds, however, the apical test strategy may be questioned because not enough is known about the ability of the animal to compensate for a deficit in such a way that overall performance is normal, nor is there very good evidence on the degree of dysfunction required in a system before the apical behaviour is affected. The data of Hicks and D'Amato (1978) provide the best available evidence bearing on this point. Their data suggests that animals can perform many tasks normally with rather substantial amounts of CNS tissue loss. If compensatory mechanisms prove to be factors of major importance in assessing functional impairments, then the optimal safety assessment strategy could turn out to be the use of a series of tests as specific as it is possible to develop. At this point the issue is unresolved, but that very fact should serve as a caution to those developing behavioural test systems: that it is too early in the process to endorse or refute the apical test approach and the best intervening strategy might be described as one which combines the apical and specific test approaches into a comprehensive test system. Moreover, tasks should be sought that have been tested against agents reported in the literature to be neurobehavioural toxins in developing animals as the best currently available assurance of test validity.

Thus far the overall strategy for behavioural testing within the Japanese and British/French guidelines has been discussed without regard to what capacities should be tested. Both the Japanese and the British/French guidelines place a considerable amount of emphasis on the assessment of sensory functions. Certainly, some testing of sensory capacities is appropriate, since an animal cannot perform many tasks requiring more complex functions if it suffers from a sensory deficit in the modality to which the animal must respond in a particular test. On the other hand, learning, memory, problem solving, curiosity, activity rhythms and other more complex psychological functions probably represent the area where behavioural testing offers its greatest unique contribution to the detection of potential toxins. If this is correct, then the British/French guidelines might be notably improved by modifying the current 'behavioural impairment' requirement to, perhaps, 'testing for learning and memory impairments, including phases examining acquisition, extinction, reversal learning or complex problem solving, is required as well as a measure of exploration and spontaneous locomotor activity'. In the Japanese guidelines, at least two items require clarification. Firstly, what number of sensory functions must be assessed and restrictions on them determined (such as whether tests of vision must always be done); and secondly, the requirement of a test of emotionality is not clear. There are many experimental paradigms that have been interpreted as being reflections of emotional state, but there is little agreement or uniformity in the behavioural literature on this topic. It might be wiser in the long run to simply modify this term or to define it with examples from the literature as to which general paradigms assessing emotionality will be considered acceptable. Some clarification of this point might help to avert future problems that could place either the regulatory agency or the drug manufacturer in an uncertain position.

In a similar vein, too little discussion has focused on what might be termed the depth of analysis that is desired. To what level must behavioural functions be examined? Is it sufficient, for example, to determine only that the test animals are not blind, deaf, anosmic, etc.; or is it desirable to examine the precision with which sensory capacities can be used? Obviously, the more intense the examination, the greater the opportunity for observing a defect, but it is equally obvious that a comprehensive examination could go on almost infinitely. A philosophy that balances test sensitivity with practical utility, therefore, represents the best resolution of this problem. In other words, the goal is to encourage procedures which would, at a minimum, demonstrate that the test animal can both detect a stimulus in the modality in question and alter its behaviour in some way as a result of detecting the stimulus. In this way some assurance can be given that a complete perceptual process, rather than merely a simple perceptual reflex, can be appraised within the examined modality.

For all the flaws in the existing and proposed behavioural teratology guidelines, their net effect on the field seems to be salutory. They have spurred industry to begin to grapple with the issue of possible long-term behavioural abnormalities of new compounds and to begin developing assessment techniques. The private sector will probably struggle with these requirements for a while, but ultimately they will probably, partly in conjuction with university-based researchers and partly on their own, develop sound strategies to meet both the letter and spirit of these new guidelines. A second benefit derived from the guidelines has been the impetus they have had upon the behavioural sciences to promote the development of practical, applied test systems in the area of animal psychology. The application of scientific knowledge has proved to be a profound asset to both the public and science in other fields and it is difficult to believe that that will not also be the case in behavioural teratology. Finally, these regulations have begun to engender interest in and support for behavioural teratology, effects that have allowed this specialty to develop. This is not to say that behavioural teratology is a mature scientific discipline as yet, but it is certain that it is currently experiencing a remarkable rate of growth, growth which should help it to find a permanent place in the neurosciences even after the novelty has dissipated.

Already the literature in behavioural teratology has grown to the point that a comprehensive review is impossible in anything less than an entire book, so this review will of necessity be selective. We have selected those areas that constitute some of the major veins of research in this field. We have also selected topics with particular reference to the establishment of the principles of behavioural teratogenesis. Before discussing these specific areas, however, a brief overview of the breadth of behavioural teratology will be presented.

The reader is also referred to earlier reviews that present different perspectives on the field (Joffe, 1969; Barlow and Sullivan, 1975; Coyle *et al.*, 1976; Hutchings, 1978; Rodier, 1978).

Parenthetically, we would like to introduce a new term that will be used throughout the remainder of this chapter, psychoteratology. In the past the field has been known as behavioural teratology and this term is likely to remain in use, but we suggest that by analogy with such terms as psychopharmacology, psychobiology, psychophysiology and psychopathology the term psychoteratology is more suitable and more consistent with current nomenclature for specialty areas that interface psychology with other disciplines.

Table 9.1: Compounds Reported as Being Experimental Behavioural Teratogens

Class	Agent	Reference	Species
Alcohol	Ethanol	See Table 9.4	Various
Amino Acids	Phenylalanine and/or *p*-chlorophenylalanine	Vorhees *et al.* (1981)	Various
Anticonvulsants	Phenobarbital	Murai (1966)	Rat
		Zemp and Middaugh (1975)	Mouse
		Middaugh *et al.* (1975)	Mouse
		Yanai and Tabakoff (1979)	Mouse
		Martin *et al.* (1979)	Rat
	Diphenylhydantoin	Ata and Sullivan (1977)	Rat
Anaesthetics	Halothane	Bowman and Smith (1977)	Rat
		Smith *et al.* (1978)	Rat
	Phencyclidine	Jordan *et al.* (1979)	Rat

Antidepressants	MAO Inhibitors	Werboff et al. (1961a, b)	Rat
	Tricyclics	Coyle and Singer (1975)	Rat
	Lithium	Rider et al. (1978)	Rat
Antimitotics	Hydroxyurea	See Table 9.3	Rodents
	5-Azacytidine	See Table 9.3	Rodents
	Methylazoxymethanol	See Table 9.3	Rodents and Ferret
	X-Irradiation	Joffe (1969)[1]	Rodents
		Hicks and D'Amato (1978)[1]	Rodents
		Tamaki and Inouye (1979)	Rat
		Schneider and Norton (1979)	Rat
	Co[60]	Ordy et al. (1978)	Monkey
Antineurotics (Anxiolytics)	Benzodiazepines	Fox et al. (1977)	Mouse
		Butcher and Vorhees (1979)	Rat
		Barlow et al. (1979)	Rat
		Harris and Case (1979)	Rat
		Kellogg et al. (1980)	Rat
	Meprobamate	Werboff et al. (1961a, b)	Rat
		Werboff and Havlena (1962)	Rat
		Werboff and Kesner (1963)	Rat
		Werboff and Dembicki (1963)	Rat
		Kletzkin et al. (1964)	Rat
		Hoffeld and Webster (1965)	Rat
		Murai (1966)	Rat
		Hoffeld et al. (1968)	Rat
Antipsychotics (Neuroleptics)	Phenothiazines	Werboff and Dembicki (1962)	Rat
		Werboff and Havlena (1962)	Rat
		Werboff and Kesner (1963)	Rat
		Hoffeld and Webster (1965)	Rat
		Murai (1966)	Rat
		Jewett and Norton (1966)	Rat
		Hoffeld et al. (1968)	Rat
		Clark et al. (1970)	Rat
		Golub and Kornetsky (1974; 1975 a, b; 1978)	Rat
		Smith et al. (1975)	Rat
		Vorhees et al. (1979a)	Rat
		Ordy et al. (1966)	Mouse
	Reserpine	Werboff and Dembicki (1962)	Rat
		Werboff and Havlena (1962)	Rat
		Werboff and Kesner (1963)	Rat

257

Antipsychotics (Neuroleptics)	Reserpine	Hoffeld and Webster (1965)	Rat
		Murai (1966)	Rat
		Jewett and Norton (1966)	Rat
	Butyrophenones	None	
Cannabinoids	Marijuana	Fried (1976)	Rat
		Abel (1979a, b)	Rat
Cholinergics	Phytostigmine	Richardson *et al.* (1972)	Mouse
	Diisopropylfluoro-phosphate	Richardson *et al.* (1972)	Mouse
	Scopolamine	Richardson *et al.* (1972)	Mouse
	Nicotine	Abel *et al.* (1979)	Rat
		Peters *et al.* (1979)	Rat
Food Additives[2]	Allura Red AC (Red No. 40)	Vorhees *et al.* (1980d)	Rat
	Antioxidants (BHT, BHA, TBHQ)	Stokes and Scudder (1974)	Mouse
		Vorhees *et al.* (1980a, b, h)	Rat
	Aspartame	Brunner *et al.* (1979)	Rat
	Brominated vegetable oil	Vorhees *et al.* (1980c)	Rat
	Calcium carrageenan	Vorhees *et al.* (1979b)	Rat
	Erythrosine (Red No. 3)	Vorhees *et al.* (1980e)	Rat
	MSG	Vorhees *et al.* (1979b)	Rat
		Stokes and Scudder (1974)	Mouse
		Stokes *et al.* (1972)	Mouse
	Tartrazine (Yellow No. 5)	Sobotka *et al.* (1977)	Rat
Hormones	ACTH	Simon and Gandelman (1977)	Mouse
	Adrenalectomy	Smith *et al.* (1975)	Rat
	Gonadotrophics	Whitsett and Vandenbergh (1978)[1]	Various
		Reinisch *et al.* (1978)	Rat
		Gandelman *et al.* (1979)	Mouse
Metals	Lead	Snowden (1973)	Rat
		Reiter *et al.* (1975)	Rat
		Brady *et al.* (1975)	Rat
		Driscoll and Stegner (1976)	Rat
		Padich and Zenick (1977)	Rat
		Tesh and Prichard (1977)	Rat

Metals	Lead	Zenick *et al.* (1978, 1979 a,b)	Rat
		Verlangieri (1979)	Rat
		Flynn *et al.* (1979)	Rat
	Methylmercury	Spyker *et al.* (1972)	Mouse
		Sobotka *et al.* (1974)	Rat
		Zenick (1974)	Rat
		Spyker (1975)	Mouse
		Hughes and Annau (1976)	Mouse
		Zenick (1977)[1]	Rodents
		Dyer *et al.* (1978)	Mouse
		Musch *et al.* (1978)	Rat
		Eccles and Annau (1978)	Rat
		Hughes and Sparber (1978)	Rat
Miscellaneous	Anabolic steroids	Bertolini *et al.* (1979)	Rat
	Atmospheric pressure	Graessle *et al.* (1978)	Rat
	Barbital	Harris and Case (1979)	Rat
	Carbon monoxide	Fechter and Annau (1977)	Rat
		Garvey and Longo (1978)	Rat
	α-Methyl-*p*-tyrosine	Lydiard and Sparber (1977)	Chicken
	Polychlorinated biphenyls	Tilson *et al.* (1979)	Mouse
	Reticular stimulation	Golub *et al.* (1977)	Rat
	Actinomycin D	Mele and Jensh (1977)	Rat
	Microwaves	Jensh *et al.* (1978)[3]	Rat
Narcotics	Heroin	Lasky *et al.* (1977)	Rat
	Methadone	Soyka *et al.* (1978)	Rat
		Peters, M.A. (1978)	Rat
		Hutchings *et al.* (1979 a, b)	Rat
		Zagon *et al.* (1979a, b)	Rat
		Grove *et al.* (1979)	Rat
	Morphine	Davis and Ling (1972)	Rat
		Sobrian (1977)	Rat
		Glick *et al.* (1977)	Rat
		Peters, M.A. (1978)	Rat
		Kirby (1979)	Rat
	Naloxone	Vorhees (1981)	Rat
	Propoxyphene	Vorhees *et al.* (1979a)	Rat

Nutrition (general)	Undernutrition	Leathwood (1978)[1]	Rodents
		Zamenhof and Van Marhtens (1978)[1]	Rodents
		Peters, D.P. (1978)	Rat
	Essential fatty acid deficiency	Lemptey and Walker (1978)	Rat
	Zinc deficiency	Halas *et al.* (1977)	Rat
		Sandstead *et al.* (1977)	Rat
	Excess iron	Kochever *et al.* (1977)	Rat and Monkey
Pesticides	Carbofuran	Avery and Spyker (1978)	Mouse
	Diazinon	Spyker and Avery (1977)	Mouse
Salicylates	Acetyl salicylate	Butcher *et al.* (1972b)	Rat
	Methyl salicylate	Vorhees *et al.* (1980g)	Rat
	Sodium salicylate	Kimmel *et al.* (1974)	Rat
Solvents	Carbon disulphide	Hinkova and Tabacova (1978)	Rat
	Chloroform	Burkhalter and Balster (1979)	Mouse
	Perchloroethylene	Nelson (1979)	Rat
Stimulants	*D*-Amphetamine	Clark *et al.* (1970)	Rat
		Middaugh *et al.* (1974)	Mouse
		Zemp and Middaugh (1975)	Mouse
	Caffeine	Sobotka *et al.* (1979)	Rat
		Butcher *et al.* (1980)	Rat
	Fenfluramine	Vorhees *et al.* (1979a)	Rat
Stress	Restraint	Herrenkohl and Whitney (1976)	Rat
		Barlow *et al.* (1978)	Rat
		Meisel *et al.* (1979)	Rat
	Cold	Villescas *et al.* (1979)	Rat
	Shock	Smith *et al.* (1975)	Rat
		Sobrian (1977)	Rat
		Rohner and Werboff (1979)	Mouse
	Shock of handling	Hutchings and Gibbon (1970)	Rat
	Drug-induced stress	Joffe (1977)	Rat
	Various	Joffe (1978)[1]	Rodents

Table 9.1: continued

Vitamins	Hypervitaminosis-A	See Table 9.2	Rat
	Thiamin deficiency	Bell and Stewart (1979)	Rat

[1] Review articles.
[2] All food additive experiments cited as unpublished and originating from the author's laboratory may be obtained from the author (C.V.V.) or from the United States Food and Drug Administration Bureau of Foods, 200 C Street, Washington, D.C. 20204, USA.
[3] Agent tested for behavioural teratogenicity, but none found.

III. Review of Experimental Behavioural Teratology

A. *Survey of Behavioural Teratology*

Table 9.1 shows a referenced summary of most of the behavioural teratology literature. In areas where the literature is extensive or where the literature may be viewed as pertaining to psychoteratology but in which that was not its original thrust, secondary sources have been cited. Examples of such areas are research on the effects of X-irradiation, malnutrition and sex hormones. Fortunately, fairly recent reviews of these areas already exist.

Several points bear mentioning on inspection of Table 9.1. The scope of research is extensive, suggesting that behavioural teratology embraces virtually every category of chemical and physical agent though to have toxic potential. However, the literature is unbalanced. Overwhelmingly, it is pharmaceutically oriented followed by nutritional factors and industrial waste-product categories (e.g. methylmercury and lead). Pesticides and solvents are under-represented, as are radiations other than X-rays.

The range of the agents listed in Table 9.1 might at first glance appear alarming, but as with compilations of agents that are morphological teratogens these data do not necessarily constitute a statement of imminent health hazard to humans. A more realistic appraisal of the studies listed in Table 9.1 is that psychoteratologists are discovering that almost any biologically active chemical or physical agent can be behaviourally teratogenic if administered in large enough doses at vulnerable periods of development. This concept is the equivalent of the well-known axiom in toxicology that 'anything can be toxic if given in large enough quantities'. It is too early in the evaluation of behavioural teratogens to draw many conclusions about what categories of agents are the most active at disrupting behavioural development, because the number of studies in the various categories are more a reflection of bias brought to the field from other areas than they are an accurate index of toxic potential. The only suggestions that seem justified at this early stage of development of psychoteratology are: (1) that all agents that have been found to be CNS teratogens and that have been tested at lower, non-malforming doses for behavioural abnormalities, have been found to be psychoteratogenic; and (2) in addition to CNS teratogens, many compounds that may be classified as psychoactive (and usually psychotropic) are also found to be psychoteratogenic even if they are not CNS teratogens at higher doses. Whether this latter concept will withstand exhaustive scrutiny remains to be seen, but it does suggest that psychoactive drugs should be a major area of interest in future psychoteratology research.

B. *Behavioural Teratology of Hypervitaminosis-A*

An area that has received sustained interest over a period of more than 10 years has been the behavioural consequences of prenatal exposure to large doses of vitamin A. Vitamin A is of interest to psychoteratologists because it is one of the most thoroughly studied morphological teratogens. Among the terata produced by vitamin A are malformations of the CNS; indeed, CNS malformations are the most prominent form of defect if vitamin A is given during early organogenesis (Kalter, 1968). Because the history of psychoteratology and vitamin A are closely intertwined, what follows is a brief account of the role of research on this compound in the early development of the field.

Malakhovskii (1969) in the Soviet Union was apparently the first to demonstrate that hypervitaminosis-A was a potent behavioural teratogen at doses below which physical malformations are observed. Independently, Butcher *et al.* (1972a) in the United States also demonstrated the capacity of vitamin A to produce behavioural defects at doses just below the teratogenic threshold for the induction of morphological abnormalities. This observation was followed closely by a parallel study showing the same phenomenon for another well-studied teratogen, aspirin (Butcher *et al.*, 1972b). These studies established perhaps the first principle of psychoteratology, that CNS teratogens are behavioural teratogens at doses at or

Figure 9.1: Theoretical Set of Dose-Response Curves Showing the Relationship between the Three Primary Manifestations of Teratogenesis

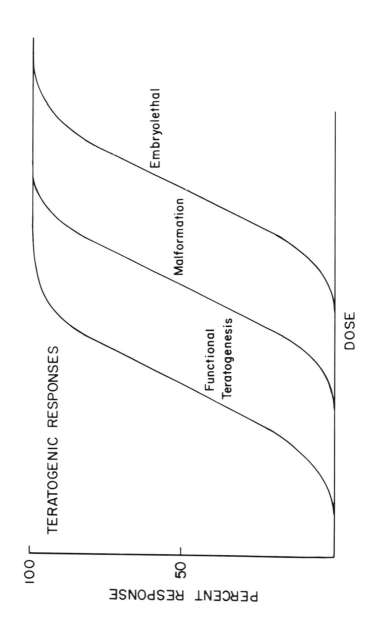

below the morphological no-effect level and established the concept of three end-points in teratology, each with its own dose–response curve (Fig. 9.1). The left curve in Figure 9.1 is designated 'functional' to indicate that this represents, at least potentially, all types of defects that might not be visible morphologically but are demonstrable through some test of the offspring's adaptive capacity. Overwhelmingly, functional assessments have been of behavioural and neurological performance. Neurochemical, immunological, hormonal and other physiological parameters have been discussed but have received only limited attention. A fourth curve has also been added by several authors in recent years: a curve intervening between the functional and malformation curves that represents offspring growth. It is not entirely clear, however, whether the growth curve will always intervene between the functional and malformation curves or whether for some agents it will prove to be isomorphic with or even to the left of the functional effects curve. A great deal more will have to be learned about the relationship between growth and functional development before this point can be resolved, but it is clear that there are at least some cases where these two curves can be dissociated — cf. propoxyphene (Darvon) and prochlorperazine (Compazine) (Vorhees *et al.*, 1979a).

These early experiments with hypervitaminosis-A were not the first in psychoteratology. Several studies appeared in the early and mid 1960s by Werboff, Hicks, Meier, Furchtgott and others using either ionizing radiation or psychoactive drugs (see Joffe, 1969). However, not until the experimental findings of Butcher *et al.* and Hutchings *et al.* on vitamin A, Rodier on 5-azacytidine, and Spyker on methylmercury were published in the early 1970s, did psychoteratology emerge as a specialised area of teratology. These investigators brought together the disciplines of behaviour and teratology because they carefully related their work to the concepts and phenomena of teratology, a focus absent in the earlier work. Thus although psychoteratology existed before 1972, it was not a coherent discipline until that time.

The next important step in psychoteratology emerged from the work of Hutchings *et al.* (1973, 1974). They demonstrated that hypervitaminosis-A could also produce behavioural abnormalities in the offspring when the prenatal exposure occurred later in gestation than organogenesis (organogenesis being the period when the embryo is most vulnerable to disruptions producing major malformations). Moreover, Hutchings' work also provided evidence for two other principles that have become axiomatic in the field. The first is that the type and pattern of behavioural defect produced is a function of the stage of development at which the agent is administered. This concept is a direct extrapolation from teratology, in which it has long been known that the type, frequency and even the magnitude of malformation is a function of the stage of development at which the agent acts. Knowledge of this concept in teratology does not diminish the importance of Hutchings' demonstration that this principle applies to psychoteratogenic responses as well, since proof of this concept for behaviour was by no means accepted before that time. The second principle that may be inferred from Hutchings' work was that fetal susceptibility to insult from an agent decreases with advancing development. Thus, Hutchings and associates had to administer more vitamin A on gestational days 16 and 17 to obtain behavioural effects than they did on days 13 and 14. This relationship has subsequently been reaffirmed by others. An example of this and the concept of the period–effect interaction in vitamin A research is shown in Table 9.2 (Vorhees *et al.*, 1978). Using a constant dose, Vorhees *et al.* (1978) demonstrated that activity effects are produced by treatment during early organogenesis and learning deficits in homing behaviour by treatments later in organogenesis, while swimming-maze deficits could be demonstrated by treatment at either of these periods. Moreover, at this dose, effects later in development, during the third trimester, were not found. More dramatic demonstrations of period–effect interactions may be found in the work of Rodier (see Table 9.3).

Few studies have looked systematically at dose–response relationships in psychoteratology and this is an area that clearly requires more attention. The only study on this topic with vitamin A was done early in the research on this compound and demonstrated a problem that tends to plague reproductive studies generally: that the sensitive zone for producing the effects desired is invariably narrow, so that if widely different doses are given the nature of the response changes dramatically (Vorhees, 1974). This point is well known in teratology, where one dose may produce no apparent effect, the next higher dose may produce malformations, and the next higher dose may produce resorptions (embryolethality) with few remaining fetuses. In behaviour a similar circumstance occurs; one may rapidly step from a no-effect dose to a psychoteratogenic dose, to a malforming dose that yields few or no viable offspring (Vorhees, 1974). If a narrow dose range is selected then all the doses may be psychoteratogenic, but the problem then becomes that it is difficult to distinguish the doses based on a single end-point (Vorhees, 1974). This latter problem does not appear quite so often in teratology, where routine examinations tend to reveal all or nearly all types of possible malformations, but in

265

Table 9.2: Behavioural Consequences of Prenatal Hypervitaminosis-A in Rats

Reference	Dose (IU/kg body weight/day)	Treatment (Day(s))[1]	Strain	Fostering	Physical effects	Behavioural tests	Behavioural results
Malakhovskii (1969, 1971)	600 000	9	Albino	No	No malformation No histological difference	Activity Shock-squeaking 1-way escape conditioning Choice avoidance	Decreased Decreased Decreased Increased errors
Butcher *et al.* (1972a)	100 000	8–10	S-D	Yes	No significantly different malformations No weight difference	Biel water maze	Increased errors
Hutchings *et al.* (1973)	240 000	13–14	Wistar	Yes	No malformations or histological differences; decreased weight and delayed eye opening	Operant-CRF variable interval 40 seconds S+/S− S− latency	No difference No difference Increased S− errors Decreased
Hutchings and Gaston (1974)	360 000	16–17	Wistar	Yes	No malformations, histological differences, weight differences or developmental delays	Operant-CRF variable interval 40 seconds stimulus (S+/S−) S− latency	No difference Decreased acquisition Decreased S+ acquisition No difference
Vorhees (1974)	10 000 25 000	8–10	F-344	No	No malformations, weight differences or litter-size differences	Open field Y-Maze-avoidance	Decreased at 100 000 only Decreased

Table 9.2: continued

Dose	Reference	Strain		Days	Effects	Test	Result
40 000							Decreased
							Decreased
100 000					Smaller litters, increased mortality and decreased weight		Increased
80 000	Vorhees *et al.* (1978)	S-D	Yes	5–7 8–10 11–13 14–16 17–19	Decreased weight 11–13	T-maze	Increased errors 11–13
						Photocell activity	Increased 8–10
						Biel water maze	Increased errors 8–10 and 11–13
40 000	Vorhees *et al.* (1979a)	S-D	No	7–20	Decreased weight before weaning, no differences after weaning	Cliff avoidance	Delayed
						Righting	Delayed
						Swimming development	Delayed
						Negative geotaxis	Delayed
						Open field 18″	Increased rearing
						Open field 36″	Increased ambulation and rearing
						Spontaneous alternation	No difference
						Biel water maze	No difference
						Wheel turn avoidance	Increased
						Passive avoidance	No difference
						Rotorod	Decreased

Column headings (right): -discrimination, -activity, -latency

[1] Gestational age adjusted in all studies to the day of conception set equal to day 0 of pregnancy.
S-D = Sprague-Dawley.

267

behavioural analyses where end-points are time consuming and must be used selectively it has been difficult to show clear dose–response relationships. It may be that the number of behavioural tests conducted per experiment will have to be increased substantially before good dose–response patterns will be described, or that tests possessing greater sensitivity will have to be developed. The former approach is becoming more widely adopted but it is too early to determine how much power has been gained. Promising examples, however, may be found in the recent work of Vorhees *et al.* (1979a) on psychotropic drugs and on food additives (Table 9.1), especially brominated vegetable oil (Vorhees *et al.*, 1980a).

In summary, the history of research into the psychoteratogenic effects of hypervitaminosis-A is a microcosm of the development of the entire area of behavioural teratology. Hypervitaminosis-A has proved to be a fruitful compound for behavioural studies and it continues to be studied from a variety of perspectives. Examples include its use to validate new behavioural measurement techniques in psychoteratology (Adams, 1980) and its use as a positive control technique in a wide-range test battery for comparison with agents of unknown psychoteratogenic potential (Vorhees *et al.*, 1979a).

C. *Behavioural Teratology of Antimitotic Agents*

Some of the most interesting work in psychoteratology has come from studies on the behavioural effects of drugs that inhibit mitosis (Table 9.3). The studies presented in Table 9.3 are not shown in strictly chronological order, but instead are grouped by investigator and shown chronologically within investigators. The work by Butcher and colleagues on hydroxyurea was a direct outgrowth of that described in the preceding section. One of the points of using this drug was that microscopic examination of neural tissues within a few hours after drug administration showed massive cell death at high doses. Thus, here was an agent whose mechanism of action was better understood and whose cellular effects were clearly demonstrable. What was also interesting about hydroxyurea was that at lower doses the drug produced an initial phase of cell death but at 48 hours after the treatment no significant cell loss was in evidence. Experiments with antimitotic agents have shown that this is because exogenously produced cell death, if below some threshold amount, can be adjusted by compensatory reductions in normal, so-called programmed, cell death.

It was of interest to know, in part, whether these cellular compensatory

Table 9.3: Behavioural Consequences of Prenatal Exposure to the Antimitotic Drugs Hydroxyurea (HU), 5-Azacytidine (5-AC) or Methylazoxymethanol (MAM) in Rodents

Reference	Dose (IU/kg body weight/day)	Treatment (Day(s))[1]	Strain	Fostering	Physical effects	Behavioural tests	Behavioural results
Butcher et al. (1973)	HU 375 or 500	12	Rat (Wistar)	Yes	No difference in birth weight, no major malformations, increases in kinked tails	Activity / Biel water maze	No difference / Increased errors at 500
Butcher et al. (1975a)	HU 500 or 625	12	Rat (Wistar)	Yes	No difference in malformations, but reduced weight	Activity / Biel water maze	No difference / Increased errors
Butcher et al. (1975b)	HU 500	12	Rat (S-D)	No	Increase in minor malformations and reduced weight at birth and at testing	Air righting / Forelimb strength / Rope climbing	Delayed / No difference / Impaired
Brunner et al. (1978)	HU 150	6 9 12 15 18	Rat (S-D)	No	Increase in hydrocephalus and microphthalmia	Surface righting / Air righting / Swimming development / Pivoting / Startle	No difference / No difference / No difference / No difference / No difference
Rodier et al. (1975)	5-AC 8	14 18 PN2[2]	Mouse (DUB-ICR)	No	Reduced weight and cell no. in specific brain regions	Surface righting / Pivoting	Delayed at 18 and PN2 / Increased at 14 and PN2

Table 9.3: continued

Study	Agent	Days	Species		Findings	Test	Result
Rodier *et al.* (1975)	5-AC 8	14 18 PN2[2]	Mouse (DUB-ICR)	No		Tremors Activity Gait Passive avoidance	Present at 18 and PN2 Increased at 14 Abnormal at 14 and PN2 Increased at 14
Rodier (1977)	5-AC 8	15 17	Mouse (DUB-ICR)	No	Reduced weight and cell no. in specific brain regions	Activity Passive avoidance Active avoidance	Increased at 17 Impaired at 17 Decreased at 15 and increased at 17
Rodier *et al.* (1979)	5-AC 0.5 and 1	at 11 at 13	Mouse (DUB-ICR)	No	Reduced body and brain weight	Surface righting Air righting Passive avoidance Active avoidance Activity Olton spatial maze	No difference Delayed at 11 Impaired at 13 Increased[3] Decreased at 11 No difference in rewards, but increased rigidity in problem solving
Haddad *et al.* (1977)	MAM 15	32 37 38 41 PN0[2] 10	Ferret	No	Primarily cerebral malformations at 32, 37, 38 primarily cerebellar malformations at 40, 41 and PN0	Locomotion	No difference at 32, 37, 38 and 40 Ataxia at 41 and PN0

Table 9.3: continued

					Microencephaly		
Haddad *et al.* (1979a)	MAM 20 or 30	15	Rat	Yes		T-Maze	Impaired reversal learning
						Visual placing	Delayed
Haddad *et al.* (1979b)	MAM 15	32 38 40	Ferret	No	Lissencephaly, hydrocephaly at 32; less effects at 37 and 38; cerebellar malformations at 40 and PN1	Appetitive discrimination reversal	No difference
		20 10 PN1[2]				Lashley III Maze	Impaired at 32
						Hebb-Williams	Impaired at 32
						Maze	Impaired at 32

[1] Treatment days adjusted to day of conception as day 0.
[2] PN: postnatal age; other ages are days of gestation.
[3] Day 11 group significant only using scaled scores.
S-D = Sprague-Dawley.

mechanisms are adequate to maintain completely normal development or if they result in some compromise to ultimate functional capacity. Butcher's data (Table 9.3) showed that at doses near the threshold for net cell reduction, clear behavioural impairments could be demonstrated, but not at lower doses. Brunner *et al.* (1978) subsequently demonstrated that moderate doses of hydroxyurea that produce a low incidence of effects, such as microphthalmia and hydrocephalus without net cell loss and no reduction in brain weight, produced no apparent effects on behavioural development. However, no adult behavioural tests were performed in this experiment; all of the behavioural findings were based on tests of early development.

The work of Rodier using 5-azacytidine (Table 9.3) is particularly interesting because it took the examination of cell loss to a finer level of analysis using quantitative histological and autoradiographic techniques. In a series of experiments Rodier showed that subtle brain damage that would not be detected by standard teratological techniques resulted in profound behavioural abnormalities in the offspring. Moreover, Rodier demonstrated that the stage of development of each brain structure determined which structures would be most profoundly affected by drug treatment on a given day, and that in certain cases knowledge of which structures were disrupted was predictive of the kind of behavioural defects one would later find in the offspring. For example, drug administration during the period when cell layers of the hippocampus were being laid down preferentially resulted in preferential cell loss in that structure and these offspring subsequently showed disruptions in passive avoidance behaviour, the same pattern seen in adult animals with electrolytic lesions of the hippocampus.

Passive avoidance and its relationship to hippocampal damage is but one example of the effects Rodier has found in the 5-azacytidine-exposed offspring. The behavioural patterns seen in the offspring in Rodier's studies are complex but what is salient is that the changes seen could be related to the structures sustaining the largest amount of cell loss from drug treatment at each given time during development. Of course, instances exist where different exposure periods produce behavioural changes in one direction at one point, the opposite direction at another point and the original direction at still a third point, as illustrated by the passive avoidance effects, but two considerations must be borne in mind when considering such effects. Firstly, the overall pattern of effects were different for each exposure point, confirming the concept of the period–effect interaction for psychoteratology as predicted from teratology. Secondly, in some tasks, such as passive avoidance, the task is structured in such a way that only a very limited set of responses is possible. Limitations in the range of responses measured, however, in no sense mean that impaired passive avoidance in progeny treated on day 13 is necessarily equivalent to impaired passive avoidance in progeny treated on day 17. It is easy to imagine that impaired passive avoidance performance could be produced by a variety of alterations in psychological processes. As so often occurs in behaviour, the behaviour measured provides only a hint at the intervening psychological processes and in some settings the behaviour may not be an adequate differential marker of distinctly different changes in brain functioning.

Finally, the work of Haddad *et al.* is presented in Table 9.3. This work is somewhat different in thrust because here the behavioural manifestations of a clearly defined and major brain anomaly are presented. The anomaly of interest is microcephaly in some cases, lissencephaly in others and a comparison of cerebral versus cerebellar reductions in another. Nevertheless, these studies show that with increasing severity of treatments producing overt CNS pathology, but still viable offspring, increasingly dramatic behavioural defects are demonstrable. Haddad's work is the most decisive in refuting the oft expressed remark from psychoteratology detractors that behaviour is in some sense scientifically imprecise or that effects upon it are nebulous and not clearly related to the degree of pathological severity. Haddad and Rodier have both done important work in that region of the spectrum shown in Figure 9.1 where the functional and pathological curves overlap, and their work forms the bridge to work shown in Table 9.4 on alcohol and other work in behavioural teratology on psychotropic drugs, food additives and other agents, where the magnitude of the exposure to the test agent is to the left of the end of the malformation curve shown in Figure 9.1. It should be recognised from an inspection of Figure 9.1 that experiments carried out using doses below those on the malformation curve are almost automatically at the lower end of the functional effects curve, since to be at the upper end of the curve would mean overlapping the malformation curve. Most of the time, therefore, psychoteratologists are working with phenomena that are expressed in only a minority of the individuals examined, at least with agents having dose–response relationships similar to those illustrated in Figure 9.1. There are times when the curves are further apart, as is apparently the case with propoxyphene (Darvon) (Vorhees *et al.*, 1979a), but this general problem accounts largely for the heavy emphasis in psychoteratology on group performance differences rather than upon individuals, as is often the case in some other research areas.

D. *Behavioural Teratology of Ethanol*

The congenital effects of prenatal alcohol exposure in humans were rediscovered in the late 1960s and early 1970s. Excellent reviews of the human literature on what Jones and Smith (1973) called the fetal alcohol syndrome (FAS) may be found by Clarren and Smith (1978) and Thompson (1979). The FAS is of particular interest to psychoteratologists because mental retardation is the most serious and perhaps the most common symptom of the disorder. The other major and common symptoms are growth retardation (both pre- and postnatally) and a fairly characteristic set of minor facial anomalies that led to the initial recognition of this syndrome. Other anomalies also occur and include microcephaly and joint and cardiac defects, but at much lower incidences than the symptoms described above. The syndrome of FAS is generally regarded as representing only the effects observed at high doses of alcohol exposure and little is known about the occurrence, severity and nature of effects that may be occurring at moderate and low doses. Little is also known about period–effect relationships or about the interaction of alcohol with other factors. To resolve these many issues there has emerged a flood of research on the development of animal models of FAS. Thus far all of the published animal models of FAS have concentrated on rodents. The earlier work has been reviewed by Abel (1980). Here we give a brief review of that work extended to include more recent findings. A summary of the FAS research in animals is shown in Table 9.4. No dramatic and consistent pattern of effects has yet emerged; however, some trends are beginning to appear.

Because of the nutritional problems attendant to alcohol administration considerable attention has been given to nutritional control procedures, and this concern seems well founded. Three basic strategies have been used:

(1) Alcohol has been given by gavage.
(2) Alcohol has been mixed in the drinking water; with either of (1) or (2) controls that are pair-fed to match the experiments for food and/or fluid intake are usually included.
(3) Total liquid diets, in which a portion of the calories are given as either alcohol to the experimental group or sucrose to the controls.

Table 9.4: Behavioural Consequences of Prenatal Exposure to Alcohol in Rodents

Reference	Dose (g/kg body weight/ day)	Method of treatment	Treatment (day(s))	Species (strain)	Fostering	Pair-fed controls	Physical effects	Behavioural tests	Behavioural results
Abel (1978a)	1 or 2	Gavage	0–22	Rat (L–E)	Yes	Yes	None relative to pair-feds	Pup retrieval Spontaneous alterations 1-Way avoidance Water maze Discrimination	Reduced at 2 No difference No difference No difference No difference
Abel and Dintcheff (1978)	4 or 6	Gavage	0–22	Rat (L–E)	Yes	Yes	Lengthened gestation, reduced weight and increased mortality	Inclined plane Rotorod	Reduced at 6 Impaired at 4 and 6
Abel and York (1979)	1 or 2	Gavage	0–22	Rat (L–E)	Yes	Yes	None relative to pair-feds	Open field Free field	No difference No difference
Abel (1979a)	4 or 6	Gavage	0–22	Rat (L–E)	Yes	Yes	Not reported	Open field Step-down latency Spontaneous alterations Sleep time	Reduced Increased at 6 in males No difference No difference
Abel (1979b)	4 or 6	Gavage	0–22	Rat (L–E)	Yes	Yes	Not reported	Cannibalism	Increased

275

Table 9.4: continued

Reference	Dose	Route	Period	Species			Maternal effects	Test	Result
Abel (1979c)	4 or 6	Gavage	0–22	Rat (L-E)	Yes	Yes	Reduced weight at 5 months	2-Way avoidance / Water maze	Impaired in females / No difference
Bond and DiGiusto (1976)	14	Drinking	0–22	Rat (Wistar)	No	No	Not reported	Open field / Alcohol preference	Increased ambulation and rearing / Increased
Bond and DiGiusto (1977a)	13.3	Drinking	0–22	Rat (Wistar)	No	No	Slight reduction in maternal weight	Open field	Increased ambulation
Bond and DiGiusto (1977b)	13.3	Drinking	0–22	Rat (Wistar)	No	No	Not reported	2-Way avoidance	Impaired
Bond and DiGiusto (1978)	12.6	Drinking	0–22	Rat (Wistar)	Yes	No	None	2-Way avoidance / Hebb-Williams maze	Impaired / No difference
Branchey and Friedhoff (1976)	12	Drinking	10–22	Rat (?)	No	Yes	None relative to pair-feds	Open field	Increased ambulation
Buckalew (1977)	Approx. 2	Drinking	Gestation and Lactation	Rat (?)	No	*No* controls	Increased mortality and reduced weight	Observation	Reduced responsiveness

Table 9.4: continued

Reference	Dose	Route	Gestation and Lactation	Species		*No* controls		Alcohol preference	
Buckalew (1979)	approx 1.4–2.3	Drinking	Gestation and Lactation	Rat (?)	No		Not reported	Alcohol preference	Increased
Caul et al. (1979)	2, 4, 6 or 8	Gavage	10–14	Rat (S–D)	No	Yes	None relative to pair-feds	Developmental milestones Open field	No difference Increased ambulation at 4, rearing at 4 and 8, groom at 8, and start speed at 8
								Y-Maze avoidance	Increased avoidance at 6[1] and 8 and discrimination at 8
Demers and Kirouac (1978)	1.2–1.5	Intra-venous	5–18	Rat (S–D)	Yes	No	Increased mortality	Developmental milestones	Delayed head, shoulder and pelvis elevation, air righting, climbing, walking and negative geotaxis
Ewart and Cutler (1979)	17	Drinking	Pre-conception to adulthood	Mouse (CFW)	No	No	Reduced weight and delayed further development	Social interactions	Reduced social encounters and increased evasiveness

277

Table 9.4: continued

Reference								Social interactions	
Krsiak et al. (1977)	1	Gavage	0–21	Mouse (?)	No	No	None	Social interactions	Increased aggressiveness and activity
Martin et al. (1977)	13.8–15.3	Drinking and sub-cutaneous	Gestation and Lactation[2]	Rat (S-D)	No	Yes	Lengthened gestation, increased mortality, reduced weight, delayed eye opening, no mal-formations	Righting	No difference
								Forward locomotion	Reduced
								Operant:	
								Constant reinforcement frequency	Reduced reinforcement
								Fixed ratio reinforcements −10	Reduced reinforcement
								Fixed ratio reinforcements −10–10	No difference
								Direct reinforcement latency −15 seconds	Increased reinforcement
								Shock	No difference
								Shock + Constant reinforcement frequency	Reduced reinforcement
Shaywitz et al. (1979)	Dosage not given[3]	Drinking	2–22	Rat (S-D)	Yes	Yes	Reduced weight gain	Righting	No difference
								Negative geotaxis	No difference
								Cliff avoidance	No difference

278

Table 9.4: continued

Reference	Dosage	Route	Days	Species			Physical effect	Behavioural measure	Result
Shaywitz *et al.* (1979)		Drinking	4–19[4]	Rat (L–E)	No			Air righting	Delayed
								Activity	Increased
								Shock escape latency	Increased
								2-Way avoidance	Impaired
Riley *et al.* (1979a)	12.96 or 6.66	Drinking		Rat (L–E)		Yes	Reduced weight gain at 12.96	Spontaneous alterations latency	Increased
Riley *et al.* (1979b)	12.96, 8.26 or 4.18; 14.19; 13.78 and 6.78	Drinking	4–19; 5–15; 4–19[4]	Rat (L–E)	No	Yes	Reduced weight gain and increased mortality at higher doses	Shock T-maze Errors	
								– Acquired	No difference
								– Reversal	Increased
								Nose-poke frequency	Increased at 12.82, 8.26 and at 14.19
								Head-dipping frequency	Increased at 13.78
Ginsburg *et al.* (1975)	Dosage not given[5]	Drinking	Pre-conception to PN14 and to sires	Mouse (DBA and C57BL)	Yes	No	Reduced weight and delayed eye and ear opening in DBA	Audiogenic seizures	Increased
Yanai and Ginsburg (1976)	10–15 (gestation) 12–28 (lactation)	Drinking	Pre-conception through PN14	Mouse (DBA and C57BL)	No	No	None	Predation	Decreased in DBA

Table 9.4: continued

Yanai and Ginsburg (1977)	10-15 (gestation) 12-38 (lactation)	Drinking	Pre-conception to PN14	Mouse (DBA and CF7BL)	No	No	No	Reduced weight and delayed ear opening in DBA	Startle Righting	No difference No difference

[1] Increased avoidance performance in the 6 g dose group in study 1 but not in study 2.
[2] A second group receiving alcohol only during lactation is not described here.
[3] Maternal blood alcohol concentrations at 8am on day G18 was 197 ± 48 mg%.
[4] Adjusted to time of conception = day 0 of pregnancy.
[5] Maternal blood alcohol at peak night concentrations was 40–45 mg%.
S-D = Sprague-Dawley; L-E = Long-Evans.

Even a cursory examination of the data in Table 9.4 reveals that these approaches are not equivalent. For example, gavage procedures produce maternal weight reductions at doses of 6–8 g/kg body weight/ day, while *ad libitum* liquid diet treatments produce small or no weight reductions at alcohol doses of 13 g/kg body weight/ day or higher. Thus, it is clear that in terms of general toxicity, bolus administrations are quite different from more continuous self-administered doses of alcohol. If this applies to maternal toxicity it may also apply to fetal toxicity, including post-natal behaviour. Investigators working on FAS will have to resolve this difficulty eventually; and the best approach may be a 'within laboratory' study directly comparing the two treatment methods using identical behavioural end-points.

Higher doses (within the range of doses given by gavage) appear to produce reduced activity in Long–Evans rats (Abel's studies) and increased activity in Sprague–Dawley rats (Caul's studies) (see Table 9.4). For example, Abel reports impaired rotorod and active avoidance acquisition, whereas Caul finds increased active avoidance acquisition. Abel also reported reduced inclined plane and step-down performance, while Caul reported increased discrimination performance. The dietary studies show increased activity in Wistar, Sprague–Dawley and Long–Evans rats, if for the latter one is willing to interpret Riley's dependent measures as indicative of activity level. In avoidance responses, the dietary studies have shown impaired avoidance in both Wistar and Sprague–Dawley rats. No other effects emerge, although the operant learning impairment shown by Martin *et al.* (1977) and the impaired reversal learning shown by Riley *et al.* (1979a) may provide additional evidence for the concept that FAS offspring have compromised learning capacities. In mice of the DBA strain alcohol, when given in the drinking water, appears to increase seizure thresholds and predatory behaviour. Unfortunately, the mouse experiments generally lack adequate controls and include only a few behavioural end-points.

Riley *et al.* (1979a, b) has suggested that FAS offspring exhibit behavioural characteristics that may indicate an impairment of normal response inhibition mechanisms. This concept also fits with the data of Caul *et al.* (1979), but does not easily accommodate the finding of impaired FR-10 operant performance observed by Martin *et al.* (1977), or the reduced avoidance performance found by Shaywitz *et al.* (1979) and Bond and DiGiusto (1978). These points cannot be resolved from the other experiments presented in Table 9.4 because they either lack controls (Buckalew, 1977, 1979) or lack matched controls (Demers and Kirouac,

1978; Ewart and Cutler, 1979; Ginsburg *et al.*, 1975; Yanai and Ginsburg 1976, 1977). The experiments by Bond and DiGiusto (1976, 1977a, b, 1978) also lack pair-fed controls but since at their treatment levels they report no, or only very minor, maternal weight changes, their data does not appear to be compromised.

Thus we see that the reported data on FAS is difficult to compare because of the numerous differences between experiments, even in the species, strain and stock of animals used. These differences may eventually prove to be a strength of FAS models by increasing the generality of the findings, but they presently appear to be an obstacle to discerning general principles. The instances of known strain differences in behaviour are numerous and will not be cited here, but in terms of open-field activity only the Long-Evans rat has shown decreased activity in FAS offspring, in all others it has increased.

Another troublesome aspect of the published data on animal FAS is the period of alcohol exposure. Most studies have simply given alcohol throughout gestation, but Caul *et al.* (1979) have used a more discrete exposure period (gestation days 10–14) as have Riley *et al.* (1979a, b,) (gestation days 5–15 and 14–19) and Demers and Kirouac (1978) (gestation days 5–18). (The last study is unusual in other respects, however, including the use of intravenous alcohol administration.)

Finally, some of the inconsistencies between studies may be attributable to the maternal rearing variable. Some have used fostering procedures, some have not, but unfortunately most of the studies that were concerned about this issue elected to merely by-pass it by fostering all offspring to surrogate dams. Only Shaywitz *et al.* (1979) used a cross-fostering procedure and their data suggests that there may be a significant maternal contribution from dams exposed to alcohol before parturition on the offspring they rear. By several criteria Shaywitz found that saline-exposed offspring reared by former alcohol-treated dams more closely resembled the offspring of alcohol-treated dams reared by alcohol-treated dams than alcohol-exposed offspring reared by control dams. While this point is hardly crucial to the issue of demonstrating an enduring behavioural impairment in animals exposed to alcohol early in life, it does raise the possibility that the effects of early alcohol may be mediated by two mechanisms; direct fetal exposure and postnatal maternal effects. A more thorough exploration of this point may help to clarify the differences between Abel's findings (Abel, 1978, 1979a, b, c, d), where fostering is always included, and the work of Bond and DiGiusto (1976, 1977a, b, 1978), Branchey and Friedhoff (1976), Caul *et al.* (1979), Martin *et al.* (1977), and Riley *et al.* (1979a, b), where there was no fostering.

The final question is whether the FAS models will be successful or not. As this is an empirical question, it can be stated only that the work looks promising, if not altogether consistent. Hyperactivity and/or hyperreactivity (or conversely, impaired response inhibition in Riley's perspective, which may be similar) appear to be the most promising elements. Much more work is needed on measures of complex learning along the lines of Riley's reversal learning paradigm (Riley *et al.*, 1979a) and Caul's Y-maze avoidance–discrimination measures (Caul *et al.*, 1979). A nonhuman primate model might also be appropriate in the future, as well as more attention to the dosage, method of administration, blood concentrations, period of exposure, fostering and related methodological issues.

IV. Principles of Behavioural Teratology

As noted in the introduction, one of the reasons that behavioural teratology gained acceptance in the 1970s was because the investigators of this period related their research to the principles and concepts of teratology. Thus, the following principles are framed in a teratological perspective:

(1) Psychoteratogenicity is expressed as delayed behavioural maturation, impaired rates of learning, abnormal activity, impaired adaptation and problem solving, and other indices of compromised behavioural competence.

(2) The type and magnitude of the response is a function of the type of agent administered.

(3) The type and magnitude of the response is a function of the dose of the agent.

(4) The type and magnitude of the response is a function of the stage of development at which the agent acts.

(5) The type and magnitude of the response is a function of the genetic milieu of the target organism.

(6) The type and magnitude of the response is a function of the environment of the target organism, i.e., maternal and placental metabolic influences before birth and maternal metabolism, behaviour and living environs after birth.

(7) Psychoteratogenic agents are those that are CNS teratogens or those that may be classified as psychoactive agents.

(8) Psychoteratogenesis is a manifestation of abnormal development that is demonstrable at doses of the agent at or below which malformations are induced.

(9) The period of susceptibility to psychoteratogenesis is isomorphic with the period of CNS development, and the period of maximum susceptibility corresponds to the period of maximum susceptibility to structural and physiological abnormalities of the CNS.

(10) Not all agents that are capable of producing malformations are psychoteratogens.

More detailed statements on the organising principles of teratology may be found in the writing of Wilson (1977).

The first principle shown is analogous to the principle in teratology that teratogenesis is expressed as embryolethality, malformation, impaired growth or impaired functional development. To reiterate, the latter includes behaviour as well as functionality in other systems (immunological, neurochemical, hormonal, biochemical, etc.). Within the confines of behavioural analyses the manifestations of psychoteratology cannot be enumerated definitively because the methods which will ultimately serve to define these outcomes are still undergoing active development. Thus, those behavioural manifestations listed in principle (1) are clearly appropriate, but there will undoubtedly be more in the future that will have to be added as they become defined.

Principles (2) and (3) are not unique to psychoteratology, nor even to teratology, but have their origins in basic pharmacology – i.e. that the unique characteristics of the agent determines its biological activity which, in turn, determines its toxicity, and, whatever the agent used, the dose that reaches the tissue site where it acts (the target organ) determines its effects, be they pharmacological or toxicological.

Principle (4) is perhaps the single most important one that is unique to the developmental sciences; namely, that during development, especially during early development, the stage of maturation at which the agent reaches the organism is a major determinant of what kind of effect will be produced and how severe the effect will be. In a certain sense this principle has been a cornerstone in making teratology (and therefore also psychoteratology) a unique discipline within toxicology. This principle is tantamount to the statement that at any two points in development that one might select for exposure to an agent, the organism will be so different that it is as if one were dealing with an entirely different animal. The magnitude of difference between any two time points during development is especially dramatic during early development, when most teratological phenomena occur.

Principle (5) concerns the importance of the genetic background against which all teratogens and psychoteratogens act. Principle (5) has usually been ignored in psychoteratology, a situation that must clearly be remedied in the future. Thus, although there is a substantial documentation in teratology of the interaction of genetic characteristics with various teratogenic agents using inbred mouse strains, there is practically nothing known about this interplay as it would be reflected in behaviour. The work of Yanai and Ginsburg (1976, 1977) in Table 9.4 on FAS represents one of the few attempts to examine more than one strain of mice with behavioural evaluations, but much more extensive work is needed.

Principle (6), on environmental influences, is undoubtedly of even greater concern to psychoteratology than teratology. Not only are environmental factors an area of traditional concern to the behavioural sciences, but the proximate environment to the fetus and neonate, the maternal organism, is an especially critical determinant of behavioural development. The special symbiotic relationship between mother and fetus/infant is such that no consideration of one is ever complete without the other. An obvious concern has been the extent to which the maternal organism can serve as a conduit for the transmission of the test agent to the offspring long after prenatal treatment of the mother has ceased. Psychoteratologists have been equally concerned, however, about whether the prenatal treatment procedure has in some way altered the maternal organism's infant-rearing behaviour. Both of these problems can be, and have often been, dealt with through the use of fostering (i.e. surrogate mothers), or in a few cases even by artificial rearing. There is little doubt that these solutions work, but they exact a heavy toll upon the experimenter in terms of resources. Before the conduct of any experiment in psychoteratology it is always worth considering whether the maternal–control procedures are fully justified by the probable outcome of the experiment. Maternal-control procedures are clearly requisite when a compound is under investigation as part of a continuing programme of research on an agent and the experimenter is committed to investigating its effects in depth. On the other hand, as a first examination of a compound, or in experiments conducted as part of a screening process, or for that matter in experiments in which prior work has already tested for maternal influences and found none, the routine inclusion of maternal–control procedures appears unwarranted.

Principle (7) cannot yet be considered to be as firm as principles 1–5, although it is fair to say that there are no data that contradict it. That CNS teratogens are always demonstrably psychoteratogens at doses below those producing frank CNS dysmorphology, is a secure, albeit not too surprising, concept in behavioural teratology. The second part of the principle, however, is a more recent and slightly more tentative concept. Nevertheless, it has clearly been demonstrated that there are psychoactive agents that produce no malformations at any dose (or if they do they are not CNS malformations) but which none the less produce behavioural abnormalities. At very high doses, drugs of this type tend to produce maternal toxicity before any signs of embryopathy can be shown. Thus, the maternal intolerance may, for these drugs, preclude teratogenesis in the sense of malformations. With few exceptions (the main exceptions being thalidomide, alcohol and anticonvulsants) psychoactive drugs appear to have a very low potential for producing malformations based on animal experimentation. Yet their potential as psychoteratogens is rather pervasive (Table 9.1). The doses required to induce psychoteratogenesis are generally very much above customary therapeutic levels, but it must be emphasised that the dose–response relationships are very poorly understood in psychoteratology and no firm judgment about the lower end of the curve is currently possible.

Principle (8) is a rather obvious one, in that if an agent produces major malformations at a given dose then that dose is not appropriate for trying to assess behaviour. What is less obvious about principle (8) is that it leaves the no-effect level for teratogenesis, in its broadest sense, open-ended. When malformations were the left-most curve in the spectrum of teratogenic phenomena (Fig. 9.1), or even growth impairment, it was fairly straightforward to determine a no-effect level at the tail-end of the curve. With the addition of psychoteratogenesis, this point has become clouded because at present we know only that this curve is to the left of the others, but we do not know much about its exact shape. Once this information is obtained then the no-effect level will once again be establishable for any test agent, but it is likely that the inclusion of behavioural end-points will tend to make the no-effect level of a drug more susceptible to qualifications, simply because the methods used to assess animals behaviourally will probably never be as sensitive as those available for assessing human behaviour, hence a gap in certainty is always likely to exist. This problem is not as serious as it may sound, because through the application of appropriate safety margins allowances can be judiciously applied that will allow for this gap in our comparative methodology.

Principle (9) is essentially no more than a statement of psychoteratology's commitment to the biological basis of behaviour, i.e. that all behaviour arises from structural and functional (biochemical) interactions that reside within the CNS, interactions that are ultimately determinable by physicochemical means. There is, however, a secondary element in principle (9) that is proffered here as an hypothesis for which some data exists, but for which a great deal more is needed; namely, that for a given dose of an agent, one will discover that the most severe effects will be produced by exposures that occur during organogenesis compared with exposures at any other time. This principle has been demonstrated countless times for the induction of malformations, but it has not been well investigated for growth or behavioural development. A few studies exist which support the application of this precept to psychoteratology; examples are the work of Vorhees *et al.* (1978) on vitamin A and that of Rodier on 5-azacytidine (1975, 1977, 1979); but the existing examples have thus far included only agents that are potent CNS teratogens. Careful period–response studies with agents that are not malformation inducing (many psychoactive drugs) have yet to be done. Thus, we offer the concept of organogenesis being the most sensitive period for inducing behavioural effects as a challenge which deserves more vigorous investigation.

Finally, principle (10) is a strictly tentative generalisation offered here for its possible heuristic value, not because there is a large amount of data to support it. Nevertheless, there are some data from a study by Butcher *et al.* (1975b) which demonstrated very clearly that acetazolamide, which is a potent teratogen, especially of the forelimbs and preferentially malforming to right forelimbs in rodents, did not affect problem solving or other behaviours not dependent on forelimb strength. This principle is also offered because it is a logical extension of the concept already implied in some of the other principles; namely, the concept of specificity of action, i.e. that many agents possess a high degree of target specificity which is presumably translated in a developing system into effects that produce focused defects. Thalidomide in man is a classic example of a highly specific, very potent human teratogen that is not psychoteratogenic. Thus, we may reasonably expect that other examples of teratogenesis will be found that will not affect psychological development.

Before leaving the principles of behavioural teratogenesis, another issue deserves to be mentioned. This issue concerns the context or perspective in which experiments in psychoteratology or any area within toxicology are done. One of the essential dilemmas in all of toxicology testing is that which exists between the modelling approach and the approach of sensitivity maximisation; or, expressed slightly differently, the problem is between safety assessment and basic toxicology. When expressed in the terms of modelling versus sensitivity, the dilemma is whether one tests compounds with the aim of modelling probable human exposure as closely as possible or whether one exaggerates the exposure conditions to maximise the ability of the test system to detect differences. When expressed in terms of safety versus toxicology, the dilemma is whether one devises the test system to mimic the real world or whether one regards all compounds as toxic at some dosage and focuses upon the phenomenology of toxic effects as the point of ultimate interest.

Psychoteratology cannot escape this dilemma, although it is unlikely that those working in this area will completely resolve it, any more than have those working in any of the other toxicological specialties. An example which illustrates this point fairly clearly for behavioural development, albeit after primarily early postnatal rather than prenatal exposure, are the studies on monosodium glutamate (MSG). Without recounting the evidence in detail, there is little doubt that MSG is a neurotoxin in developing rodents when injected parenterally at high doses during early life. The neurotoxic effects include lesions in the region of the arcuate nucleus and have been demonstrated in many laboratories (e.g. Olney, 1969, Olney and Ho, 1970; Olney *et al.*, 1971; Inouye and Murakami, 1974; Takasaki, 1978a). Further, it is clear that when MSG is administered so as to produce neuropathological effects, abnormal behavioural, growth and sexual manifestations are also demonstrable (Olney, 1969; Araujo and Mayer, 1973; Pizzi and Bernhardt, 1976; Nemeroff *et al.*, 1977; Inouye and Murakami, 1974; Pizzi *et al.*, 1977; Pradhan and Lynch, 1972; Berry *et al.*, 1974). It is equally apparent that humans do not inject MSG into themselves, and experiments attempting to model human dietary exposure routes in rodents have found no brain lesions (Takasaki, 1978b) and essentially no adverse effects on behaviour (Vorhees *et al.*, 1979b). This example illustrates that some agents, such as MSG, may exhibit overt developmental neurobehavioural toxicity when conditions for the induction of neuropathology are optimised, but that when conditions are structured for purposes of safety assessment the practical risks appear to be low. There is also data suggesting that a somewhat similar situation may be obtained with caffeine. In very high doses caffeine produces an increase in the incidence of malformations when administered by gavage, but when given in the drinking source caffeine produces only minor and apparently transitory lags in structural (bone), growth and functional (neuro-behavioural) development that do not appear to represent a major health hazard (Butcher *et al.*, 1980). Indeed the risks appear to be sufficiently mild that regulatory decisions on caffeine seem somewhat unlikely.

It appears that the most thorough analysis of the safety of any agent would be one that approached the problem from both of the perspectives cited above. In terms of psychoteratological phenomena the best stance that is currently available is to begin with high doses and bolus administrations to maximise test sensitivity and determine at what dose, if any, behavioural toxicity can be demonstrated. If no psychoteratogenicity is demonstrable when conditions for toxicity are maximised than the need for additional psychoteratology testing is obviated. If the agent shows substantial psychoteratogenic potential, then it should also be evaluated using a safety assessment model to discover if the health risks are of practical significance at human dose ranges and by routes and patterns of exposure analogous to those of human usage.

V. Mechanisms of Behavioural Teratogenesis

Ultimately the aim of most of the research in psychoteratology is to discover the mechanisms which underlie such phenomena. Despite this very clear goal, there are very little data in the psychoteratology literature on mechanisms. This somewhat paradoxical situation is not too surprising, however, when one considers that to be able to investigate a mechanism one must first know something about the phenomenon of interest. Thus, one of the stages most research endeavours pass through is one which is descriptive and phenomenological, and that is precisely the category into which most of the psychoteratology literature fits. It is interesting that psychoteratology is still received by those outside the field in diametrically different ways. Some regard it with interest and tolerance, recognising that it is passing through its formative stages, while others are impatient and critical, believing that it should get on to mechanistic issues, as if investigating mechanisms were a simple matter of intent, rather than recognising that the methods and description of the phenomena must reach a certain level before mechanistic research becomes truly fruitful. Premature efforts to investigate mechanisms run the risk of investigating two unknowns simultaneously, i.e. trying to find an unknown origin for an undefined phenomenon, an impossible predicament.

In the last few years, however, the field has become 'ready' to turn to mechanistic research. This does not mean that the descriptive work has to or should cease, but that a sense has developed within the area that enough is known about some of the phenomena in psychoteratology to begin to search for explanations on another plane. Research on mechanisms is not monolithic and can be pursued at several levels. Firstly, there are what may be called behavioural mechanisms. In this approach one attempts to isolate a single behavioural construct from which a variety of specific behavioural effects may be seen to flow. The value of this approach is that it not only provides a unified conceptualisation of the behaviour, but equally as important, it serves as a bell-wether for what to examine at the next level of explanation. The second level we will present is the anatomical, or more precisely the histological, in which explanations for behavioural phenomena are sought in morphology, but at the cellular rather than at the organ level. Finally, we will mention mechanisms at the biochemical level of explanation which is the level often referred to as though it were synonymous with the concept of mechanism of action.

Recently, it was demonstrated that 75 mg/kg body weight of propoxyphene (Darvon) administered on days 7–20 of gestation in rats produced a collection of behavioural abnormalities in the offspring at various ages and by a variety of tests (Vorhees, 1979c). The effects observed in the progeny included decreased negative geotaxis turning times, increased pivoting, increased pre- and postweaning open-field ambulation and rearing and decreased preweaning open-field start–exit times, facilitated wheel-turn avoidance, and impaired rotorod performance and swimming development. The thread which unifies most of these effects is hyperarousal, which may be defined as hyperactivity and hyperreactivity. Hyperactivity was seen in the two open-field tests and on the measure of pivoting locomotion and hyperreactivity, i.e. a magnified response to a challenge stimulus, was seen in enhanced negative geotaxis and active avoidance performance. This explanation provides a good fit to most of the data and provides the basis for a clearly testable hypothesis in future experiments. The remaining effects seen in the propoxyphene-exposed offspring are more tentatively ascribed to hypoadaptability. This concept fits the rotorod performance particularly well since this test punishes animals that fail to adjust rapidly to the changing demands of the accelerating tread. Moreover, hyperarousal and hypoadaptability are not mutually exclusive concepts, in fact we believe they reflect an underlying defect in which the heightened arousal state is inextricably related to the diminished flexibility of these animals to adapt to changing task demands. Nevertheless, propoxyphene-exposed animals have no apparent difficulty with what we might call static problem solving as in the Biel maze, in which there is only one solution and the objective is to minimise errors to an otherwise unchanging problem.

The hyperarousal–hypoadaptability explanation also leads one to the prediction that behaviours requiring the inhibition of responding, such as passive avoidance, should be impaired. It is interesting that although not statistically significant, the passive avoidance data on the propoxyphene-exposed offspring showed that they performed less well than animals from any other drug-treated group in this study, including those exposed to hypervitaminosis-A (Vorhees *et al.*, 1979a).

Another example of a behavioural mechanistic explanation is that of Riley *et al.* (1979a, b) in their studies on an animal model of the fetal alcohol syndrome (FAS). They have shown that on several test paradigms, including reversal learning and passive avoidance, FAS offspring exhibited an inability to inhibit inappropriate responses. Riley *et al.* have also shown that the hyperactivity that characterises a number of their studies on animal models of FAS may be conceptualised as a failure to inhibit normal exploratory behaviour. Here again, the value of this analysis of the behavioural deficit in FAS animals is that it will enable this concept to be tested in explicit terms in future work and provides a firm basis from which to explore neurochemical mechanisms.

The next level of explanation that deserves consideration is that which examines the cellular changes associated with psychoteratogenic effects. At present Rodier's work stands as the best example of this approach, work which has already been reviewed in this chapter (see Section II (C)). However, this brief review can in no sense do justice to this elegant research and there is no substitute for reading the original work of Rodier, particularly the paper summarising her early work (Rodier, 1977). With that advice we will defer any further discussions of the histological approach to mechanisms.

The final level of explanation to be discussed here is the neurochemical. Studies in psychoteratology that have sought neurochemical explanations for the behavioural abnormalities observed have been rare. Middaugh (Middaugh *et al.*, 1974; Zemp and Middaugh, 1975) demonstrated that C57BL mice injected daily with 5 mg/kg body weight of *D*-amphetamine during the last third of pregnancy showed reduced brain norepinephrine levels at birth, which then rose to above normal levels at 21 and 30 days of age in the offspring. Dopamine levels, on the other hand, were elevated only at 30 days of age in the offspring. Behaviourally, the animals showed no increases in activity at 13–31 days of age, but were hyperactive at 75 days of age, by which time brain catecholamines were no different than in controls. These data demonstrate one of the difficulties with neuro-chemical analyses as explanations for behavioural abnormalities, i.e. that often no simple relationship exists between a given neurochemical event and the behavioural phenomena being measured. While it is true that fairly good correlations have been obtained between neurotransmitter changes and behaviour in psychopharmacology, it is less apparent that this approach will be as straightforward in psychoteratology where the drug acts on the organism early and one measures the neurochemical and behavioural consequences at a point far removed from that exposure period. Of course it may be argued that by measuring other neurotransmitters, metabolites or turnover or perhaps by measuring cyclic nucleotide receptor systems, a more adequate correlation would be obtained, but in view of the temporal displacement problems the strategy of simply measuring more neurochemical events does not appear to be a likely solution.

Rech *et al.* (1980) have recently demonstrated that methadone administered on days 5–22 of gestation in rats produced decreased norepinephrine, dopamine and serotonin levels in brains of 21-day-old offspring as well as reductions in several neurotransmitter metabolites, but by 90 days of age virtually all of these neurochemical changes had dissipated. By contrast, the methadone progeny exhibited facilitated shuttle-box acquisition at 90 days of age. While it could be suggested that additional measurements of still more neurotransmitters and of their turnover might reveal the relationships between prenatal methadone exposure and day 90 shuttle-box avoidance behaviour, it is not clear that such would be the case. While it is not surprising to learn that the first few studies to embark on this line of research have not uncovered solid correlations, it is nevertheless somewhat discouraging to confront the prospect that the kinds of approaches that provided the first explanatory insights in psychopharmacology are apparently providing a less auspicious entrée for psychoteratologic analyses.

VI. Implications and Conclusions

It has been the objective of this chapter to provide a selected overview and analysis of research in psychoteratology with an eye towards those topics that are of greatest current interest in the field. Thus, we have discussed government regulations to the extent that they encompass assessments for potential psychoteratogenic effects and we have surveyed the literature and discussed some of the research in the areas of hypervitaminosis-A, antimitotic agents and alcohol. From these we have derived a list of principles that seem to govern psychoteratogenic phenomena, even though many of the principles are not firmly established. These principles will hopefully serve an heuristic or even provocative function to stimulate further research. Finally, we briefly discussed some of the directions being taken in research into psychoteratogenic mechanisms.

Lest we lose sight of the goal, however, let us review several examples of human psychoteratogenesis. The most important example is un-doubtedly the fetal alcohol syndrome (FAS). Clarren and Smith (1978) have stated that FAS may be the 'most frequent known teratogenic cause of mental deficiency in the Western World'. If this appraisal of the signifi-cance of FAS is correct then research in psychoteratology is not merely of academic interest. The effect of this disorder alone may ultimately outweigh that of a tragedy even of the magnitude of thalidomide, if for no other reason than the sheer number of childbearing women and women of childbearing age who use and misuse alcohol. Clarren and Smith (1978) believe, as do most of those working in the fetal alcohol area, that FAS as defined in the scientific literature represents only the most extreme cases of the effects of fetal alcohol exposure. Presumably there are much larger groups of children that have been subjected to compromised development as a result of more moderate alcohol exposures that are undetected, examples perhaps of the concept of covert embryopathy.

A more circumscribed but none the less very real problem in psycho-teratology has been documented in methylmercury poisoning (Minimata disease) and more recently the description of three or perhaps four fetal syndromes related to various anticonvulsant medications. The latter have included the fetal barbituate syndrome (Smith, 1977), the fetal phenytoin syndrome (Hanson and Smith, 1975), the fetal tri-methadone syndrome (Feldman *et al.*, 1977), and most recently the fetal primadone syndrome (Shih *et al.*, 1979). Each of these syndromes exhibits a composite of both physical and psychological defects of which the psychological defects presage the most serious long-term outcome. What is unsettling about the detection of these disorders is that in each case the initial cause for concern was the observation of the physical defects. It is alarming to consider that had these physical defects not occurred concomitantly, these disorders would almost certainly have been missed. Ultimately, the affected children would have undoubtedly been identified, at least by the time they were in elementary school, as learning disabled, but by that time it is unlikely that the disorders could have been related back to their mother's prenatal medical history, with the resultant loss of the cause–effect connection. Thus, the disturbing prospect remains that there could be a defect at large in the environment that compromises

Behavioural Teratogenicity

intellectual and emotional development without concomitant physical signs, a case of covert embryopathy that might escape detection if we do not aggressively undertake efforts to develop a more complete understanding of the phenomena we call psychoteratology.

Acknowledgement

This work was made possible in part through support from NIH Grant HD-05221.

References

Abel, E.L. (1978a) *Psychopharmacology, 57*, 5-11
—— (1978b) *J. Pharmacol. Exp. Ther., 207*, 916-21
—— (1979a) *Behav. Neural Biol., 25*, 406-10
—— (1979b) *Behav. Neural Biol., 25*, 411-13
—— (1979c) *Pharmacol. Biochem. Behav., 10*, 239-43
—— (1979d) *Neurobehav. Toxicol., 1*, 285-7
—— (1980) *Psychol. Bull., 87*, 29-50
Abel, E.L. and Dintcheff, B.A. (1978) *J. Pharmacol. Exp. Ther., 207*, 916-21
Abel, E.L. and York, J.L. (1979) *J. Stud. Alcohol, 40*, 547-53
Abel, E.L., Dintcheff, B.A. and Day, N. (1979) *Neurobehav. Toxicol, 1*, 153-9
Adams, J. (1980) *Teratology, 21*, 25A (Abstract)
Araujo, P.E. and Mayer, J. (1973) *Am. J. Physiol., 225*, 764-5
Ata, M.M. and Sullivan, F.M. (1977) *Br. J. Pharmacol., 59*, 494P (Abstract)
Avery, D.L. and Spyker, J.M. (1978) *Society for Neuroscience, 4*, (Unpublished Abstract)
Barlow, S.M., Knight, A.F. and Sullivan, F.M. (1978) *Teratology, 18*, 211-18
Barlow, S.M., Knight, A.F. and Sullivan, F.M. (1979) *Teratology, 19*, 105-10
Barlow, S.M. and Sullivan, F.M. (1975) in *Teratology: Trends and Applications* (Berry, C.L. and Poswillo, D.E., eds.), pp. 103-20, Springer-Verlag, New York
Bell, J.M. and Stewart, C.N. (1979) *J. Nutr., 109*, 1577-83
Berry, H.K., Butcher, A.E., Elliot, L.A. and Brunner, B.L. (1974) *Develop. Psychobiol., 7*, 165-70
Bertolini, A., Bernardi, M., Poggioli, R., Genedani, S., Castelli, M. and Ferrari, W. (1979) *Experientia, 35*, 635
Bond, N.W. and DiGiusto, E.L. (1976) *Psychopharmacologia, 46*, 163-5
Bond, N.W. and DiGiusto, E.L. (1977a) *Psychopharmacology, 52*, 311-12
Bond, N.W. and DiGiusto, E.L. (1977b) *Psychol. Rep., 41*, 1269-70
Bond, N.W. and DiGiusto, E.L. (1978) *Psychopharmacology, 53*, 69-71
Bowman, R.E. and Smith, R.F. (1977) *Environ. Hlth. Pers., 21*, 189-93
Brady, K., Herrara, Y. and Zenick, H. (1975) *Pharmacol. Biochem. Behav., 3*, 561-5
Branchey, L. and Friedhoff, A.J. (1976) *Ann. N.Y. Acad. Sci., 273*, 328-30
Brunner, R.L., McLean, M.S., Vorhees, C.V. and Butcher, R.E. (1978) *Teratology, 18*, 379-84
Brunner, R.L., Vorhees, C.V., Kinney, L. and Butcher, R.E. (1979) *Neurobehav. Toxicol., 1*, 79-86
Buckalew, L.W. (1977) *Res. Commun. Psychol. Psychiatr. Behav., 2*, 179-91
Buckalew, L.W. (1979) *Addict. Behav., 4*, 275-7
Burkhalter, J.E. and Balster, R.L. (1979) *Neurobehav. Toxicol., 1*, 199-205
Butcher, R.E. (1976) *Environ. Hlth. Pers., 18*, 75-8
Butcher, R.E. and Vorhees, C.V. (1979) *Neurobehav. Toxicol., 1*, Suppl. 1, 207-12
Butcher, R.E., Brunner, R.L., Roth, T. and Kimmel, C.A. (1972a) *Life Sci., 11*, 141-5

Butcher, R.E., Hawver, K., Burbacher, T. and Scott, W. (1975a) in *Aberrant Development in Infancy* (N. Ellis, ed.), pp. 149-60, Erlbaum, Potomac, Maryland
Butcher, R.E., Hawver, K., Kazmaier, K. and Scott, W. (1975b) in *Basic and Therapeutic Aspects of Perinatal Pharmacology* (Morselli, P.L., Garattini, S. and Sereni, F., eds.), pp. 171-6, Raven Press, New York
Butcher, R.E., Scott, W.J., Kazmaier, K. and Ritter, E.J. (1973) *Teratology, 7,* 161-6
Butcher, R.E., Vorhees, C.V. and Kimmel, C.A. (1972b) *Nature New Biol., 236,* 211-12
Butcher, R.E., Wootten, V. and Vorhees, C.V. (1980) *Final Report. National Coffee Association,* USA
Caul, W.F., Osborne, G.L., Fernandez, K. and Henderson, G.I. (1979) *Addict. Behav., 4,* 311-22
Clark, C.V.H., Gorman, D. and Vernadakis, A. (1970) *Develop. Psychobiol., 3,* 225-35
Clarren, S.K. and Smith, D.W. (1978) *N. Engl. J. Med., 298,* 1063-7
Collins, T.F.X. (1978) *J. Environ. Pathol. Toxicol., 2,* 141-7
Coyle, I.R. and Singer, G. (1975) *Psychopharmacology, 44,* 253-6
Coyle, E., Wayner, M.J. and Singer, G. (1976) *Pharmacol. Biochem. Behav., 4,* 191-200
Davis, W. and Ling, C. (1972) *Res. Commun. Chem. Pathol. Pharmacol., 3,* 205-14
Demers, M. and Kirouac, G. (1978) *Physiol. Psychol., 6,* 517-20
Driscoll, J.W. and Stegner, S.E. (1976) *Pharmacol. Biochem. Behav., 4,* 411-17
Dyer, R.S., Eccles, C.U. and Annau, Z. (1978) *Pharmacol. Biochem. Behav., 8,* 137-41
Eccles, C.U. and Annau, Z. (1978) *Society for Neuroscience.* Vol. 4 (Abstract)
Ewart, F.G and Cutler, M.G. (1979) *Psychopharmacology, 62,* 247-51
Fechter, L.D. and Annau, Z. (1977) *Science, 197,* 680-2
Feldman, G.L., Weaver, D.D. and Lovrien, E.W. (1977) *Am. J. Dis. Child., 131,* 1389-92
Flynn, J.C., Flynn, E.R. and Patton, J.H. (1979) *Neurobehav. Toxicol., 1,* Suppl. 1, 93-103
Fox, K.A., Abenschein, D.R. and Lachen, R.B. (1977) *Pharmacol. Res. Commun., 9,* 325-38
Fried, P.A. (1976) *Psychopharmacology, 50,* 285-91
Gandelman, R., Simon, N.G. and McDermott, N.J. (1979) *Physiol. Behav., 23,* 23-6
Garvey, D.J. and Longo, L.D. (1978) *Biol. Reprod., 19,* 8-14
Ginsburg, B.E., Yanai, J. and Sze, P.Y. (1975) in *Research, Treatment and Prevention: Proceedings of the Fourth Annual Alcoholism Conference of the National Institute of Alcohol Abuse and Alcoholism* (Chafetz, M.E., ed.), pp. 183-204, NIAAA, Rockville, Maryland
Glick, S.D., Strumpf, A.J. and Zimmerberg, B. (1977) *Brain Res., 132,* 194-6
Golub, M.S. and Kornetsky, C. (1974) *Develop. Psychobiol., 7,* 79-84
Golub, M. and Kornetsky, C. (1975a) *Develop. Psychobiol., 8,* 519-24
Golub, M.S. and Kornetsky, C. (1975b) *Psychopharmacologia, 43,* 289-91
Golub, M. and Kornetsky, C. (1978) in *Neuro-Psychopharmacology,* Vol. 2, (Deniker, P. *et al.* eds.), pp. 1395-401, Pergamon Press, Oxford
Golub, M., Kornetsky, C. and Bernier, J. (1977) *Physiol. Behav., 18,* 581-5
Graessle, C.A., Ahbel, K. and Porges, S.W. (1978) *Bull. Psychonom. Soc., 12,* 329-31
Grant, L.D. (1976) *Environ. Hlth. Pers., 18,* 85-94
Grove, L.V., Etkin, M.K. and Rosecrans, J.A. (1979) *Neurobehav. Toxicol., 1,* 87-95
Haddad, R., Lee, M.H., Rabe, A., Zatz, Y., Canlon, B. and Dumas, R. (1979a) *Teratology, 19,* 28-9A (Abstract)
Haddad, R., Rabe A. and Dumas, R. (1979b) *Neurotoxicology, 1,* 171-89
Haddad, R., Rabe, A., Dumas, R., Shek, J. and Valsamis, M.P. (1977) *Teratology, 15,* 33A (Abstract)
Halas, E.S., Reynolds, G.M. and Sandstead, H.H. (1977) *Physiol. Behav., 19,* 653-61
Hanson, J.W. and Smith, D.W. (1975) *J. Pediatr., 87,* 285-90
Harris, R.A. and Case, J. (1979) *Behav. Neural Biol., 26,* 234-47
Herrenkohl, L.R. and Whitney, J.B. (1976) *Physiol. Behav., 17,* 1019-21
Hicks, S.P. and D'Amato, C.J. (1978) in *Studies on the Development of Behaviour and the Nervous System,* Vol. 4, *Early Influences* (Gottlieb, G., ed.), pp. 35-7, Academic Press, London
Hinkova, L. and Tabacova, S. (1978) *Acta Nerv. Super. (Praha), 20,* 12-14, (Abstract)
Hoffeld, D.R., McNew, J. and Webster, R.L. (1968) *Nature (London) 218,* 357-8
Hoffeld, D.R. and Webster, R.L. (1965) *Nature (London) 205,* 1070-2
Hughes, J.A. and Annau, Z. (1976) *Pharmacol. Biochem. Behav., 4,* 385-91
Hughes, J.A. and Sparber, S.B. (1978) *Pharmacol. Biochem. Behav., 8,* 365-75

Hutchings, D.E. (1978) in *Studies on the Development of Behaviour and the Nervous System*, Vol. 4, *Early Influences* (Gottleib, G., ed.), pp. 7-34, Academic Press, London
Hutchings, D.E. and Gaston, J. (1974) *Develop. Psychobiol., 7*, 225-33
Hutchings, D.E. and Gibbon, J. (1970) *Psychol. Rep., 26*, 239-46
Hutchings, D.E., Gibbon, J. and Kaufman, M.A. (1973) *Develop. Psychobiol., 6*, 445-57
Hutchings, D.E., Feraru, E., Gorinson, H.S. and Golden, R.R. (1979a) *Neurobehav. Toxicol. 1*, 33-40
Hutchings, D.E., Towey, J.P., Gorinson, H.S. and Hunt, H.F. (1979b) *J. Pharmacol. Exp. Ther., 208*, 106-12
Inouye, M. and Murakami, U. (1974) *Congenital Anomalies, 14*, 77-83
Jensh, R.P., Ludlow, J., Weinberg, I., Vogel, W.H., Rudder, T. and Brent, R.L. (1978) *Teratology, 17*, 21A
Jewett, R.E. and Norton, S. (1966) *Exp. Neurol., 14*, 33-43
Joffe, J.M. (1969) *Prenatal Determinants of Behavior*, Pergamon Press, London
—— (1977) *Physiol. Behav., 19*, 601-6
—— (1978) in *Studies on the Development of Behaviour and the Nervous System*, Vol. 4, *Early Influences* (Gottlieb, G., ed.), pp. 197-44, Academic Press, London
Jones, K.L. and Smith, D.W. (1973) *Lancet, 2*, 999-1001
Jordan, R.L., Young, T.R., Dinwiddie, S.H. and Harry, G.J. (1979) *Pharmacol. Biochem. Behav., 11*, Suppl. 1, 39-45
Kalter, H. (1968) *Teratology of the Central Nervous System*, University of Chicago Press, Chicago
Kandall, S.R. (1977) in *Drug Abuse in Pregnancy and Neonatal Effects* (Rementaria, J.L., ed.), pp. 116-28, Mosby, St. Louis
Kellogg, C., Tervo, D., Ison, J., Parisi, T. and Miller, R.K. (1980) *Science, 207*, 205-7
Kimmel, C.A., Butcher, R.E., Vorhees, C.V. and Schumacher, H.J. (1974) *Teratology, 10*, 293-300
Kirby, M.L. (1979) *Develop. Neurosci., 2*, 238-44
Kletzkin, M., Wojciechowski, H. and Margolin, S. (1964) *Nature (London), 204*, 1206
Kochever, J.W., Martin, J.R., Appleby, B.D., (1977) *Bull. Psychonom. Soc., 10*, 49-52
Krsiak, M., Elis, J., Poschlova, N. and Masek, K. (1977) *J. Stud. Alcohol, 38*, 1696-704
Lasky, D.I., Zagon, I.S. and McLaughlin, P.J. (1977) *Pharmacol. Biochem. Behav., 7*, 281-4
Leathwood, P. (1978) in *Studies on the Development of Behaviour and the Nervous System*, Vol. 4, *Early Influences* (Gottlieb, G., ed.), pp. 187-209, Academic Press, London
Lemptey, M.S. and Walker, B.L. (1978) *J. Nutr., 108*, 358-67
Lodge, A. (1977) in *NIDA Symposium on Comprehensive Health Care for Addicted Families and their Children* (Beschner, G. and Brotman, R., eds.), pp. 79-85, National Institute on Drug Abuse, Rockville, MD
Lydiard, R.B. and Sparber, S.B. (1977) *Develop. Psychobiol., 10*, 305-14
Malakhovskii, V.G. (1969) *Bull. Exp. Biol. Med., 68*, 1230-2
—— (1971) *Bull. Exp. Biol. Med., 71*, 254-6
Martin, J.C., Martin, D.C., Lemire, R. and Mackler, B. (1979) *Neurobehav. Toxicol., 1*, 49-55
Martin, J.C., Martin, D.C., Sigman, G. and Radow, B. (1977) *Develop. Psychobiol., 10*, 435-46
Meisel, R.L., Dohanich, G.P. and Ward, I.L. (1979) *Physiol. Behav., 22*, 527-30
Mele, J.M. and Jensh, R.P. (1977) *Teratology, 17*, 44A (Abstract)
Middaugh, L.D., Blackwell, L.A., Santos, C.A. and Zemp, J.W. (1974) *Develop. Psychobiol., 7*, 429-38
Middaugh, L.D., Santos, C.A. and Zemp, J.W. (1975) *Pharmacol. Biochem. Behav., 3*, 1137-9
Murai, N. (1966) *Tohoku J. Exp. Med., 89*, 265-72
Musch, H.R., Bornhausen, M., Kriegel, H. and Greim, H. (1978) *Arch. Toxicol., 40*, 103-8
Nelson, B.K. (1979) *Teratology, 19*, 41A (Abstract)
Nemeroff, C.B., Grant, L.D., Bissette, G., Ervin, G.N., Harrell, L.E. and Prange, A.J. (1977) *Psychoneuroendocrinology, 2*, 12-19
Olney, J.W. (1969) *Science, 164*, 719-21
Olney, J.W. and Ho, O.L. (1970) *Nature (London), 227*, 609-10
Olney, J.W., Ho, O.L. and Rhee, V. (1971) *Exp. Brain Res., 14*, 61-76
Ordy, J.M., Briezzee, K.R., Beavers, T. and Medart, R. (1978) *Society for Neuroscience, 4*, St. Louis (Unpublished Abstract)
Ordy, J.M., Samorajski, T., Collins, R.L. and Rolsten, C. (1966) *J. Pharmacol. Exp. Ther., 151*, 110-25

Padich, R. and Zenick, H. (1977) *Pharmacol. Biochem. Behav., 6*, 371-5
Peters, D.A.V., Taub, H. and Tang, S. (1979) *Neurobehav. Toxicol., 1*, 221-5
Peters, D.P. (1978) *Physiol. Behav., 20*, 359-62
Peters, M.A. (1978) *Proc. West. Pharmacol. Soc., 21*, 411-18
Pizzi, W.J. and Barnhardt, J.E. (1976) *Pharmacol. Biochem. Behav., 5*, 551-57
Pizzi, W.J., Barnhardt, J.E. and Fanslow, D.J. (1977) *Science, 196*, 452-4
Pradhan, S.N. and Lynch, J.F. (1972) *Arch. Int. Pharmacodyn. Ther., 197*, 301-4
Rech, R.H., Lomuscio, G. and Algeri, S. (1980) *Neurobehav. Toxicol., 2*, 73-5
Reinisch, J.M., Simon, N.G., Karow, W.G. and Gandelman, R. (1978) *Science, 202*, 436-8
Reiter, L.W., Anderson, G.E. and Cahill, D.F. (1975) *Environ. Hlth. Pers., 12*, 119-23
Reuhl, K.R. and Chang, L.W. (1979) *Neurotoxicology, 1*, 21-55
Richardson, D.L., Karczmer, A.G. and Scudder, C.L. (1972) *Fed. Proc. Fed. Am. Soc. Exp. Biol., 31*, 596 (Abstract)
Rider, A.A., Simonson, M., Weng, Y.S. and Hsu, J.M. (1978) *Nutr. Rep. Int., 17*, 595-605
Riley, E.P., Lochry, E.A., Shapiro, N.R. and Baldwin, J. (1979a) *Pharmacol. Biochem. Behav., 10*, 255-9
Riley, E.P., Shapiro, N.R. and Lochry, E.A. (1979b) *Pharmacol. Biochem. Behav., 11*, 513-19
Rodier, P.M. (1977) *Teratology, 16*, 235-46
—— (1978) in *Handbook of Teratology, Research Procedures and Data Analysis*, Vol. 4, (Wilson, J.G. and Fraser, F.C., eds.), pp. 397-428, Plenum Press, New York
Rodier, P.M., Reynolds, S.S. and Roberts, W.N. (1979) *Teratology, 19*, 327-36
Rodier, P.M., Webster, W.S. and Langman, J. (1975) in *Aberrant Development in Infancy: Human and Animal Studies* (Ellis, N., ed.), pp. 177-85, Erlbaum, Hillsdale, New Jersey
Rohner, E.C. and Werboff, J. (1979) *Develop. Psychobiol., 12*, 39-48
Sandstead, H.H., Fosmire, G.J., Halas, E.S., Jacob, R.A., Strobel, D.A. and Marks, E.O. (1977) *Teratology, 16*, 229-34
Schneider, B.F. and Norton, S. (1979) *Neurobehav. Toxicol., 1*, 193-7
Shaywitz, B.A., Griffieth, G.G. and Warshaw, J.B. (1979) *Neurobehav. Toxicol., 1*, 113-22
Shih, L.Y., Diamond, N. and Kushnick, T. (1979) *Teratology, 19*, 47-8A (Abstract)
Simon, N.G. and Gandelman, R. (1977) *Behav. Biol., 21*, 478-88
Smith, D.W. (1977) *Am. J. Dis. Child., 131*, 1337-9
Smith, D.J., Joffe, J.M. and Heseltine, G.F.D. (1975) *Physiol. Behav., 15*, 461-9
Smith, R.F., Bowman, R.E. and Katz, J. (1978) *Anaesthesiology, 49*, 319-23
Snowden, C.T. (1973) *Pharmacol. Biochem. Behav., 1*, 599-603
Sobotka, T.J., Brodie, R.E. and Spaid, S.L. (1977) *J. Toxicol. Environ. Hlth., 2*, 1211-20
Sobotka, T.J., Cook, M.P. and Brodie, R.E. (1974) *Biol. Psychiatr., 8*, 307-20
Sobotka, T.J., Spaid, S.L. and Brodie, R.E. (1979) *Neurotoxicology, 1*, 403-16
Sobrian, S.K. (1977) *Pharmacol. Biochem. Behav., 7*, 285-8
Sobrian, S.K. (1977) *Develop. Psychobiol., 10*, 41-51
Soyka, L.F., Joffe, J.M., Peterson, J.M. and Smith, S.M. (1978) *Pharmacol. Biochem. Behav., 9*, 405-9
Spyker, J.M. (1975) in *Behavioural Toxicology* (Weiss, B. and Laties, V.G., eds.), pp. 311-30, Plenum Press, New York
Spyker, J.M. and Avery, D.L. (1977) *J. Toxicol. Environ. Hlth., 3*, 989-1002
Spyker, J.M., Sparber, S.B. and Goldberg, A.M. (1972) *Science, 177*, 621-3
Stokes, J.D. and Scudder, C.L. (1974) *Develop. Psychobiol., 7*, 343-50
Stokes, J., Scudder, C.L. and Karczmar, A.G. (1972) *Fed. Proc. Fed. Am. Soc. Exp. Biol., 31*, 596 (Abstract)
Takasaki, Y. (1978a) *Toxicology, 9*, 293-305
—— (1978b) *Toxicology, 9*, 307-18
Takeuchi, T., Eto, N. and Eto, K. (1979) *Neurotoxicology, 1*, 1-20
Tamaki, Y. and Inouye, M. (1979) *Physiol. Behav., 22*, 701-5
Tesh, J.M. and Pritchard, A.L. (1977) *Teratology, 15*, 23A (Abstract)
Thompson, R.J. (1979) *J. Pediatr. Psychol., 4*, 265-76
Tilson, H.A., Davis, G.J., McLachlan, J.A. and Lucier, G.W. (1979) *Environ. Res., 18*, 466-74
Verlangieri, A.J. (1979) *Pharmacol. Biochem. Behav., 11*, 95-8
Villescas, R., Zanenhof, S. and Guthrie, D. (1979) *Physiol. Behav., 23*, 945-54

Vorhees, C.V. (1974) *Teratology, 10,* 269-74
—— (1981) *Neurobehav. Toxicol.* (in press)
Vorhees, C.V., Brunner, R.L., McDaniel, C.R. and Butcher, R.E. (1978) *Teratology, 17,* 271-6
Vorhees, C.V., Brunner, R.L. and Butcher, R.E. (1979a) *Science, 205,* 1220-5
Vorhees, C.V., Brunner, R.L., Wootten, V. and Butcher, R.E. (1980g) *FDA Report on Methyl Salicylate,* (Contract 223-75-2030)
Vorhees, C.V., Brunner, R.L., Wootten, V. and Butcher, R.E. (1980h) *FDA Report on Tertiary Butylhydroquinone (TBHQ)* (Contract 223-75-2030)
Vorhees, C.V., Butcher, R.E. and Berry, H.K. (1981) *Neurosci. Biobehav. Rev.* (in press)
Vorhees, C.V., Butcher, R.E., Brunner, R.L. and Sobotka, T.J. (1979b) *Toxicol. Appl. Pharmacol., 50,* 267-82
Vorhees, C.V., Butcher, R.E., Brunner, R.L. and Sobotka, T.J. (1980a) *Fd. Cosmet. Toxicol.* (in press)
Vorhees, C.V., Butcher, R.E., Brunner, R.L., Wootten, V. and Sobtaka, T.J. (1980b) *FDA Report on Butylated Hydroxyanisole* (Unpublished)
Vorhees, C.V., Butcher, R.E., Brunner, R.L., Wootten, V. and Sobotka, T.J. (1980c) *FDA Report on Brominated Vegetable Oil* (Unpublished)
Vorhees, C.V., Butcher, R.E., Brunner, R.L., Wootten, V. and Sobotka, T.J. (1980d) *FDA Report on FD and C Red Dye No. 40* (Unpublished)
Vorhees, C.V., Butcher, R.E., Brunner, R.L., Wootten, V. and Sobtka, T.J. (1980e) *FDA Report on FD and C Red Dye No. 3* (Unpublished)
Werboff, J. and Dembicki, E.L. (1962) *J. Neuropsychiatr., 4,* 87-91
Werboff, J. and Havlena, J. (1962) *Exp. Neurol., 6,* 263-9
Werboff, J. and Kesner, R. (1963) *Nature (London), 197,* 106-7
Werboff, J., Gottlieb, J.S., Dembicki, E.L. and Havlena, J. (1961a) *Exp. Neurol., 3,* 542-55
Werboff, J., Gottlieb, J.S., Havlena, J. and Word, T.J. (1961b) *Paediatrics, 27,* 318-24
Whitsett, J.M. and Vandenbergh, J.G. (1978) in *Studies on the Development of Behaviour and the Nervous System,* Vol. 4, *Early Influences* (Gottleib, G., ed.), pp. 73-106, Academic Press, London
Wilson, J.G. (1977) in *Handbook of Teratology,* Vol. 1, *General Principles and Etiology* (Wilson, J.G. and Fraser, F.C., eds.), pp. 309-55, Plenum Press, New York
Wilson, J.G., Kalter, H., Palmer, A.K., Hoar, R.M., Shenefelt, R.E., Beck, F., Earl, F.L., Nelson, N.S., Berman, E., Stara, J.F., Selby, L.A. and Scott, W.J. (1978) in *Pathology of Laboratory Animals,* Vol. 2, (Benirschke, K., *et al.,* eds.), pp. 1817-1946, Springer-Verlag, New York
Wilson, G.S., McCreary, R., Kean, J. and Baxter, J.C. (1979) *Paediatrics, 63,* 135-41
Yanai, J. and Tabakoff, B. (1979) *Psychopharmacology, 64,* 325-7
Yanai, J. and Ginsburg, B.E. (1976) *Physiol. Psychol., 4,* 409-11
Yanai, J. and Ginsburg, B.E. (1977) *Clin. Exp. Res., 1,* 325-33
Zagon, I.S., McLaughlin, P.J. and Thompson, C.I. (1979a) *Pharmacol. Biochem. Behav., 10,* 743-9
Zagon, I.S., McLaughlin, P.J. and Thompson, C.I. (1979b) *Pharmacol. Biochem. Behav., 10,* 889-94
Zamehof, S. and Van Marhtens, E. (1978) in *Studies on the Development of Behaviour and the Nervous System,* Vol. 4. *Early Influences* (Gottlieb, G. ed.), pp. 149-86, Academic Press, London
Zemp, J.W. and Middaugh, L.D. (1975) *Addict. Dis., 2,* 307-31
Zenick, H. (1974) *Pharmacol. Biochem. Behav., 2,* 709-13
—— (1977) in *Behavioural Toxicology: An Emerging Discipline* (Zenick, H. and Reiter, L.W., eds.), pp. 3-1 to 3-21, US Environmental Protection Agency, Research Triangle Park, North Carolina
Zenick, H., Padich, R., Thatcher, T., Santistevan, B. and Aragon, P. (1978) *Pharmacol. Biochem. Behav., 8,* 347-50
Zenick, H., Pecorraro, F., Price, D., Saez, K. and Ward, J. (1979a) *Neurobehav. Toxicol., 1,* 65-71
Zenick, H., Rodriquez, W., Ward, J. and Elkington, B. (1979b) *Develop. Psychobiol., 12,* 509-14

CHAPTER TEN

DEVELOPMENTAL ENZYME PATHOLOGY
Keith Snell

CONTENTS

I. General Considerations of Developmental Toxicity

For many years it has been recognised that chemicals present in the environment or administered therapeutically pose a hazard to the unborn fetus to whom they may be transmitted via the maternal circulation. The most overtly recognisable adverse effect of exposure to a toxicant in this manner is either intrauterine fetal death or birth of the fetus with anatomical malformations (see reviews by Wilson, 1973; Smithells, 1976). The identification of such 'teratogenic' effects is now a part of all toxicological evaluation studies (see Beck, Chapter 1; Palmer, 1977). However, it is also becoming recognised that gross teratogenic effects are only a small part of the potential hazard facing the developing organism during its progress towards adulthood (see Vorhees and Butcher, Chapter 9, and also Barlow and Sullivan, 1975; Harris and Simonopolous, 1976; Thornburg and Moore, 1976). Apart from frank congenital malformations, prenatal toxicity may also manifest itself as functional aberrations, such as behavioural or biochemical abnormalities, which may remain latent before being expressed at later stages of development. It follows from the nature of the defect that such functional abnormalities are likely to be induced during organogenesis itself or even at later stages when the development of individual organs is complete but the establishment of inter-organal regulatory networks is still developing. An extreme example of a latent toxic response is seen in the case of transplacental carcinogenesis, where the action of a carcinogen prenatally does not manifest itself in the form of tumours until later in life (see Kleihues, Chapter 8). Organogenesis is not a synchronous event for all organs so that the timing of the toxic insult during development not only determines the type of abnormality (anatomical or functional) but also the organ which is affected (see Williams, Chapter 4). In the rat the period of organogenesis is from about day 5 to day 15 of gestation and the organ-specific spectrum of malformations resulting from exposure to a teratogen will vary according to the precise time of exposure within that period (Wilson, 1973). Thus, in terms of structural teratogenic effects (resulting in anatomical malformations) the period of organogenesis constitutes a 'sensitive' or 'critical period'. Other factors will influence the 'critical periods' for other types of developmental toxicity, if indeed this concept is applicable in these situations.

One crucial factor determining developmental toxicity, and especialy transplacental carcinogenicity, is the maturity of the enzyme systems that metabolise foreign compounds. In many cases such metabolism leads to the formation of reactive intermediates which are the ultimate progenitors of toxic or carcinogenic actions. The enzymic machinery for foreign-compound metabolism develops in the liver late in gestation and in the early postnatal period (see Pelkonen, Chapter 6, and also Eriksson and Yaffe, 1973; Gillette and Stripp, 1975; Dickerson and Basu, 1975). This period could therefore constitute another critical developmental period for toxicity. Druckrey and others have shown that this applies strikingly to transplacental carcinogenesis and particularly to tumours arising in the central nervous system (Druckrey, 1973; Kleihues, Chapter 8).

Other factors which may contribute to the developmental susceptibility of the immature animal to toxic insult and which may form the basis for further critical periods include the immaturity or absence of: membrane barriers governing intestinal absorption (Koldovsky, 1972; Henning and Kretchmer, 1975) and transport across the blood–brain barrier (Nyhan, 1961; Shapiro, 1971; Cremer *et al.*, 1976); renal excretory capacity (Baxter and Yoffey, 1948; Capek and Jelinek, 1956; Bernstein, 1972), protein-binding capacities in blood and other tissues (Kobyletzki, 1971); and differences in pathways of intermediary metabolism (Greengard, 1971; Snell and Walker, 1973a; Baquer *et al.*, 1973; MacDonnel and Greengard, 1974; Snell, 1981a) and in the cellular composition of tissues (Tennyson, 1970; Pease, 1971; Greengard *et al.*, 1972).

The susceptibility of the developing animal to a particular toxic agent and the nature of the toxic response are of course also dependent on the site of action of the agent. In the prenatal period, apart from direct interactions with the fetus after the transplacental transmission of the agent by the mother, toxic substances can also act on the placenta or on the mother to produce secondary effects in the developing fetus. Interference with placental function could lead to defective nutrient transport (see Beck, Chapter 1; Williams, Chapter 4). In addition developmental aberrations can also arise through alterations in the umbilical blood flow or in the amniotic fluid volume. Effects on the mother may result in biochemical or endocrinological disturbances or nutritional deficiencies which can have secondary effects in the fetus which interfere with organ maturation and functional development. One can envisage two situations in which prenatal exposure to a toxic agent might take place. There might be a single accidental exposure of the pregnant female to the toxicant at a critical developmental stage. This could be due, for example, to ingestion of a batch of contaminated foodstuff by the mother, as was the case in recent incidents in Japan and Iraq of methylmercury poisoning (Magos, 1975). Damage to the developing fetus may not be overtly manifest as anatomical malformations at birth, but may be exhibited as behavioural or metabolic abnormalities which perhaps remain dormant until later in life. *Metabolic teratogenesis* (Snell *et al.*, 1977) or *psychoteratogenesis* (Vorhees and Butcher, Chapter 9) are terms which describe the development of functional disorders at birth, or later in development, after early prenatal exposure of the developing fetus to a toxic agent. Alternatively, continuous exposure to the toxic agent may occur because of persistent intake by the mother of an environmental contaminant or because of long-term use of therapeutic agents. The continuous exposure of the developing fetus to a toxicant could result in functional disturbances at any subsequent developmental stage.

The mother continues to play a significant role in developmental toxicology in the postnatal period. Environmental toxic agents can affect the developing neonate directly or postnatal exposure to fat-soluble toxicants by ingestion with the maternal milk can occur. Lipophilic chemicals (such as the halogenated hydrocarbon insecticides like DDT) are accumulated in body fat, and during pregnancy and lactation the body burden will be greater due to the increased amounts of maternal fat. Moreover, during lactation the explosive increase in lipid material in the mammary gland, coupled with a marked increase in the blood flow, will make this organ a particularly significant store of lipophilic toxicants which will be excreted into the milk and subsequently ingested by the developing infant. For example, the concentrations of organochlorine pesticide residues in human milk exceed those accepted in other foods, which is a cause for much concern (Egan *et al.*, 1965; Quinby *et al.*, 1965; Matsumura, 1975; Woodard *et al.*, 1976; Rogan *et al.*, 1980). Toxic agents may also be ingested in the milk by the developing neonate simply as a result of transfer from the maternal blood-stream into the secreted milk fluid.

As with all toxic reactions, developmental abnormalities will be expected to exhibit dose-response relationships. Teratologists have long held the view that there is a no-effect level of a toxic agent which is below the threshold at which teratogenic or embryo- or fetolethal effects begin to appear. It is now clear that this is not so and that sandwiched between this no-effect dosage and the threshold for teratogenicity is a dosage range over which developmental functional disorders may be induced (see Chapter 9). Since this range is lower than that at which other types of developmental toxicity are produced, functional abnormalities probably constitute the most serious hazard of toxic agents to which developing organisms may be exposed.

II. Early Detection of Developmental Toxicity

One of the problems associated with functional developmental toxicity is that although an increased vulnerability of developing animals to toxic agents is apparent, the consequences may not manifest themselves until later developmental stages. The latency could arise because the damaged process does not become fully functional until later in life or because compensatory mechanisms are present that inititially mask the defect but which themselves change during development. This obviously poses a problem of early detection and, moreover, if the derangements are functional in nature they may present as subtle sub-clinical disturbances causing further difficulties in toxicological evaluation studies. Because of the subtleties of the derangements sensitive toxicological methods of detection have been proposed for their investigation, such as behavioural tests (Spyker, 1975a, b; Brimblecombe, 1968) and tests of the occurrence of specific developmental events (Shapiro *et al.*, 1970; Spyker, 1975a, b), and examples are shown in Table 10.1.

The rationale for these tests is that the parameters measured involve very precise co-ordinated response of neural and endocrine systems. Experience has shown that the central nervous system is the most vulnerable organ in the developing animal, both because of its own functional immaturity and also the absence of the protective blood–brain barrier until later life. Thus, microneuroanatomical lesions could be produced which are not expressed at that time but which later manifest themselves

Table 10.1: Evaluation of Developmental Toxicity

(i)   Morphological characteristics: posture, fur condition.
(ii) Growth: body and organ weights, and rate of growth.
(iii) Maturation events: age of ear and eye opening, acquisition of fur.
(iv) Specific reflexes: righting reflex, corneal reflex, swimming reflex.
(v)   Activity: hyper- or hypoactivity measurements at various ages; open-field tests.
(vi) Learning ability: maze tests and conditioning response tests.
(vii) Sexual parameters: age of sexual development; reproductive efficiency; fertility rate.

as developmental or behavioural abnormalities, both of which are dependent on neural integrity. The dependence on endocrine status also makes these parameters useful as indicators of general impairments of body function which are likely to be reflected in hormonal balance in the animal.

We have explored the potential value of the use of biochemical parameters, particularly enzymes, as indicators of developmental disturbances. Analysis of the developmental profiles of over 80 rat liver enzymes indicated that these could be divided into a number of characteristic patterns that correlated with known metabolic adaptations which occur during pre- and postnatal development of the rat (Snell, 1971). The major adaptations of carbohydrate, protein and lipid metabolism are shown in Figure 10.1, and these patterns are mirrored by the activities of key enzymes in the various metabolic pathways during development. These patterns may be further resolved, on the basis of the age of first appearance of the enzyme activity, into three temporal groups (Greengard, 1971; Snell, 1971) which Greengard has denoted as the fetal, neonatal and suckling clusters (Fig. 10.2 a, b and c, respectively). The appearance of a characteristic enzyme at a specific development stage should therefore serve as a sensitive indicator of the developmental competence of the animal at that age, and the use of developmental enzymes for this purpose has been referred to as 'enzyme pathology' (Greengard, 1977). This will reflect not only the inherent normal functioning of hepatic tissue but also general body function and neural integrity. This is because the evolution of enzymes at the various developmental stages is critically dependent on the presence and co-ordination of hormonal and environmental factors (see Vernon and Walker, 1968, Greengard, 1971; Snell and Walker, 1972, 1974; Feigelson, 1973). Table 10.2 shows the specific influences which have been implicated in controlling developmental enzyme accumulations.

Figure 10.1: Metabolic Adaptions During Neonatal Development of Rat Liver. A, Nucleic acid synthesis (circles), amino acid oxidation and urea synthesis (lines); B, glycolysis and lipid synthesis (lines), fatty acid oxidation and ketogenesis (circles); C, glycogen synthesis (lines) and gluconeogenesis (circles). B, birth; A, adult. Results are expressed as percentage of adulthood; left-hand scales, lines; right-hand scales, circles.

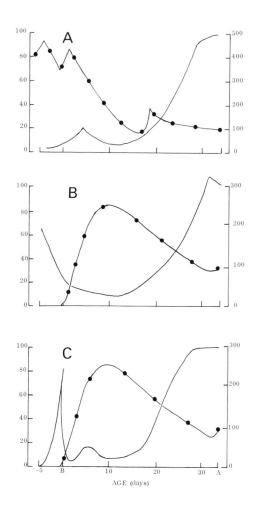

Source: Data compiled from Greengard (1971, 1973); Snell (1971, 1980a); Walker (1971).

306

Figure 10.2: Enzyme Clusters During Neonatal Development of Rat Liver. (a) Fetal cluster; (b) neonatal cluster; (c) weanling cluster. Enzymes appearing in more than one cluster show a biphasic developmental accumulation. B: birth.

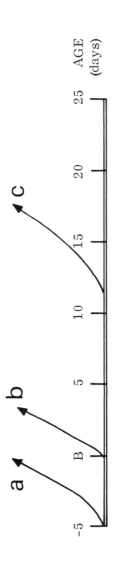

(a) glycogen
glucose 6-phosphatase
glycogen synthetase
glycogen phosphorylase
NADPH-cytochrome c dehydrogenase

(b) PEP carboxykinase
serine aminotransferase
glyoxylate aminotransferase
fructokinase
palmityl CoA synthetase
glycerol kinase
glucose 6-phosphatase
alanine aminotransferase

(c) glucokinase
alanine aminotransferase
tryptophan dioxygenase
NADP-malate dehydrogenase
ATP-citrate lyase
xanthine oxidase

Source: Enzymes are compiled from data of Greengard, 1971; Snell, 1971; Snell and Walker, 1972, 1974.

307

Table 10.2: Factors in Developmental Enzyme Accumulations

	Fetal period
Hormonal:	Adrenal corticoids
	Thyroid hormones
	Pituitary
Nutritional:	Maternal glucose supply
	Perinatal period
Hormonal:	Pancreatic hormones
Nutritional	Carbohydrate-to-lipid transition
	Postnatal period
Hormonal:	Pituitary-adrenal axis activated
	Thyroid hormones
	Insulin
Nutritional:	Lipid-to-carbohydrate transition
	Adolescent period
Hormonal:	Oestrogen-neuroendocrine interaction

As well as enzyme activities, other biochemical parameters can also serve as sensitive parameters of normal development, since they show characteristic modifications at specific stages of development. This is particularly so during the perinatal period, where hormones and metabolites in the blood undergo rapid and marked changes in the newborn animal in response to its transition from the uterine to the extrauterine environment (Snell and Walker, 1973b; Girard *et al.*, 1973).

In terms of toxicity evaluation one is always concerned with the problem of extrapolating from data obtained in experimental animals to man. It is therefore pertinent to know whether the developmental enzyme changes observed in the rat also occur in the same way in man. For obvious reasons it is difficult to obtain data on the changing pattern of enzyme activities throughout human fetal and postnatal development. However, it is possible to examine this question even if data are only available from a single fetal age-group by relating the enzyme activities to those found in adult liver. Such a comparison has been carried out by

Greengard (1977) who found that enzymes measured in the second trimester human fetal liver fell into discrete groups depending on the fractional activity (compared to adult liver activity) which they exhibited at this stage. There was good agreement between the fractional activities characteristic of these various enzyme groups in human fetal liver and the developmental behaviour of rat liver enzymes as characterised by enzyme clusters (Fig. 10.3).

In addition to the developmental clusters shown in Figure 10.2, a further group of enzymes is included which in rat liver shows high activity before birth but then declines postnatally to low adult values. Enzymes belonging to this cluster in rat liver show greater than adult values in human fetal liver. Enzymes associated with the other clusters in rat liver show evidence of similar clustering in human fetal liver and the pattern obtained (Fig. 10.3) suggests that the *sequence* of enzyme development in human liver closely resembles that in rat liver. This further implies that the physiological mechanisms involved in developmental enzyme changes in the two species must also be analogous. Thus, deviant developmental enzyme patterns observed in the rat in the experimental situation may be considered as being of direct relevance to man. Furthermore, any disturbances in the fetal environment which resulted in developmental enzyme aberrations may also have a similar genesis in man, thus providing clues as to the age of onset and possible toxic mechanisms.

In the following sections I will consider the application of developmental enzyme pathology to various examples of developmental toxicity which result in metabolic functional abnormalities. In view of the newness of the concepts there is virtually no material in the literature to draw upon, hence all of the examples will be from work in my own laboratory.

III. Prenatal Developmental Toxicity

A. *Metabolic Teratogenesis by Methylmercury*

The environmental hazards of organomercury compounds have been well recognised since the large-scale outbreaks of poisoning in Japan and Iraq in the 1950s and 1960s (Magos, 1975). Overt neurological dysfunction is the most striking sign of toxicity in experimental and clinical situations (Hunter and Russell, 1954; Miyakawa, *et al.*, 1970; Chang and Hartman, 1972) and this criterion is used as a basis for setting safety standards.

Figure 10.3: Developmental Enzymes in Human Fetal Liver. (a') Fetal enzymes; (a) fetal cluster; (b) neonatal cluster; (c) weanling cluster. Human fetal liver enzymes (numbered) are arranged beneath the enzyme cluster to which the rat liver enzymes belong. 1, thymidine kinase; 2, phosphoserine phosphatase; 3, ornithine decarboxylase; 4, hexokinase; 5, glucose 6-phosphate dehydrogenase; 6, pyruvate carboxylase; 7, glutamate dehydrogenase; 8, phenylalanine hydroxylase; 9, carbamoyl phosphate synthetase; 10, fructose bisphosphatase; 11, arginase; 12, aspartate aminotransferase; 13, glucose 6-phosphatase; 14, ornithine carbamoyltransferase; 15, UDP-glucuronyltransferase; 16, PEP carboxykinase; 17, phenylalanine-pyruvate aminotransferase; 18, alcohol dehydrogenase; 19, alanine-2-oxoglutarate aminotransferase; 20, glucokinase.

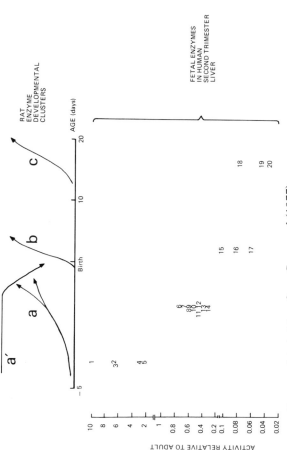

Source: Enzyme data is taken from Greengard (1977).

Distribution studies have shown that methylmercury is concentrated in the liver (Norseth and Clarkson, 1970; Takahashi *et al.*, 1971; Ware *et al.*, 1974a), and ultrastructural evidence for hepatotoxicity after acute or chronic methylmercury exposure of rats has been presented (Desnoyers and Chang, 1975a, b), emphasising the potential role of this organ as a target for organomercury toxicity.

Exposure of pregnant women (Bakir *et al.*, 1973) or animals (Reynolds and Pitkin, 1975) to methylmercury is known to result in rapid placental transfer and at birth the highest concentration of methylmercury is found in the liver (Garcia *et al.*, 1974). Ultrastructural evidence for fetal liver damage after injection of pregnant rats with a single small dose of methylmercury during gestation has been obtained (Ware *et al.*, 1974b). No information as to any functional hepatic derangement was given, although the newborns showed no gross teratological malformations. It is known that mice treated with similar low doses of methylmercury during gestation give birth to overtly normal pups who develop subtle behavioural deviations between weaning and puberty. Later in life more overt disturbances of a neurological and immunological nature become apparent (Spyker, 1975a, b). Thus, the manifestation of toxicity after fetal exposure to methylmercury appears to be developmentally related and, in view of the ultrastructural evidence for hepatic abnormalities at birth (Ware *et al.*, 1974b), measurements of biochemical parameters were made in the late fetal and perinatal periods.

Methylmercury was administered as a single injection on the ninth day of gestation at low doses (4 or 8 mg/kg body weight) which have been estimated to represent a fetal exposure of about 3-6 ppm (Ware *et al.*, 1974b). At these low doses, in common with other workers, no toxic effects were observed in the mother and, moreover, no evidence of anatomical malformations or other overt toxic symptoms were detected in methylmercury-exposed progeny at the ages at which biochemical investigations were made in the present study.

There was a dose-related decrease in liver glycogen and glucose 6-phosphatase (chosen as parameters on the basis of Fig. 10.2) in late fetal animals exposed to methylmercury *in utero* on day 9 of gestation (Fig. 10.4). These parameters were chosen not only because they undergo marked developmental changes at this time, but also because of their implications for carbohydrate metabolism which assumes crucial physiological importance in the perinatal period (Snell, 1981b; Snell and Walker, 1978, 1973b, c). Postnatal rats showed a dose-related decrease in body weight after *in utero* exposure to methylmercury (Snell *et al.*, 1977) and

Figure 10.4: Effect of Methylmercury (MeHg) on Fetal Liver Glycogen Concentration and Glucose 6-Phosphatase Activity. The open circles show the natural developmental patterns for liver glycogen and glucose 6-phosphatase in untreated animals during the later fetal period (means of 3-5 determinations; K. Snell, unpublished work). The columns show glycogen concentrations and glucose 6-phosphatase activities in livers of fetuses (20.5 days' gestation) of mothers exposed to methylmercury, at the doses indicated, on day 9 of gestation. SEM of 12-25 determinations (glycogen) or 4-9 determinations (glucose 6-phosphatase) are shown by vertical bars. B: birth.

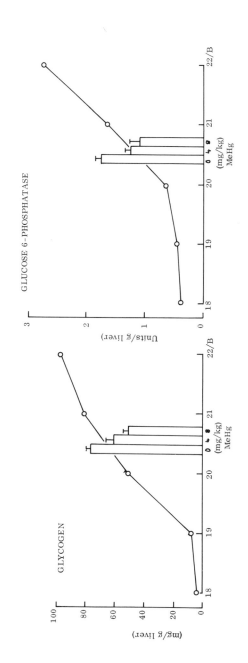

Source: Data taken from Snell et al. (1977).

Figure 10.5: Adaptations of Carbohydrate Metabolism at Birth. Further details in Snell (1981b).

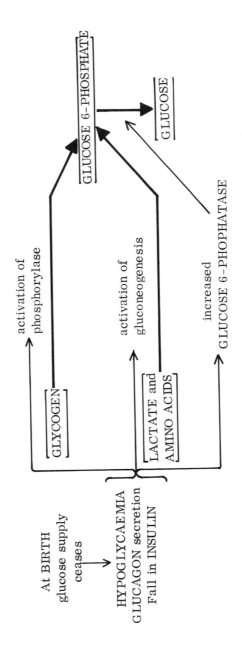

this effect persisted beyond weaning. A retardation of body growth during postnatal development was also observed by Spyker (1975b) in mice exposed to low doses of methylmercury *in utero*.

Interpretation of the biochemical changes observed in response to methylmercury exposure requires a description of the adaptations of carbohydrate metabolism that take place at birth and these are shown schematically in Fig. 10.5 (see also Snell, 1981b). Before birth the normal rat fetus builds up an enormous store of liver glycogen. At birth this store of glycogen is mobilised to supply blood glucose which falls precipitously after the abrupt cessation of the transplacental glucose supply. Correction of the natural transient postnatal hypoglycaemia is achieved both by breakdown of liver glycogen and activation of hepatic gluconeogenesis, the process by which non-carbohydrate precursors are synthesised into glucose. Both metabolic pathways generate glucose 6-phosphate as a common intermediate and liberation of free glucose from this metabolite is catalysed by glucose 6-phosphatase, which increases in activity after birth in a second phase of developmental accumulation (Fig. 10.2b). These events appear to be largely under the control of the pancreatic hormones, glucagon and insulin, whose blood concentrations change rapidly in a reciprocal fashion after birth.

Functionally, the inhibition of glycogen deposition in methylmercury-exposed rats before birth (Fig. 10.4) may compromise the correction of neonatal hypoglycaemia because of reduced glycogen stores at birth. In addition, the reduced activity of glucose 6-phosphatase in the liver of methylmercury-exposed fetuses (Fig. 10.4) may impair the capacity for free glucose formation from either glycogen breakdown or gluconeogenesis (see Fig. 10.5). Indeed it has been shown that animals exposed to methylmercury *in utero* exhibit a more profound and prolonged phase of hypoglycaemia at birth, which is associated with decreased liver glycogen concentrations and a reduced rate of glycogen mobilisation (Snell *et al.*, 1977). It is tempting to speculate that the degree and persistence of the neonatal hypoglycaemia observed in methylmercury-exposed rats may result in glucose deficiency in the brain, which is still undergoing differentiation and development at this age, and so may contribute to the pathogenesis of the behavioural and neurological disturbances observed in these animals in later life (Spyker, 1975 a, b). The eventual correction of blood glycaemia which occurs in the animals postnatally is undoubtedly due to the activation of gluconeogenesis and the production of glucose in the liver by this means. The postnatal phase of glucose 6-phosphatase accumulation also eventually takes place (Snell *et al.*, 1977), so that there is no permanent constraint on hepatic glucose formation.

The mechanisms by which methylmercury exerts its metabolic terato-genic effect remain speculative at present. As far as direct effects on the fetus are concerned, these could be directed either at the liver itself or at other organs. In view of the ultrastructural findings of Ware *et al.* (1974b) in hepatocytes, it is reasonable to consider the liver as the primary site of the defects in hepatic metabolic parameters. Methylmercury may have a deleterious effect on the liver-cell genome, modifying either the integrity or the regulation of expression of genes controlling the production of enzymes or other proteins during developmental transitions. This is considered unlikely, since such a disturbance would be likely to produce major alterations in hepatic function that would challenge cellular viability. In fact, the modification of the late-fetal developmental accumulation of glucose 6-phosphatase by methylmercury (Fig. 10.4) is relatively small. For this reason it is also unlikely that methylmercury is having a direct specific inhibitory effect on the glucose 6-phosphatase enzyme.

The ultrastructural observations of Ware *et al.* (1974b) emphasise intracellular disturbances in the morphology of endoplasmic reticulum and mitochondria of hepatocytes at birth. It is noteworthy that glucose 6-phosphatase and glycogen are associated with the endoplasmic reticulum of the cell and during this period of development major morphological changes take place in this subcellular component (Dallner *et al.*, 1966; Pollack and Duck-Chong, 1973). Methylmercury may interfere with these developmental changes in endoplasmic reticulum morphology resulting in decreased biochemical activities associated with this organelle. The inclusion of mitochrondrial aberrations in methylmercury action is also a strong possibility, since this organelle has been shown to be a sensitive target of mercury action in adult (Desnoyers and Chang, 1975a, b; Al-Shaikhaly and Baum, 1977) and fetal liver (Ware *et al.*, 1974b). Indeed, Fowler and Woods (1977) have described a loss of respiratory control and decreased activities of membrane-associated enzymes in mitochondria of fetal rats exposed transplacentally to low doses of methylmercury. The consequent impairment of mitochondrial biogenesis and function during a developmental period when major changes occur in cellular mitochondrial content and mitochrondrial metabolism (Jakovcic *et al.*, 1971; Herzfeld *et al.*, 1973, Pollak, 1975) may prejudice the cellular capacity for energy generation leading to possible interference with macromolecular synthesis, including glycogen and enzyme proteins.

Interference with placental function or disturbances of maternal metabolic or endocrine status could have indirectly influenced fetal hepatic development. Interference with transplacental nutrient supply is unlikely to be included in the hepatic effects of methylmercury in our studies, since no evidence of growth retardation or reduction in body weight was found between control and exposed animals before birth (Snell *et al.*, 1977). Similarly, maternal disturbances are unlikely to be included, since there were no obvious signs of toxicity in methylmercury-treated dams and weight gain and food consumption were normal.

This study of the effect of methylmercury, administered to pregnant rats on a single occasion and at low doses which do not result in frank teratogenesis, shows that functional toxicity which previously could be detected only in later life as behavioural and neurological disturbances, can be detected in late-fetal and newborn animals using developmental biochemical parameters. The nature of the metabolic teratogenic effects provides information on the pathogenesis of the later functional disturbances and on the mechanisms of these subtle actions of methylmercury on the developing organism.

B. *Transplacental Toxicity of Actinomycin*

Actinomycin D is a drug with known structural teratogenic properties when administered during the period of organogenesis in the rat (Tuchman-Duplessis and Mercier-Parot, 1960). In our study the agent was injected intraperitoneally at 8.00 and 18.00 hours on day 21 of gestation to pregnant rats at a dose of 0.1 mg/kg body weight. Fetal rats were surgically delivered by caesarian section at 08.00 the following day (term) and maintained at 35°C in a humid atmosphere. Hepatic phosphoenolpyruvate (PEP) carboxykinase activity (one of the neonatal cluster of enzymes, see Fig. 10.2b) was assayed 4 hours after delivery. There was a marked (76%) inhibition of enzyme accumulation in actinomycin-exposed newborns compared with control animals (Fig. 10.6). Few exposed newborn rats survived beyond 6 hours after delivery.

Again the developmental enzyme studied (phosphoenolpyruvate carboxykinase) was selected as a parameter not only as a representative of the neonatal enzyme cluster, but also because it is a key regulatory enzyme whose increase at birth is involved in the initiation of gluconeogenesis (see Snell, 1981b; Hanson *et al.*, 1975). In the absence of gluconeogenesis, glucose homeostasis at birth is severely compromised (see Fig. 10.5). Thus, there is a greatly exaggerated postnatal hypoglycaemic

Figure 10.6: Effect of Actinomycin on Changes in Liver PEP Carboxykinase and Plasma Glucose at Birth. Upper panel: the open circles show the natural developmental pattern for liver PEP carboxykinase in untreated animals during the immediate postnatal period (means of 4–5 determinations; K. Snell, unpublished work). The columns show enzyme activity in livers of neonates (at 4 hours *post partum*) from mothers injected with actinomycin D on day 21 of gestation (see text). SEM of 5 determinations are shown by vertical bars. Lower panel: the open circles show the natural change in plasma glucose concentration in untreated animals during the immediate postnatal period, and the closed circles show plasma glucose concentrations in neonates from mothers injected with actinomycin D on day 21 of gestation. SEM of 3-4 determinations are shown by vertical bars; each determination was on plasma pooled from two animals.

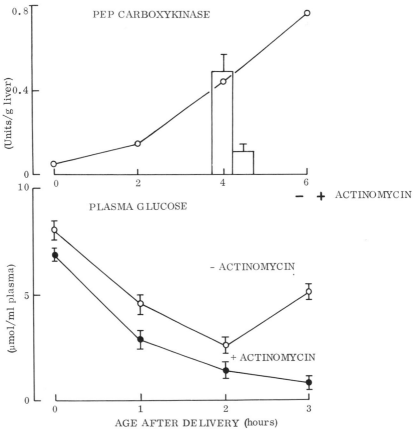

317

episode in actinomycin-exposed rats compared with controls (Fig. 10.6). Unlike control animals, where recovery from hypoglycaemia is apparent at 3 hours after delivery, actinomycin-exposed rats are unable to correct the postnatal hypoglycaemia which persists, until at the time of death plasma glucose concentrations of less than 0.5 mmol/1 were observed. In another study newborn rats were injected with actinomycin at the time of delivery and also showed an exaggerated fall in plasma glucose concentrations at birth. It was shown that in these animals glucose formation after birth was completely suppressed and gluconeogenesis from injected ^{14}C-lactate was greatly inhibited (Snell and Walker, 1973c). The transplacental exposure of fetal rats to actinomycin apparently prevents the neonatal appearance of phosphoenolpyruvate carboxykinase causing a metabolic block in gluconeogenesis. As a result of this, glucose homeostasis at birth is inadequate and as a consequence the blood glucose concentration falls to life-threatening values.

The mechanism for the transplacental toxicity of actinomycin in this situation is fairly clear. The antibiotic is known to inhibit DNA transcription and block messenger RNA formation. Thus, gene activation and expression which is necessary for the developmental appearance of phosphoenolpyruvate carboxykinase (Hanson *et al.*, 1975) is inhibited by the drug. Further evidence that it is indeed specifically the block in phosphoenolpyruvate carboxykinase development, and therefore the lack of enzyme activity, which is responsible for the disturbances in carbohydrate metabolism, rather than any non-specific toxic action of the drug, is provided by our observations with quinolinate. Quinolinate, a naturally occurring tryptophan metabolite, blocks gluconeogenesis by inhibiting the phosphoenolpyruvate carboxykinase reaction (see Snell, 1979). When this agent was injected into newborn rats at delivery, gluconeogenesis was inhibited, glucose formation was prevented and severe hypoglycaemia ensued, leading to death within a few hours (K. Snell, unpublished work). Thus, despite the normal neonatal development of phosphoenolpyruvate carboxykinase, inhibition of the enzyme reaction by quinolinate produced the same sequalae of responses as with actinomycin.

This study of the experimentally induced transplacental toxicity of actinomycin has interesting implications for the pathogenic mechanisms of fatal neonatal hypoglycaemia in human infants. A proportion of these cases may be the result of a primary genetic lesion affecting the expression of the gene coding for phosphoenolpyruvate carboxykinase. These may simply be an example of the class of genetic diseases referred to as 'inborn errors of metabolism' and which are presumed to arise as the result of

318

natural hereditable mutations. However, the possibility exists that some cases may be the result of transplacental exposure to toxic agents which have initiated developmental defects leading to metabolic aberrations.

IV. Postnatal Developmental Toxicity

A. *Translactational Nourishment Effects*

One of the difficulties in assessing translactational developmental toxicity is that untoward effects may arise not because of a direct effect of a toxic agent on neonatal development through its transmission in the milk, but rather that the agent alters the amount or composition of the maternal milk supply. Overfeeding or overnourishment of experimental animals (or humans) during suckling can lead to the development of metabolic derangements associated with obesity (insulin resistance and diabetes). On the other hand, undernourishment can lead to metabolic abnormalities associated with malnutrition or kwashiorkor. There is evidence that the amount of nourishment received in the first few weeks after birth can fix the lifetime appetite of the animal (Oscai and McGarr, 1978) so that the immediate postnatal suckling period constitutes a critical developmental period in this regard.

It is possible to experimentally alter the amount of milk consumed by suckling rats by manipulating litter size at birth so that the animals are reared in small (overnourished) or large (undernourished) litters, relative to normal litter size. This experimental manipulation has a permanent and irreversible effect on body weight gain and composition (Widdowson and McCance, 1960) despite the access of animals to food *ad libitum* after weaning. Animals reared in this way show permanent enzyme abnormalities at 20 weeks of age in liver enzymes involved in lipid metabolism (Duff and Snell, 1978) and associated with the weanling developmental cluster (Fig. 10.2c). Activities of fatty acid synthetase, ATP-citrate lyase, malic enzyme and glucose 6-phosphate dehydrogenase were increased in overnourished animals, and decreased in undernourished rats compared with normal rats (Fig. 10.7). Increases in these enzyme activities have been observed in genetically obese rats (Martin, 1974) and are associated with an increased synthesis of lipid (Elliott *et al.*, 1974). Clearly, increased hepatic lipid synthesis is one of the major factors in the deposition of fat that occurs in obesity. Changes in adiposity induced by early postnatal

319

Figure 10.7: Long-term Effect of Translactational Nourishment on Hepatic Lipogenic Enzymes. Neonatal pups were suckled from birth in a litter of 4 (overnourished), 10 (normally nourished) and 16 (undernourished) until weaning (21 days *post partum*) when they were caged in equal numbers and allowed to feed *ad libitum*. Enzyme activities were determined at 20 weeks of age. Columns are the means (bars show SEM) of 4–5 determinations.

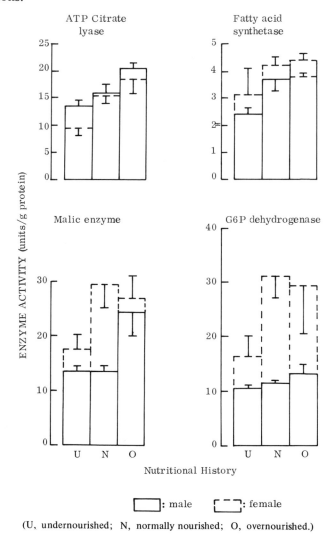

(U, undernourished; N, normally nourished; O, overnourished.)

Developmental Enzyme Pathology

nourishment is another major factor. The development of adipose tissue, and in particular the determination of the final adult complement of adipocytes, occurs during early postnatal life and has been shown to be sensitive to nutritional modifications at this age (Hirsch and Knittle, 1970).

Brain development is also completed during the early postnatal period in laboratory animals and both structural and functional changes have been induced by nutritional manipulations (Winnick and Morgan, 1979). For example, calorie deprivation of neonatal rats results in a deficiency of hypothalamic thyrotropin-releasing hormone which becomes manifest only in later life (Shambaugh and Wilber, 1974).

In assessing the possible translactational toxicity of an agent, it is obviously important to monitor the postnatal gain in body weight of the progeny. It may also be advisable to measure maternal milk production, if deviations from normal weight gain occur, to distinguish between direct and indirect effects of the agent on the developing neonate. It also follows that in toxicity-testing procedures, litter sizes should be standardised at birth and maintained at a constant size throughout the suckling period. A similar precaution should also be taken in constructing 'normal' developmental enzyme profiles (e.g. Snell and Walker, 1974).

B. *Translactational Effects of Low-Level DDT Feeding*

The hazards associated with the manufacture, usage, and environmental presence of the organochlorine pesticides have been a matter of debate for a number of years (Deichmann, 1972; Hodge et al., 1967). In the present study DDT has been used to investigate possible developmental biochemical abnormalities in rats continuously exposed to low doses of the pesticides during pre- and postnatal development. Unlike the organophosphate insecticides, DDT is considerably less lethal to suckling rats compared with adults, at least after acute exposure (Harbison, 1975). Despite the well-recognised toxicity of the organochlorine pesticides, no evidence of gross teratogenicity has been reported in any mammalian species (Chernoff et al., 1975; Deichmann, 1972; Khera and Clegg, 1969; Hodge et al., 1967), although decreased postnatal growth rates and increased neonatal mortality have been reported after prenatal or suckling exposure of mice and rats to pesticides (Virgo and Bellward, 1977; Chernoff et al., 1975; Fahim et al., 1970). Changes in behavioural responses have been detected in young adult mice exposed to DDT during maternal gestation and lactation (Craig and Ogilvie, 1974; Al-Hachim and Fink,

321

1967a, b, 1968). The administration of DDT to rats at different pre- and postnatal stages caused a stimulation of the development of some hepatic drug-metabolising enzymes in postnatal, but not fetal animals (Bell *et al.*, 1976).

Some of the developmental and behavioural effects observed may be secondary to effects on maternal lactation and nursing behaviour resulting in inadequate nutrition and nursing of the pups. Indeed effects on maternal behaviour have been reported for DDT (Paulsen *et al.*, 1975). One way of avoiding problems of maternal nursing behaviour is to use fostering procedures at birth, but in this case the influence of pesticide transmission in the milk cannot be monitored. In our study, a low level of the pesticide was used which was below the doses at which maternal nursing disturbances have been reported and in none of the experiments were any gross behavioural effects observed in the mothers, nor was maternal body weight gain or diet consumption different in pesticide-treated dams compared with control lactating animals.

p,p'-DDT ($> 99\%$ purity) was administered to pregnant female rats at 20 ppm in the diet for 4 weeks before mating and throughout gestation and lactation. Postnatal rats were weaned at 21 days on to control diets not containing pesticide. At the dose used no effects of DDT on body weight were observed in newborn rats and postnatal growth rates were comparable with untreated controls. At no time during the studies did the mothers or their progeny show any overt toxic symptoms or gross behavioural changes. Analysis of DDT residues in maternal blood and blood and liver of postnatal animals showed that the most significant exposure of developing rats to the pesticide occurred during the suckling period (Fig. 10.8). The transmission of pesticide from the suckling mother to the pup is reflected in the postnatal fall in maternal blood concentrations due to increased excretion by this route. In view of the greatly increased exposure of suckling rats to the pesticide, it was decided to concentrate on enzyme changes associated with the weanling developmental enzyme cluster (Fig. 10.2c). In addition the enzyme parameters selected (Table 10.3) included representative examples from three major areas of metabolism which are known to undergo pronounced modifications at this time (Greengard, 1971; Snell, 1971).

A slight stimulation of gluconeogenic enzyme activity in mid-suckling postnatal rats was observed in DDT-exposed animals, whereas the developmental accumulation of glucose 6-phosphate dehydrogenase was somewhat retarded in male and female DDT-exposed rats (Fig. 10.9). This enzyme shows a sexual differentiation of activity after 30 days *post partum* which

Figure 10.8: Effect of DDT Feeding During Gestation and Lactation on Maternal and Neonatal Levels in Blood and Liver. Pregnant rats were fed 20 ppm p,p'-DDT throughout gestation and lactation. The points represent the total DDT concentrations (DDT + DDE + DDD) in maternal (triangles) and neonatal (open circles) blood and in neonatal liver (closed circles). Each point shows the mean of 3–5 determinations (bars show SEM). B: birth.

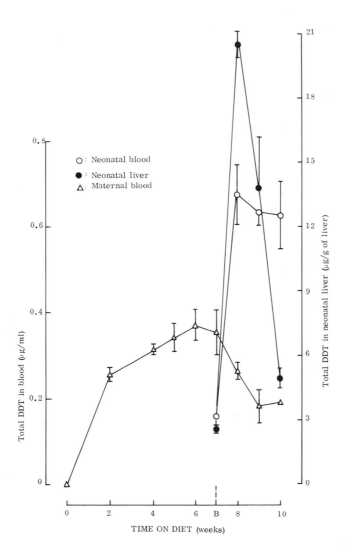

was not altered in DDT-exposed animals (Fig. 10.9). Developmental patterns for glucokinase (Fig. 10.9) and malic enzyme (malate dehydrogenase (NADP)) were similar in control and DDT-exposed rats, whereas ATP–citrate lyase and pyruvate kinase developmental accumulations were both somewhat attenuated (Fig. 10.9).

The magnitude of the interference with enzyme development by DDT was not great, nor did it show any simple relationship with the metabolic functions of the enzymes. Thus, although some enhancement of all gluconeogenic enzyme activities was observed, different glycolytic and lipogenic enzymes were variously retarded or unaffected in development.

Figure 10.9: Effect of DDT Feeding During Gestation and Lactation of Neonatal Hepatic Enzyme Development. Details as in Figure 10.8. Each point shows the mean of 4 determinations (bars show SEM). Open circles represent neonates from untreated dams and closed circles represent neonates from dams fed DDT throughout gestation and lactation. All animals were weaned on to normal control diets at 21 days *post partum.*

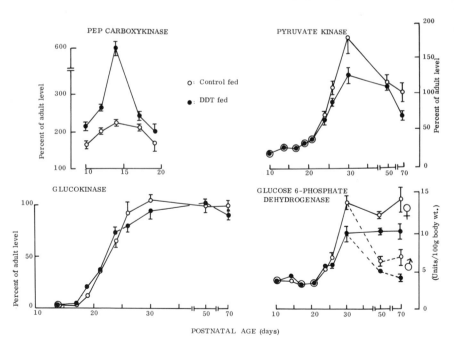

Table 10.3: Enzyme Parameters Measured in Study of Translactational Effects of DDT

	Change at Weaning[1]
Glycolytic:	
Hexokinase	0
Glucokinase	+
Pyruvate kinase	+
Gluconeogenic:	
Glucose 6-phosphatase	−
Fructose bisphosphatase	−
Phosphoenolpyruvate carboxykinase	−
Lipogenic:	
ATP–citrate lyase	+
Malic enzyme	+
Glucose 6-phosphate dehydrogenase	+

[1] Symbols refer to changes in activity during the weaning period:
0, no change; +, increase; −, decrease.

Table 10.4: Summary of Effects of DDT on Postnatal Enzyme Development

Enzyme parameter	Putative developmental inducing agent	Effect of DDT[1]
Malic enzyme	Thyroid Hormone	0
Glucokinase	Insulin/Glucocorticoids	0
ATP–citrate lyase	Insulin	−
Pyruvate kinase	Insulin	−
G-6-P dehydrogenase	Insulin (at weaning)	−
	Oestrogen (at puberty)	0
Glucose 6-phosphatase	Glucagon–cAMP	+
PEP carboxykinase	Glucagon-cAMP	+

[1] Symbols refer to modifications of developmental profiles of enzyme activities:
0, no change; +, enhancement; −, suppression.

This apparently random pattern may be partly resolved if the enzymes are categorised according to the hormonal stimuli that have been identified or implicated in triggering their developmental transitions at this age (Table 10.4).

Hormonal effects are singled out for attention here because of the reported endocrine disturbances associated with many of the actions of pesticides. Perhaps the most well-established endocrine effect of pesticides is the oestrogenic action of DDT, although this activity is largely confined to the o,p'-isomer and its metabolites (Welch *et al.*, 1969; Bitman and Cecil, 1970; Kupfer and Bulger, 1976). At high doses physiological reproductive disturbances have been noted in female rats exposed to o,p'-DDT from the mother during the perinatal period (Gellert and Heinrichs, 1975; Heinrichs *et al.*, 1971). In addition DDT and other chlorinated pesticides have been reported to have antioestrogenic and antiandrogenic actions that may disturb both male and female reproductive physiology (Thomas and Lloyd, 1973; Kupfer and Bulger, 1976; Thomas *et al.*, 1977). These effects have been attributed to the induction of drug-metabolising enzymes which are also involved in the metabolism of the steroid hormones (see Kupfer and Bulger, 1976). There was no evidence for sex-hormone mediated effects of DDT at the low doses used in our work. For example, the sex differentiation of enzyme activities in post-weaning rats is brought about by oestrogen (Feigelson, 1973), but in our work sex differentiation of glucose 6-phosphate dehydrogenase proceeded normally (Table 10.4).

Other steroid hormones may also be affected by the enzyme-inductive action of pesticides and interference with corticosteroid-mediated responses have been reported (see Kupfer and Bulger, 1976). Postnatal developmental induction of glucokinase is controlled by insulin (Wakelam and Walker, 1980) with perhaps some additional glucocorticoid effects (Greengard, 1971), but in our experiments no pesticide effects on the development of this enzyme were observed (Table 10.4). Thyroid hormones have been suggested as having a role in a wide variety of sublethal effects of organochlorine pesticides (Jefferies, 1975). The lack of effect of DDT on the development of malic enzyme (Table 10.4), which is under developmental control by thyroid hormones (Murphy and Walker, 1974), makes it unlikely that the pesticide effects could include thyrogenic or antithyrogenic actions.

The remaining enzyme activities, whose developmental accumulations are modulated by DDT, share the common property of being under pancreatic hormone control, presumably acting through a common cyclic AMP-mediated action in the liver. However, direct measurements of cyclic AMP concentrations in livers from 10-, 15- and 30-day-old DDT-exposed rats showed no significant differences from controls (Stratford and Snell, 1979).

Regardless of the mechanisms of small modulations in developmental enzyme changes, it is apparent that at the low doses used in the study (chosen to simulate known human levels at environmentally relevant exposures) there are no major developmental enzyme disturbances. The small enhancement of gluconeogenic enzymes in mid-suckling (Fig. 10.9) is not reflected in any changes in gluconeogenic function *in vivo* at this age (Stratford and Snell, 1979). Although some small DDT-related enzyme changes were still apparent at 70 days of age (Fig. 10.9), none persisted into adulthood (20 weeks). The extreme sensitivity of developmental enzyme changes as indicators of physiological and pathological modifications requires that due consideration is given to the effects observed in terms of their magnitude and their functional metabolic consequences. Similar considerations with regard to interpretation are also required in the use of behavioural parameters in toxicity testing.

V. Carcinogenesis and Developmental Enzyme Dedifferentiation

A. *Introduction*

The use of developmental enzyme clusters as an indicator system for the process of carcinogenesis has both practical and theoretical implications. Practically speaking, if specific developmental enzyme changes are a characteristic of the early stages of carcinogenesis then they would constitute a suitable test system for the screening of chemical substances for carcinogenic properties. From a theoretical standpoint the pattern of any developmental enzyme changes might provide us with some clues as to the nature of neoplastic transformation. It is well recognised that neoplastic transformation resulting in tumour formation includes a morphological loss of differentiated tissue characteristics. The differing extents of the deviation from the fully differentiated normal tissue morphology are reflected in the diversity of tumour types of common origin that can be distinguished histologically. Such morphological diversity is also reflected in biochemical phenotypic characteristics (enzymes). However, if tumours of a common cellular origin are arranged in order of growth rate, then one

327

observes a graded loss of morphological differentiation accompanied by a graded loss of enzymic parameters characteristic of the fully differentiated state (Knox, 1972, 1976). In the extreme case of rapidy growing, poorly differentiated tumours, the enzymic composition resembles closely that of the fetal stage of the cognate tissue and, moreover, rapidly growing tumours of differing tissue origins, like their fetal counterparts, resemble one another more closely in their enzymic composition than do more well-differentiated tumours.

It thus appears that the apparent diversity of cellular and biochemical characteristics in tumours arising from a common cellular origin merely reflects a spectrum of differing degrees of tissue differentiation characterised by a deletion of adult-type enzymes (or isoenzymes) and an acquisition of fetal-type (iso)enzymes. This has been referred to as the 'fetalism' of tumours (Knox, 1976). Most of the evidence for such a concept has been derived, of necessity, from studies with transplantable tumours which are available with differing growth rates and differing degrees of differentiation, and for the most part these have been hepatomas. Clearly, before the concept of fetalism of tumours can be established as a general phenomenon of cancer other tissue types and tumours arising from them must be analysed for their enzymic composition. Studies of a graded series of transplantable mammary tumours have so far reinforced the fetalism concept (Knox, 1976). A number of reviews have appeared describing the enzyme (or isoenzyme) modifications that take place in tumours and in many cases have drawn attention to the fetalism or oncodevelopmental nature of these modifications (Knox, 1967, 1976; Criss, 1971; Schapira, 1973; Goldfarb and Pitot, 1976; Weber, 1977; Uriel, 1978; Ibsen and Fishman, 1979).

The question of the origin or genesis of fetalism in tumours is clearly of significance to our understanding of the nature of cancer. Furthermore, the metabolic consequences of biochemical fetalism in tumours will be important in developing new concepts of chemotherapeutic intervention aimed at eradicating cancer cells from normal tissues. At present there are two main ideas relating to the origin of fetalism in tumours. Both require that a population of proliferating cells which are undergoing differentiation become blocked or arrested at some early stage of their differentiation as a result of events associated with neoplastic transformation. Such a cell population is suggested to have arisen either through the stimulation of putative undifferentiated stem cells whose subsequent differentiation is then arrested at some point in the ontogenic process (Potter, 1969, Pierce, 1970), or by a process of cell renewal involving retrodifferentiation, proliferation and redifferentiation with an ontogenic arrest either during retro- or redifferentiation (Uriel, 1978; Ibsen and Fishman, 1979). Whichever mechanism is relevant to tumour formation, it is clear that arrests in differentiation must be able to occur at different stages of ontogeny to account for the spectrum of tumours that are observed having differing degrees of divergence from the adult towards the fetal enzymic phenotype. Whether the carcinogenic or oncogenic stimulus causes fetalism and is therefore responsible for tumourigenesis, or whether fetalism is a cellular adaptation to the neoplastic state, are critical questions which at present are unresolved.

Enzyme changes are apparently an early feature of hepatocarcinogenesis *in vivo*, and in terms of multi-stage models of carcinogenesis it is suggested that the changes are associated with one of the steps in the initiation phase (Farber, 1980; Pitot and Sirica, 1980; Emmelot and Scherer, 1980). Thus distinct focal and nodular hyperplastic areas are rapidly produced by the administration of hepatocarcinogens which are deficient in adenosine triphosphatase, glucose 6-phosphatase and other enzymes while showing increased activities of enzymes such as γ-glutamyl transferase and DT-diaphorase. Such early lesions are considered to be 'preneoplastic' and progenitors of hepatocellular carcinoma (Farber, 1980). The early enzyme changes are a more reliable and more readily identifiable feature of preneoplastic lesions than histological criteria, which together with their objective quantitation makes them attractive as markers for screening of possible carcinogenic chemicals. No systematic studies have examined whether these early enzyme changes reflect a generalised enzymic de-differentiation or whether this process is linked to later (promotion or progression phases?) stages of tumourigenesis.

B. *Developmental Enzyme Changes during Diethylnitrosamine-Induced Hepatocarcinogenesis*

Diethylnitrosamine is an ideal choice as a carcinogen for studying early hepatic enzyme changes because it combines high carcinogenic potency with a low toxicity and is relatively specific for parenchymal cells (Nishizumi *et al.*, 1977). In our study male Wistar rats received diethylnitrosamine continuously at a dose of 10 mg/kg body weight per day in the drinking water and died from hepatic carcinoma between 14 and 15 weeks from starting the treatment. Groups of animals were killed at 2-weekly intervals and enzymes were assayed in whole liver extracts and by histochemical methods. In addition routine histological examinations were performed on portions of each liver. The enzymes used in the study were selected on the basis of their developmental characteristics (see Figs. 10.2 and 10.3), and are listed in Table 10.5. The enzymes can be further categorised (Fig. 10.10) on the basis of: those whose fetal activities are equal to or greater than the adult level; those whose fetal activities are less than the adult level; and those with negligible fetal activities.

Table 10.5: Developmental Enzymes Studied During Hepatocarcinogenesis

'High' fetal cluster (a')

Thymidine kinase
Hexokinase
Glucose 6-phosphate dehydrogenase

Fetal cluster (a)

Glucose 6-phosphatase
Aspartate aminotransferase

Neonatal cluster (b)

Phosphoenolpyruvate carboxykinase
Glutamate dehydrogenase
Glucose 6-phosphatase

Weanling cluster (c)

Glucokinase
Glucose 6-phosphate dehydrogenase
Malic enzyme

See Figs. 10.2 and 10.3 for explanation of clusters.

After only 2 weeks treatment with carcinogen changes in enzyme activities were apparent, despite a completely normal histological appearance of the liver tissue. Enzymes characterised by having low fetal activities compared with the adult were all depressed in livers from carcinogen-treated animals, whereas enzymes having higher fetal activities compared with the adult were increased in treated animals. Glucose 6-phosphate dehydrogenase activity, which has a fetal value similar to the adult, did not change appreciably at this stage of carcinogen treatment. With

Figure 10.10: Effect of Diethylnitrosamine (DEN)-Feeding on Hepatic Developmental Enzyme Activities. The left-hand panels show the enzyme activities (relative to adult activity) in fetal (20 days' gestation) liver (columns represent the means of 10–20 determinations). The right-hand panels show the liver enzyme activies (relative to the adult) during diethylnitrosamine feeding (10 mg/kg body weight; each point represents the mean of four determinations). Adult values are the means of at least 50 determinations. TK, thymidine kinase; HK, hexokinase; G6PDH, glucose 6-phosphate dehydrogenase; AAT, aspartate aminotransferase; G6P, glucose 6-phosphatase; GDH, glutamate dehydrogenase; GK, glucokinase; ME, malic enzyme; PEPCK, phosphoenolpyruvate carboxykinase.

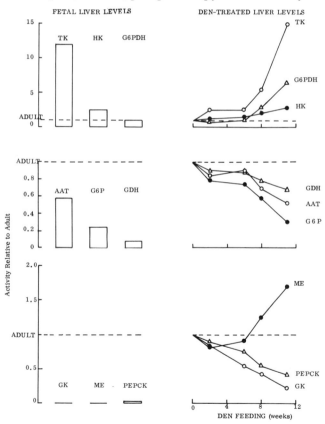

331

continued carcinogen treatment the enzyme changes became progressively more pronounced. From the sixth week of treatment glucose 6-phosphate dehydrogenase activity increased above adult values. At six weeks livers were still histologically similar to controls, but with a slight proliferation of fibrous tissue around the portal tracts and a reduction in glycogen content. By the eighth week micronodular cirrhosis was becoming evident. Mitotic figures and fat accumulation were observed in the nodules, which coincided with an anomalous progressive increase in malic enzyme activity above adult values. Histochemical analyses at this stage for glucose 6-phosphate dehydrogenase, malic enzyme and glucose 6-phosphatase activities revealed that the whole liver changes in these enzymes were more exaggerated within the histologically defined nodules. Nevertheless, the magnitude of the enzyme changes in the whole liver suggests that they may not be confined exclusively to the nodular areas.

The study shows that fetal characteristics (loss of adult enzyme and gain of fetal enzyme activities) are acquired during the course of hepato-carcinogenesis and can be detected as early as two weeks after the initiation of carcinogen treatment. Visual inspection reveals little difference in the temporal patterns of the enzyme changes between enzymes belonging to different developmental clusters (a-c, Table 10.5). However, when rank correlation statistical analysis (as described by Knox, 1976) was applied it appeared that during the early stages of carcinogenesis the pattern of liver enzymes was significantly similar to that of the five-day-old and weanling animals, and that as carcinogenesis progressed this pattern shifted towards that of fetal liver (Curtin, 1981). This finding is consistent with the notion that the development of neoplasia is associated with phase-specific blocks in a step-wise retrodifferentiation of mature hepatocytes. Histochemical analysis of the tissues showed that, for the enzymes studied, the overall changes observed in whole liver reflected similar, more pronounced, changes in preneoplastic nodules as these arose. Heterogeneous enzyme changes in different enzyme-altered foci or nodules has been reported during carcinogenesis (see Farber, 1980, and Emmelot and Scherer, 1980) but the range of enzymes investigated was not selected on the basis of developmental characteristics and so do not permit any conclusions regarding possible developmental-phase specific differences. It is clear that, regardless of the theoretical implications of the present study, the assay of a group of developmental enzymes that have characteristically high activities in either fetal or adult liver should prove a valuable system for the detection of hepatocarcinogens. The question of the specificity of the responses has still to be settled but other studies suggest that the changes in enzyme patterns during hepatocarcinogenesis differ from those found in regenerating liver after partial hepatectomy (Curtin, 1981).

Another feature of developmental enzymes and cancer is the possibility that the liver may constitute a host tissue which shows a sensitive enzymic response to the presence of neoplasms at either hepatic or extrahepatic sites. The former case is suggested above on the basis of the magnitude of the enzyme changes in whole liver extracts in the early stages of hepatocarcinogenesis. Studies in Greengard's laboratory (Herzfeld and Greengard, 1972, 1977; Herzfeld *et al.*, 1978) have shown that hepatic enzymic dedifferentiation is detectable within a few days of the subcutaneous implantation of various tumours (of the mammary gland, kidney, liver, muscle or lymphoma) into rats and the changes become more extensive as tumour growth progresses. The aetiology of this host liver response is not clear, but it may reside in the release of chemical mediators from the tumour into the circulatory system. Regardless of the mechanism, the assay of appropriate developmental enzymes in host liver may assist in the detection of latent extrahepatic tumours. Recently this work has been extended to include observations on human patients with cancers of non-hepatic origin (Herzfeld *et al.*, 1980). Again the assay of a group of 12 developmental enzymes in the host livers of these patients revealed an enzymic dedifferentiation which discriminated tumour-bearing patients from others with no neoplastic disease. The possibility that some non-neoplastic diseases may produce similar enzymic aberrations and the question of whether the human liver enzymic dedifferentiation is detectable at an early stage of cancer require evaluation before developmental enzyme analysis can assume any clinical diagnostic function. From the point of view of screening for chemical carcinogens the enzymic dedifferentiation of rat liver may permit the detection of tumour-inducing properties (at both hepatic and non-hepatic sites) at an early stage before tumour formation becomes palpable by other means.

VI. General Conclusions

Much attention is focused on the gross anatomical malformations which result from the teratogenic actions of environmental chemicals and drugs to which the developing embryo may be exposed. The hazardous effects of lower subteratogenic doses, or of exposure at later stages of gestation and in neonatal life, are more subtle. However, they are likely to occur at a greater incidence and may manifest themselves as functional disorders, such as behavioural abnormalities or as permanent metabolic disturbances. Some metabolic disturbances of unknown aetiology such as sudden infant (cot) death syndrome, respiratory distress syndrome, neonatal hypoglycaemia, maturity-onset diabetes and obesity may result from developmental biochemical abnormalities. The detection of metabolic lesions at an early stage is more likely to be successful if investigations are carried out at critical developmental periods when the homeostatic mechanisms of the organism are being called upon to cope with major physiological adaptations. These critical periods coincide with major reorganisations of gene expression, particularly in the liver, and the changing patterns of enzymes during developmental transitions would, therefore, provide the most sensitive indicators of deviations from normal differentiation. The interaction of endocrine, neural and nutritional influences in bringing about developmental transitions makes enzyme adaptations useful general indicators of the integrity of the developing organism as a whole.

These considerations guided the studies described in sections III and IV and which serve as examples of the possible applications of developmental enzyme pathology in toxicology and in toxicity testing. These are the first attempts at such applications and clearly much further work is required to refine and validate the approach. One general consideration that emerges is that it is important in toxicological applications to select developmental enzymes from a number of different metabolic pathways. These should include enzymes in pathways of metabolism which are known to undergo adaptive changes at the particular critical developmental period which is under scrutiny, and also enzymes whose developmental adaptations are controlled by common physiological stimuli. In this way not only would the detection of toxic actions be enhanced, but the possibility of gaining information on the underlying mechanisms of such actions would also be improved.

Unfortunately, the ease with which developmental enzyme adaptations can be modified by the experimental manipulation of controlling physiological influences (Greengard, 1971; Snell and Walker, 1972, 1974; Duff and Snell, 1978), while testifying to the sensitivity of enzymic parameters, poses problems on the interpretation of any effects that are observed. Ideally the significance of the enzymic aberrations should be investigated directly by appropriate studies *in vivo* or *in vitro* of the metabolic functions subserved by those enzymes. However, this would increase the complexity of the procedure and make it more cumbersome and time consuming as a developmental toxicity screen. The high degree of sensitivity and doubts as to the physiological significance of the observed changes, especially in terms of man, also affects the use of behavioural parameters as indicators of toxicity. An advantage with developmental enzyme indicators is that the magnitude of the aberration can be quantified and related to a basis of known functional adequacy — the activity of the enzyme in the mature adult. The expression of both control and deviant developmental enzyme activities as a fraction of the adult enzyme activity would reveal the quantitative significance of the differences observed. The advantages of recording enzyme activities in this way have been discussed in detail by Knox (1976) and Greengard (1977).

Another general consideration emerging from the present studies, and indeed one of the guiding principles of the use of developmental enzyme indicators is that assays of groups of enzymes, rather than of any single enzyme, will enhance the resolving power of developmental analyses, particularly if cognisance is made of the 'clustering' behaviour of the enzymes during development (see Fig. 10.2). The discriminating power of multiple enzyme analysis has been successfully employed by Knox (1972, 1976) to distinguish adult tissues from each other, and from their less differentiated counterparts at earlier developmental stages or in the neoplastic state. In section V use was made of changes in developmental enzymes to detect the transformation of normal liver to preneoplastic tissue during chemically induced carcinogenesis. Some additional considerations are necessary in selecting developmental enzymes as indicators for this purpose. It is important to include enzymes that increase in amount during biochemical dedifferentiation (fetal enzymes) as well as those that decrease (adult enzymes) in these circumstances. This avoids reliance on the loss of enzyme activities that could well result from non-specific effects related to the toxicity of the tumour-inducing chemical or related to non-neoplastic pathological events occurring in the tissue as a result of tumour growth. Again, by selecting enzymes from different pathways of metabolism as indicators of differentiation there is less chance of a non-neoplastic change, such as alterations in nutritional or hormonal status, leading to a concerted effect on all enzymes if they serve different metabolic functions. With a range of developmental enzyme indicators selected by these criteria, it is unlikely that any non-specific physiological or pathological factor would result in changes in all the enzymes in the direction characteristic of the dedifferentiated state.

The studies reported in this chapter are a first attempt to systematically apply the principles of developmental enzyme pathology to the analysis of toxicological problems associated with the detection of teratogenicity, developmental toxicity and carcinogenicity. I believe that such analyses will prove valuable not only in the detection of abnormalities of cellular function but also in elucidating the underlying mechanisms by which the various abnormalities are produced and, in some cases, in predicting the possible long-term pathophysiological consequences. In the latter case this would raise the possibility of therapeutic or prophylactic intervention to correct or diminish the early developmental aberrations and so block the evolution of deleterious functional disorders. The validation of the usefulness of developmental enzyme pathology as a toxicological tool can come only from further fundamental and applied studies in different areas where toxicity evaluation is required. It is my hope that this chapter will introduce the topic of developmental enzyme pathology to a variety of investigators in toxicology, but more importantly that it might encourage others to initiate investigations in this area.

Acknowledgements

It is a pleasure to acknowledge the assistance of Sheila Ashby, Stephen Barton, Nicola Curtin, David Duff and Michael Stratford in different parts of the work described here. We are grateful for the financial support provided by the Medical Research Council, the Science Research Council, the Cancer Research Campaign, the British Diabetic Association and Shell Research Ltd. in various aspects of these studies.

References

Al-Hachim, G.M. and Fink, G.B. (1967) *Psychol. Rep., 20*, 1183-7
Al-Hachim, G.M. and Fink, G.B. (1967) *Psychol. Rep. 22*, 1193-6
Al-Hachim, G.M. and Fink, G.B. (1968) *Psychopharmacologia, 12*, 424-7
Al-Shaikhaly, M.M. and Baum, H. (1977) *Biochem. Soc. Trans., 5*, 1093-5
Bakir, F., Damluji, S.F. and Amin-Zaki, L. (1973) *Science, 181*, 230-41
Baquer, N.Z., McLean, P. and Greenbaum, A.L. (1973) *Biochem. Biophys. Res. Commun., 53*, 1282-8
Barlow, S.M. and Sullivan, F.M. (1975) in *Teratology: Trends and Applications* (Berry, C.L. and Poswillo, D.E., eds.), pp. 103-20, Springer-Verlag, Berlin
Baxter, J.S. and Yoffey, J.M. (1948) *J. Anat., 82*, 186-96
Bell, J.U., Hansell, M.M. and Ecobichon, D.J. (1976) *Toxicol. Appl. Pharmacol., 35*, 165-77
Bernstein, J. (1972) *Am. J. Pathol., 66*, 16a
Bitman, J. and Cecil, H.C. (1970) *J. Agric. Food Chem., 18*, 1108-12
Brimblecombe, R.W. (1968) *Mod. Trends Toxicol., 1*, 149-74

Capek, K. and Jelinek, J. (1956) *Physiol. Bohemoslov.*, *5*, 9-14
Chang, L.W. and Hartmann, H.A. (1972) *Acta Neuropathol.*, *20*, 122-38; 316-34
Chernoff, N., Kavlock, R.J., Kathrein, J.R., Dunn, J.M. and Haseman, J.K. (1975) *Toxicol. Appl. Pharmacol.*, *31*, 302-8
Craig, G.R. and Ogilvie, D.M. (1974) *Environ. Physiol. Biochem.*, *4*, 189-99
Cremer, J.E., Braun, L.D. and Oldendorf, W.H. (1976) *Biochim. Biophys. Acta.*, *448*, 633-7
Criss, W.E., (1971) *Cancer Res.*, *31*, 1523-42
Dallner, G., Siekevitz, P. and Palade, G.E. (1966) *J. Cell Biol.*, *30*, 73-117
Deichmann, W.B. (1972) *Arch. Toxicol.*, *29*, 1-27
Desnoyers, P.A. and Chang, L.W. (1975a) *Environ. Res.*, *9*, 224-39
Desnoyers, P.A. and Chang, L.W. (1975b) *Environ. Res.*, *10*, 59-75
Dickerson, J.W.T. and Basu, T.K. (1975) in *Enzyme Induction* (Parke, D.V., ed.), pp. 27-77, Plenum Press, New York
Druckrey, H. (1973) *Xenobiotica*, *3*, 271-303
Duff, D.A. and Snell, K. (1978) *Biochem. Soc. Trans.*, *6*, 160-1
Egan, H., Goulding, R., Roburn, J. and Talton, J. O'G. (1965) *Br. Med. J.*, *2*, 66-70
Elliott, J., Dade, E., Salmon, D.M.W. and Hems, D.A. (1974) *Biochim. Biophys. Acta, 343*, 307-23
Emmelot, P. and Scherer, E. (1980) *Biochim. Biophys. Acta, 605*, 247-304
Eriksson, M. and Yaffe, S.J. (1973) *Ann. Rev. Med.*, *24*, 29-40
Fahim, M.S., Bennett, R. and Hall, D.G. (1970) *Nature (London), 228*, 1222-3
Farber, E. (1980) *Biochim. Biophys. Acta, 605*, 149-66
Feigelson, M. (1973) *Enzyme, 15*, 169-97
Fowler, B.A. and Woods, J.S. (1977) *Lab. Invest.*, *36*, 122-30
Garcia, J.D., Yang, M.G., Wang, J.H.C. and Belo, P.S. (1974) *Proc. Soc. Exp. Biol. Med.*, *147*, 224-31
Gellert, R.J. and Heinrichs, W.L. (1975) *Biol. Neonate, 26*, 283-90
Gillette, J.R. and Stripp, B. (1975) *Fed. Proc. Fed. Am. Soc. Exp. Biol.*, *34*, 172-8
Girard, J.R., Cuendot, G.S., Marliss, E.B., Kervran, A., Rieutort, M. and Assan, R. (1973) *J. Clin. Invest.*, *52*, 3190-200
Goldfarb, S. and Pitot, H.C. (1976) *Front. Gastrointest. Res.*, *2*, 194-242
Greengard, O. (1971) *Essays Biochem.*, *7*, 159-205
Greengard, O. (1973) *Biochemical Bases of the Development of Physiological Functions*, S. Karger, Basel
Greengard, O. (1977) *Paediatr. Res.*, *11*, 669-76
Greengard, O., Federman, M. and Knox, W.E. (1972) *J. Cell. Biol.*, *52*, 261-72
Hanson, R.W., Reshef, L. and Ballard, F.J. (1975) *Fed. Proc. Fed. Am. Soc. Exp. Biol.*, *34*, 166-71
Harbison, R.D. (1975) *Toxicol. Appl. Pharmacol.*, *32*, 443-6
Harris, J.S. and Simonopoulos, A.P.(1976) *Maternal and Child Health Research: Developmental Processes and Long-Term Effects of Disturbances in Development*. Report of Division of Life Sciences, National Research Council, Washington, DC
Heinrichs, W.L., Gellert, R.J., Bakke, J.L. and Lawrence, N. (1971) *Science, 173*, 642-3
Henning, S.J. and Kretchmer, N. (1975) *Enzyme, 15*, 3-23
Herzfeld, A. and Greengard, O. (1972) *Cancer Res.*, *32*, 1826-32
Herzfeld, A. and Greengard, O. (1977) *Cancer Res.*, *37*, 231-8
Herzfeld, A., Federman, M. and Greengard, O. (1973) *J. Cell Biol.*, *57*, 475-83
Herzfeld, A., Greengard, O. and McDermott, W.V. (1980) *Cancer, 45*, 2383-8
Herzfeld, A., Greengard, O. and Warren, S. (1978) *J. Natl. Cancer Inst.*, *60*, 825-8
Hodge, H.C., Boyce, A.M., Deichmann, W.B. and Kraybill, H.F. (1967) *Toxicol. Appl. Pharmacol.*, *10*, 613-75
Hirsch, J. and Knittle, J.L. (1970) *Fed. Proc. Fed. Am. Soc. Exp. Biol.*, *29*, 1516-21
Hunter, D. and Russell, D.S. (1954) *J. Neurol. Neurosurg. Psychiatr.*, *17*, 235-45
Ibsen, K.H. and Fishman, W.H. (1979) *Biochim. Biophys. Acta, 560*, 243-80
Jakovcic, S., Haddock, J., Getz, G.S., Rabinowitz, M. and Swift, H. (1971) *Biochem. J.*, *121*, 341-7
Jefferies, D.J. (1975) in *Organochlorine Insecticides* (Moriarty, F., ed.), pp. 131-230, Academic Press, London
Khera, K.S. and Clegg, D.J. (1969) *Can. Med. Ass. J., 100*, 167-72

Knox, W.E. (1967) *Adv. Cancer Res., 10*, 117-61
—— (1972) *Am. Sci., 60*, 480-8
—— (1976) *Enzyme Patterns in Fetal, Adult and Neoplastic Rat Tissues*, 2nd ed, S. Karger, Basel
Kobyletzki, D. (1971) in *Prenatal Infections* (Tahlhammer, O., ed.), Georg Thieme-Verlag, Stuttgart
Koldovsky, O. (1972) in *Nutrition and Development* (Winick, M., ed.), pp. 135-49, John Wiley, London
Kupfer, D. and Bulger, W.A. (1976) *Fed. Proc. Fed. Am. Soc. Exp. Biol., 35*, 2603-8
MacDonnel, P.C. and Greengard, O. (1974) *Arch. Biochem. Biophys., 163*, 644-55
Magos, L. (1975) *Br. Med. Bull., 31*, 241-5
Martin, R.J. (1974) *Life Sci., 14*, 1447-53
Matsumura, F. (1975) *Toxicology of Insecticides*, pp. 469-73, Plenum Press, New York
Miyakawa, T., Udo, N., Hatton, E. and Tatitsu, E. (1970) *Acta Neuropathol., 15*, 45-55
Murphy, G.M. and Walker, D.G. (1974) *Biochem. J., 144*, 149-60
Nishizumi, M., Albert, R.E., Burns, F.J. and Bilger, L. (1977) *Br. J. Cancer, 36*, 192-7
Norseth, T. and Clarkson, T.W. (1970) *Arch. Environ. Hlth., 21*, 717-27
Nyhan, W. (1961) *J. Pediatr., 59*, 1-4
Oscai, L.B. and McGarr, J.A. (1978) *Am. J. Physiol., 235*, R141-4
Palmer, A.K. (1977) in *Current Approaches in Toxicology* (Ballantyne, B., ed.), pp. 54-67, John Wright and Sons, Bristol
Paulsen, K., Adesso, V.J. and Porter, J.J. (1975) *Bull. Psychonomic Soc., 5*, 117-19
Pease, D.C. (1971) *Cellular Aspects of Neural Growth and Differentiation*, University of California Press, Berkeley
Pierce, G.P. (1970) *Fed. Proc. Fed. Am. Soc. Exp. Biol., 29*, 1248-58
Pitot, H.C. and Sirica, A.E. (1980) *Biochim. Biophys. Acta, 605*, 191-215
Pollak, J.K. (1975) *Biochem. J., 150*, 477-88
Pollak, J.K. and Duck-Chong, C.G. (1973) *Enzyme, 15*, 139-60
Potter, V.R. (1969) *Can. Cancer Conf., 8*, 9-30
Quinby, G.E., Armstrong, J.F. and Durham, W.F. (1965) *Nature (London), 207*, 726-8
Reynolds, W.A. and Pitkin, R.M. (1975) *Proc. Soc. Exp. Biol. Med., 148*, 523-6
Rogan, W.J., Bahniewska, A. and Damstra, T. (1980) *New Engl. J. Med., 302*, 1450-3
Schapira, F. (1973) *Adv. Cancer Res., 18*, 77-153
Shambaugh, G.E. and Wilber, J.F. (1974) *Endocrinology, 94*, 1145-9
Shapiro, S. (1971) in *Brain Development and Behaviour* (Sterman, M.B., McGinty, D.O. and Adinolfi, A.M., eds.), pp. 307-34, Academic Press, New York
Shapiro, S., Salas, M. and Vukovich, K. (1970) *Science, 168*, 147-50
Smithells, R.W. (1976) *Br. Med. Bull., 32*, 27-33
Snell, K. (1971) 'Studies on Glyoxylate Aminotransferases in Animal Tissues', PhD Thesis, University of Manchester
—— (1979) *Biochem. Soc. Trans., 7*, 645-9
—— (1981a) in *Biochemical Development of the Fetus and the Neonate* (Jones, C.T., ed.), Vol. 2, Elsevier/North-Holland, Amsterdam, in press
—— (1981b) in *Carbohydrate and Energy Metabolism in Extrauterine Adaptation* (De Meyer, R., ed.), pp. 81-105, Martinus Nijhoff Pub. B.V., The Hague
Snell, K. and Walker, D.G. (1972) *Biochem. J., 129*, 403-13
Snell, K. and Walker, D.G. (1973a) *Enzyme, 15*, 40-81
Snell, K. and Walker, D.G. (1973b) *Biochem. J., 132*, 739-52
Snell, K. and Walker, D.G. (1973c) *Biochem. J., 134*, 899-906
Snell, K. and Walker, D.G. (1974) *Biochem. J., 144*, 519-31
Snell, K. and Walker, D.G. (1978) *Diabetologia, 14*, 59-64
Snell, K., Ashby, S.L. and Barton, S.J. (1977) *Toxicology, 8*, 277-83
Spyker, J.M. (1975a) in *Behavioural Toxicology* (Weiss, B. and Laties, V.G. eds.), pp. 311-44, Plenum Press, New York
Spyker, J.M. (1975b) *Fed. Proc. Fed. Am. Soc. Exp. Biol., 34*, 1835-44
Stratford, M.R.L. and Snell, K. (1979) *Biochem. Soc. Trans., 7*, 902-4
Takahashi, T., Kimura, T., Jato, Y., Shiraki, H. and Ukita, T. (1971) *J. Hyg. Chem., 17*, 93-107
Tennyson, V.M. (1970) in *Developmental Neurobiology* (Himwich, W.A., ed.), pp. 47-116, Thomas,

Springfield, Illinois

Thomas, J.A. and Lloyd, J.W. (1973) in *Pesticides and the Environment, a Continuing Controversy* (Deichmann, W.B., ed.), pp. 43-51, Intercontinental Medical Book Corp., New York

Thomas, J.A., Schein, L.G. and Donovan, M.P. (1977) *Environ. Res., 13*, 441-50

Thornburg, J.E. and Moore, K.E. (1976) in *Perinatal Pharmacology and Therapeutics* (Mirkin, B.L., ed.), pp. 269-354, Academic Press, New York

Tuchmann-Duplessis, H. and Mercier-Parot, L. (1960) in *Congenital Malformations* Ciba Foundation Symp. (Wolstenholme, G.E.W. and O'Connor, C.M., eds.), p. 115, Little, Brown and Co., Boston

Uriel, J. (1978) *Adv. Cancer Res., 23*, 127-74

Vernon, R.G. and Walker, D.G. (1968) *Biochem. J., 106*, 331-8

Virgo, B.B. and Bellward, G.D. (1977) *Res. Commun. Chem. Path. Pharmacol., 17*, 399-409

Wakelam, M.J.D. and Walker, D.G. (1980) *Biochem. Soc. Trans., 8*, 384-5

Walker, D.G. (1971) in *The Biochemistry of Development* (Benson, P.F., ed.), pp. 77-95, Heinemann Med. Books Ltd., London

Ware, R.A., Burkholder, P.M., Chang, L.W. and Cashwell, R.J. (1974a) *Fed. Proc. Fed. Am. Soc. Exp. Biol., 33*, 227

Ware, R.A., Chang, L.W. and Burkholder, P.M. (1974b) *Nature (London), 251*, 236-7

Weber, G. (1977) *N. Engl. J. Med., 296*, 486-93, 541-51

Welch, R.M., Levin, W. and Conney, A.H. (1969) *Toxicol. Appl. Pharmacol., 14*, 358-67

Widdowson, E.M. and McCance, R.A. (1960) *Proc. Roy. Soc., Ser. B, 150*, 188-206

Wilson, J.G. (1973) *Environment and Birth Defects*, Academic Press, New York

Woodard, B.T., Ferguson, B.B. and Wilson, D.J. (1976) *Am. J. Dis. Child., 130*, 400-3

Winnick, M. and Morgan, B.L.G. (1979) in *Contemporary Metabolism*, Vol. 1, (Freinkel, N., ed.), pp. 165-80, Plenum, New York

339

NOTES ON CONTRIBUTORS

Felix Beck, Professor of Anatomy, University of Leicester Medical School, England

Nigel A. Brown, Department of Pharmacology, George Washington University Medical Center, Washington DC, USA

Richard E. Butcher, Psychoteratology Laboratory, Children's Hospital Research Foundation, Cincinnati, Ohio, USA

Ruth M. Clayton, Institute of Animal Genetics, University of Edinburgh, Scotland

Bengt Danielsson, Department of Toxicology, University of Uppsala, Sweden

Lennart Dencker, Department of Toxicology, University of Uppsala, Sweden

Sergio E. Fabro, Department of Obstetrics and Gynaecology, Columbia Hospital for Women, Washington DC, USA

Mont R. Juchau, Department of Pharmacology, University of Washington, Seattle, Washington, USA

Paul Kleihues, Department of Neuropathology, University of Freiburg, German Federal Republic

Olavi Pelkonen, Department of Pharmacology, University of Oulu, Finland

Keith Snell, Department of Biochemistry, University of Surrey, Guildford, Surrey, England

Sven Ullberg, Department of Toxicology, University of Uppsala, Sweden

Charles V. Vorhees, Psychoteratology Laboratory, Children's Hospital Research Foundation, Cincinnati, Ohio, USA

Kenneth E. Williams, Department of Biochemistry, University of Keele, Staffordshire, England

Ahmet Zehir, Institute of Animal Genetics, University of Edinburgh, Scotland

INDEX